Revised and Updated Edition

365 DAYS OF SPENDING TIME WITH JESUS

KEVIN JOHNSON

BETHANYHOUSE
a division of Baker Publishing Group
Minneapolis, Minnesota

Published by Bethany House Publishers
11400 Hampshire Avenue South
Bloomington, Minnesota 55438
www.bethanyhouse.com

Bethany House Publishers is a division of
Baker Publishing Group, Grand Rapids, Michigan

Printed in the United States of America

Library of Congress Control Number: 2017945991

ISBN 978-0-7642-1999-3

Cover design by LOOK Design Studio

17 18 19 20 21 22 23   7 6 5 4 3 2 1

To Lyn
The Love of My Life

To Nate, Karin, and Elise
The Lights in My Smile

Contents

Day 1
Total Devotion

From the mass tragedy of 9/11 to the latest headline-grabbing acts of violence, terrorists of every creed and shade of crazy aim to disrupt our lives. Whether imported or homegrown, they want to make our every moment feel uneasy. Most of all, they plot to turn us against each other. If hatred wins and love loses, without a doubt they have succeeded.

Don't ever mistake acts of terrorism for *devotion*. What terrorists do is *deviation* from everything right and good. They think their twisted brand of wickedness is worth killing for—even dying for. They couldn't make any clearer why Jesus is worth living for.

Read Romans 12:1

What kind of devotion does Jesus want from you?

Terrorists ooze such damaged commitment that you can watch what they do, then do the exact opposite:

You aren't trying to gain heaven as a suicide bomber. God offers you eternal life as a free gift.

You don't burn with cruel inhumanity. Your commitment to Jesus overwhelms you with compassion.

You don't work for a distant, menacing God. You lovingly serve the Savior who walked in your shoes and died in your place.

You don't unleash death on the innocent. You usher the guilty into life.

Total devotion isn't a one-shot mission. It's an attitude you can adopt this instant and apply moment by moment. It's gratefully offering your whole self to God. It's clinging tight to the Lord of the universe and letting him rule over every inch of your existence.

When you consider what Jesus has given you—from breath to eternal life and every good thing in between—you know in your heart he deserves nothing less.

You're not a dead fool. You're a living sacrifice. That's total devotion.

And so, dear brothers and sisters, I plead with you to give your bodies to God
because of all he has done for you. Let them be a living and holy sacrifice—
the kind he will find acceptable. This is truly the way to worship him.

Romans 12:1 NLT

Day 2
Snooze and Lose

As Sophia snoozed her wake-up alarm for the third time, her mom rapped on her bedroom door and yelled to see if she was awake. "It's eight o'clock, Sophia. We leave for church in half an hour!"

Sophia dragged herself to the kitchen, erupting in her usual whine. "Why do we go to church? Can't we take some Sundays off? You and Dad should go by yourselves." Sophia thought Sunday school was okay, a chance to chat with her friends while the teacher blathered on. But wasting a second hour in a worship service made her crazy mad. Sophia said church band sounded like a cow moaning in labor—and she couldn't figure out why the pastor got so worked up about stuff she cared nothing about.

One of these days, Sophia told herself, *I'm staying home. And I'm not going back.*

Read Colossians 1:10

Why would anyone want to "please God in every way"?

Before we decide to trust God for ourselves, stuff like knowing, following, and enjoying God feels about as important as a stash of old Happy Meal toys lost in a backyard sandbox. Instead of recognizing God as King of the universe, we want to rule our own lives. We might even strike a pose as open rebels against God.

You probably know the facts on how God hatched a plan to bring us back to himself. Even though we deserve death for our sins (Romans 6:23), Christ suffered that punishment for us. He died on the cross in our place so we can be forgiven (Colossians 1:21–23).

Being convinced of those facts gives you enormous reason to choose total devotion to Jesus. You admit, *I've been wrong, God. I thought you weren't worth it. I disobeyed you.* You become God's friend. *I accept the gift of forgiveness and life you offer through Christ.* Suddenly it makes sense to follow him every moment of every day, because you've realized the infinite value of living close to him. After all, if he's rescued you and brought you into his kingdom of love, he deserves every bit of your life.

> So that you may live a life worthy of the Lord and please him in every way:
> bearing fruit in every good work, growing in the knowledge of God.
>
> *Colossians 1:10*

Day 3
To Die or to Die

"Hurry up!"

Aiden's toes nudged toward the cliff edge. It looked like a mile down to the swirling river below, but truthfully, the rock where he stood was just high enough to cause a mild episode of heart pounding and hyperventilating. Unless the water was running low. Which it was.

Jumping the cliff was the initiation required to hang out with the older neighborhood kids. The test started as a joke. One by one a select group of guys and girls had braved the leap.

If Aiden didn't jump, he would be banished to the group of kiddos not allowed to tag along, meaning the choice to jump was between potential physical harm on one hand and certain social death on the other. And if Aiden's parents found out he was cliff jumping—well, that would end in another form of death.

"So are you jumping—or not?"

Read Mark 8:31–38

What did Jesus identify as the toughest thing about following him?

Choosing to follow Jesus might leave you feeling caught between a rock and *the* Rock (Isaiah 26:4). If you ignore your friends' demands, you could face humiliation and rejection. Yet if you do wrong—mistreating yourself, others, and/or Jesus—you know that God will be less than pleased. Either way causes you pain.

Jesus understood that obeying God's plan to save the world from sin meant he would be mocked and hated, then killed on the cross. Nevertheless, he was totally determined to obey God.

Jesus said that if you choose to be devoted to him, you must imitate him—deny yourself and take up your cross. Swap your way for his way—completely. Obey him even when it hurts—like those times you feel you've been pierced with nails and all you can do is twist in pain.

Daring to stick with Jesus sometimes feels like you've been strung up to die. But Jesus promises that his way leads to life.

> Then he called the crowd to him along with his disciples
> and said: "Whoever wants to be my disciple must deny
> themselves and take up their cross and follow me."
>
> *Mark 8:34*

Day 4
Look Out Below

From your perch atop your 110-story office tower, you ponder how you rocketed to the top. A little lawn-mowing service, a few baby-sitting jobs, some lucrative investments, and *bam*—you sit on a sizable fortune.

You purchased a city block, then built the skyscraper with your name in big glittery letters. Downstairs is a garage packed with your favorite cars—and up top sits your personal helicopter emblazoned with your corporate logo. Thousands of workers in the tower below answer to you. It's all yours.

Your feet? Propped up on the desk. Your nose? Higher than the sky. Your bank account? Bigger than the gross national product of Slovenia. You call the shots. You run the show. You're your own boss. And you're only fifteen.

Just wait until you get your driver's license and move away from Mom and Dad.

Read John 12:25–26

Who runs your life when you're out and about on your own?

Even if you occupy the top spot in your own office tower, there's still Someone high above you.

Whether your kingdom consists of half a bedroom, a bunk bed, and a few video games—or a dorm room, a microwave, and a wheezing old Chevy—or condos, cars, corporations, and techno-toys that defy imagination—you're not the master of the universe. You don't even rule your own life.

There's no escape: You serve *somebody*. The Bible says you're a slave either to wrong or to right (Romans 6:19), either to death or to life (Romans 8:6), either to Satan or to God (Ephesians 2:1–10).

Trying to run your own life is like taking a leap off your office tower. It might feel daring and doable, but you won't fly. Life without God is a death spiral as sure as gravity. Giving yourself back to God—sticking close to him, obeying his commands—is what sends you soaring.

Growing up is your chance to choose for yourself to follow Jesus—to fly with the real Master of the universe.

Whoever serves me must follow me; and where I am, my servant also will be.

John 12:26

Day 5
On Your Mark

Wrapped in a ginormous sumo suit, you waddle to the starting line for a ten-thousand-meter race. Eyeballing other runners, you wonder why everyone else is dressed so funny. You struggle to bend over to take your mark, accidentally rolling into motion just as the starting gun fires.

You pick yourself up and wobble down the track, observing that it's hard to move when you're blown up like a balloon. And as the pack of runners tears away, you look down and spot one more problem. Your sumo flip-flops are on the wrong feet.

Read Hebrews 12:1–3

How should you dress for the race to follow Jesus?

Wrapping yourself in a sumo suit works great if your goal is to bounce your way to last place. But if you hope to run well, you strip to essentials and slip on the most supportive shoes you can find.

As Christians, we have a race laid out for us. On the far side of the finish line is an eternity in heaven with God and his people. Our race course isn't a sprint—it's a marathon that demands determination and devotion. To run well—doing life tight with Jesus—we toss off anything unnecessary for the race.

Sometimes we come to the race carrying loads of stuff as out-of-place as a jumbo wrestling suit—like having a social calendar that leaves no time for Christian friends, or doing activities that keep you too busy for time alone with God.

Those are good things out of control. Even worse is when we let bad things take hold of our lives. Sin takes us out of the race. It leaves us sprawled on the track until we ask God for forgiveness and let him pick us up.

You only run fast and free as a Christian when you get rid of anything that tangles you up. Now is the time to take note of how you're geared up for the run—and toss everything that slows you down.

> Let us throw off everything that hinders and the sin that so easily
> entangles, and let us run with perseverance the race marked out for us.
>
> *Hebrews 12:1*

Day 6

The Finest Things

With the entire contents of her closet spread out on her bed, Samantha calls Lauren to plot party wear. "I don't know. . . . Huh? . . . I can't wear *that*. I'll never wear that again. Don't you remember? The last time I did, Luke called me 'bubble butt.' . . . Sure, I suppose we could both dress up. That would make everyone else look bad. . . . Yeah, I guess the green outfit would be okay. . . . Yeah, I know. It's cute. You don't think it makes me look like an elf, do you? I don't want anyone to laugh at me this time."

Read Matthew 6:25–34

When you aim to live totally devoted to Jesus,
what goal should you keep top of mind?

Clothes aren't the only things in life that can consume us. Drooling over the latest tech, drilling nonstop to make the soccer team, unlocking every last level of your favorite video game . . . none of these things are bad, but sometimes they squeeze out things that are even better.

You *need* clothes and food and a few other things. You *want* fun and money and lots of other things. Yet God wants to help you focus on even bigger stuff.

Jesus tells you to seek first God's kingdom and righteousness. To seek God's *kingdom* means wanting what he wants. That's giving God your heart. To seek his *righteousness* means looking for ways to love him and others. That's giving God your life. And God makes an extraordinary promise to those who chase him hard. He vows to take care of everything else you really need in life.

None of this means you're so spiritual you don't have to think about the ordinary stuff of life. Birds dig worms and flowers drink. And it's not a bad idea to lay out clothes for the next day so you aren't late for school. But you're running toward the wrong goal if you always panic about what to wear and yet never ponder how to live.

For the pagans run after all these things, and your heavenly Father
knows that you need them. But seek first his kingdom and his
righteousness, and all these things will be given to you as well.

Matthew 6:32–33

Day 7
Marshmallows

The campfire flared, lighting up a dozen dirty, sweaty faces.

"So what are you into? What makes you happy?" someone asked Makayla. No one had been able to figure her out. Nothing seemed to thrill her.

"Money makes me happy," Makayla said. "I want to be rich."

"How come?"

"I like to go to the mall." She flashed a look that meant, *Isn't that obvious, you stupid people?* She did dress like she knew her malls.

"What do you do when the malls close?" someone prodded.

"Not much."

"And that's fun?" someone else asked.

Makayla sensed no one was impressed. "Marshmallows!" she said suddenly. "I like marshmallows." She smooshed a marshmallow between her fingers to demonstrate her sincerity. "Marshmallows make me happy."

The last question to her fell unanswered as she looked away, into the fire. "So what happens when the marshmallows are gone?"

Read 1 Corinthians 3:10–15

What parts of life can you count on to last forever?

Life is full of thrills and peak moments: an afternoon kicking around with friends, a *whoosh* down a water slide, a favorite song in your headphones, scoring the winning goal, your dog jumping at the door for you after school. They're marshmallows. Roasted sugar. Hot on a stick. Fast yet delicious. Lick your lips to get it all.

But is that all there is?

God made marshmallows to enjoy. He also points out that only things connected to him last forever. Anything built on Jesus—enjoying things his way, doing his will, following him—matters for eternity. Anything done without him—leaping into sin, doing your own thing, jumping out-of-bounds—will be gone in a flash.

God offers you more than a fluffy friendship. He invites you to total devotion.

> If anyone builds on this foundation using gold, silver, costly stones, wood, hay or straw, their work will be shown for what it is.
>
> *1 Corinthians 3:12–13*

Heaven's Gate

Standing outside the gates of heaven, you scope out the ticket booth with the shortest line. When you finally reach the front of the line, you pull wads of yellow sticky notes from your pockets.

"What are these?" the ticket lady asks.

"It's everything nice I've ever done," you say. "I've been keeping track."

"I'm sorry, but those won't get you in."

The girl behind you nudges past you. She hands the lady a ticket with big letters that say *Admit One*.

You push back to the ticket lady. "You've made a mistake," you protest. "I've got all the proof I need right here. I've been really good."

The ticket lady turns back to the girl. "Welcome, Sadie. Go on in."

The lady glances back at you. "You can't buy tickets here," she says. "The tickets were free. Back on earth."

You rip the ticket from the lady's hands and stare at it, looking for a secret code or a hint of where it came from. "Where did you get this? Who could possibly give you a free pass to heaven? I've been good my whole life just to get here."

"Didn't you hear?" the girl replies. "Jesus was giving them away."

Read Ephesians 2:8–9

What gets you friendship with Jesus—and eternal life in heaven?

There's a danger in total devotion. It's this: You might begin to think that your spiritual goodness somehow earns you friendship with God and a free pass to his forever home.

No, Jesus doesn't hand out actual tickets to heaven that say *Admit One*. There's no such thing as a *Get Out of Hell Free* card. But don't forget this fact: Your total devotion doesn't earn you a place in heaven. The love you live out for God is your way of expressing thanks for everything God has done for you.

God already loves you completely. When you trust Christ, he saves you, forgiving you and promising you life in heaven. You can't take credit for that.

> God saved you by his grace when you believed. And you can't take credit for this; it is a gift from God. Salvation is not a reward for the good things we have done, so none of us can boast about it.
>
> Ephesians 2:8–9 NLT

Day 9

Lost and Alone

Caroline left camp minus her phone and GPS, planning an easy run through the forest. She figured she had a couple hours of daylight to loop the trails near camp and get back with no problem.

Somewhere along her run, Caroline got off the main path, and as she plunged deeper among the trees, branches whipped her face and scratched her arms and legs. She suddenly realized that little about the path looked familiar. Just trees, rocks, and more trees and rocks.

Scared, Caroline ran faster but recognized even less. As darkness grew, she was spun around and halfway out of her mind. Fright overwhelmed her. On the shore of a lonely, isolated lake, she crumpled from exhaustion, utterly lost.

Read 2 Timothy 3:14–17

*How does the Bible help you find your way
when you want to follow God?*

Some lost people panic. Other people refuse to admit they're in a sad spot. They run farther and faster down the wrong path because they're too embarrassed to admit they're going the wrong way.

Other lost people stay calm. They're not shy about seeking out directions. They backtrack in the woods. They find a sign. They admit they need help figuring out exactly where they are and getting to where they want to go.

If you want to get unlost in the woods, you've got to stop to get directions. If hikers hadn't found Caroline and led her out of the forest, it's tough to say how her story might have ended.

If you want to get unlost in life, the Bible is the place to look. It teaches you to know God and shows you the way to real life.

Getting directions doesn't work if the details aren't clear. The Bible is "breathed by God," providing perfect directions from the perfect God. If you look to God's Word for instruction, you can trust what it says. It's your unique guidebook written by the ultimate guide, God himself.

> All Scripture is inspired by God and is useful to teach us what is
> true and to make us realize what is wrong in our lives. It corrects
> us when we are wrong and teaches us to do what is right.
>
> *2 Timothy 3:16 NLT*

Day 10

Hunger Pains

"My Sunday school class signed a pledge to read the Bible from cover to cover this year," Scott moaned. "Until January 23, I was flying—all the way through Leviticus and halfway into Numbers. Then I crashed. I suppose I should feel good I made it as far as I did. That's three and a half books. But I still think God is mad at me that I didn't do way better."

Know what? Getting to know God isn't supposed to be a pain.

Read John 6:28–35

What drew people to Jesus?

You probably don't need someone to watch over you and force you to eat. Apart from serious eating issues, you eat when you're hungry. Your stomach growls, and you munch until you fill up.

Whether you know it or not, you have the same kind of natural hunger for God. Your questions, problems, doubts, triumphs, failures, the things you love and hate, your dreams of things you want to be or do—those are like a growling stomach prompting you to get closer to God by spending time with him and his Word.

When you glance at a restaurant menu, you never say, "Give me one of everything, please," then try to down it all. And you don't have to eat the Bible all at once. Start with a few of its choicest morsels. Over time, you can plow through the rest of the menu.

If you always come to your Bible telling yourself, "I'm doing this because I have to," or "I need to finish the Bible by next month or else," you'll lose your appetite for God. And don't just focus on all the spiritual vitamins, amino acids, and complex carbs you're getting. Who wants a plateful of *that*?

As you open your Bible, focus instead on the enormous coolness of getting closer to God. Jesus promises that he's the kind of food that leaves you salivating for more—food that satisfies better than anything else. Living close to him is something you do because you want to, not because you have to.

> Then Jesus declared, "I am the bread of life. Whoever comes to me will never go hungry, and whoever believes in me will never be thirsty."
>
> *John 6:35*

Day 11
Out on a Limb

The man's spotless business suit got rumpled and grimy as he heaved himself up into the tree. When his pants caught on a sharp twig and there was a loud *riiiiiipppp*, people below him on the ground burst out laughing. After a couple more noisy grunts, the guy settled on a branch that sagged under his weight.

The people? Your friends. The tree-climbing sloth? Your dad, trying to get a better shot as he videoed your first game of the season.

Why would your dad—or your mom or whoever—do that? Because they want to see you—and show you off.

Read Luke 19:1–10

Why would anyone want to see Jesus so bad?

Zacchaeus (Zack-KEY-us) scaled a tree to see Jesus because he had heard that Jesus loved the unlovable—and Zacchaeus wasn't exactly adored by the masses. A corrupt tax collector, he cheated his countrymen and aided the Roman enemies who occupied his country. Lower than slime, this traitor was the baddest of the bad.

Yet Jesus picked Zacchaeus to share dinner with him. Why?

Jesus kept strolling past the people snickering at Zacchaeus—people on the ground who thought they were good enough to deserve Jesus' friendship. Zacchaeus knew he had a need. He proved it by going out on a limb just to glimpse Jesus. People laughed at his unabashed need, but everyone present needed a forgiver, master, and friend just as much. They *all* should have scampered up a tree.

You are special to God. He sent his Son, Jesus, to live and die and rise again for you. And he comes now. "Here I am!" he says. "I stand at the door and knock. If anyone hears my voice and opens the door, I will come in and eat [fellowship] with that person, and they with me" (Revelation 3:20).

Being like Zacchaeus is how you open that door. Admit you need Jesus—and don't care who sees you.

> When Jesus reached the spot, he looked up and said to him,
> "Zacchaeus, come down immediately. I must stay at your house
> today." So he came down at once and welcomed him gladly.
>
> *Luke 19:5–6*

Day 12
The Wall

For nearly thirty years following World War II, eastern Germany was walled off from western Germany—city from city, family from family, friend from friend. East Germans suffered through pollution, poverty, and brutal repression of politics and religion. They could barely dream of the freedoms enjoyed in the West, on the far side of the wall. Anyone who tried to escape the East met razor wire, land mines, and machine guns.

You would never willingly choose to live locked inside a wall, separated from everything you enjoy, in a country that's pretty much a prison cell. Yet you and every person who has ever lived are expert wall builders. We choose to separate ourselves from God and his goodness.

Read Luke 15:11–24

Why does the son in the story distance himself from his dad?

Deep inside, we're all a lot like that wandering son. Some of us battle openly to do things our way. Others of us are scared to step out of line, although if we thought we could sin and get away with it, we might act a lot more like this son.

Sin makes it impossible for us to be God's friends. Each time we disobey—when we sin by what we think, say, or do—we lay a brick between ourselves and God. He doesn't build the wall—*we* do each time we choose to sin. Separation grows brick by brick.

The division starts now and can last forever. If we refuse God's way of demolishing the wall—Jesus—we will discover that when we die, the wall cements for eternity (Romans 6:23). We'll find ourselves cut off from God and everything good. Nothing will tie us to family or friends or God on the other side of the wall.

The son came home to his waiting father. Our Father is waiting for us too, so that we can be friends again with him. He sent his son, Jesus Christ, to tear down the wall we've built. It's a job only he can do.

> But while he was still a long way off, his father saw him
> and was filled with compassion for him; he ran to his son,
> threw his arms around him and kissed him.
>
> *Luke 15:20*

Day 13
Tear Down the Wall

You've been dying to drive for years. With your game deck outfitted with custom chair, weighted steering wheel, and genuine gas and brake pedals, you've mastered every NASCAR videogame ever invented. If anyone was ready for the road, it was you.

One night your parents get picked up by friends for a couples' date night. You seize your opportunity. You buckle into the family roadster and back into the street. *No problem*. You shift into drive and ease forward. *Flawless*.

You're halfway down the block when you meet an oncoming car. In half a heartbeat, you realize that a zillion laps around a virtual track never equipped you for real-world traffic coming *at* you. You panic, veer right, and clip a parked car.

waiting for whatever punishment your parents dish out.

Read Isaiah 53:4–12

These verses predict that Jesus will take the punishment others deserve. Whose blame does he take?

Jesus did something crazy beyond imagination: He had never sinned, he deserved no punishment, yet he took God's consequence for sin—death—so we wouldn't have to. He was pierced for *our* evil, crushed for *our* wrong.

Jesus died for everyone, but God requires each of us to accept that fact. We need to tell the truth about our wrongdoing and take responsibility for our sin. You can do that by praying, "God, I've sinned. I've broken your rules and disappointed you. God, I know that Jesus died in my place." That's the beginning of being a Christian.

When you accept the fact that Jesus took your punishment, you have a fresh chance to stick tight with God now and forever: "The payment for sin is death. But God gives us the free gift of life forever in Christ Jesus our Lord" (Romans 6:23 NCV). Christ demolishes the wall of sin between you and God. Not a brick stands. Not a pebble is left—not even a speck of dust. It's all been washed away by Christ's blood.

> But he was pierced for our transgressions, he was crushed
> for our iniquities; the punishment that brought us peace
> was upon him, and by his wounds we are healed.
>
> *Isaiah 53:5*

Day 14
The Principal's Office

Think for a moment how you feel when a teacher sends you to the principal's office. You no doubt clutch your heart with joy and skip happily down the hall, looking forward to your principal's hearty congratulations for your scholarship and outstanding behavior. As you think about meeting with the person who inspires all your intellectual pursuits, you anticipate sparkling conversation. In fact, you're so grateful that you're already mentally composing the thank-you note for the faculty member who suggested this opportunity for warm interaction with your principal.

Yeah . . . not so much. Unless your behavior is flawless and your report card puts you at the top of your class, warmth might be the last thing you feel on your way to see the big cheese.

Read Hebrews 10:19–22

How is getting close to God different from going to see your principal?

If your principal indeed were your good friend, you'd have a radical change of attitude about your invitation to his office. You might need a load of imagination to picture this, but try: Your principal—emphasis on *pal*—is an amazing teacher, counselor, enforcer, and friend rolled into one. Whatever the problem—homework, relationships, the school bully, loneliness—your principal gets you through the rough spots. If your principal were your best friend, instead of getting *sent* to the principal, you would *run* to the principal.

This same radical change happens between you and God when the wall of sin and separation crumbles. You go to God's presence without fear because Jesus has won you total friendship with God.

Before becoming a Christian, we rebel, hate rules, make excuses for sin, and fear death and hell—the ultimate detention. After accepting Jesus as Savior and Lord, we learn friendship, trust, forgiveness, and openness to correction—looking forward to eternity in heaven with God, our best friend.

Don't be afraid to go to God. His door is always open. Jesus flung it open with his blood.

We have confidence to enter the Most Holy Place by the blood of Jesus.

Hebrews 10:19

Day 15
Eleven against One

Holly didn't know what to say to Mrs. Kim. "I have gymnastics three days a week after school," she protested. "My evenings are piano on Mondays. Ballet on Tuesdays. Community theater on Thursdays. I baby-sit most Saturday nights. I have lots of homework too."

"All I'm asking for is Wednesday. You're saying you can't work on the yearbook just one night a week?" Mrs. Kim replied. "You know that turning this down means you can't be editor next year, don't you? We'll be looking for *experience*."

"I know," Holly said. Then she decided to tell Mrs. Kim the real reason. "Wednesday is the only night of the week I can go to youth group."

Read Hebrews 10:23-25

How can you keep your friendship with God fresh?

The author of Hebrews just told his readers about their wild new friendship with God through Christ. Now he explains how to keep that friendship fresh—and the key is simple: Keep getting together with other followers of Jesus.

Lots of influences try to tear down your faith. So you need to reinforce and rebuild yourself and your Christian friends through encouragement—talking, praying, just sharing the ups and downs of following Jesus. Constantly missing church or youth group hurts not just you but the Christians you could be helping.

When church collides with another activity, maybe you can reschedule one or the other. When you can't, church shouldn't always come last, even when that means disappointing advisors or friends, or missing future opportunities. Sometimes you gotta say no to a good activity to say yes to a better one. Getting and giving encouragement is that important.

You would have to be a fool to walk out on a football field to take on a whole team by yourself. You would look up, see eleven mammoths charging toward you, and run crying off the field. Why do you think you can stay in the game alone as a Christian? You need your team or you won't survive.

> Let us consider how we may spur one another on toward love
> and good deeds, not giving up meeting together, as some are
> in the habit of doing, but encouraging one another.
>
> *Hebrews 10:24-25*

Day 16
Cold Wet Ooze

You're frolicking barefoot in a park, teeing off on your favorite disc golf course. Just as you let fly a sure hole-in-one, you feel a cold, wet ooze between your toes. You shriek, busting out your funkiest dance moves as you paw the ground, scraping off a gift from a rogue dog owner who failed to pick up after their Saint Bernard.

Know it or not, the apostle Paul had something like that in mind when he wrote this next chunk to the Philippian Christians.

Read Philippians 3:7–11

*What's the most important thing in life—and
what does Paul call everything else?*

Before Paul met Jesus, he had a long list of things he thought were important. Now, however, he calls them "rubbish," using a word that means "worthless trash" or "garbage" or, to be more vivid, "dung." Compared with knowing Christ, he says, everything else is like dancing in you-know-what. Paul shares the shocking truth that the *best* thing in life isn't what we have or what we do but who we know: Christ.

That may sound like over-the-top devotion, spiritual weirdness for parents and pastors, but not for you. Yet here's what it looks like in real life: It's wanting more than anything else to hang close to God, living your life the way God desires, whether that decision brings suffering or success. Being a believer is more than following rules, going to church, and trying hard not to beat up your smaller siblings. It's being best friends with the Lord of the universe, aiming to know, enjoy, and serve God completely in everything you do.

Thinking you can live close to God isn't a cotton-candy dream that melts in the wind and rain—when you try to make it work at home, in school, or with friends. Paul's faith was tested by beatings, stonings, shipwrecks, and persecutions, yet he (and lots of other believers) agree with this: One short day lived close to God is better than a thousand without him (Psalm 84:10).

I consider everything a loss because of the surpassing
worth of knowing Christ Jesus my Lord. . . . I consider them
garbage, that I may gain Christ and be found in him.

Philippians 3:8–9

Day 17

Get Up and Go On

"I QUIT," Carlie screamed as she dangled up high in a ropes course. Her on-lookers far below couldn't tell whether her face was wet from tears or sweat, but she was clearly shaking. "I can't find a foothold! I keep slipping! I can't do this anymore! Lower me down!"

Climbers don't always reach the summit. Sooner or later, even the greatest musicians miss a note. No genius ever pulls straight A's on every assignment, quiz, and exam from their days as a kindergarten punk all the way through a PhD program.

Being a Christian isn't any different. You can be sure that *no one* pulls it off perfectly. *No one* lives a flawless Christian life. If we think we live without sinning, we're fooling ourselves (1 John 1:8).

Paul acknowledged that truth. Just after he wrote that everything was dung compared to knowing Jesus, he fessed up to his readers that he wasn't perfect. He was totally devoted to God, but sometimes even this great servant of the Lord missed his step.

Read Philippians 3:12–14

How can you overcome mistakes and mess-ups?

The more assignments you mess up at school, the harder it is to keep trying. It's easy to conclude that working harder won't change your grade and that you're doomed to failure. When there's no room for extra help and do-overs, falling short in one class after another might make you think that school isn't for you.

When Paul talks about "forgetting what is behind," he's trying to guard you against giving up. He wants you to know that when you admit your sin, God forgives you and picks you up so you can press on toward the goal of knowing Christ completely. So don't ever give up on following Christ just because you fall down.

There's no such thing as a Christian who never stumbles. Real Christians are the ones who get up and go on.

> But one thing I do: Forgetting what is behind and straining
> toward what is ahead, I press on toward the goal to win the prize
> for which God has called me heavenward in Christ Jesus.
>
> *Philippians 3:13–14*

Day 18

Look-Alikes

The next time you point and laugh at someone's total weirdness, ponder this fact: If someone looks odd to you, you can bet you look at least as odd to them. And if you're part of a group snickering at another group, you can multiply that indisputable fact by however many people you're hanging out with. If you spot a clump of people sporting the same weird look, for example, you can be sure they easily see that you and your friends share your own special brand of weirdness—everything from hair and clothes to expressions and gestures.

Picture your tribe through the eyes of other groups at school. It's easy for you to pick out other cliques and clones. But you and your friends look just as cookie-cutter to others as they look to you. Spend enough time with someone and you eventually resemble each other in how you think, talk, and act.

The same thing happens spiritually. Your character is shaped by the people you hang out with. When you spend time with Christ—talking with him, reading his Word, and sticking close to his friends—you start to resemble your Lord.

Read Galatians 5:19–26

*What qualities rub off on you, thanks to the
Holy Spirit, as you get to know God?*

This passage starts by describing what people can look like without God—full of rebellion, ranging from sexual immorality to drunkenness, jealousy, and selfishness. If you make people who are dead-set against God your very closest friends, don't be surprised when those qualities rub off on you. But as you choose to live close to Jesus, you begin to pick up all his good qualities, some of which are listed in verses 22 and 23.

That's the best part of the look-alike thing. As you know Jesus better, people will begin to notice that you look more and more like him (1 Corinthians 3:18). No one can fault you for being his look-alike ("against such things there is no law"). People can't criticize you for being loving, joyful, peaceful, patient, kind, good, faithful, gentle, and self-controlled. If they do, it just shows how messed-up they are.

But the fruit of the Spirit is love, joy, peace, forbearance, kindness,
goodness, faithfulness, gentleness and self-control.

Galatians 5:22–23

Day 19
Total Healing

Minutes after the car crash, paramedics wheeled fourteen-year-old Alec into the emergency room, where a doctor washed the boy's wounds and sent him home. The doctor didn't stitch up Alec's bleeding cuts, didn't set his broken bones, and failed to treat his internal injuries, leaving Alec bent and broken.

If a doctor ever treated someone we love so terribly, we'd scream with fury and sue for millions. So it's odd when we get upset as God goes beyond washing our sins to fixing the full depth of our spiritual problems. We like having our sins forgiven and knowing that we'll go to heaven, but we get miffed when God wants to do surgery on our sin.

If sin is bad enough for Jesus to die for it, then it's bad enough for us to get rid of it. God saves us not just from the punishment of sin but from the power of sin to rule and ruin us.

Read 2 Corinthians 5:14–15

Why did Jesus die for you?

God is the Great Physician who wants to heal us totally, and forgiveness is just the first part of his cure for sin. The second part is remaking us from the inside out so we stop living for self and start obeying him. God doesn't give us one without the other. Because Christ has died, our old sinful lives have died—and we have been born anew to live a better life.

You might wonder how some people manage to live consistently for God. There's nothing mysterious about how that happens. Once forgiven, we become friends with God. Then the Lord uses that relationship to change us. His Holy Spirit lives in us, teaches us through the Bible, and empowers us beyond our natural abilities (Romans 8:1–17). That takes time, and like surgery, sometimes it hurts. But in the end, we grow closer and closer to who God wants us to be.

God loves us too much to leave us twisting in pain, with our sin and selfishness untreated.

> For Christ's love compels us, because we are convinced that one died for all, and therefore all died. And he died for all, that those who live should no longer live for themselves but for him who died for them and was raised again.
>
> *2 Corinthians 5:14–15*

Day 20

Total Weirdness

Some Christians claim to be the greatest people who ever walked the earth, as if every other human being is a complete mess and knows nothing about morality, love, or truth. But you don't have to hang out with Christians for long to realize that some churchfolk detest anyone different from them in color, gender, beliefs, or a hundred other features. These hypocrites, shams, and liars turn every conversation into an angry confrontation; if you had to sum them up in a word, you might say they're downright *mean*. They're nothing like the Jesus you meet in the Bible.

As a Christian, you know you're supposed to be different from people who don't follow Jesus. But how weird do you have to be?

Read Matthew 22:34–40

*What does Jesus say are the two huge ways you
show you are totally devoted to him?*

Jesus didn't leave any doubt about how his followers are supposed to stand out from other people. We're the people (1) learning to love God totally ("love God with all your heart and with all your soul and with all your mind") and (2) learning to love others unselfishly ("love your neighbor as you love yourself").

That really *is* a wild kind of weird, because you won't find a lot of people—young or old—following Jesus' command.

Too many people who claim to follow Jesus ooze selfishness—at school, home, with friends, at work. They consistently put their own interests first in their private lives and the public square. They wrap themselves in hatred and do nothing to help a hurting world (Matthew 23:1–39).

In our crowded world, a Christian actually living as Jesus expects really stands out. In fact, living up to God's biggest commands may actually help you make friends. True, your love for God may make others think you're a little off. But your love for people may convince them that you're not. If your actions and words show that you care about others as much as you care about yourself, not everyone will call you *weird*. A lot of them may call you *friend*.

Jesus replied: 'Love the Lord your God with all your heart
and with all your soul and with all your mind'.... And the
second is like it: 'Love your neighbor as yourself.'

Matthew 22:37, 39

Day 21
Saved from the Drain

As Chloe ran sobbing into the restroom, Steven looked incredibly pleased with himself. His cruel words aimed at Chloe indeed were spot-on funny. But Janika was fed up with Steven's thermonuclear sarcasm. "You're so mean!" she seethed. "How can you treat her like that? What's wrong with you?"

Matt rushed to rescue Steven. "Don't blame him. He can't help it. It's just the way he is. It's his personality."

"Actually, it's his biochemistry," Martina suggested. "Steven should see a psychiatrist for a prescription."

"What's wrong with *you*?" Alexa butted in. "He's just sarcastic, nasty, and obnoxious. He needs to say he's sorry and shut up."

Read Ephesians 4:17–24

Can you help it if you're bad?

If you jump into a scalding hot tub and lay there lazily until your skin turns red . . . and soak longer until your skin rots . . . and linger in the tub still longer until one day you dissolve into bits of flesh and whoosh down the drain—now, that would be *your* fault.

Paul uses big words in this passage to say that apart from God, people want to stay stuck in a tub of sin. You lose your grip on what's right. You lounge in sin so long that your heart becomes numb with hatred and your mind dead with rebellion.

But God made a way out of badness. Christ lived so you could see what God is like, and he died and rose so you could be made right with God. When you accept the fact that Christ rescued you, you want no more part of sin (Titus 2:11–12). As you soak in God's truth—the Bible—you start to think differently. God works in you. You hate sin. You chase what's good. And that emerges in how you act. You decide to get out of the tub before you wash down the drain.

> You were taught, with regard to your former way of life, to
> put off your old self, which is being corrupted by its deceitful
> desires; to be made new in the attitude of your minds. . . .
>
> Ephesians 4:22–23

Day 22

Busted

There was no escape for Ella after picking on her little brother one too many times. Ella loved Trevor, of course. She felt sorry for him, true enough. His developmental disabilities were major enough to make school tough and making friends tougher. And Ella knew she needed to be nicer.

Ella always felt like she had to pitch in more than her fair share, and she couldn't figure out why Trevor's challenges had to make her own life miserable. "I'm the big sister who always has to put her little brother first," she complained. "I never get to do what I want."

Early one morning, Ella had to once again watch her brother while their parents ran errands. When they arrived home, Trevor was gone. They found a note on his bed that said, "I don't know why Ella hates me. I'm running away."

Ella's dad found Trevor two blocks away at a friend's house, but not before Ella's mom called 9-1-1 and the police rolled up to take a report.

Read Romans 7:21–25

What's your problem when you can't seem to do what's right?

Cuffed like a criminal, blinded by a spotlight, plugged into a lie detector and forced to be honest, none of us lacks shortcomings. We know the rules. Yet we fail to keep them perfectly, no matter how hard we try.

Some of our failings are like an annoying hunk of hair that always sticks up wrong. No matter how much product you slather on, as soon as you drop your guard—*fuh-wang!* Other flaws, though, aren't small. They matter way more than bad hair.

Even after we've decided to follow Jesus, sin still hounds us (Hebrews 12:1). Part of us wants to do what's right. Part of us doesn't. We can blame others, make excuses, or hide our faults, but it always comes back to one fact: There's something wrong inside us. We're at war within ourselves.

Admitting when we're a mess inside opens the way for God to fix us. Being a Christian isn't just knowing the rules. It's not even knowing when you've broken them. It's relying on the Master to change you from the inside out.

What a wretched man I am! Who will rescue me
from this body that is subject to death?

Romans 7:24

Day 23
The Living Dead

When Hunter was little and heard that the Holy Spirit lived inside him, he imagined a tiny Jesus living in his heart like a garden gnome carving out a home in a tree. Or something like that.

Hunter's current idea of what his Sunday school teacher called "the indwelling of the Holy Spirit" was no more accurate. When he heard that the Holy Spirit was constantly there to help him to do right, he sat back and waited for it to happen. *I'm gonna instantly turn into Mother Teresa,* Hunter thought. *Make that Father Teresa.*

Hunter was surprised when the same old temptations were, um, *tempting.* So he decided to just sit back and wait some more, confident that at any moment, God would zap him good.

Read Romans 8:9–17

How does Holy Spirit living inside you change you?

As you become more and more like Jesus, you don't become any less *you*—the best parts of how God made you are unique. God doesn't erase your personality. He doesn't overwhelm everyday emotions with perpetual bliss and good cheer. He doesn't vacuum out your brain. And he doesn't convert you into a GPS-guided robochristian who acts holy at the flip of a heavenly switch.

You still feel. You still think. You still act. You still react.

Here's what actually happens. You have a new relationship with the God of the universe. You no longer dread God. You can, in fact, call him "Abba" ("Father," or even "Daddy"). He isn't simply "out there" somewhere. God himself lives *in* you through his Spirit.

The Bible says the Spirit produces love, joy, peace, patience, kindness, goodness, faithfulness, gentleness, and self-control in you (Galatians 5:22–23). He helps you understand God's commands so the part of you hostile to God begins to fade away. And real change happens as you listen and obey, one small choice after another, that adds up to a new you.

> And if the Spirit of him who raised Jesus from the dead is living
> in you, he who raised Christ from the dead will also give life to
> your mortal bodies through his Spirit who lives in you.
>
> *Romans 8:11*

Day 24

Staying Alive

"These—they're the best. Get some." Micah grabbed a shoe off the shelf and shoved it in Dylan's face.

Dylan peered at the price inside the heel and put the shoe down. "My parents will only pay half. I have to wait until I save the rest."

Micah pointed at his own shoes. "How do you think I got these?" Dylan shrugged. "I put them on and walked out." Micah started to rummage through a shelf full of shoe boxes. "What size do you want?"

Dylan grabbed Micah's arm to stop his digging. "My parents—I'd get three feet inside the house and they'd want to know where I got them."

"Your parents don't have to see them," Micah reasoned. "Keep them in your locker and change at school. You want the shoes or not?"

Read Romans 6:11–14

When did you decide to dump evil?

Imagine that a guy with biceps bigger than your head tries to drag you into a boxing ring to knock your head off. What's the best strategy to stay safe? (a) Throw a right jab and a left hook and hope you don't bust your hand; (b) jump on the guy's back and try to rip off his ear; (c) bark like a seal and pray for pity; or (d) stay out of the ring in the first place.

Smart choice.

Just before the passage you read, Paul says that all Christians have "died with Christ." When you became a Christian—whether that process was quick or slow, yesterday or a long time ago—God acted in you. Christ died *for* your sin, but you also died *with* Christ *to* sin. God moved you "from death to life," raising you up with Christ, forgiving you, wiping your conscience clean, giving you a heart that's alive toward him.

You died to sin, so stay dead. You committed yourself to following God, so grow in that commitment to him. You made up your mind to dump evil, so keep it made up. You decided to get out of the ring, so stay out.

Do not offer any part of yourself to sin as an instrument of
wickedness, but rather offer yourselves to God. . . .

Romans 6:13

Day 25
Bad and Good

You jab your friends to pay attention to the best part of the movie. An alien is oozing toward the mothership after destroying the entire town. The town's lone survivor rigs a photon ray bazooka from cornstalks and a rusty muffler. One shot and the alien explodes into a gazillion globs—that is, until he re-combobulates in the sequel.

As you and your friends leave the theater, you sigh with relief that evil has been crushed. But as your eyes get accustomed to the bright sun outside, you realize your bikes are gone, ripped off during the movie.

Read Malachi 3:13–4:3

*What does God promise you when it's tough
being good in a bad world?*

In the real world, evil rarely ends as quickly as in a make-believe movie. It might make you wonder if God cares at all about stopping evil.

The people in the book of Malachi noticed the same things you see every day: cheaters get A's, evil people get rich, and snotty girls nab all the trendy clothes and cute guys.

The believers in Malachi's day survived by reminding one another that the success of bad people isn't the whole story. In God's judgment at the end of time, evildoers will be punished, and those who follow God will romp like frisky calves set free from their pen.

Don't ever think that God doesn't notice evil or that he doesn't feel your pain. Just the opposite. That's why he sent Christ—to end wrongdoing and give people a chance to obey him. God, however, is patient. He holds off his righteous punishment, offering time for people to repent (2 Peter 2:9; 3:9).

That doesn't mean you should relax and tolerate evil. Change what you can in your own life and within arm's reach. Work together with peers and parents and authorities to confront bigger evils like poverty. And if you feel overwhelmed by evil, be patient. Remind yourself that God sees you. He won't forget your faithfulness.

But for you who revere my name, the sun of righteousness will rise with healing in its rays. And you will go out and frolic like well-fed calves.

Malachi 4:2

Day 26

Bondservant of God

You shiver with fright in the corner of a dark closet, terrified that the men who invaded your home will find you. Thugs suddenly rip open the door and drag you out. They toss you in the back of a truck, then into a rough cargo plane for a jarring ride to a jungle hideout. Once there, the men make clear you have an either/or choice. Either you work long days in the hot sun for them, or they let you starve to death.

Attitude check: How glad would you be to serve your captors?

Read Exodus 21:1–7

Why would a slave ever choose to stay with his master?

In Bible times, people sold themselves to pay back debts. Not long ago, Africans were kidnapped, brutalized, and forced to serve against their wills. And even today, slavery in a variety of hideous forms still persists.

Exodus 21 shows a different kind of slave, one who voluntarily said "no" to freedom so he could stay with his master. His master took the slave to a doorpost and pierced the slave's ear. That pierced ear showed that the slave was forever his "bondservant," someone who serves a master because he *wants* to.

That's some wild devotion. Was it crazy? The bondservant didn't think so. He chose to work hard for his master out of gratitude for what the master had given him—security, love, a family, food, a home.

Paul proudly called himself a bondservant of Jesus Christ (check Romans 1:1 for an example). Paul was so sure of God's love that he chose to obey God in every way he knew, with unflinching willingness and excitement. Paul understood that unlike human masters, God is a righteous and good master. God gives us "every good and perfect gift" (James 1:17), from life itself to his never-ending love.

God doesn't twist your arm to make you serve him. He never beats you into submission. He earns your respect, trust, and love. Once you're sure that God loves you and wants the best for you, then it's not crazy—or hard—to love him back.

His master must take him before the judges. He shall take him to the door or the doorpost and pierce his ear with an awl. Then he will be his servant for life.

Exodus 21:6

Day 27
Swine Diving

You were washing down chunks of chocolate chip cookie dough with chugs of Red Bull at your best friend's birthday party when you decided to break your personal record for the number of sugar packets consumed in one sitting. You were close to busting the record when someone yelled, "SWINE DIVE!" and the whole party headed upstairs.

Over and over you leapt oh-so-elegantly off a dresser and belly flopped on the bed. When the bed crashed through its frame to the floor, your friend's dad sent you home. Enough was enough. He declared you officially out of control.

You think you're funny. Hilarious. A legend in your own mind. You claim you aren't to blame. It was the sugar and caffeine that put you over the edge.

Read Proverbs 25:28

What good is self-control?

Getting a sugar buzz isn't the only way to lose control of yourself. A guy who misuses drugs has misplaced his brain. A girl who gets drunk and winds up in bed with a stranger loses her body—and maybe her health or her future or her life.

When you lose self-control, you're like an ancient city with broken-down walls. You lack protection. You have no power over who comes in or goes out or what they do. Letting yourself run wild can destroy you.

God respects you enough to make *you* ultimately responsible for yourself. He gives you parents and teachers and other authorities to instruct and shape you. But ultimately you answer to God for yourself. Having authority over yourself is God's gift that allows you to follow him for yourself—not because you have to, but because you want to.

You abuse that gift whenever you give control of yourself to anything or anyone other than God. You might as well bind your hands, gag your mouth, and unplug your brain. If you don't control yourself, something else will.

Like a city whose walls are broken through is a person who lacks self-control.

Proverbs 25:28

Day 28
Scrub Your Heart

Cooper and his science partner both torched holes in their desks with Bunsen burners, but it wasn't Cooper who got caught. "You're in charge, Cooper," his teacher called out as he escorted Cooper's pyro pal to the principal. Cooper congratulated himself on his promotion to teacher. *Not bad.*

After school, Cooper scored points at a quickmart by turning in his brother for shoplifting three candy bars and a soda—for him. "Come back in a couple years and I'll give you a job, son," the manager said. Cooper patted himself on the back. *Impressive.*

And that evening, Cooper's Bible study leader frowned as she picked up glass from a shattered classroom window. "We're going to sit here until someone claims responsibility," she scowled, "except for Cooper. You may go." *I'm too good,* Cooper thought as he exited class.

Read Matthew 23:25–28

What does God think of spiritual fakes?

The Bible isn't lying when it says that we all sin (1 John 1:8). It makes equally clear that forgiveness is always available when we confess our sin to God (1 John 1:9). God knows that being a Christian means we're in process. We're not perfect.

Jesus nevertheless had a major problem with people who try hard to look good on the outside while they let evil run wild on the inside. He called them "hypocrites," a word that comes from the masks worn by actors in ancient Greek theaters, who would cover their faces to play a role. The exaggerated masks hid who they really were, and when it comes to true faith, that kind of deceit is a truly bad thing. In fact, the harshest words Jesus ever spoke were aimed at spiritual fakes.

While slugging it out with the hypocrites, however, Jesus explains that our lives are like cups. Scrubbing the outside doesn't guarantee the inside is clean. But if we wash the inside first, the outside will sparkle as well.

Want a life where your outsides match your insides? Let Jesus clean out your heart.

On the outside you appear to people as righteous but on the
inside you are full of hypocrisy and wickedness.

Matthew 23:28

Day 29
Crybaby

Standing on a little hill across the street from school, Caitlin puffed a cigarette as Bus 93 passed by. *I hate people. They're all staring at me. I hope they like what they see.* Caitlin never rode the bus with the kids from her neighborhood anymore. She walked to school early to spend time with her new friends on the hill.

Back in elementary school, Caitlin was an easy target because she always knew the answers, always finished on time, always did what she was supposed to do. Kids called her "Crybaby Caitlin" because she always wailed whenever she got the smallest wittle owie.

One day, Caitlin decided she was tired of being good. She found some rebels who welcomed her into their clan, and almost overnight she transformed herself into a chain-smoking, attitude-spewing monster.

Read Galatians 6:9

What do you do when you're sick of being good?

Some days you don't know how much longer you can keep doing good. *I should get suspended so I fit in better. If I do too well I'll get made fun of. If I laugh at their mean jokes they'll like me more.* So you give up and give in.

But choosing between being bad and being obnoxiously good aren't your only options. You can choose to be good God's way.

You're repulsively good if you remind people how good you are. Or if you do good to make others look bad. Or if you live to keep rules instead of keeping rules to live.

Being good God's way requires a different attitude. You choose God's way because you trust that sooner or later it leads to life. You quietly and steadily do what's right because you believe God's promise that good behavior has good results.

God commands you to do good not to ruin life but to give life. Being bad is tossing your life away. Being obnoxiously good is a sure way to be boring and friendless. Being good—being obedient God's way—sets you up for God's best.

Let us not become weary in doing good, for at the proper
time we will reap a harvest if we do not give up.

Galatians 6:9

Day 30
Invisibility

Madeline couldn't recall how long she had been invisible. There were moments, of course, when people saw *parts* of her—awful parts, usually. Like the day Madeline caused a commotion at school when kids saw a faceless nose topped by a gigantic zit floating through the halls.

Sometimes teachers saw Madeline's hand raised in class, usually after she scored well on a test. The teachers wondered how a hand could wave without being connected to a body. After a couple days, however, the hand faded from their sight.

And once Madeline was eating in the cafeteria at a table full of people, though no one knew she was there. She was leaning forward on her chair when the chair shot out from under her and skidded across the lunchroom. Madeline splattered on the floor, and for a split second *everyone* saw her.

Halfway through eighth grade, Madeline and her family moved. Her old school transferred her records, teachers crossed her name off class lists, and another student took over her locker to be closer to friends. But no one at school could remember what the girl who had moved away looked like.

Read Psalm 25:16–21

What hope do you have when you feel lonely?

God didn't design you to float through life alone. He created you to be friends with other people and with himself. He built you a brain, injected you with feelings, and put you in a pack of human beings instead of sending you out to live solo. He set you loose to help and be helped by others and to worship him. Everything about the way God made you shows that he destined you to know and love him and others.

But there's a problem. While God made us for outrageously intense friendships, we've messed up. We've strained our relationships with both God and people. That's why at times everybody feels like Madeline—invisible, distant, and friendless.

When you feel alone, God hears your every cry. And he has a plan to usher you into the friendships he designed for you to enjoy. He wants to show you how to be a friend worth having—and find friends who count.

Turn to me and have mercy on me, because I am lonely and hurting.

Psalm 25:16 NCV

Day 31
Rolling Boulder Test

You knew you were in trouble when Kristin, Brianna, and Aubrey interrupted your lunch. "We have a simple test," Kristin announced with a wicked grin. "If a boulder the size of a house were rolling down a hill and was about to kill all three of us—and if you could save only one of us—who would it be?"

You think, *Hmmm . . . that's not so hard. I could easily live without Brianna.* But you're not stupid. *This is a trap. Two of them will hate me. And the one I save will think I'm cruel for letting the other two get crushed.*

You're pretty sure that saving someone from a boulder is *not* what friendship is really about, but the threesome isn't looking for a philosophical discussion. So you stall for time. "Um, could you rephrase the question?"

Read 1 John 3:11–16

How do we know what love is really like?

Life without friendship is like life without air. That's why you feel like your umbilical cord has been severed when you can't text, call, message, or otherwise communicate. It's why being grounded is no fun. It explains why you feel awful when you eat lunch alone or when everyone seems paired off and you're not. Honestly, it's why the first thing you do when you enter a crowd is to look around for anyone you know. It's true: Next to knowing God, having good human relationships is the most important thing in the world (Matthew 22:35–39).

If you belong to God, it changes how you treat people. In fact, love is the big test of whether or not you know God (1 John 4:7–8).

Love is only love when it's demonstrated in real life. You don't get many chances to be a hero and save a friend from a tumbling boulder. You do get opportunities every day to love in less showy ways. Life is a series of endless moments to be kind, to encourage, to admit you're wrong, or to refrain from hurtful habits like jealousy, lust, anger, and selfishness.

Jesus' death passed the true-life friendship test. A promise to save a friend from an imaginary rock? You can do better.

This is how we know what love is: Jesus Christ laid down his life for us.
And we ought to lay down our lives for our brothers and sisters.

1 John 3:16

Day 32
Shopping for Friends

You're not a kid anymore. And your life is like an all-school garage sale: Just like stuff you lived with for so long—toys, clothes, games, vacation souvenirs, whatever—old friends go on the table for cheap. A few are hard to part with, but you figure another table will have better stuff.

Some friends, after all, don't fit so good. They used to feel as comfortable as a favorite pair of jeans, but now not so much. There's nothing wrong with them, so you worry about just ditching them. Other old friends spew nastiness and gossip, and these days you're more mature than that. A few friends are boring or broken—like childhood buddies you used to play baseball or Barbies with who now toy with alcohol, drugs, and sex.

It's not always easy to know at a garage sale what to sell and what to keep—or, if you're buying, what's a bargain and what's a rip-off. It's the same way when you're shopping for friends.

Read Philippians 2:19–24
What kind of friends should you hunt for?

Paul didn't make the Christians in the city of Philippi go garage-sale shopping for a high-quality friend. He packed up his buddy Timothy and shipped him off to meet his dear friends in Philippi.

Timothy was a rare person. While everyone else only thought about their own lives and interests, there was one thing that always mattered most to Timothy: doing what Christ wanted.

You don't need friends who like you when you do wrong.

You don't need people who applaud you for being comical when you drink or chill when you smoke weed.

You want friends who are totally devoted to God and help you get closer to him.

With each year that passes, the less your friends are dictated by where you live or a classroom seating chart—and more to do with interests you share, like sports, music, school subjects, or hobbies. When you go shopping for friends, your best investment are the ones who are interested in God.

For everyone looks out for his own interests, not those of Jesus Christ.

Philippians 2:21

Day 33
Think Small to Think Big

Alisha elbowed William. "Isn't that the boy who moved in across the street from you?" She pointed to a guy moping all alone down the hallway at school. He didn't look at anyone. He just looked afraid.

"I guess so," William answered. "He was at the bus stop this morning. He sat a couple seats away from me—would you quit looking over there? He'll see us." He turned the other way so the new kid wouldn't spot him.

Alisha glared at William. "You're pathetic. I'm going to go say hi and welcome him to school."

"Just leave him alone," William argued. "He's fine. I'm sure he'll make friends. He has to fend for himself like everyone else."

William pulled at Alisha when she started to head in the new kid's direction. "Let's *go*," William begged. "He'll think I want to be his new best friend."

Read Mark 9:30–32

What does it mean to be "like Christ" in how you treat people?

Why are you here on planet earth? To consume oxygen? To master video games? To inhale the contents of your parents' refrigerator? To rule the world?

Think bigger. You're here to become like Christ (2 Corinthians 3:18). You're destined to do the things he did (Ephesians 2:10). God put you on this planet to be a servant like your Master (Mark 9:35). But what does *that* look like?

As his death on the cross loomed only days away, Jesus openly told his disciples that he was about to suffer and die. They didn't get it. They thought that Jesus would crush his enemies and seize power as king of the world. They assumed that being his followers meant ruling along with him and getting rid of people they detested. They didn't understand that being like Jesus means laying down your life for others' good.

Jesus-style servanthood is putting your love into action for all people. Like new kids. And enemies. And losers. People you know and people you don't. Even if your acts of servanthood cost you everything.

The Son of Man is going to be delivered into the hands of men.
They will kill him, and after three days he will rise.

Mark 9:31

Day 34
Makeover

Alexis rolled over, glanced at the clock, groaned, and bolted out of bed. *Not again!* She had eight minutes to fix a disaster. She had nothing clean to wear—everything was in the washer, sopping wet. She pulled her bedhead into a ponytail and tugged on a hat.

A sprint to the bus stop spared her from a long, late walk to school, and she dropped panting into the first open seat. Bad choice. Morgan smiled sweetly at Alexis. "Sleep through your alarm again?" she inquired. "That's twice this week, isn't it?"

Once up on a time, Morgan had loaned a stack of teen magazines to Alexis, an act of pity on someone she regarded as the ugly neighbor girl. Alexis toiled to follow their beauty tips, but it was like trying to follow a blueprint to build an aircraft carrier. And Alexis once again felt miserably average. She dreamed of having Morgan's flawless face and bikini-ready body. She wished she could get plastic surgery on her life.

Read Titus 3:3–8

How do you put a stop to jealousy?

Beauty queens claw and whine to stay in the spotlight and score their own talk shows. Champion athletes try to stay in the game as armchair sports commentators. Jealousy doesn't end when you get what someone else has, because sooner or later you get bumped from your throne.

Your only hope is to be happy with what you have.

God doesn't do plastic surgery to make you into someone else. He does, however, perform a heart transplant that remakes your attitude. Paul told Titus that before we meet God, we're wrapped up in malice (a desire to harm or spite others) and envy (unhappiness at what someone else has or can do). Yet when we accept God's kindness, we begin to see we have everything we truly need—God's acceptance, his forgiveness, the promise of living in eternal paradise with him, and friendship right now with his Holy Spirit.

Compared to that, the stuff that others have—that we don't—is nothing.

We lived in malice and envy, being hated and hating one another. But when the kindness and love of God our Savior appeared, he saved us....

Titus 3:3–5

Day 35
Bragging Rights

"Strike three! That's the game!" the umpire hollered. Runners trotted in from first and third, and the scorekeeper recorded another loss for the Panthers. "You're out, son," the ump said a bit more gently as Hunter stood in the batter's box, still trying to figure out what had blown by him. "Next time."

Hunter was barely out of the box when David jumped him. "You whiffed! You always whiff! You lost the game!"

"Me? I wasn't the only one who got out," Hunter shot back.

"You're a loser. Almost the whole team is a bunch of losers. I don't know why I play on this team. I hit, I run, I score—then you whiff."

Jake joined David in walloping Hunter, and others trotted over to see what the noise was about. "The two of us," Jake bragged, "could beat the rest of you put together."

Read Jeremiah 9:23–24

When is it okay to brag?

You can argue with a friend about who's taller, but you both look short next to the starting center for the Lakers. You can debate who's smarter, but Einstein wouldn't have asked either of you for help with his homework. Likewise, God reminds us that next to him we don't measure up. "To whom will you compare me?" God asks in Isaiah 40:25. "Or who is my equal?"

God's goal isn't to pound us into the ground like a kid hunting ants with a baseball bat. Here's his point: The things we brag about are imperfect, powerless, and broken down. It's pointless to feel overly proud of brains that misfire, beauty that fades, muscles that go flabby, or money that flushes down the drain in ways we can't predict.

It's right to enjoy the good things God gives us. Even so, our confidence and security is God himself—not some ugly brute of a God, but One perfect in kindness and goodness. God is "righteous in all his ways and faithful in all he does" (Psalm 145:17).

Having a friend like that *is* something worth bragging about.

> Let him who boasts boast about this: that they have the
> understanding to know me, that I am the Lord.
>
> *Jeremiah 9:24*

Day 36

Don't Apologize for You

"*That* isn't the Little Dipper. It's over *there*," Jada argued.

"Actually, it's that set of stars up there," Lauren said quietly. "See the handle? And the dipper?" Lauren was surprised. *They didn't laugh at me.* Dazzled by the night sky outside the city, kids on the church retreat actually seemed to listen to her. So Lauren pointed out other constellations. Then Mars and Jupiter. One of the kids, though, said she was making stuff up. Lauren got quiet again.

"Ignore him," one of the adult leaders advised. Then he asked how she knew so much. Lauren never told anyone she was into astronomy because it would only make her feel even more like she came from another planet. She didn't care about clothes, got bored putting on makeup, and thought most boys needed to grow up. But this time she let some of her enthusiasm out. The leader thought Lauren should bring her telescope on the next retreat.

Maybe she would.

Read Psalm 138

How can you learn to be bold about who you are?

Different probably isn't high on your list of what you want to be when you grow up. You might like a classmate no one else does so you pretend to swoon over a popular person you think is stupid. Or you know that people are about to bad-mouth your music or your hobbies so you clobber them before they clobber you. True, sometimes it's socially acceptable to be strange—but only if the crowd says so.

That's what the "gods" and "goddesses" around you think. But the real God has some amazing news about who you are.

You are the work of God's hands—and he won't abandon you. He made you unique—and he will show you his purpose for you. His heart is with you wherever you go—and when you ask for help, he will make you bold.

God delights in nothing more than seeing you live as the masterpiece he made you (Ephesians 2:10). He deserves praise for how he designed you—no matter what others think. When you're shy about revealing the real you, he is your source of power to break out and be yourself.

When I called, you answered me; you greatly emboldened me.

Psalm 138:3

Day 37
Don't Roll Over

Sabina knew something was wrong as soon as she picked up her backpack. *This is too light,* she thought. She kicked herself for forgetting her homework. . . . But then she recalled that she *had* put her homework in the bag.

Someone's been in my stuff. Fumbling to unzip her bag, she dumped it upside down. Only two library books fell out—none of her spiral notebooks. Worst of all, her typed-up oral report and all the notes she used to put it together were gone.

The next day, her teacher wouldn't buy Sabina's story about a stolen paper—even when a girl named Kennedy stood up and read Sabina's report, word for word. With all her notes and everything gone, Sabina had no way to prove Kennedy had read *her* paper.

Sabina was dead.

Read 1 Peter 4:8

Are you supposed to roll over and play dead after someone hurts you?

When someone does you wrong, you might long to let loose the pit bulls.

Jesus gave you a better way to confront wrong. He said to start by talking to the person who hurt you. If getting face-to-face doesn't resolve the situation, take someone with you to back up what you say. And if that doesn't work, you can appeal to people in authority, like parents, teachers, principals, or pastors (Matthew 18:15–17).

However those tactics turn out, there's one more step to take. When you've done all you can do to set a situation straight, it's time to let love "cover" the wrongs you have suffered.

To cover a pile of sins obviously doesn't mean to act like wrongs never happened, or Jesus would never have given you that script for fighting back his way. But it does mean you forgive others as God has forgiven you (Colossians 3:13). You quit broadcasting blame (Proverbs 17:9). You do your best to live at peace (Romans 12:16).

You don't have to roll over when someone wrongs you. But you do need to call off the dogs.

Above all, love each other deeply, because love covers over a multitude of sins.

1 Peter 4:8

Day 38
Right Place, Right Time

Elijah joked with a clump of friends as they waited to buy movie tickets. When a group of guys from church walked up and spotted him, they looked less than friendly. It felt like they were spying on him.

Sitting in the movie, Elijah couldn't figure out why his Christian friends were upset. He wasn't sneaking into some terrible movie he shouldn't see; and Elijah knew his parents would never let him go to the movie his Christian friends headed in to see.

When Elijah darted out for a bucket of popcorn, one of his church friends followed him to the lobby. Cody pounced. "What are you doing with those guys?"

"They're my friends from down the block," Elijah explained.

Cody wasn't convinced. "You shouldn't hang around with them. You're going to turn into one of them. They're going to ruin you."

Read Luke 15:1–2

Can Christians have non-Christian friends?

You can be fairly sure you're in the wrong place at the wrong time with the wrong crowd if police officers bust down the doors and shoot in tear gas.

But people and places and situations don't have to be unmistakably evil to be risky to your faith. The Bible, for example, makes clear that Christians shouldn't be "unequally yoked," roped together with non-Christians. Making those folks your only friends sooner or later will keep you from obeying God (2 Corinthians 6:14).

But that doesn't mean God wants you to run and hide from non-Christians. When the Pharisees criticized Jesus for spending time with sinners—including the lowest life-form of that society, tax collectors—Jesus retorted that he was like a doctor rushing to help the wounded and dying.

Jesus went where he was needed most. He wasn't making an excuse to have out-of-bounds fun. His goal was to invite people to meet God. What's yours?

The Pharisees and the teachers of the law muttered, "This
man welcomes sinners and eats with them."

Luke 15:2

Day 39

Squashed

"I don't want any," Olivia protested. "Not my thing. In fact, I need to go."

Olivia darted out the front door of Sarah's house. It didn't take her long to get home—after all, her best friend lived just three doors down. But it was long enough for Olivia to realize that something about their friendship had been changing. It had been months since they had a sleepover and weeks since they had hung out for more than a few minutes. Nothing like the old days.

Olivia couldn't believe it when Sarah handed her a baggie with a few prescription pills and told her to try one. *Sarah? Really?!*

Read Galatians 1:3–12

When is it worst to give in to peer fear?

You don't live in this world by yourself. It's crowded. You bump into people. They shove back. Sometimes they gang up and squash you. You inevitably get molded into a new shape.

You've heard that before. Parents, teachers, and public service commercials have been telling you since you were two that peers have the potential to crush you.

But peer pressure isn't all bad. If not for peer fear, you'd still pick your nose in public. You can't live isolated from your peers, and a lot of times it's fine to fit in. God doesn't intend for Christians to lives in their own private bubble, clueless about when it's *okay* to conform.

Yet you can never be all that your peers want you to be. In one area—your faith as a Christian—it's never right to be squashed by the forces that surround you. The facts that Christ died and rose for you, forgives you, and deserves your full obedience aren't ideas open for negotiation. You don't dump them to win points with people.

Sometimes you can act, talk, dress, and think in a way that is wonderful both to God and people. Other times you can't. It's a choice. Then it's no contest whose opinion matters more.

Do you think I am trying to make people accept me? No, God is the One I am trying to please. Am I trying to please people? If I still wanted to please people, I would not be a servant of Christ.

Galatians 1:10 NCV

Day 40
Screen Surfing

A hundred and sixty-two channels, and Nina's top choices were a demo of lesser-known spreadsheet features, a shopping network dedicated to ceramic kittens, and a local-access rerun of a third-grade boys' basketball game. Even the endless variety of videos and clips streaming online struck Nina as worse than boring.

Nina agreed with her parents that her school's dances weren't the best place to spend an evening. She'd been there. She'd seen what went on. So she didn't go. Normally she didn't feel left out because she always found something else to do. But this time her friends weren't around, her mom was traveling for work, and her dad was entertaining Nina's sick little brother.

So at seven o'clock that evening as the dance was starting, Nina curled up on her bed and stared at the wall, imagining the fun she was missing.

Read Psalm 1:1-6

What does God promise you when you feel left out because of him?

Some days you might feel like a lone tree on the prairie, bent by the wind, scraggly for lack of water. No one lops a gushing hose at your roots. No one trims you to look like a giraffe or a flamingo. You fear you'll lose your leaves, shrivel up, then tumble away in the wind.

Maybe you worry you'll be forever left out if you refuse to wallow with the wicked or saddle up with sinners or mess around with those who mock God. Your imagination might roar with all the fun you'll miss.

It's time to ground yourself in reality. You're not the one who needs to worry about wilting. Look at what God promises his people: They drink from his streams. They sprout fruit. They stand in his presence. He watches over every detail of their lives. And here's what happens to those who distance themselves from God: They lack roots—no water, no food, no life. They're dried-out chaff (the husks left over from threshing wheat). They blow away in the hurricane of God's wind.

Doesn't sound like you're missing much.

Blessed is the one
who does not walk in step with the wicked
or stand in the way that sinners take
or sit in the company of mockers.

Psalm 1:1

Day 41
I Gag

Megan rolled her eyes when her new science partner walked up and bobbed her hair from side to side. "I was so glad when I found out you were my partner!" Felicity chirped. "If I hadn't gotten paired up with you, I was gonna flunk. Everyone says you're a brainiac, you know."

Every day since then, Megan slaved over science experiments while Felicity giggled with her friends at another table. Felicity explained that helping out would require goggles, and that goggles meant significant hair repair—which was obviously not acceptable. So Megan was stuck. If she didn't do the work, she and Felicity would be partners again—in summer school.

Read Matthew 18:15–17

What can Christians do when someone treats them badly?

Christians are supposed to "turn the other cheek," right? Yes, Jesus uttered those familiar words (Matthew 5:38–39). But Jesus was talking about not taking tooth-for-tooth revenge—like shattering a rack of test tubes over Felicity's head. He never said you shouldn't try to solve problems.

No one likes a nag. You've got to overlook little offenses or you'll drive yourself crazy (Proverbs 19:11). But if you find a wrong too big to let go, Jesus says to talk to that person directly. You need a brave heart and gentle words. It's far more difficult than moaning or gossiping about the problem, but it's also more effective, especially if you're ready to apologize for any wrongs you might have done.

If speaking to the person doesn't work, Jesus gives further steps, like taking a friend or two with you—not to gang up on the person but to back up your accusations. After you've done your best with the first two steps, you can go to someone in authority for help.

Jesus' solution does away with whining, stewing, tattling, and behind-the-back complaining. It's also radically realistic. Jesus recognizes that you can't fix every problem, and—as a last resort—he recommends that sometimes you need to take a break from people who mistreat you.

> If your brother or sister sins, go and point out their fault, just between the two of you. If they listen to you, you have won them over.
>
> *Matthew 18:15*

Day 42

Explosions

All season long, Nick and his lacrosse teammates had fought hard to become a fierce team, able to dominate almost any opponent that faced off against them.

But as Nick watched a game-winning goal hit the net and kill their team's chance at the league championship, he exploded. "Christopher!" he screamed. "You idiot! You call yourself a goalie? How could you have let that by? If it weren't for you, at least we would have had a chance in overtime."

KaBOOM. Christopher walked away, choking back tears. (Real men don't whimper, after all—at least when others are looking.)

Read 1 Peter 5:5

*How can you put a friendship back together
after you've blown it apart?*

When you battle with friends, it's like you've dynamited a giant hole in the ground, shoved others in, and tumbled after them.

You might wonder why you need to undo the damage you cause when you've hit, bit, spat upon, betrayed, cheated, lied to, gossiped about, or otherwise hurt someone.

For starters, it gets tense down in that hole you dug. Fighting leaves you friendless. And there's another huge reason. Christ has accepted you just as you are, flaws and all. As Christians, we're commanded to accept others as completely as God accepts us (Romans 15:7).

Peter points out your only way to climb out of the pit: humility.

Your first foothold is asking forgiveness from God (1 John 1:9) and from the person or people you hurt (Matthew 5:23–24). If you pretend you did nothing wrong, you just dig yourself deeper. There are other footholds that let you climb out of the pit little by little: See a situation through others' eyes. Let go of your ego. Remember others' needs, not just your own. Show love through concrete actions.

When you do those things, you and your friends will find your way out of the pit.

All of you, clothe yourselves with humility toward one another,
because, "God opposes the proud but shows favor to the humble."

1 Peter 5:5

Day 43
Over the Edge

"I'm going over. It looks like fun." With that announcement, your friend climbs over the edge of a cliff—a stupid stunt, like bungee-jumping without the bungee. Unless you do something in the next split second, she'll plummet to the bottom of a gorge.

You throw her a rope. What do you do next? Do you (a) let go of the rope and yell, "Buh-bye!", (b) heroically wedge yourself into a tree and pray you don't get rope burn, (c) run to your youth group and lead a Bible study about your friend's brainlessness, or (d) tie the rope to an enormous rock and find some people to help you pull your friend to safety?

Read Galatians 6:1–2

How can you help hurting friends?

Friends and classmates jump over spiritual, moral, and emotional cliffs all the time. What can you do about it?

Abandoning friends isn't cool. You've got a relationship—a rope attached to your friend. Galatians says you can pull people back up by helping carry their "burdens," a word that means a load too large for any one person to lift.

But helping friends out of danger is tricky. They might need more help than you alone can provide, like with depression or substance abuse. You don't want to get dragged over the same cliff. Just when you think your spiritual heft will keep you safely anchored on top of the cliff, that's the moment their weight will *fuh-whang* you over the edge (1 Corinthians 10:12).

Any choice but *d* is unwise. You've got an immovable Rock to which you can anchor your fallen friends. Pray for them. Ask God to help you to encourage, persuade, and befriend, and to know how to model faith for the person who needs more of Jesus.

And find help. Rescuing your friends single-handedly might seem heroic, but it's stupid. You don't get a second chance if your friends strike the bottom of the gorge—and take you with them.

> Brothers and sisters, if someone is caught in a sin, you who
> live by the Spirit should restore that person gently.
>
> *Galatians 6:1*

Day 44
Ready, Aim, Fire

Radar sweeps the horizon. *Zzzt. Zzzt. Zzzt.* Stunningly pretty girl at two o'clock floating through the lunchroom. She turns the head of every guy who sees her, but no one knows her name. They dare each other to introduce themselves to the new girl.

Meanwhile, the girls are also at it. Fresh from study hall, Amanda eagerly reports on Santiago. "His smile is so cute!" she squeals. "He said hi to me. He's so nice." As hearts *thump thump thump*, the girls conclude that Santiago is everything a girl could want in a guy—friendly, funny, considerate, and supremely beautiful.

Read 1 Corinthians 13:4–7
What qualities should you look for in a guy or a girl?

Smart hunters know what they're looking at before they take aim. *I heard something . . . over there . . . the bush moved . . . BLAM BLAM BLAM* isn't good strategy. Before you know whether you're aiming at a deer, a tree, or your hunting partner, you've shot something or someone dead.

The same is true for hunting guys or girls. Don't aim your heart at someone you're not sure you want to hit. The person you set your sights on right now actually matters. Why? The kind of person you get crushes on becomes the kind of person you want to date. The kind you date becomes the kind of person you love and want to spend your life with.

The "Love Chapter" of the Bible—1 Corinthians 13—tells what to look for in a significant other: patience, kindness, humility, good manners, unselfishness, an even temper. Someone who forgives, does right, and never stops wanting God's best for you and your relationship. That adds up to someone totally devoted to Christ. That's your target. Don't waste yourself on anything less.

You can't spot those qualities from a glance across the lunchroom or from a smile in study hall. You have to watch someone for a long time to know for sure what you're aiming at.

Love does not delight in evil but rejoices with the truth.

1 Corinthians 13:6

Day 45
Bladder Buster

The movie is half over when you feel a tiny jab. *I can wait*, you decide. *I can make it.* But a while later—with a half hour of movie remaining—there's no ignoring the pressure. You try to forget the two-liter bladder buster you guzzled before the movie started.

You cross your legs. You uncross them. You try to relax. Your back screams pain. Your feet tap-dance.

You lose it.

Wrong time. Wrong place. If only you had been more careful about what you had to drink, you would have been able to wait.

Read Genesis 2:19–25

Why is marriage a big deal?

Back in the Garden of Eden, Adam had a literal zooful of friends. But God made Adam a partner so he could have someone to share his life with at the deepest level of body and soul.

Nowadays marriage is the same big deal. It's a man-and-woman promise in God's presence to love each other until death parts. To couples who commit themselves to that unending friendship, God gives the gift of sexual love as an amazing wedding present. Hebrews 13:4 says, "Marriage should be honored by all, and the marriage bed kept pure." To keep marriage "pure" means to save sex and all that leads up to it for God's time and place.

As you get older, however, your body and emotions get impatient. If you truly want to choose God's best for your life—if you want to wait for sexual love until marriage—you can't be stupid about what you take into your life right now. Pornography, movies, videos, music, dirty jokes, lust, dating without boundaries—all these things add to the pressure you feel.

Some of those are like sips. Some are gallon gulps. You have a choice about what you drink—what you look at, listen to, and think about. It's better to watch what you drink than to wait in misery—or to lose it all.

The man said, "This is now bone of my bones and flesh of my flesh."
Genesis 2:23

Day 46

Which Row to Hoe

Sebastian and Nora met in social studies class. It was a magical combo. Sebastian was funny, Nora was shy, and their teacher was so nearsighted and hard of hearing that he didn't notice them sitting next to each other in the back of the room. All semester long, Sebastian and Nora wrote notes, whispered, and laughed.

Sebastian wasn't a Christian and Nora was, but Nora liked Sebastian because he paid attention to her. He said she was pretty. She couldn't understand why he hung out with the people he did—they looked kind of wild—but . . .

Read 2 Corinthians 6:14–7:1

What does God say about relationships between
Christians and non-Christians?

Make no mistake: Jesus told Christians to reach out and enlarge God's family, and that only happens if you make friends with non-Christians.

Yet a tug-of-war starts when a Christian is "yoked" to an unbeliever, lashed together like two oxen plowing a field. Two things can happen. You can fight about how and where to plow, and rip each other's heads off, or you can give in and let the non-Christian drag you down a row you shouldn't go. Forcing a non-Christian to go down your row is never an option, by the way. Jesus doesn't *make* us come to him. He invites us.

Being best friends, going together, dating, or marrying are all relationships that yoke. But sports teams, jobs, clubs, or other activities that demand total commitment can also control you in a bad way.

No non-Christian will join you completely in living your faith—in belonging to God and making him the most important thing in your life. You're not headed toward the same goals or holding the same standards. God wants your closest friends to be people you can pull together with—toward the goal of knowing and following him better.

> For what do righteousness and wickedness have in common?
> Or what fellowship can light have with darkness? What does
> a believer have in common with an unbeliever?
>
> *2 Corinthians 6:14–15*

Day 47

In This Corner

Jake hated baby-sitting his younger brother and sister. Tuesday was grocery day, and once again Jake's mom reminded him to come straight home from school so she could run to the store. Talking at lunch, Jake's friends made other after-school plans—nothing big, just playing basketball—and they mocked him about going home to play Mommy.

That afternoon, Jake's mind bounced back and forth: *Go. Don't go. Go. Don't go.* It would have gone on forever—except that the last bell rang and his friends were leaving. He had to decide.

Being stuck between friends and parents is like a boxing match—friends in one corner, parents in another. At the bell they dance into the ring. They don't fight each other. They come after *you*. If you listen to your parents, friends might hit you hard. Listen to the wrong friends, and parents rampage.

Read Proverbs 1:8–19

What big bad influences does the father warn his son against?

The bad guys in Proverbs wanted the son to help ambush an innocent man. Jake's friends just wanted him to shoot hoops, but by encouraging him to break his mom's trust, they were still pushing him into doing wrong. Friends, enemies, and everyone in between can pressure you the same way. They want to tell you how to talk, think, feel, and act. Sometimes what they suggest doesn't agree with what your parents expect. Or what God wants, for that matter.

Like Jake and the son listening to his dad in Proverbs, you need to figure out what's true and right—what's really best for you. The "sinners" offered the son easy-to-grasp benefits: being part of their group and sharing in the plunder, enough to meet any need. Your peers might make big promises too, like popularity, excitement, or adventure. Parents argue those promises are a sucker punch—a wallop that will catch you by surprise when you least expect it.

Who's right? What's best? You're dead center in the boxing ring with both sides are coming at you. It's time to think hard about your parents and the job God gives them.

My son, if sinful men entice you, do not give in to them.

Proverbs 1:10

Day 48
From Mars with Love

Your suspicions about your parents' true origin arose the first time you flipped through their high school yearbooks. All those pointy heads and spaced-out faces. What's up with that? Your parents aren't the only ones who look like they're from another planet. So do most of their classmates.

The truth hits you like an electric jolt. *My parents were part of a massive alien invasion.*

Your theory explains a lot. You've always wondered why your parents argue about finer points of warp drives when they watch *Star Trek*. Suddenly you have answers to your deepest questions—like why your dad has a forest of nose hairs and why your mom constantly bemoans her age and weight. *If she were back on Mars,* you calculate, *she'd be 47 percent younger—and tons lighter!* Only one question still begs for an answer. How can your parents pilot a flying saucer 250 million miles but not be able to figure out their smartphones?

Read Psalm 68:6
What's God's plan for you to get along in your family?

It's beyond strange. You can be enjoying a perfectly normal conversation with your parents when suddenly you're sucked into a Martian Moment, a throbbing instant when their utter weirdness convinces you they're from another planet.

But if your parents are Martians, what does that make you? You're a chip off the old planetoid. You're not as alien to one another as you might think. When your parents say, "You'll understand when you have kids," you actually understand what they mean—sometimes. There's a lot of them in you—and a lot of you in them. You'll probably be a parent someday. And your parents definitely were once your age, although it might have been a long time ago in a distant galaxy.

God knows exactly where your parents came from. He wants to help you get along with them when it feels like they hover. And for all those times when they're nowhere nearby, he wants to teach you to follow *him.*

God sets the lonely in families, he leads out the prisoners with singing;
but the rebellious live in a sun-scorched land.

Psalm 68:6

Day 49
The Parental Mind

As you try to understand your parents, you might feel as if you're at the helm of as starship blasting into an uncharted sector of the universe. Other explorers, you've heard, have died trying to squeeze their vessels into so tiny a space. Contrary to all previous data, however, you discover the mind of your parents isn't empty. Actually, it's bigger than it looks from the outside, and once you figure a way in, you bump into some astonishing stuff.

Lots of days your parents are pretty okay. Other times, you might wonder if your parents have anything in their heads besides a slow computer churning out one command: MAKE CHILD MISERABLE.

Your wondering isn't wholly wrong. The truth is that your parents *are* programmed at the factory to follow one extraordinary command.

Read Proverbs 22:6

What job does God give to parents?

Parents understand that they have one goal: to raise children to become adults who can survive and thrive on their own. They aim to move their children from dirtying diapers to changing them, from spending money to earning it, from being parented to parenting.

All parents have that programmed into their brains—and you do too, as you'll discover when you have kids. Christian parents also understand that training a son or daughter in "the way they should go" ultimately means raising that child to follow Jesus in every area of life.

That one job has countless duties. God expects parents to protect their children (Hebrews 11:24), provide for them (1 Timothy 5:8), and discipline them (Hebrews 12:7, 11). Besides that, he expects all parents to love him and teach their children to do the same (Deuteronomy 6:5–7).

Knowing your parents have those four assignments might make you nervous. That's because you're programmed to want to grow up and thrive on your own. That's what makes growing up so interesting.

Start children off on the way they should go, and even
when they are old they will not turn from it.

Proverbs 22:6

Day 50
Waiting Up

Lily was supposed to be home an hour ago. Where is she? She always calls if she's late. We shouldn't have let her go with Riley.

When Lily gets home, sees the lights on, and finds her parents pacing the living room and nervously stuffing themselves with chips, how will she react? If she had been home on time, their waiting up might have seemed cute and comforting. Tonight, however, she'll probably get angry when her parents ask why she was late.

Parents are the people who wait up for you to make sure you get home safely. They keep the lights on. But you might not always like those lights shining bright. Some days, in fact, you want to turn your parents off and on like a switch. You want them on when you can use them—and off when they're a hassle.

Read Ephesians 6:1–3
What does it mean to "honor your parents"?

Your parents no doubt embarrass you at times. Your dad might wear his favorite Hawaiian shirt, cargo shorts, sweat socks, and dress shoes to a school event. Other times they make you angry. But you've done the same to them—like when you barfed at the supermarket checkout, or when the police brought you home for hurling rocks at cars. Your parents didn't stop caring for you.

Honor is pretty much how you treat your parents when you want something from them. You show respect. You hear their side. You obey. But there's a world of difference between wanting to honor them and just sucking up to them to grant your wish. Honoring your parents is treating them well with no expectation of a payoff.

Parents deserve nothing less than that honor, even when they embarrass you or you disagree. And as you learn to honor them day after day, they'll learn to trust you enough to not wait up. Or at least they'll pretend to go to sleep.

Your parents keep the lights on for you. Don't shut 'em off on them.

Children, obey your parents in the Lord, for this is right.

Ephesians 6:1

Day 51

Hound Dog

Jamal just wanted to hang out with friends. His dad just wanted to know what they would be doing. "You never trust me!" Jamal yelled. When his dad announced that Jamal was grounded for the weekend and told him to go to his room, Jamal just glared. Then he grabbed his jacket and headed out the door.

Jamal was absolutely right. His parents don't trust him.

But he's overlooking another truth. He doesn't trust his parents. Once upon a time, he thought his parents knew everything. Now he calls them idiots. Once he thought they were caring. Now he complains when they're too much in his business.

Read Proverbs 4:3–4

What do parents know?

It's normal for your insides to churn when your parents start a sentence with "I expect you to . . ." or "You'd better not . . ." or "When I was your age . . ." But get this: Parents know *lots* about *lots of things*. And they know *something* about *pretty much everything*. Parents are usually more than happy to spout advice. So what do you do when that advice spills over on you?

Trust is complex. It results from you believing that (1) your parents have wisdom you can learn from, (2) they want what's best for you, and (3) they're part of how God guides you. Trust means hearing and obeying your parents even when you're convinced they're wrong and you're right.

If you trust your parents enough to obey, something amazing happens. Eventually, you gain more freedom than you ever imagined.

When you don't trust your parents, you're like an untrained pup. Ignoring their advice in favor of making your own mistakes means you're a wild little beast, not the mature young adult you want to be. If your parents sense that you don't listen to them, don't be surprised if they keep you on a short leash. And don't blame them when you try to gnaw through the leash and end up chewing off your leg.

When I was a young boy in my father's house and like an only child
to my mother, my father taught me and said, "Hold on to my words
with all your heart. Keep my commands and you will live."

Proverbs 4:3–4 NCV

Day 52
Obnoxious Parents

Emma poked at her phone, ready to hit *send* on a party invitation. "Okay, Dad. Everything's filled in except the end time." Then she brought it up again: "Can they sleep over or not?"

"Don't ask again," her dad snapped. "I told you *no*. When your friends sleep over, you're out of control. Remember last time? Screaming through the house and running into walls at four in the morning!"

What's Emma's next move?

Does honoring and obeying her parents mean Emma should give up and play dead? From the outside looking in, it's hard to tell who's right—maybe Emma, maybe her dad—but here's a great fact: God doesn't just tell daughters and sons how to act. He has rules for parents too.

Read Ephesians 6:4

What key thing does God tell parents never to do?

God wants parents to provide and guide with love. Kids are supposed to listen and learn. But we all mess up. And sometimes you'll feel your parents are the ones who fall short.

Parents might embarrass you. They may pay more attention to whatever they're doing than to you. You might think they're too strict about your friends, music, attitude, bedtime, schoolwork, social life, or a hundred other things. Exasperation is what you feel when you've pulled out your hair and want to pull out their hair too.

What can you do when your parents irk you?

You can learn to speak up. Instead of screaming or plotting your escape from their control, your best approach is to respectfully *appeal* to them like you would bring a well-prepared case to a judge. You offer reasons: "I think I should be able to . . . and this is why." You present evidence: "I've proven myself in these instances." You ask for a decision: "What do you think?"

Then accept your parents' decision, as you do the authority of a judge. Parents have the final say. *What* you say and *how* you say it will impact their decision. And if not this one, the next.

Fathers, do not exasperate your children; instead, bring
them up in the training and instruction of the Lord.

Ephesians 6:4

Day 53
Guess I'll Keep Them

It looked like a rock slide had dropped on Mason and swallowed him up. When the pile cleared, Mason lay pretzel-shaped on the football field.

Even from the bleachers, his parents could see something was wrong. When Mason didn't get up, his coach ran in from the sideline. Mason writhed in pain, his leg broken.

"Where's my dad?" Mason cried as they took him off the field. "Get my dad and mom!"

Since the day you were born, your parents have been letting go, little by little, allowing you to grow more independent. At one point, they held your hand wherever you went. Now they're content to watch you from the stands.

Sometimes you're glad to spot them in the front row. Other times you wish they would disappear under the bleachers and maybe never come back. But they're the first ones who come running when you need them. They're probably the people you want most when trouble hits.

Read Luke 2:40–52

Did Jesus ever mess up his parents? How did he work it out?

Jesus never sinned (Hebrews 4:15). He never strayed from God's plan or disobeyed God's commands. That doesn't mean he never perplexed his ol' ma and pa.

In this famous Bible scene, it wasn't as if the Joseph Carpenter family of Nazareth drove off and forgot twelve-year-old Jesus at a rest stop. Joseph didn't glance in the backseat and turn to Mary and say, "Have you seen Jesus? Oops!" Traveling to the Passover Feast caravan-style with a crowd of other people, Joseph and Mary likely assumed Jesus was with friends or cousins. It took a day to realize he was gone, a day to travel back, and a day to search.

Jesus was fine. He wasn't spray-painting graffiti on camels or sleeping on a sewer grate. That wasn't the point. Mary and Joseph knew it was their job for a few more years to keep track of their son. And Jesus knew he still needed his parents. He went home.

> "Son, why have you treated us like this? Your father and I have
> been anxiously searching for you." . . . Then he went down
> to Nazareth with them and was obedient to them.
>
> *Luke 2:48, 51*

Day 54
Cinderfella

Just like every Saturday morning, Caden did a sparkling job washing his mom's car. He picked bugs off the grille and hood, hand-dried the car, and polished the windows. Then he went back inside his family's apartment to do a pile of dishes and dust the furniture.

He finished his chores by vacuuming dust creatures from under the couch—and from under his snoozing brother. Caden kicked hard at the end of the couch, but his brother barely stirred. *I'm going to change my name to Cinderfella,* Caden moaned to himself. *I do all the work around here.*

Read Genesis 4:1–9

Why do siblings sometimes not get along?

If you have brothers or sisters, you probably get mad at them more than at anyone else. That's nothing new.

The first family feud was no pillow fight. It started when God disapproved of Cain's attitude in worship. Cain blamed everyone but himself: *God—what a slave driver. See if I ever bring him another offering. And Abel—that kiss-up gets to play with sheep while I break my back farming. Dad and Mom always loved him more.* Instead of straightening things out with God, Cain took his anger out on Abel.

Cain's fight with his brother actually began as a fight with God. The Lord had warned Cain that if Cain pushed him away, sin would take over his heart and his life. The instant Cain stopped wanting to please God, a family feud was all but inevitable.

Cain thought Abel made him look bad. Your brothers and sisters will give you plenty of real and imagined reasons to get angry—laziness, meanness, hitting, stealing, tattling . . . You have a choice between striking back or obeying God.

When you choose to do right and invite God to help you to love your unlovable siblings, you slam the door shut on sin. When you make your home God's home, you crush sin's fingers in the door.

> But if you do not do what is right, sin is crouching at your
> door; it desires to have you, but you must rule over it.
>
> *Genesis 4:7*

Day 55
Don't Blame Me

Krystal and Ellie had a pact. Everyone else in their friend group walked around with their heads wrapped in high-end headphones, making Krystal and Ellie feel left out. So they agreed that neither would buy headphones until they both could.

When Ellie showed up at school wearing new headphones, Krystal fumed. But the next day she showed up in a pair she swiped from her older brother's room. Nolan forgot them when he went back to college, and he wouldn't be home for a month.

The plan worked until Krystal dropped the headphones during passing time and a kid behind her stepped on them, cracking one side and scratching the other. Krystal shrugged. As soon as she got home from school, she stashed the headphones back in Nolan's room.

When Nolan came home and discovered his busted headphones, he immediately blamed his other sister. Krystal breathed a sigh of relief. She was off the hook.

Read Proverbs 28:13

What good thing happens when you admit wrongdoing?

You're headed for trouble when you don't 'fess up at home—a mess only gets messier. Take Krystal. She borrowed an expensive toy without asking, treated it carelessly, hid the evidence, and let her sister take the heat. She also made fitting in with her friends more important than peace with her family. She had a lot to confess to both God and her family.

It's never easy to admit you've blown it. Saying "I did it" instead of "Not me! Not me!" feels awful. But you're guaranteed a bad time if you hide what you've done wrong.

How come? Because God sees wrongdoing, and he won't let you succeed as long as you hide your sin. Yet if you admit your wrong and resolve to do right, he promises his great forgiveness.

Your family might rub your shortcomings in your face. But the situation will only get worse the longer you hide your sin.

> If you hide your sins, you will not succeed. If you confess
> and reject them, you will receive mercy.
>
> *Proverbs 28:13 NCV*

Day 56

Nightmare Coaster

Justin lounged in the family room, munching on carrots and casting video clips on the big screen. Not much was especially good, but he nudged up the volume to drown out his parents' fight in the next room. A few minutes later his dad went out the door with a suitcase.

"Hey, Dad!" Justin yelled. "Where—?" Dad was out the door before Justin could finish. *Another business trip?* Justin wondered.

A couple days later Justin found out his dad hadn't left on business. He had left for good.

Having parents split is like being dragged onto a roller coaster that thunders out of your nightmares. No one checks to see if you're safely buckled in. You loop, twist, and plunge, hanging on to whatever you can. Even when divorce is a biblical response to an awful problem, it's never a kiddie ride.

Read Psalm 62:1–8

What good is God when family life gets that scary?

The best amusement park roller coasters worry you enough to wonder, *What if . . . ? What if I fall out? A rail breaks? I get sick?* Deep down, however, you're sure you're safe—or you wouldn't ride. On the nightmare coaster of divorce, however, you don't have a choice whether or not to ride, and you're seldom sure what's ahead: *Who will I live with? Will we have enough money? What will happen to me?*

You do have a promise to hang on to as you face the ride: God will keep you safe. When you're weak, he's your fortress. You can tell him whatever you think and feel, even yell at him when you need to. God won't stop the roller coaster—you'll still face unexpected dips and turns. But you can have peace and confidence in him.

The one thing worse than being on the nightmare coaster is riding alone—having no one to scream with, lock arms with, or sigh in relief with. Friends and a supportive parent, pastor, or counselor can ride part of the way. And God has the stomach to always stick with you (Hebrews 13:5).

> [God] is my mighty rock, my refuge. Trust in him at all times, you people; pour out your hearts to him, for God is our refuge.
>
> *Psalm 62:7–8*

Day 57

In the Trunk

Kira and her younger brother, Colin, stood at the front of the church while a band oozed a hipster version of "Here Comes the Bride." *Bride?* Kira had never thought of her mom as a bride. When her mom reached the altar, everyone up front stood at attention—Kira by her mom, and Colin next to Ryan, his stepbrother-to-be.

Colin was all smiles. He was getting a new playmate, plus a new dad to do fun stuff with.

Kira wasn't so sure. Her stomach knotted. She despised Ryan—*little brat*—but she would put him in his place soon enough. Kira's bigger fear was losing her mom. As long as Kira could remember, they had been best friends. It was rough when her mom started dating. Now Kira would have to share her all the time.

Read Romans 12:18

*What's your job when you have to get along
with people you're not sure you like?*

It's hard to know what to expect of a new family arrangement. Kira's mom and Colin each hoped that having a new family would be better than being alone, but Kira dreaded losing the one relationship she knew she could count on. Same situation, different expectations, maybe different outcomes.

Relationships are like driving a car. When it comes to friends, you're usually in the driver's seat, usually getting to pick who rides along. With classmates or teammates, you get some choice, sort of like being a backseat driver. When it comes to family, you get no control. You're all stuffed in the trunk together, like it or not.

You help decide whether the trunk is cozy or cramped. Every family feels crunched at times, but you can at least control whether it's *you* doing the elbowing, shoving, and kicking. You can decide not to bang on the inside of the trunk or drill into the gas tank and drop in a match. You can't control who's in the trunk, but you can control yourself.

If it is possible, as far as it depends on you, live at peace with everyone.

Romans 12:18

Day 58
Never-Ending Love

"My dad keeps trying to push his way into my life," Steven fumed. "Until a few months ago, he was never around. Now he's having a midlife crisis, and it hits him that he's been a workaholic. He always went to work before I got up and came home after I was in bed. He never knew when I needed anything, so I started mowing yards and walking dogs and everything else to make my own money. I'm sorry, but I don't need him now."

It's easy to forget to feed a fish—it doesn't make noise. It's harder to forget to feed a dog—it scratches and yelps when it's hungry. It should be impossible to forget about a kid—they can use words and actions to scream for what they need. But it happens. Some parents neglect their children.

Read Lamentations 3:22–24

Does God's love for you ever run out?

At some time or other, almost everyone feels ignored by their parents. And it's easy to think a friend's parents are nicer, more understanding, more easygoing with rules, more there-when-you-need-them-and-not-when-you-don't. In better moments, though, your parents seem pretty good. You get along. You talk things over and work problems out.

But in some families, relationships are totally neglected. A parent may work too much just to buy nice stuff. They give material things but never time or attention. Others escape into hobbies or into too much activity at church. A mom or dad may up and leave. And a few parents are just cold. It's as if their voicemail says, "I'm sorry, but we're unavailable. We don't plan to return your call."

God never forgets his children (Isaiah 49:16). His comfort and compassion never quit (Lamentations 3:22–23). His love "reaches to the heavens" (Psalm 36:5). And nothing in all of creation can ever separate us "from the love of God that is in Christ Jesus our Lord" (Romans 8:39).

God loves you now. And his love lasts forever.

Because of the Lord's great love we are not consumed, for his compassions never fail. They are new every morning; great is your faithfulness.

Lamentations 3:22–23

Day 59

Outta Here!

Abby hid behind the doorway when her eighteen-year-old brother punched his fist through the living room wall. "I hate you!" Gavin screamed at his parents. "I'm sick of your stupid rules. You never listen to me. You treat me like I'm a baby. I'm an adult. I can run my own life!" The front door slammed hard after Gavin, and his motorcycle roared as he drove off.

Gavin spent the next couple of weeks at a friend's house, then moved in with some older guys. Abby couldn't believe the hole in the wall or the way Gavin treated their parents, but she was a little jealous that her brother got to be out on his own.

It's normal to dream about growing up and moving out. It's a fantasy, though, to think that being out from under your parents makes everything perfect.

Read Joshua 24:14–21

What does Joshua vow his family will do?

Life isn't a game. That's why parents usually shelter you from the cold facts of life: If you're mouthy, you get fired. If you're unruly, you get bounced out of your apartment. If you're lazy, you starve. More than that, when you leave home you don't escape rules. Instead of parents, you get professors and roommates and bosses—and then a spouse and kids to answer to. And you never know when you might boomerang home to the same old bedroom and same old parents.

In fact, there's no such thing as "running your own life." When you're out on your own, maybe with a family to care for, life presents you with only two choices: *I will follow and obey God*, or *I will choose another god*.

Look out: Picking another god means signing up for slavery and death (Romans 6:20–23). You leave what you think is a prison and wind up in a zoo. It might look like a nice place to visit, but you wouldn't want to live there.

Happiness and freedom comes from choosing to enjoy God and his will for you no matter where you're at (Psalm 37:3–4). It's better to enjoy your place in God's family than to be a baboon locked up in a zoo.

But as for me and my household, we will serve the Lord.

Joshua 24:15

Day 60
The (Im)perfect Family

Sitting behind the Martins in church, you'd think they leapt from an ad for a trendy store—all perfect with their stylin' clothes, hip hair, and orthodontically perfect smiles. Every family in church wishes they could be the Martins. Or at least pretend for a while.

But no one saw the Martins on the way to church, when Ana once again mangled Cameron's fingers for saying that a boy she likes has a face like a fish. And when the family hums along in church, no one can tell that Mom and Dad haven't spoken to each other for the last three days.

Read Galatians 5:14

How can you make your home a happier place?

If you compare your family to the *image* of people like the Martins, you might feel cheated.

So join their family for a while. Want to be Cameron, getting your fingers torqued until they touch your wrist? Or how about Ana, who apparently has never learned a happier way to deal with her brother? Or how about swapping places with either of them, always wondering why Mom and Dad can't agree on anything?

If you could see inside families that seem to be so much better than yours, you'd find that no family is perfect. So what do you do about yours?

God offers a simple rule that can transform the inhabitants of your house into some of your best friends: Love your neighbor—as in your mom, dad, sisters, brothers, whoever else lives in your house—just as you love yourself.

The family is a web of relationships you can't escape. It forces you to learn to love, to forgive, to talk about what hurts, to put God and others first, to get help when the family breaks. And get this: Whatever lessons you refuse to learn now can become problems that, until you learn to solve them, will haunt all your relationships for the rest of your life.

If you want your family to work well, work hard at working together. Your closest neighbors share the same roof.

The entire law is fulfilled in keeping this one command:
"Love your neighbor as yourself."
Galatians 5:14

Day 61
The Facts of Life

Five minutes into your test, you're still staring at the first question. *I know this one,* you tell yourself. X *equals* Y *squared plus 4.* You plug in the numbers. No go. You try again. X *equals the square root of the inverse of* Y. You mind goes dark. More minutes pass. You're still stuck. You chew the eraser off your pencil and start gnawing on the wood.

Breathe. The answer in there somewhere. You close your eyes, rock back and forth, and try to remember your teacher working the problem on the board. Your brain spits random facts. *Abraham Lincoln. December 7, 1941. Sacagawea.*

You're not even hitting the right memory sector. You need one measly bit of data. It's lost. You freeze.

You know that as soon as you slap your blank test on the teacher's desk, every fact you've forgotten will all come whooshing back. You consider slamming your head onto the desk, hoping it will crack open and leak something smart onto your paper.

Read Exodus 20:1–3

What one task does God put at the top of your to-do list?

Your head is full of things you need to remember. Test stuff. Street smarts. Life skills. Details about friends, fractions, and facial scrubs. How do you keep it all straight?

When God wanted his people to understand the crucial facts about obeying him, he didn't put it on TV or even post it online. He didn't send his list in a tweet. He carved it in stone. And at the top of the list is one unforgettable thought: *God is Lord over all.* And because of his absolute greatness, you are to put no person or thing above him in your life. He's worth your total devotion.

That's the ultimate command of the Living God. You can forget a lot of things—but not this, the big fact of life. Whether you're hanging out at home or out on your own, it's at the top of your must-do list.

> I am the Lord your God, who brought you out of Egypt, out of the
> land of slavery. You shall have no other gods before me.
>
> *Exodus 20:2–3*

Day 62
Busting Loose

"Mom and Dad," Owen groveled. "I'm sorry."

The umpteen other times Owen had gone on a church retreat, he had listened to the youth pastor's Bible talks and figured they were for all the bad boys and girls. God was trying to get into their *thick* heads, not his.

This time, though, God knocked some sense into Owen. He felt shock waves rumble through as he recognized his Sunday school arrogance—how he thought he was better than other people, how he had a cruel habit of dissecting people with his words, how at home he'd been on a six-month rampage about homework and chores.

When he got home to talk to his mom and dad, it all dumped out again.

"Hey, tough guy," his dad said, trying to brush aside the sorrys. "It's okay."

"No, Dad, it's not," Owen persisted. "I've been hurting *you*. I've been hurting *me*. I've disrespected *God*. I don't want to be that way anymore."

Read Colossians 3:5–9

Why is God so big on changing you?

Sin causes staggering pain. Don't be surprised if you feel a spasm of sadness when you realize how bad sin actually is. Psalm 107 says it well: "Some sat in darkness and deepest gloom, imprisoned in iron chains of misery. They rebelled against the words of God, scorning the counsel of the Most High" (vv. 10–11 NLT).

All sin chains you, even if you think your sin is "not so bad." Yet God aims to set you free. Listen again to the psalm: "He led them from the darkness and deepest gloom; he snapped their chains" (v. 14 NLT).

Saying yes to God's offer of forgiveness in Jesus frees you from the *penalty* of sin. But there's a second chain God wants to break: the *pain* of sin.

God wants you to grab hold of his forgiveness. But he also wants to lead you into his cool freedom from hurting yourself and others. Breaking that second chain starts with realizing you need to bust loose. Only then will you allow God to set you free to obey him totally.

Because of these, the wrath of God is coming. You used
to walk in these ways, in the life you once lived.

Colossians 3:6–7

Day 63
Defused

When Jenna chose a seat right in front of Miles at opening night of the school musical—the perfect spot for him to stare at her while pretending to watch the stage—his heart climbed into his throat and almost choked him. *An hour and a half of watching Jenna watch the show.*

Miles knew the Bible's principles about guy-girl stuff: Control yourself (1 Thessalonians 4:3–5). Keep your thoughts clean (Matthew 5:28). Sex is for marriage (Hebrews 13:4). And don't hook yourself to non-Christians (2 Corinthians 6:14). Once Miles even thought he'd heard God say, "Don't go near Jenna." *Thanks, God,* his brain mouthed back. *You didn't have to say that. She looks at me like I look at broccoli.*

Several months later, everyone discovered Jenna's well-hidden secret: A friend had pulled her into a serious drinking habit, which had led to a load of other ugly situations. Miles felt sorry for her. And he wondered what his own life might be like had he ever gotten Jenna as his girlfriend.

Read Psalm 119:43–48

Why obey God?

It seems like a strange game. Each day a total stranger sends you a tiny electronic gizmo and some assembly directions in the mail. Day by day, piece by piece, you put the parts together. One day, after you've followed all the steps, you wake up. You've got a ticking bomb taped to your chest, ready to explode.

Life has the potential to blow up in your face when you follow the wrong directions. Good thing God is head of the bomb squad.

God keeps you from blowing up your life in a couple of ways: Sometimes he powerfully arranges your circumstances to keep you out of harm's way, but he's also given you the Bible. His commands are like instructions for spotting a bomb as it's being built. His rules steer you away from unnecessary pain and point you to real life (John 10:10). If you trust that God wants what's best for you, then follow his good instructions.

I will always obey your law, for ever and ever. I will walk about in freedom, for I have sought out your precepts.

Psalm 119:44–45

Day 64

Stand, Walk, Run

Dominic waves to his parents as they drive off. "See you later! Have fun!"

Dominic knows *he'll* have fun. As he shuts the front door he wonders why his parents said not to have anyone over. *What are they worried about? Don't they trust me?*

A few minutes later the half dozen friends he invited arrive—followed by a dozen he didn't invite. A guy Dominic barely recognizes carries in armfuls of beer and asks directions to the fridge. A girl breaks out bottles of stronger stuff. The house gets loud. Things fall off walls.

Dominic runs to the bathroom and locks himself in. *What to do? Call the cops on my own party?* Don't bother. The neighbors already made the call. Red and blue lights flash in the driveway. Dominic hears a knock at the front door and a scramble of people out the back. The officers are nice enough, but they promise to hang around and wait for Dominic's parents to get home.

Read Psalm 119:30–32

Does obeying God ever get easy?

If you obey your parents only because they can ground you for life, then you'll always struggle to do right. You'll concentrate more on how to break rules than how to keep them.

It's the same with obeying God. You only eagerly choose his best when you trust him above anything else. That doesn't happen all at once, but *how* it happens isn't hard to understand: *You stand.* You "choose the way of truth" (verse 30). You tell God you want him and his way. *You walk.* You "hold fast to God's statutes" (verse 31). Even though you worry that you'll fall and grind your face in the dirt, you obey. Your trust grows. *So you run.* You "run in the path of God's commands" (verse 32). Your heart is "set free" or "enlarged," which means "swollen with joy" (Isaiah 60:5), and "a breadth of understanding" (1 Kings 4:29).

Over and over, God proves that he's kind, wise, and practical. When you're convinced his ways work, obeying isn't such a struggle.

I run in the path of your commands, for you have broadened my understanding.

Psalm 119:32

Day 65
It's Funny Until You . . .

With dual dart guns cocked and ready, Andrew charges from behind the futon, puts a gun on each side of Morgan's head, and pulls the triggers. *Fwank! Thunk!* Andrew laughs as he retreats to reload while Morgan fakes pain. Then from the other room comes a yell that halts the war: "It's funny until you put an eye out! Stop it right now."

We disregard rules we think are stricter than necessary: Cross the street only at crosswalks, don't run in the hall, use inside voices . . . Breaking those rules doesn't seem to carry the big bad consequences threatened by rule makers, so we take our chances.

In the same way, some people ignore God's warnings about right and wrong because they think they're too harsh, difficult, or old-school. But if you take God seriously and choose not to join others' out-of-bounds activities, they tend to think you're just as unreal.

Read Psalm 119:89–96

What makes God worth obeying?

Sooner or later, even most believers wonder why they bother to obey God.

Well, it doesn't hurt to remember that the Lord crafted heaven and earth, so he gets to make the rules and set consequences for breaking them. But there are bigger reasons to obey than the fact that God has power to roast his enemies.

Of all the rule makers in your world, only God combines earth-shaking power, flawless wisdom, and total love. The result? Perfect judgment about what's right and what's wrong, what builds up and what tears down. Not one of his rules is dumb or out-of-date, and not one is meant for anything less than your good.

That's what God's faithfulness is all about. The mocking of people who don't understand can't undo the perfection of God's ways—his "laws," "precepts," "statutes," and "commands." You get shook by their laughter and threats only if you forget the boundlessness of God's wisdom and care.

If your law had not been my delight, I would have perished in my affliction.

Psalm 119:92

Day 66
Be the Beanstalk

Kylie sat in the very back at Bible study, leaning against the rear wall of a room where dozens of students packed tight each week. For years, she had wanted that coveted spot, waiting her turn until she was among the oldest students in the group.

For the first several weeks in the back, Kylie thought she had scored the best seat ever. After a few more studies, however, she was surprised to be wishing for a place closer to the front. Something was finally clicking inside her. The speaker's talks suddenly made sense. The Bible passages each week seemed really relevant to her life. Instead of more or less ignoring God week after week, she wanted more of the good changes she was experiencing.

Kylie decided that looking through a forest of heads each week meant she would never get all she could out of Bible study. So she decided to take a stand, determined to make it cool to sit up front.

Read Mark 4:1–9 and 15–20

What makes a Christian strong?

Becoming spiritually mature doesn't mean you never drift off in youth group, snooze during a sermon, or forget to read your Bible. But if you want to get closer to Christ, it shows in how hard you listen.

The word of God—the message of his care, his commands, and Christ's death for our sake—is like seed. God flings it in all directions. Some drops on hard paths, where it settles on the surface and is snatched away. Other seed lands in rocky outcroppings, where it springs up but dies for lack of roots or water. Still other seed grows up among thorns, the kind of worries and distractions that choke a young plant.

But some seed falls on good soil—on those who pay attention to God's words, trust them, and act on them. Their lives explode with growth, producing a hundred times the amount of the seed that was sown.

Each time you hear God's Word, it's your chance to be rich dirt. You can choose to listen or not, believe or not, obey or not. Live up to what you know and you'll grow. Don't and you won't.

> Other seed fell on good soil. It came up, grew and produced a
> crop, multiplying thirty, some sixty, some a hundred times.
>
> *Mark 4:8*

Day 67

Dodging the Bullet

Saying no was supposed to be so easy.

One word. No. That's all I have to say.

A dozen solid reasons to stay away from weed flashed through Jake's brain. His teachers had lectured him. His youth pastor made him role-play sketchy situations. And for as long as Jake could remember, his parents had drilled him about choosing right over wrong.

But Jake never expected the temptation to hit so soon. Or to be so tantalizingly simple to get away with undetected. Or to come from such a good friend. And in the moment, nothing about doing the right thing felt very easy.

Read Matthew 4:1–11

Did Jesus ever struggle to do right?

Here's how we usually picture this passage: The devil attacks. Jesus flexes his muscles, flashes a perfect smile, and rattles off a few Bible verses. The devil whimpers and walks away in defeat. No fuss, no agony. Temptation bounces off Jesus like a bullet off Superman's chest.

But that's not what went down.

Jesus fought temptation the same way we have to—the hard way. Satan came at an opportune time, after Jesus had been fasting alone in the wilderness for forty days. Jesus was hungry—and Satan offered him bread. The Lord was about to embark on a life of servanthood—and Satan offered to make Jesus king of the world. Jesus knew he was headed to the cross—and Satan dared him to test God to save his skin.

Jesus fought back with truth. But Satan didn't depart for long (Luke 4:13). Though the Bible doesn't describe more face-to-face confrontations, the battle went on. It says that Jesus was tested just like we are (Hebrews 4:15).

Struggling against temptation never feels good. When the temptation bullet comes your way, it hits, rips, rattles around inside, and goes out your backside. Jesus understands that pain. When he sees you struggle, he doesn't blow you off. He would never stand by and do nothing. He wades in to help (Hebrews 4:16).

Then Jesus was led by the spirit into the wilderness to be tempted by the devil.

Matthew 4:1

Day 68

Pop Quiz

Mom and Dad looked sympathetic. "We know how you feel, Hanna," they explained. "But we don't have any choice about moving. It'll be okay. God's going with us, you know. You'll see."

I'm going to die, Hanna thought. *It's not even summer. If we have to move, why do we have to do it in the middle of a school year?*

While Hanna said good-byes to her friends, she hatched a plan. She decided to walk to her new school so no one would see her sitting alone on the bus. She would dart from class to class, looking like she knew where she was going. And she would bypass the lunchroom and hide in the library so no one would notice her lack of friends.

God? she said to herself. *What does he care?*

Read John 6:5–13

What does Jesus want most from you?

Jesus had a situation on his hands. A crowd of five thousand was swarming toward him. It was time to eat, and the Lord gave his disciples a pop quiz: "Where are we getting lunch?" he asks. "How are we going to feed this hillside of people?" Jesus isn't punching up directions to the nearest Taco Bell, and he doesn't need a volunteer to cough up a year's worth of salary. He simply wants to know what his closest followers actually think of him.

Not one of the disciples answers the quiz correctly. Philip mumbles about the expense. Andrew mentions a kid with a tiny snack of fish and bread. The disciples all assume Jesus has made the lunch problem *theirs* to solve. On their own, they don't see a solution.

But Jesus just wants them to ask for his help. "Crack the bread in half, Jesus," he longs for them to say. "Start passing it around and there will be food for everyone. *We* can't feed the crowd, but *you* can." What Jesus wants from his disciples—from his followers back then and from us now—is trust. It wasn't a trick question. It was a trust question.

"Where shall we buy bread for these people to eat?" [Jesus] asked this only to test him, for he already had in mind what he was going to do.

John 6:5–6

Day 69
God in a Box

You might not think you have God in a box. But you do. The only question is the size of your container.

A tiny box says that Jesus is a good teacher, a guy much like any other human being. He's full of nice words, but he's really nothing special. A tiny Jesus that fits comfortably in a tiny box isn't the Jesus of the Bible.

A medium box says that Jesus is fully God, born as a baby who grew up, went to the cross for the sin of humankind, and rose from the dead to make his point. That's a better box. In fact, a wonderful box. But there's more.

The biggest box comes without a lid. It says that Jesus your Savior and Lord is with you right now. You can choose to carry him with you wherever you go, yet you can never control him. And you never know when he'll bust out the top.

Read Mark 6:45–52

Why trust Jesus?

That can't be Jesus. As Jesus walks across waves through the mists of night, the disciples are bewildered. They imagine they've seen a ghost. He reaches them and the wind dies down.

The disciples didn't get it. They didn't figure out Jesus' real identity. They couldn't fathom his power over *everything*. Even when Jesus did things only God could do, they were clueless. Sure, they knew Jesus was a cut high above them. But he was *infinitely* greater. He was God himself, all-powerful, come to earth as a human being. They had Jesus in box, even though the universe itself isn't enough to contain him.

It isn't just power, though, that makes Jesus a hero. You would fear him if he threatened to evaporate you with a blast from his finger, but you wouldn't willingly like, love, or obey him.

Jesus is total power paired with perfect goodness. That's what makes him worth trusting—worth obeying. He isn't just able to feed the crowds. He offers bread that satisfies forever (John 6:35). He doesn't just walk on water. He's the One who says, "It's me! Don't be scared!"

Immediately he spoke to them and said, "Take courage! It is I. Don't be afraid."

Mark 6:50

Day 70
Booked Solid

"I can't—really," Ashleigh protests. "Here—look at my calendar." Ashleigh pops open her locker and flips out a giant calendar. Madeline pages through it month by month. Tuesday—the night Madeline's youth group met—was scribbled full for weeks.

"See?" Ashleigh pokes at the Tuesdays. "I volunteer at the animal shelter every Tuesday evening for the next eight weeks. I'll put you down for February 17."

Madeline counts on her fingers. "That's *twelve* weeks."

"I help at Children's Hospital two Tuesdays after that," Ashleigh explains, "and I need to keep a couple weeks open for emergencies."

"Sure," Madeline says. "I understand. You just said you wanted to come to a Bible study sometime. You know—all those questions you had when your grandpa died. . . . We have stuff on other nights sometimes."

"Sorry!" Ashleigh apologizes. "It wouldn't matter. I'm booked solid."

Read Matthew 19:16–22

What can you do when good stuff gets in the way of Jesus?

Lots of things in life are good. But they aren't so good if they keep you from following Jesus—like trying too hard to be popular (Galatians 1:10), overrating the size of your brain (1 Corinthians 1:28–29), doing right just to show off for others (Matthew 6:2–4), or getting too busy for God (Luke 10:40–42).

Jesus said there's something more important than all the other good things we can do. It's getting hold of God himself (Matthew 6:19–34). He pointed out that the young man had done everything right—except love God above anything else. The man didn't kill anyone, steal anything, or disrespect his mother. When Jesus invited him to follow—and to dump his luggage first—the man couldn't bear to leave his mountain of wealth behind.

You became God's friend not through what you *do* but because of what Jesus *did*. Yet your acts of obedience let you experience God's care. If you truly want to follow Jesus, you have to let go of what's good when it keeps you from grabbing what's best.

Sell your possessions and give to the poor, and you will
have treasure in heaven. Then come, follow me.
Matthew 19:21

Day 71
Deepest Regrets

"Bailey is a Jesus-lover!" Peyton taunted. "That's why Bailey won't kick butt on the rink."

Bailey knew she dug as deep as any other player on her hockey team. But that didn't stop the team from joining Peyton in pouncing on Bailey.

"It's true. She prays at lunch." *How could she tell?* Bailey wondered. *I don't stand up and yodel.*

"And she reads a Bible in the library." *Not that much.*

"It's why she sucks up to all the teachers." *I just pay attention.*

"So?" Bailey finally spoke up. "Those things don't make me a Christian." *Well, technically not. They don't* make *me a Christian. But I do them* because *I'm a Christian.*

The dodge didn't distract anyone. "So are you or aren't you?"

Read Luke 22:54–62

What did Peter do when people accused him of being Jesus' friend?

When you make it your aim to obey Jesus, sooner or later someone won't like it. They'll laugh at you or insult you or just ignore you.

You don't have to give people unnecessary reasons to hate you. The Bible doesn't say, "Go ye forth and rub thy faith in thy neighbor's face just to make sure you get insulted." But it does coach you to be honest and unashamed: "Live such good lives among the pagans that, though they accuse you of doing wrong, they may see your good deeds and glorify God" (1 Peter 2:12).

Those are words from the guy who three times denied he knew Jesus only hours after swearing he would go with Jesus to prison and death (Luke 22:31–34). When soldiers swept in and captured Jesus, Peter feared for his life and tried to hide. Just as Jesus had predicted, Peter claimed three times not to know him.

One look from Jesus was enough for Peter to understand what he had done.

The Lord turned and looked straight at Peter. Then Peter remembered the word the Lord had spoken to him: "Before the rooster crows today, you will disown me three times." And he went outside and wept bitterly.

Luke 22:61–62

Day 72
Sob Stories

Adrianna buried her face in her pillow. *Sobs.*

Her church's third youth pastor in four years had resigned, and her youth group had once again imploded. She could count her close Christian friends on her two big toes. *Lonely sobs.*

It felt like everyone her world was into sports. She liked drama and music. *Bored sobs.*

Adrianna kept reminding herself of words she'd memorized from 2 Timothy 2:22—to "*pursue* righteousness, faith, love and peace, along with those who call on the Lord out of a pure heart." But what had that gotten her? *Angry sobs.*

And she'd heard that the guy she liked thought of her as his sister. *Ugh.* She had discovered a profound truth: No one ever asks his sister to a movie. Not that her parents would let her go. But it would be nice to be asked. *Broken sobs.*

Read 2 Samuel 22:32–37

How do you keep obeying God when you feel like quitting?

Anyone who claims your life as a believer will be stress free obviously missed Jesus' message in John 16:33: "Here on earth you will have many trials and sorrows" (NLT). But in addition to that straight-up truth, the Bible presents loads of promises that God will help you obey him even on days when you bawl in your pillow.

Sift through this passage for some of those amazing promises: God is your Rock. He arms you with strength. He makes your way perfect. He gives you biceps that can bend a bronze bow. And he makes your feet dance like a deer on mountain tip-tops.

All through the Bible are more assurances. Some of the choicest: God points you "along the right paths for his name's sake" (Psalm 23:3). He gives "the desire and the power to do what pleases him" (Philippians 2:13 NLT). And he "is able . . . to accomplish infinitely more than we might ask or think" (Ephesians 3:20 NLT).

Some days you have reasons to cry. But you also have reasons to dance.

He makes my feet like the feet of a deer; he causes me to stand on the heights.

2 Samuel 22:34

Day 73
Don't Go Solo

As his home for the next seventy-two hours, Jack picked a strip of land jutting into a backwoods lake. If he could get by with nothing more than a sleeping bag—building his own shelter, starting his own fire, snaring his own food—he would pass his survival skills test.

Halfway through Jack's second day, swarms of biting flies swept in. He ducked into his sleeping bag for protection—head and all—but he baked like a pig in a blanket. Even though he was almost crying, he crawled back out.

Later that night, Jack was back in the bag wishing he had found more to eat. A storm blew up, and ferocious winds nearly rolled him off the point. Jack left his site and tore through the rain to a rock outcrop not far away. As he slid into a crevice, he knew he had flunked the test. But he was safe.

Read Luke 1:26–38

Why run to God when you feel overwhelmed?

Obeying Jesus doesn't transform your life into a cushy campout in a posh RV. Flies will still bite at your arms, and storms will still blow your way. So when you know you can't make it alone, you're smart to run for cover.

When an angel knocked at Mary's door and announced that God had an astounding plan for her life, Mary had a whopper of a question: *How can I have a son? I've never been with a man.* Yet her baby wouldn't be made the ordinary way. He would be formed by the Holy Spirit. Moreover, Jesus wouldn't be an ordinary baby. He was God's Son, Savior of the world.

People will still talk, Mary must have thought. *I'll be an outcast.* In fact, even Joseph considered breaking their engagement until God let him in on the big plan (Matthew 1:19).

As Mary contemplated the Lord's plans for her life, she saw both wonder and terror. But she knew where to run for safety. She stayed strong by hiding in the Rock (Isaiah 26:3–4). Mary knew who to trust.

There's no such thing as a merit badge for trying to survive life solo. You only fail if you don't hide in the Rock and end up getting blown away.

> "I am the Lord's servant," Mary answered. "May your word to me be fulfilled."
>
> *Luke 1:38*

Day 74

Honest to God

"It's not fair!" Alyssa was furious. "He failed half of us." When she saw Mr. Wilder's office empty and unlocked before school, she rampaged. Alyssa cleared the top of his desk and yanked the desk drawers onto the floor.

Then her friend Kendra joined in, smooshing a peanut butter sandwich all over a microscope stored behind Mr. Wilder's desk. Alyssa froze. "Kendra! What are you doing?"

"They'll never figure out we did it. They'll think it was the guys."

That day Alyssa told Mr. Wilder she needed to talk after class. "I messed up your desk," she confessed. "I'll help you pick stuff up, and then I'll go see the principal."

"You're going to be hungry at lunch today, aren't you?" he prodded.

"I didn't do that!" Alyssa argued. "Honest!"

"You'll have to explain that at the office, Alyssa. I don't believe you."

Read Psalm 51:1–12

Why bother to admit that you're wrong?

David wrote Psalm 51 after he had an affair with Bathsheba—and then ordered her husband killed so he could take her as his wife. That's big-league sin. But to God, there's not much difference between David's sin and ours. All sin builds a wall between us and God.

Sin hurts everyone, but it pains God more than anyone. He's the "you" in "against you, you only have I sinned." David couldn't make excuses with God, the ultimate judge. His only hope was to come clean and plead for mercy.

David wanted God to forget his "transgressions," to stop being angry with him, and to fix their friendship. That's a request God always grants. He forgives those who admit what they've done wrong (1 John 1:8–9). David also knew it would be dishonest to grab God's forgiveness, then go and sin more. So he asked God to help him be happy doing what God required.

Growing up means you begin to see yourself as you really are. Growing a devoted heart begins when you're truthful to God and yourself.

Against you, you only, have I sinned and done what is evil in your sight;
so you are right in your verdict and justified when you judge.

Psalm 51:4

Day 75
The Secret Service

Why the president wanted to visit your school, no one knew. But one day your principal announced *the* president was coming. The head of the U.S. of A. And your principal launched a school-wide essay contest: "What I Want to Ask the President."

Whoever won the contest would have lunch with the president. You wanted to win bad. Not for the opportunity to discuss fine points of immigration policy, but to snap the ultimate selfie with the infamous leader of the free world. So you titled your entry "Why I Want to Party with the Prez."

When you lost the contest, you plotted ways to get the president's attention. Then you saw bomb-sniffing dogs nosing around lockers and secret service agents with machine guns under their suit coats banging through ventilation ducts. You decided that squatting in front of the podium and playing "Hail to the Chief" on your armpit wasn't a good move. You didn't want the president to launch a nuclear warhead at your locker. It's not good to mess with the prez.

Read Proverbs 9:10

Should you be afraid of God? Why—or why not?

God calls Christians closer to himself than you'll ever get to a president. He offers to be your friend (Revelation 3:20), and because Christ died for your sins, you have a constant access to the God of the universe (Hebrews 10:19–22). That beats any invitation to the Oval Office. But knowing God is more than just hanging out with the big cheese.

To "fear God" doesn't mean you're scared spitless. God is totally powerful. That might push you away. Yet God is totally loving. That pulls you toward him. Put those together: You're drawn to God in awe.

The book of Nahum illustrates how to think about God. He's a "jealous and avenging God" (1:2) and he "will not leave the guilty unpunished" (1:3). But God is also "a refuge in times of trouble" (1:7). He "cares for those who trust in Him" (1:7).

The fear of the Lord is the beginning of wisdom, and
knowledge of the Holy One is understanding.

Proverbs 9:10

Day 76

I've Had Enough

"Dad, everyone at school has a bigger house than us," Dylan moaned. "And the stuff they wear to school every day costs so much money. I'll never have friends." Dylan wanted to remake his image. *Now.*

Dylan's dad understood, and he promised to do what he could. A few days later, they piled into the car for a trip to the mall. When Dylan noticed they were taking a detour to a different part of the city, his dad waved off his questions.

"Dylan," his dad finally said, "before we go shopping, I want you to see something. Not so you feel guilty, but so you remember what we've got." They stopped in front of a run-down house hardly bigger than Dylan's friends' playhouses. Windows were broken and garages were sprayed with graffiti.

"I know we don't have a huge house," Dylan's dad said, "but we have a lot to thank God for. I haven't come by here since you were little. This is where I lived with your grandpa and grandma when I was born."

Read Matthew 5:3

How can you be wildly happy, no matter what?

Matthew 5:3–11 contains what Bible buffs call the "Beatitudes" (say it like "be" plus "attitudes"). In some Bibles, these bites of truth start with the word *Blessed*, as in "*Blessed* are the poor in spirit." It's just as correct to use the word *Happy*, like other Bibles do, as in "*Happy* are the poor in spirit." If being blessed sounds weird to you, being happy probably sounds a lot more appealing.

When it comes to being thankful, Jesus is saying more than "Have an attitude of gratitude," though that's crucial (1 Timothy 6:17).

His point is this: You might feel short on friends. You might be have less than everyone else at school. But you've still got God. People who are poor in spirit—or just plain poor—possess the kingdom of heaven.

Having an enormous house or a hip wardrobe won't make your life perfect. When you've got God, you've got what matters most.

Blessed are the poor in spirit, for theirs is the kingdom of heaven.

Matthew 5:3

Day 77
Spiritual Survival

SHWOOP! FINGAFINGAFINGA! SPRANKkank kank!

A manhole cover blows off the street, catches air like a Frisbee, and lands at your feet. But you think there's no time to waste staring at the sewer lid. Intergalactic aliens dead ahead!

You've been minding your own business, walking homeward when a couple real sewer-cloggers block your path. Thanks to all the stranger-danger and self-defense lessons you've gotten in school, you punt the aliens back to where they came from, preserving life as we know it on planet earth.

Not surprisingly, you're recruited into the government's ultrasecret anti-alien corps. You get the standard-issue dark suit and shades. You wave bye-bye to your parents and siblings, and your identity is erased. You've attained ultimate awesomeness. You're a one-person, alien-busting army.

Read John 15:1–4

Why do you need God?

Someday you'll get an amazing job and move out on your own. But you'll never get by all on your own. You still need a paycheck. Groceries. Electricity to charge your laser blaster. And maybe you still expect someone to wash your dirty undies.

The next time you think you're ultracompetent and completely self-sufficient, poke your belly button and ponder this: Once upon a time, you were tucked inside your mama's tummy, kept alive through a cord.

You're just as dependent right now. And you always will be. You're designed to draw life from God.

God will never cut your spiritual umbilical cord and announce, "You won't be needing that anymore. Might as well knot it off and let it dry up and fall off." You'll never outgrow your connection to God. You draw life from him like a branch from a vine; you can't do *anything* disconnected from him.

Your belly button is a distant memory of physical dependence. And you'll never stop needing God.

A branch cannot produce fruit alone.

John 15:4 NCV

Day 78
Ready to Ride

You stash your rental snowboard in a slot on the gondola and jump inside for your ride to the top of the mountain. "You know," says one of your gondola buddies, "an Italian air force jet plowed into a lift just like this. Everyone fell like three hundred feet. Twenty people died, and the pilot got off with nothing."

You eye the horizon uneasily. As you ascend, the town at the foot of the mountain gets smaller and smaller, then disappears. Above you looms a couple thousand feet of mountain you couldn't even see from the bottom. You exit the gondola and glance around. Never mind that all the green signs scream "Beginner." You see a cliff around every curve as you strap in.

As you turn and face downhill, you manage to squeak out just one question: "Is this the only way down?"

Read Psalm 118:6

How much do you trust God to care for you when you follow him?

Life is full of slopes bigger than what you're prepared for at the moment. If you dive down a monster hill before you're ready, you can count on trouble. If you vow till-death-do-we-part to your middle school crush, for example, or commit yourself to a career before you've finished algebra, even God's help might not keep you from feeling you're going too far too fast.

There are also out-of-bounds slopes you never want to go down. True, God forgives and fixes us. He might be able to bring you back if you fly off the backside of a mountain. But that's not an excuse to go flatten yourself on a tree.

There's really only one way to get down the mountain of life in one piece. When you aim to live close to God, you can relax in the protection of the Great Instructor. When you obey his commands and stay on the right route, you can be sure you'll enjoy his presence. You might not be thrilled to ride every inch of the hill. You might feel shocked when he sends you down steep runs. But you'll survive with a smile.

If being totally devoted to God were always easy, you wouldn't need to trust your Instructor. But if you're sure he protects you, you fear nothing.

The Lord is with me; I will not be afraid.

Psalm 118:6

Day 79
Do What We Want

The plan seemed so mean. But Hailey wanted to fit in, and everyone was watching. So she agreed to the dare.

Hailey strolled over to the table where Jackson sat alone, nose buried in a calculus textbook. She wrapped her arms around his neck from behind and whispered "Jackson, I'd love it if you asked me to the dance."

This was *truly* cruel. Hailey had her arms around the nerdiest boy in school, and now she was supposed to tell him it was all a joke.

You pick the ending: (a) Hailey jumps back, yells "Just kidding!" and wins a crowd of mean new friends, or (b) as Jackson turns to answer Hailey, his hair smears grease across her face and he drools on her shoes. But Hailey can't bear to break his heart, and when they show up hand-in-hand at the dance, the school's social elite are unimpressed.

Read Proverbs 29:6

When do you feel forced to choose between friends and God?

Peer pressure isn't always glaringly obvious, but it might as well be. The crowd always makes its threat clear: "*If* you do what we want, *then* we'll like you."

Contrary to some sermons you might hear, you don't *always* have to choose between popularity with people or popularity with God. But you're delusional if you think you *never* have to rebel against your peers to follow God.

Jesus was clear that those who trust in him are on a wildly different path from those who don't. "Wide is the gate and broad is the road that leads to destruction and many enter through it," he said. "But small is the gate and narrow the road that leads to life, and only a few find it" (Matthew 7:13–14).

Picture it like this: You can often reach across and grab the hand of someone walking that path away from God. The Lord doesn't want you to let go of those folks; he wants you to pull them to his path of life. But there are times when people going the wrong way try to tug you over to their path. Those folks are headed into snares set by their own sin. You don't want to get snagged along with them.

Evildoers are snared by their own sin, but the
righteous shout for joy and are glad.

Proverbs 29:6

Day 80
Night-Light Fright

One dark and stormy night, every scary movie Marcus had ever watched came crawling into his nightmares. Vampires tiptoed up behind him and fanged him. Men with disfigured faces jumped from behind corners and slashed him. Mutant aliens crawled down his throat and hijacked his body. Terrorists kicked down his door and sprayed his bedroom with bullets. Dolls sprang to life, chased him down the street, gnawed on his ankles—then strangled him.

And those were just the previews. The main feature involved demons crawling out of sewer grates to snatch his soul to hell.

In a sweat, Marcus shook himself awake. For the next month, he slept with the lights on.

Read Philippians 4:6–7

What can you do when you're scared or worried? What happens if you follow the Bible's instructions?

You have a choice about whether you watch movies that fill your brain with freaky scenes that make you toss and turn all night. But other scary situations invade your life and terrorize you against your will.

You might be fizzling your life away feeling anxious about bad stuff that will never happen. Jesus was smart when he said, "So don't worry about tomorrow, for tomorrow will bring its own worries" (Matthew 6:34 NLT). But other threats to your health and happiness are real and present dangers. They don't lurk in your tomorrows. They're in your face today. Maybe life at home is tense. Or you have killer tests and tryouts to endure. Or you clash with friends. Or you're puzzled about getting a grown-up body.

All these things can lead to high anxiety. Yet you can dump all your worries on God, because he cares for you (1 Peter 5:7).

God won't fix every stressful thing in your life. Yet his response to your prayers is so certain that you can thank him ahead of time for his answers. He invites you to worry about nothing—and tell him about everything.

> Don't worry about anything; instead, pray about everything. Tell God what you need, and thank him for all he has done.
>
> Philippians 4:6 NLT

Day 81

Breathe

Forty days without food will stress your body to the point of breaking. Three or four days without water will take you to the brink of death. A few minutes without air will permanently fuzz up your brain. A few minutes more, and you're done.

Your body needs air more than anything, and it does three crucial kinds of breathing. There's *breathing hard*—like when you haul your body through a long run. There's *breathing for others*—mouth-to-mouth emergencies. And there's *breathing you do all the time*—those short, sweet, automatic bursts that happen all day long.

Prayer is like breathing. Your spiritual life can't survive without it. And just like you do three kinds of breathing, you can fill your life with three kinds of prayer.

Read 1 Thessalonians 5:17

How often does God expect you to pray?

You might wonder if God is joking when he says to pray continually. It sounds like a job that might wear out the world's greatest saints.

So how can you pray all the time?

By praying different kinds of prayer at different times.

There's *praying hard*. That's setting aside time just to pray—for yourself, friends, family, your whole world! It's a spiritual workout that's easy to skip, but it causes you steady growth.

There's code-red *prayer for others*. Those are the emergency prayers—like when a friend's parents are divorcing or a family member is critically ill. Mouth-to-mouth moments don't come every day.

When the Bible says to "pray continually," it means a third kind of talking to God, *prayer all the time*—conversing with him wherever you go and whatever you do. That kind of prayer can become a habit as automatic and easy as the twelve breaths you take every minute of every day.

If prayer isn't part of your moment-to-moment life, you can jump-start your breathing. Just say, "God, I think . . ." or "God, I feel . . ." or "God, I need . . ." and tell him what's going on in your heart, as often as you want.

Pray continually.

1 Thessalonians 5:17

Day 82
Talk to a Star

Imagine winning a contest to meet a superstar—say, your all-time favorite actress. A black limo picks you up for a ride to a glistening hotel where guards hold back screaming fans. A couple of freakishly large bodyguards with no necks meet you and escort you up to the star's room. The door cracks open, you dart inside, and you're standing just inches from a celebrity you would sell your best friend to meet. What do you say?

After scraping your jaw off the floor, you would probably hit three themes: "I'm glad to meet you" (you're thrilled to be her friend). "You're the best actress in the whole world" (you think she's an uber-great person). "Your last movie was so cool" (you love specific things she's done).

You might wonder what to say to God when you pray. Someone once said that the word *PRAY* is a reminder of four things to do in prayer: Praise . . . Repent . . . Ask . . . Yield. When you're at a loss for words to pray, *praise* is a great place to start.

Read Psalm 18:25–36

What kinds of things does David praise God for?

Knowing you might fumble your words if you met a movie star, you would probably think ahead of time what to say—maybe even write it out. Applauding God with praise might take that kind of practice for you. But you can start with the same three kinds of things you would say to a star: Express friendship ("God, I'm thrilled to be your friend"), worship God for who he is ("You're an amazing God"), and thank God for his concrete acts ("Thanks for helping me get my homework done"). The book of Psalms is jam-packed with things to say.

You might squirm if you think that praise has to be gushy poetry. Read the book—there's nothing stiff, elegant, soft, or formal about the Psalms. Praise at its simplest is just using your mouth to applaud God, telling him he's great, in whatever words sound natural coming from you. Say what you mean and mean what you say, telling God what you think of him.

For who is God besides the Lord? And who is the Rock except our God?

Psalm 18:31

Day 83
True Believers

Gabrielle strode to the front of the church, bowed her head, and shut her eyes tight. "God, I thank you that we are not like the teens of this world who indulge in illegal drugs and promiscuous sex. We have Bible studies three evenings a week. We go on summer missions trips to help the needy. We witness nonstop. We strive to follow your commands completely—and then some. We are not like scum who don't know you." She opened her eyes, smiled, and thumped her Bible. "Amen!"

Tyler sat in the back pew with his face in his hands. He had slipped in late, after a whopper fight with his parents. "God, I don't think I can ever be what you want me to be. Please forgive me."

Read Luke 18:9–14

Would God rather have you act holy—or get honest?

God doesn't hear your prayers because you rack up points doing good or refraining from doing bad. God listens because Christ died and rose for you. No, God isn't happy with sin. Yet he's even less happy if we're too proud to acknowledge that we sin against fellow human beings and against him in what we think, say, and do.

The second ingredient in PRAY is the *R: Repentance.* Repentance means to admit sin is sin. If you're repentant, it means you come to God in humility, realizing you need forgiveness.

Think how awkward you feel talking to your parents when you've done something wrong they don't know about. You dodge them. You avoid looking them in the eye. You sweat if they ask too many questions. But as soon as you open up, your relationship relaxes. It's the same with God. The person who hides sin from God is miserable, but the one who admits sin is happy and free (Psalm 32:1–6).

Remember how sin erects a wall between you and God? Asking for forgiveness prevents bricks from piling up. It keeps communication open. When you pray, take time to deal with anything you need to clear up between you and God.

The tax collector stood at a distance. He would not even look up to heaven,
but beat his breast and said, "God, have mercy on me, a sinner."

Luke 18:13

Day 84

God Is No Grouch

You started your math homework right after school. You worked through dinner and long past your bedtime, but your brain is still spinning. And the next day when you raise your hand for help, the teacher calls your question stupid and mocks you in front of the class. How embarrassing and frustrating!

A friend who puts off working together on a project . . . or a store manager who won't help you find what you need and instead follows you around the store expecting you to shoplift just because of your age . . . You think, *Fine. You don't care? I don't need you. I'll do it myself.*

Read Luke 11:5–13

How does God respond to your requests?

A man has an unexpected visitor show up at his door in the middle of the night. The host, though obligated by his culture to pop out of bed and feed the visitor, has nothing to serve. So he bangs on a friend's door to borrow bread. Upset, the friend grouches about the wee hour and slams the door. But the man bangs and bangs. In the end, the friend gets worn down and gives in, loaning the bread just to get rid of his noisy neighbor and go back to bed.

The *A* in PRAY is for *ask*. It's the part of prayer where you ask God to provide for your needs and wants—and it's the part most of us know best. The problem? If you think you're bugging God to do something he doesn't want to do, you'll never bother to ask.

Jesus wants you to know that God is the total *opposite* of the midnight grouch—neither is he a belittling teacher, a flaky friend, or a cranky manager. You aren't inconveniencing God when you ask him to meet your needs.

Jesus even uses a bizarre comparison to show God's eagerness to answer your prayers. No human father, he says, would give his child a snake instead of a fish, or a scorpion instead of an egg. If earthly fathers—sinners who make mistakes—can muster that much compassion, you can be sure your perfect heavenly Father won't fail to give you good gifts.

Ask and it will be given to you; seek and you will find;
knock and the door will be opened to you.

Luke 11:9

Day 85

Lord, You Pick

"No, you can't get a new bike this year," Jayden's dad replied. "Next year."

"All my friends have new ones," Jayden countered. "I don't want to ride my old one anymore." Jayden's dad flashed a look that said, *Discussion ended*.

By next summer, Jayden had grown into a sweet new adult-sized bike. His friends looked like giants on their tiny rides.

Jayden's dad had evaluated whether he needed the bike—and concluded that it would be best to wait a year. God does the same thing when you ask. He isn't a cosmic candy machine—put in the right stuff, hit a button, and expect the treat of your choice. In prayer, the final choice isn't up to you. The decision belongs to God.

Yield is the fourth part of PRAY. It means having an attitude that says, "God, answer this as you see best, according to your plan, not mine."

Read Luke 22:39–46

How did Jesus yield to God's choice before he went to the cross?

Jesus knew that dying for the world's sins would be more painful than anyone could imagine. He even wondered aloud whether there was another way to save the world, saying, "Father, if it is possible, don't let me go through this." But he closed his prayer with an attitude that yielded to his Father's plan, leaving the choice to God. He prayed, "Not my will, but yours be done."

Jesus trusted that his Father knew best. He accepted his Father's answer without complaint. He said to God, "You pick. You decide." He trusted that whatever God's answer was, it would be the best. Not the easiest. Not the most comfortable. But the best.

God has an incredible plan for you (Jeremiah 29:11). Ask for what you want, but don't forget to let God have his perfect way.

> [Jesus] withdrew about a stone's throw beyond them, knelt down and prayed. "Father, if you are willing, take this cup from me; yet not my will, but yours be done."
>
> *Luke 22:41–42*

Prayer Abuse

Somewhere in the high channels of your TV and the not-too-distant reaches of the internet—wedged between the shopping networks and the black-and-white reruns—there exists the Preacher Zone.

A few occupants of the zone preach truth. Loads of others epitomize the crime of prayer abuse. *Prayer: It makes every dream come true! Just follow my formula, donate to me, believe hard enough, and BAM! God answers every prayer. Get an A on every test, make acne vanish, always play your violin in tune, and sink every just-as-the-buzzer-sounds shot from half-court. Keep your parents from fighting, your dog from dying, and your best friend from moving away.*

Really?

Read John 15:7–14

How do you know if a promise about prayer is too good to be true?

Jesus indeed said, "Ask whatever you wish, and it will be given you." But there's a crucial condition: *If* you remain in him and his words remain in you, *then* God will give what you ask. "To remain" means you live like a branch that stays connected to the vine. Having the Lord's words "in you" means you're shaped by his promises, values, and priorities.

That doesn't mean God answers only the prayers of uber-spiritual people. It just means that if you live close to God, you'll want what God wants, and he'll gladly grant that request. You'll ache for things that make you more like Jesus, with the goal of showing God's greatness—his glory.

Even so, you don't always get what you want. Why? Because no one prays perfectly within God's will. Sometimes it's easy to spot prayer abuse—like praying to score a fake ID so you can sneak into a party. You don't get what you ask for because your motives stink (James 4:3).

Sometimes you can't comprehend why God doesn't answer a prayer like you thought he should. Only God sees the best possible answer to your every request. Trust him to give it to you.

If you remain in me and my words remain in you, ask whatever you wish, and it will be done for you.

John 15:7

Day 87

Jesus' Prayer

"O God, who reigneth in the heavenlies," droned Mr. Clark, "we thank thee for plucking us from the mire of iniquity and designating us your progeny." Translation? "God of the universe, thanks for freeing us from sin and for calling us your children."

Prayers don't have to be loud, long, and lovely, using weird words that otherwise never pass your lips.

Read Matthew 6:5–13

What did Jesus teach his disciples to pray about?

Jesus let his followers in on a couple sacred truths: (1) Praying in public to get attention is a no-go, and (2) long prayers don't get better answers than short ones. Then the Lord gave his disciples a sort-of pattern to follow. He didn't say "pray these words"—though there's nothing wrong with that—but "pray something like this."

The "Lord's Prayer" he taught them has several parts: "Our Father in heaven, hallowed be your name." That's praise—saying people should recognize God as holy. "Forgive us our debts, as we forgive our debtors." That's repentance—asking forgiveness for sins.

Other points are the *ask* part of PRAY. Some are spiritual. "Your kingdom come, your will be done on earth as it is in heaven" implores God to rule our lives and world. "Lead us not into temptation" asks that God would keep evil from luring us away. Another request is exceedingly practical. "Give us today our daily bread" reminds us we should pray for things we need to survive and thrive—food, a roof over our heads, clothing, work, help at school, family harmony, and solid friends.

Jesus' sample prayer is *straightforward*—it's about talking with God, not impressing people. His prayer is *sure*—he talks to God as Father, confident of an answer. And his prayer is *simple*—it skips the fancy words and asks straight-up for the things we need.

This, then, is how you should pray: "Our Father in heaven, hallowed be your name, your kingdom come, your will be done on earth as it is in heaven."

Matthew 6:9

Day 88
Rip a Hole in the Roof

Diamond teetered out the exit of the girls' locker room, looking pained and dazed. Friends spotted her and ran over. "What's wrong?"

"I think I broke my arm." Brilliant insight, considering her arm looked like a piece of hanger art, bent in three new directions. How Diamond managed to slip by the phys ed teacher no one could figure out. But she was in such a daze that her friends took her by the hand—the unbusted one—and led her to the school nurse, who rushed her to help.

Read Mark 2:1–12

How did the paralyzed man's friends help him get healed?

People all around you need assistance getting to Jesus. While Jesus doesn't go on tour like he did back in Bible times, you can still bring people to him through prayer.

Like the man stuck on a stretcher, some friends might not be able to get to Jesus by themselves. They might be too sick or depressed to pray. Their need could be so big that no human can handle it alone, like a parents' divorce, a dad's heart attack, or a sibling's suicide. Or the friends, classmates, parents, or others you care about might be so unaware of their need for God's help that they would never pray for themselves.

Jesus healed the paralyzed man not just physically but spiritually. You might not always see such specific results from your prayers—sometimes God has a different plan. Other times the person you pray for may continue to resist God—like a parent who has an affair and refuses to come home. God would like to fix the situation, but the person won't let him.

Even so, *your* faith allows God to act. Your prayers can help a friend get healed, find hope, or become a Christian. God won't force himself on anyone, but praying for your friends is like opening a crack in the door to invite God into the situation. You can rip a hole in the roof and bring your concerns right to God.

> Some men came, bringing to [Jesus] a paralyzed man, carried
> by four of them. Since they could not get him to Jesus because
> of the crowd, they made an opening in the roof . . .
>
> *Mark 2:3–4*

Day 89

Prayer Changes Things

The bumper sticker on the car declared that PRAYER CHANGES THINGS. The car, however, didn't look like evidence that prayer works. The ancient beater coughed black smoke as it rumbled slightly sideways down the highway. Prayer hadn't miraculously gotten that owner a better car—or even a better job so he could get a better car. Not only that, a wheelchair logo on the license plate signaled a persistent handicap. If God answers prayer, why didn't he heal the driver?

Have you ever prayed and it seemed God didn't hear? You prayed for your parents—they still got divorced. You prayed for your grandparents—they got sick and died. You prayed for a friend—the one who moved away. Or you prayed for smaller things—good grades, a spot on the team, a role in a play—and yet your prayers seemed to go unanswered.

The apostle Paul said he asked God multiple times for help dealing with a "thorn in the flesh," maybe an enemy, maybe an illness. Although we don't know exactly what Paul endured, we know his story's outcome.

Read 2 Corinthians 12:7–10

What did Paul's prayer change?

Prayer didn't change Paul's circumstances. It changed Paul.

The apostle's problem was so bad that he triple-asked God to take it away. In the end, God said no. But the Lord promised Paul strength even in his agony.

Paul concluded that he needed the thorn to keep from becoming proud of his amazing spiritual insights. The thorn made him depend on God, and he discovered that God was closest when he struggled. While the thorn was no less painful, Paul learned that God could use the thorn for good.

When you pray and don't see the answers you want, look around for what God might be doing in you and through you. Prayer will *always* change you *if* you pray in faith, trusting that God hears and cares. Prayers that seem to fail produce Christians who succeed.

Three times I pleaded with the Lord to take it away from me. But he said to me,
"My grace is sufficient for you, for my power is made perfect in weakness."

2 Corinthians 12:8–9

Day 90
All Ears

"Not now!" Jada's dad barked. "I'm worn out—and I have work to do!"

"But I need help with math," Jada repeated. "It's due tomorrow."

"You're going to have to figure it out yourself," her dad answered. "Maybe if you and your sister didn't fight all the time I'd have energy to help you."

Jada's mom rushed to calm Dad down. "What do you think it's like for your father?" she said. "He works all day long and comes home and hears you screaming at each other."

By then, Jada's little sister was pulling at her dad's pant leg. "Will you take me to the park?" Dad flashed a bit of tenderness, then flew off again.

"I have to work," he said, pulling his coat on. "I'm going back to the office. Good night." Jada winced when the door slammed behind him and wondered why she even tried to talk to her dad.

Read Psalm 27:7–14

Why does God sometimes seem hard of hearing?

Talking to a parent can be like reasoning with a rock. Or having an annoying pebble in your shoe. Some kids react by clamming up. If you can talk back and forth well with your parents, you're fortunate. You probably know friends who can't.

God isn't like a parent who can't hear or won't talk. But sometimes he feels far away. Even David begged God to listen and respond.

David hints in Psalm 27 at reasons God goes quiet: (1) to teach you to seek him more; (2) so you learn not treat him like a toy you put on the shelf; (3) to remind you to trust that he accepts you—that if you admit your sin to him, he never holds it against you (Psalm 103:12); or (4) to check whether you want to follow him badly enough that you cry out for him to show you how.

In the end, God has one giant goal for you. He wants you to trust that he is God and he is good.

Wait for the Lord; be strong and take heart and wait for the Lord.

Psalm 27:14

Day 91
Church Is Booooring

Whap! Your pastor slaps the pulpit, an annoying habit he uses to drive home key points. As usual, it works. Everyone stops rustling. Only a gurgling baby disturbs the silence.

Until you shake the pew, that is, while reading an unusually humorous note passed to you by your best friend. Your face contorts. You attempt to stifle a laugh, only to produce an ear-shattering snort. Suddenly you feel every eye turned your way. You look up to see the pastor glaring down at you, one eyebrow raised. You pull it together and begin rehearsing your excuse for later: *Church services are so boring. . . .*

Read Deuteronomy 6:4–9
How can you get excited about church?

Church isn't always fun. It's often designed for adults. It's partly aimed at the serious goals of learning and correction. To top it off, your most vivid experience of worship might be "Get up. Get dressed. Get in the car. Sit still and shut up."

Assuming you're not a rebel totally hostile to God, the biggest reason church services are a bore is lack of understanding. Grown-ups are supposed to explain what following Jesus is all about. Some don't—at least not in a way that grabs you. So you need to get answers for yourself.

For starters, try to understand *what's happening in the service*. Ask what's going on. Watching a sporting event without knowing the rules will bore you stupid. If you don't understand the players at church, why you sit or stand, or what the lyrics or sermon mean, you'll shrivel up from boredom. If you can follow what's going on, you might learn to like it.

Then ask your parents *why they go to church*. Why aren't they bored? Watching a game on TV all by your lonesome with the sound off is a guaranteed snooze. You need to feel the *oomph* of the crowd to stay engaged. So find out why God matters to your parents. Why did they start attending? When? Why do they keep going? What makes worshiping God so significant that you have to get up, get dressed, get in the car, sit still, and shut up?

These commandments that I give you today are to be on
your hearts. Impress them on your children.

Deuteronomy 6:6–7

Day 92

Big Baby

Layla felt claustrophobic every time she heard it: "We go to church because it's the right thing to do." Whenever Layla wondered out loud why she had to go to church, her mom tossed her the same tired line.

To Layla, "the right thing to do" was painfully, agonizingly, excruciatingly mind-numbing. She'd tried everything to escape. Like screaming. And cold stares. Layla even tried pulling the covers over her head and ignoring her mom. She discovered that the only thing worse than going to church was getting dragged feet first from bed and showing up with her hair and face in a mess.

Layla wanted a real reason for this twice-a-week habit—something more than "just because."

For now, Layla's mom was winning. Before long, Layla would be too big to be dragged to the car.

Read Psalm 95:1–11

What does it mean to worship God?

God is all-powerful: Lord, Master, Judge. He's all-kind: the Giver of forgiveness through Christ. Yet if you fail to perceive this mind-boggling perfection, then worshiping God makes no sense. The coolest parts of being a Christian crumble into rules and ritual. You miss out on enjoying a moment-by-moment relationship with your God. Following Jesus with other believers becomes nothing more than "the right thing to do."

God himself is the reason for everything you do as a Christian. And church is an unshakable invitation to bow before him. Your *mouth* worships. You tell God how great he is. You "shout aloud to the Rock," the one who rescues you from sin. Your *heart* worships too. You acknowledge that you belong to God. You agree that his will is good. And you worship with your *life*, giving yourself to him out of thankfulness for what he's done for you (Romans 12:1).

God doesn't drag you to church. He calls you there so you can grasp his greatness.

Come, let us bow down in worship, let us kneel before the Lord our maker; for he is our god and we are the people of his pasture, the flock under his care.

Psalm 95:6–7

Day 93
No-Brainer

You stare up from an examination table, mesmerized by your brain floating overhead. Laser probes shoot at the pink lump of wrinkled jelly from a dozen different directions. It wriggles.

"Basically empty, compared to ours," an alien space doctor finally announces to his colleagues. *They must have figured out that I flunked my last science test. My parents don't even know that.* After the alien doctor reinserts your brain, a scan of the rest of your body begins. *I can't wait to hear the results.*

"Muscular structure: unremarkable. Molecular composition: mostly water. Chemical value of creature in earth money: six dollars and two cents."

"Note the bad haircut," another doctor interjects.

"Of course. I think we all agree with my recommendation: vaporize."

Read Colossians 3:5–14

What do you want people to notice when they look at you?

When God made us, he planned that people would see *him* when they saw us. Unfortunately, sin has deformed our features, so that we no longer look like God.

Quiz time: If you gave God, who is utterly perfect, the chance to give you a fresh makeover to look more like him, which of the following would best describe you? (a) The wardrobe and plastic good looks of Ken or Barbie; (b) the classic musical talents of the Beatles; (c) the brains of Einstein; (d) the vertical jump of Michael Jordan; or (e) none of the above.

In heaven you'll receive a new body that may or may not include choices a, b, c, or d. But for now, God's first concern is something else: He wants to remake your *character* so that you think, feel, speak, and act like him.

The "old self" is human nature deformed. It's all the things that make you ugly and unlike God. The "new self" is just the opposite. Day by day, it looks more like God. If you let him, he sculpts you to resemble him.

When people probe your life, you want them to notice more than brains, looks, or talent. They should see a new you who looks more and more like God.

Therefore, as God's chosen people, holy and dearly loved, clothe yourselves with compassion, kindness, humility, gentleness and patience.

Colossians 3:12

Day 94
Don't Look Now

Thumbs up: You stroll into school just in time to hear an announcement over the school's intercom that your "Save the Stray Cats!" poster won first prize from the state Animal Humane Society. *Thumbs down:* Your social studies teacher gives you detention for your desktop celebration dance. *Thumbs up:* Your best friend hugs you for explaining geometric proofs. *Thumbs down:* Your significant other dumps you like yesterday's trash. *Thumbs down:* Sitting in a lunch-hour detention for your desktop dance, you receive an after-school detention for passing notes.

Some days you gotta wonder: Why does half the world love you—and the other half seem to hate you?

Read Psalm 19:7–14

How does the Bible tell you who you are?

Picture this: You blow your nose and miss the tissue, boogering your collar. Your neck, however, can't quite twist to spot the problem. Minus a quick horrifying glance in a mirror, you could walk around wearing a big greenie for a long time. Some people point, laugh, and walk away. Others don't want to interfere with your accessorizing. Still others call you a trendsetter. Only a real friend would whisper in your ear and speak truth.

All of us have flaws we can't see. Yet the evaluations, opinions, and judgments we hear from others aren't always accurate. Their criticisms can be too harsh. Or their unfailing support can be too kind. They might not know the difference between right and wrong. Even our own consciences can goof.

What others think of you matters. How you measure up in your own eyes is truly important. But above all else, God's opinion rules. You probably won't hear a booming voice from heaven, but you can hear God speak in the Bible, teaching you right from wrong through his "laws," "statutes," "precepts," and "commands." You can listen to him without fear because he doesn't speak up to hurt you. Every word is packed with love, meant to help.

He's definitely that priceless friend who whispers in your ear.

> The law of the Lord is perfect, refreshing the soul. The statutes of the Lord are trustworthy, making wise the simple. . . . But who can discern their own errors? Forgive my hidden faults.
>
> *Psalm 19:7, 12*

Day 95
Price Tags

Cheap. Worthless. Highly Valuable. Famous. Forgotten. Priceless. All day long, people tag you with what they think you're worth. You might spin right around and tag others. With a glance, stare, jab, or snicker, you assign value. *Low. High. Average. Negative twelve.*

Some kids' price tags say they're worthless, like the kid who sits behind you in math—everyone agrees Charlie is the dumbest person in your grade. Or you might laugh with your friends at Ashlyn when her unemployed dad drives up in a junker truck.

Other people's tags are so high-ticket that they make *you* feel like a clearance sale leftover. Some cliques bar you from entering because you fall miserably below their standards. Classmates who look light-years ahead of you might make you wonder if you'll ever grow up. Or guys or girls at church might seem so spiritual that you doubt you really count with God.

God puts a different price tag on people. You wear a tag that says you're infinitely valuable.

Read 1 Peter 1:18–19

How much did God pay for you?

God thinks that compared to you, even gold is worthless trash. When God wanted to reignite a friendship with you, it cost him the incalculable price of the death of his Son, Jesus. Cash registers can't count that high! Yet that's the price tag God glues on you and everyone else on earth. That's how much he thinks you're worth.

Given that fact, no one ever deserves to be tagged as a reject. And you can shut out any voice that says you are anything less than God's prized daughter or son.

When God looks at the world, everyone is equally valuable to him. No one is on sale. No one is an ugly shirt with six markdowns, with a tag that says, "You're worthless. No one wants you." Your price tag says the same thing as all the others in the world: *Jesus loves me and died for me.*

> You were bought, not with something that ruins like gold or silver, but with the precious blood of Christ, who was like a pure and perfect lamb.
>
> *1 Peter 1:18–19* NCV

Day 96
Looking Good

Sarah frowned at her bedroom mirror. *Comb. Brush. Curler. Product 1. Flat-iron. Product 2.*

Then, for the third time that morning, she bolted into the bathroom to wet down her hair to start all over. Time after time, major hair mishap.

Maybe you're not uptight about your hair; maybe you try on multiple outfits every morning. Or you're lured to mirrors throughout the day, just to check your look. Or you habitually double-check your deodorant by sniffing your pits.

Uh-huh. Time for more deodorant.

Read Micah 6:8

What is God scoping out when he looks at human beings?

Even if the whole world were blind, you probably wouldn't appear in public unwashed and dressed in a trash bag. Face it: You primp for a whole lot of reasons. Partly to stay clean and healthy and feel okay about yourself. But maybe even more to please others. You might think you look good only if others say so. Guys worry as much as girls.

Some people *will* judge you by your looks. Your task is to decide how much you'll let their view of you dictate your life.

The ugliest people in the world polish their surfaces but never go deeper. God—and anyone worth impressing—knows that looks aren't everything. He's pleased when he looks at you and sees authentic righteousness, kindness, and humility. He never wonders, "Did your hair turn out? Are your muscles bigger this week than last?" He asks, "Do you work hard? Can your parents trust you? How's your heart? Is it committed to me? How's your head? Are you so *over*confident it's too big to fit through a door?"

God made you awesomely good-looking, and he indeed wants you to take care of yourself. But he made you to please him through your attitudes and actions, not to be a slave to looking good.

> The Lord has told you, human, what is good; he has told you
> what he wants from you: to do what is right to other people, love
> being kind to others, and live humbly, obeying your God.
>
> *Micah 6:8 NCV*

Day 97
Good for Something

Ben was treading in deep water and gasping for breath. By midyear, his grades were dismal. His basketball coach benched him when he tripped and sprained his toe in the season opener—and broke the leg of the team's star center. His nursing home boss told him he annoys the residents—that they would rather be lonely than listen to him. Teacher after teacher pointedly informed Ben that he can't sing, act, or draw—and that he should try to find himself somewhere else. In a burst of explorative ingenuity, he signed up for a Chinese class at a community center—only to find out that "Ben" sounds just like the Mandarin word for "stupid."

Ben's mom tried to comfort him. "Everyone's good at something, dear," she cooed. "You'll find something."

"Quit it, Mom!" Ben moaned. "You're my mother. You have to like me. I'm an idiot!"

Read Romans 12:1–8

How do you discover what you're good at?

Some days you might feel like a child only a mother could love. But sometimes mama is super right: *Everyone* is good at something. The Bible makes the same point: God gives *everyone* gifts.

So how do you discover what you're good at? Some tactics:

Don't expect applause. Just because no one says "Wow!" doesn't mean you bombed. A few gifts put you up front where people *ooh* and *aah*, but acts of kindness, giving, encouraging, or serving rarely get praise.

Give it a real try. You can't try something once—or not at all—and draw a conclusion. Most gifts take practice.

Be yourself. You might feel odd even when you're doing exactly the right thing. The world needs you just the way you are.

Finally, you amp up your gifts when you *make yourself available to God.* It's the right response to everything God has given you. And as you follow him closely, you'll find your way.

Just as each of us has one body with many members, and these members
do not all have the same function . . . We have different gifts.

Romans 12:4, 6

Day 98
Power Steering

Megan cracks a wicked smile as her aunt and uncle and cousins roll up the driveway. Last summer her cousins called her a hick and nearly drowned her in the ocean.

Now they're on her turf. And it's winter.

Megan tosses her cuzzies some ice skates and pushes them toward a frozen pond out back. It's time to race.

Race? They wave their arms like windmills just trying to stay on their feet. Cold air hits their lungs with a cruel burn. When their toes freeze up and they whine to go inside, Megan swoops in for the kill. She buzzes circles around them. She hip checks. They smack ice.

Megan has one more cool thing for her cousins to try—licking a flagpole. "Helffffph!" they yell, their tongues frozen to the pole.

"You deserve that," Megan screams as she goes inside. "I hate you!"

Read Judges 16:23–30

How can you get good at something without getting arrogant?

The only thing bigger than Samson's pride in his strength were his muscles. So when he let his Philistine girlfriend sweet-talk him into revealing the secret of his might, God allowed his enemies to grab him and gouge out his eyes. They tossed him in prison to grind wheat like a mule (Judges 16:21).

Samson regained his power only when he was tamed—when he remembered that his strength came *from* God and should be used *for* God. Instead of using his might for himself, he handed the Philistines—a nation at war with Israel—a crushing defeat.

When you're smart or skilled, you can smear brains in people's faces—or gently clue them in on what you know. When you're strong, you can use your power to help people—or to break their thumbs. And when you're funny, you choose between cheering people up—or pounding them down.

Every day brings opportunities to your great gift. As you make your choices how to handle your superpower, remember this: Truly strong people don't have to prove their strength.

Then Samson prayed to the Lord, "Sovereign Lord, remember
me. Please, God, strengthen me just once more."

Judges 16:28

Day 99

I Was Here

"I was here," read the scribbled note. *"Did you even notice?"*

Feeling unnoticed . . . average . . . expendable is massively un-fun. Being so-so at sports means standout players grab all the attention. Doing okay at school means teachers and tutors focus on the high end and the low end of your classmates. Being a teen—no longer a kid, not yet an adult—guarantees that some people will ignore you. Getting compared to blazingly smart siblings can make you feel less-than-important at home.

Feeling doomed to invisibility can make you wish you could change your looks, age, clothes, personality, talents, brains—anything to break from the crowd to feel unique and important!

Read Jeremiah 1:4–10

How did Jeremiah respond when God told him to speak up?

When God called Jeremiah to preach, he was a teenage shepherd. He was known to no one. He was a worrier. Maybe even a coward, a guy who probably thought his sheep would make better mouthpieces for God. He reminded the Lord that he was a nobody, young and fumble-tongued.

God never saw Jeremiah that way. He aimed to use the young shepherd to challenge the people and rulers of Israel with a piercing message—a plan he hatched for Jeremiah long before the young man was born.

When God got through training Jeremiah, the prophet was anything but ordinary. God transformed him from scared shepherd to gutsy prophet. What made Jeremiah useful to God wasn't his abilities or lack of them but his total devotion to God's plan. Plenty of people are talented and smart. Few are obedient and available to God.

God chooses and uses ordinary people so that everyone will realize their skills and abilities come from God (1 Corinthians 1:26–31). Standing out in a crowd isn't what makes you matter. It's having an obedient heart that lets God lead you down the unique path he's mapped out for you.

> But the Lord said to me, "Do not say, 'I am too young.' You must go to everyone I send you to and say whatever I command you. Do not be afraid of them, for I am with you and will rescue you," declares the Lord.
>
> Jeremiah 1:7–8

Day 100

In the Spotlight

"It's a long fly ball," bellowed Jordan in a sportscaster voice as Vincente rounded first base in the middle-of-the-street ball game. "The Big V really smashed that one! What power! What grace!" Cheers became buried by laughter and the smash hit forgotten, however, as Vincente tripped over second base and skidded on the pavement, shredding his knees.

Some days you figure you'll never do any better than the Big V. But you won't always fall on your face. Sooner or later—even if just in little ways—you'll see the crowd, hear the applause, bask in the spotlight.

Applause is awesome. Compliments feel good. But awards and praise can make you an un-nice person who looks down on people, ignores old friends, and expects special treatment.

When things go well and people clap, you have a giant task. You get to learn to be great without getting big-headed.

Read Philippians 2:3–8

How did Jesus practice humility?

If anyone ever had a right to applause, it was Jesus. He's God! He possessed all the majesty and splendor of the King of the universe, yet he didn't draw attention to himself. Instead of rolling up in a limo and making a scene, he slipped quietly into the world as a helpless baby and grew up to be a servant who died on the cross for the sins of his creation.

When you're blinded by the spotlight's glare, you see only yourself. Fight that urge to think only of yourself by stepping out of the spotlight, like Jesus, through servanthood. Run away from selfishness by remembering that other people's needs matter as much as your own.

You can also share the spotlight with your Lord. After all, God is the real source of your gifts, talents, and abilities (1 Corinthians 4:7). When people applaud you, applaud God! Tell him thanks for your success, and remember that he's more important than anything you achieve (Jeremiah 9:23–24).

Do nothing out of selfish ambition or vain conceit. Rather,
in humility value others above yourselves.

Philippians 2:3–5

Day 101

No-Stick Jesus

Gianna whirled and pretended to dig in the bottom of her locker, her long hair hiding her wet eyes. *ZIT FACE!* reverberated in her brain. *How could Ashley say that? She's my friend. My best friend. Everyone heard!*

Gianna ditched the bus after school and walked home alone, cutting through backyards so Ashley couldn't look out from her house across the street and see her. That night, Gianna fell asleep rehearsing all the awful things she could have said about Ashley. *Next time.*

Sticks and stones may break our bones, but being called names hurts even worse. We're supposed to be Teflon people, like slippery pans that let food slide out. But it's never that easy. When careless cooks scratch Teflon, it can't do its job. When careless people nick us, their insults stick, burn, and stink: *You're ugly. You're dumb. You'll never get a boyfriend. You won't make the cut.*

Like the Bible says, "Careless words stab like a sword" (Proverbs 12:18 NCV).

Read 1 Peter 2:21–25

How did Jesus react to put-downs?

Jesus knew how to let insults slide right off. He didn't go rude in return, a response that would make him as bad as his tormentors. Instead, he trusted the Father who sees perfectly, realizing that one opinion counts more than all the others put together.

Do people who shred you know you? Possibly. But not as well as God does. Is what people say true? Maybe. But if you actually have some defect, big or small, God will tell. Gently, with great timing, helping you change. Never critically. Constructively.

By focusing on what God says about you, you have power to let insults slide off. You're the Lord's daughter or son. He loves you more than anyone else ever could. Listen for his evaluation of your words, dress, looks, attitudes, actions, sins, faults, and skills. It's God's opinion that counts.

> When they hurled their insults at [Jesus], he did not retaliate; when he suffered, he made no threats. Instead, he entrusted himself to him who judges justly.
>
> *1 Peter 2:23*

Day 102
We Are the Champions

Every spring, millions of baseball fans nearly pull a hammy trying to predict the year's World Series winner. But how can you see the end of the season before the first pitch on opening day? Wishful thinking won't win championships. Being picked as the favorite doesn't do it—what can go wrong often does. Counting on luck is a nonstarter—every team gets good and bad breaks. Even filling the bench with multimillion-dollar players can backfire.

Baseball fans—and players—would agonize less if they knew from the start who would win at the end. Knowing ahead of time, of course, kills the thrill of the game.

When it comes to your life, you're in the early days of the season. Wondering how everything will turn out is baffling. Will you win? How can you know?

Read Philippians 1:3-6

How does God promise you'll turn out when you're devoted to Jesus?

Paul was certain of one thing: Because the Philippians belonged to God, the Lord would never let them go. Until the day Jesus comes back to earth, God would keep perfecting their faith. At the end of the season, they would emerge victorious.

That was more than a happy wish. God had already started working his wonders in the Philippians. They had become believers and were spreading the good news about Jesus. As they continued as Paul's partners, God's life kept growing in them. Because God fulfills all his promises, even suffering and death couldn't rip victory out of their hands (1:22, 29).

Some days you might feel like a batter in an endless slump, like you whiff with every trip to the plate. God will coach you to better days. What's more, his eternal game plan means that you'll win big at what matters the very most: your relationship with him. If you allow God to coach you, he promises to make you a spiritual champion.

> Being confident of this, that he who began a good work in you
> will carry it on to completion until the day of Christ Jesus.
>
> *Philippians 1:6*

Day 103
Phlegmwad

Mateo glanced around the lunchroom for a friendly face, then picked an empty table. A gaggle of older girls came over, called him a phlegmwad, and said he was sliming up their spot. Mateo was new at school, but he got the hint that he should move. No worries. A kid he recognized from math class had just sat down at the next table.

Jake didn't look too barbaric, and Mateo thought he had a good shot at making a new friend. When he went over and sat down, however, the whole table ignored him. Mateo ate next to Jake and company, but he felt even more lonely than when he sat alone.

You don't have to be new at school to feel isolated. You can feel left out when strangers trounce you, friends act like enemies, or parents and family don't understand you. And because you can't see God, even he can seem like he's nowhere near.

Read Psalm 73:21–26

What can you do when you feel like a phlegmwad?

One of King David's leading musicians, Asaph (AY-saf), wrote Psalm 73 on a day he felt cut off from everyone around him. What he discovered can ease your loneliness, whatever the cause.

Asaph expected that God would instantly fix his bad situation. As an all-out follower of God, he was no doubt a friend worth having. He ought to be liked, popular, and included. In time, God surely gave him friends, but for now—doesn't sound like it. For a while, the Lord let him be alone.

Asaph discovered this: God sometimes lets you feel lonely to remind you that all you really have is him—and that he's all you need. Family can't be with you every instant. Who will you depend on? Friends move, or you just change. Who will you hang out with?

In the middle of being lonely, Asaph came to a simple conclusion: *God* is always near.

When you have no one else, you have God, and he's enough.

> Whom have I in heaven but you? And earth has nothing I desire besides you. My flesh and my heart may fail, but God is the strength of my heart and my portion forever.
>
> *Psalm 73:25–26*

Day 104

Best Buy

Ella opened the front door only to wish she had checked the peephole. *Too late.*

A man clown stepped forward with a cheeky "Hullo. We're from the Church of the Bozos down the block." He was accompanied by what appeared to be his clown kinfolk—a clown woman, clown girl, and clown boy. *Where's the clown dog?*

Ella's brain raced through a hundred ways she could simultaneously ease the door shut and dial 9-1-1. Until she suddenly she heard herself say, "Tell me more!"

The church had a sizeable clown ministry, and this Sunday was their annual clown worship service. Would she come?

The bozos seemed harmless, but Ella wasn't buying. She finally blurted what she was really thinking: "Don't you clowns know that you're scary?"

Read Matthew 13:44–46

Why did the digger swap everything he had for a treasure?

Every kind of salesperson has one goal in mind: to get you to buy something they claim will make you goofy with happiness.

God isn't selling anything. What he offers is the free gift of his friendship, greatness, presence, and guidance. He invites you to let him reign as King of your life. Yet he always lets you shop around, to choose for or against him, to love him or leave him.

Bozos don't exactly help God's pitch. If you think being a Christian means becoming a bozo, then you'll keep looking for a better deal.

Once you understand what God has for you—becoming part of the kingdom of heaven, knowing and following God—no one has to beg you, force you, or scare you into accepting God's treasure.

Being totally devoted to God won't make you weird. To be a Christian means putting trust and obedience to God first. Always. No matter what.

That's a price. But what you pay is nothing compared to what you gain.

The kingdom of heaven is like treasure hidden in a field. When a man found it, he hid it again, and then in his joy went and sold all he had and bought that field.

Matthew 13:44

Day 105
Earthshake

Put yourself in these parental shoes: Your family needs a house, and you have to choose between the only two houses for sale on the entire planet. House A is ready for immediate move-in. It's a mansion with striking features, including a party-ready pool and a deck bedazzled with multiple waterfalls. The contract for House A clearly states, however, that one day an earthquake will level the house with its owner inside. Nothing will be left—no house, no stuff, no you, no joke.

House B is a much more modest dwelling, almost barebones, but it promises to keep you snug and warm. Several clauses in the contract for House B are more than a little unusual. For starters, renovators will constantly upgrade the house—for free. And here's the strangest: Upon completion, House B will be transported to a stunning oceanside location, where it will stand until the end of time.

You control the family dollar. Which house would you choose?

Read Hebrews 12:22–29

What will survive when God shakes the world? ("They" in verse 25 refers to Israel, mentioned back in verses 14–21.)

You wouldn't be happy if you moved into a house and found yourself stuck with moldy carpet, a leaky pool, and a termite-infested deck. You would wish you had examined the house up close. When the house falls to the ground, you would beat yourself up for not believing the contract was legal, binding, and unalterable.

Lesson? Don't buy a house God has vowed to destroy.

God promises that in heaven you'll share a home where you can rock with an angel choir, a place where you'll be eternally welcome because Jesus has paid the bills and invited you in.

God's eternal home is filled with people who accept that great gift. The only other address in the universe is chock-full of folks who mock God's warning and reject his invitation. When God shakes all of creation—to keep what's worth keeping—only God's house will stand strong.

Sound scary? Not if you choose the right house.

Worship God acceptably with reverence and awe,
for our "God is a consuming fire."
Hebrews 12:28–29

Day 106
Waves

After loafing too long on the beach, Sydney started to name the seagulls that came begging for lunch. While her friends surfed and boogie-boarded, she twirled her toes in the sand and hit the hot-dog stand. Sydney wouldn't go near the water. She knew how to swim well enough, but unlike her friends, she hadn't grown up on the ocean.

Waves terrified her. Until her friends threw her in.

Waaaaaah! Sydney howled as a wave whapped her. *Woaaaaaah!* she laughed as she bobbed to the top. *Haaaaaaaah!* she shrieked as she bodysurfed to shore.

Read Hebrews 4:14–16

Do real believers ever get tempted to do wrong? How?

God doesn't command his followers to sit lonesome on the beach. The best fun is in the water—living life, playing, enjoying friends, studying, working, watching Jesus stomp on the waves. The water is where you get to smile, chuckle, and cheer.

Most waves are great fun. But you gotta watch for the ones that can knock you down and drown you.

Like a wave gone extreme, evil is often a good thing that has gone out of control, such as words (a good thing) twisted by a knife (a bad thing). Or a desire to fit in with friends churned into peer fear. Or self-respect swollen into pride. Or sex breaking the boundary of marriage. Or drugs used to hurt rather than heal.

Just like us, Jesus played in the rollicking waves of life. He had the same opportunities as we do to wade past God's boundaries. He too was tempted to swim in treacherous waters. To each temptation, Jesus said, "Good thing. But wrong time. Wrong way. No way." (See Matthew 4:1–11.)

Christians don't hide on the beach, because they know the real fun is out in the waves. But they're smart enough to watch out for waves that can take them under.

For our high priest is able to understand our weaknesses. When he lived
on earth, he was tempted in every way that we are, but he did not sin.

Hebrews 4:15 NCV

Day 107

Tummy Toaster

"My feet are really cold!" Drew shouted to friends ahead on the ski trail. "I mean it!"

"Whiner!" they all yelled back and kept moving.

A half hour later, everyone paused at a fork in the trail. "Drew—I hear your feet are cold," said Nathan, their trail guide. "Show me your feet." With one glance at Drew's right foot, he yanked up his own jacket and shirt, then knelt down and put Drew's icy foot on his bare stomach.

"Yikes!" one of the girls yipped. "That's gotta be cold."

While Nathan thawed Drew's other foot, he talked to the group. "Why didn't you stop earlier? Drew's feet are frostbitten pretty badly. We'll have to cut our day short and ski him back to the lodge."

Read 2 Timothy 2:22

Why are Christian friends so important?

You show weakness, and a friend calls you a baby. You share a secret with someone you trust, and the next day you read it scrawled on a bathroom stall. You ask for help, and forever after you're treated like an idiot.

"Who cares?" you say. "I can live without friends."

Nope. You can't. At least not without the right kind of friends.

Deciding to chase hard after God—that you want to flee evil, do right, trust God, and love others—won't work unless you follow the rest of Paul's advice: Run alongside others who are running toward God.

When your aim is to follow Jesus, other authentic followers are the only ones moving the same direction you are. It's possible that even Christians who chase after God with all their hearts might freeze you out sometimes. But if they've truly been warmed by God, they can't help sharing that warmth with you. People who are continually cold don't know God.

You need help from other Christians. Search it out. Make the most of it. You can't unfreeze your own feet.

Flee the evil desires of youth, and pursue righteousness, faith, love and
peace, along with those who call on the Lord out of a pure heart.

2 Timothy 2:22

Day 108

Upward Bound

Half a mile from Addy's house stands a mountain. Truthfully, the mountain wouldn't amount to a pimple on the face of a really rocky peak. But the ridge rises high enough to hold a seventy-meter ski jump, just a notch below full Olympic size.

Addy had no desire to hurl her body off a jump a couple hundred feet in the air. But she was awestruck by the scary-steep landing zone. In a flash of wintertime audacity, she set a goal. *Come spring, I'm running up that hill.*

As the temperature warmed and the hill thawed, Addy prepped for the big run. *Try One*: She dashed up the hill. Fifty yards up, lungs screaming and eyeballs throbbing, she stopped. *Try Two*: She managed a dozen more yards. *Try Three*: A friend hiked up with Addy, wondering all the way why anyone would want to run it. *Try Four*: A couple weeks later, Addy got halfway up before she wheezed to a halt. Aggravated, she spent the next month pounding up and down smaller hills to build stamina. *Try Five*: Addy got within spitting distance of the top. *Try Six*: Triumph! She sucked wind and wanted to stop, but step by step and breath by breath she made it up the peak.

Read Psalm 18:29–33

What can you accomplish when you get God's power?

Know it or not, there's a mountain God wants you to charge. It might not look like a mountain to anyone else, but it's an area of your life where he's challenging you to press on without quitting. Maybe it's talking to a non-Christian friend who needs to meet Jesus, or practicing good study skills to pull a grade out of the gutter, or learning to obey him consistently and bust a bad habit, or figuring out how to use your time and talents to make a difference in your world.

The test in front of you requires you to follow God step by step, try after try. If you press on, your faith will take a huge leap upward. And when you stick with it, sooner or later you'll stand on top.

God arms me with strength, and he makes my way perfect. He makes me
as surefooted as a deer, enabling me to stand on mountain heights.

Psalm 18:32–33 NLT

Day 109

Vote for Me

"The printouts I'm distributing," your school counselor drones, "suggest occupations you would likely enjoy—based on your academic achievement, test scores, and personality profiles."

Just show us the sheets. You had spent hours and hours answering questions meant to uncover your career interests. Your results, you're sure, will showcase your many gifts and multitudinous career options. You already know what you want to be: *Pro tennis player. CIA special agent. Movie producer. Jet pilot. Oceanographer.*

"Don't look at your sheets," your counselor cautions, "until I say."

You peek. Two choices. *Burger flipper. French-fry dipper.*

Read 2 Corinthians 11:23–33

What price did the apostle Paul pay to accomplish his goals?

Goals are easier to dream up than to accomplish. Paul aimed for two things in life: to know Christ (Philippians 3:7–11), and to tell the world about him (2 Corinthians 5:18–20). He considered it such a privilege to preach, that even shipwrecks and whippings couldn't force him to quit. Again and again over many years of doing ministry, he took a beating and came back to the fight.

Paul knew that actions—what you do right now—matter far more than boasting about what you'll be. You won't become a rocket scientist later if you never shoot higher than C-minus now. You won't play in the symphony as a grown-up if you never rehearse for the middle-school orchestra. You won't ever practice medicine if you don't learn how to care for your peers.

The book of James says that when you have faith—when you trust God to lead your life—that you will "persevere," that is, you'll trample over, around, or through obstacles. You'll rely on God to help you chase your dream and finish what you start.

Pain always has a purpose as you persevere. It makes you "mature," "complete," and lack nothing (James 1:2–4). So you can reach your dreams for real.

I have worked much harder.

2 Corinthians 11:23

Day 110

Bobbing Head

You doh-on't ski-ee, you doh-on't ski-ee. With the taunts of her shrimpy six-year-old cousin booming in her brain since their last family reunion, Lilly wasn't going to pass up a chance to learn to water ski.

"Lilly," her dad said, "there are two rules to follow when—er, *if* you fall. First, let go of the rope—or you get dragged face-first through the water. Second, poke your ski out of the water so other boats can see you."

When Lilly fell with a spectacular sideways wipeout, she forgot the rules. She gulped a gallon of water as she got dragged. And when she thought about creatures lurking in the deep end of the lake, she neglected to get her ski up. Back in the boat, she shook. But she felt safe. And she wanted to try again.

Read Hebrews 13:5–6

What helps you try tough stuff?

When you learn to skim on skis across water, you might fall and torque your head. Or burn your legs on the tow rope. Slamming your body and swallowing water are usually the worst part of wipeouts. That is, unless you get mowed over by a boat.

God wants you to push, to dare, to try bold new adventures. And he promises that you'll never face a situation bigger than you can handle. Check this verse: "You can trust God, who will not permit you to be tempted more than you can stand. But when you are tempted, he will also give you a way to escape so that you will be able to stand it" (1 Corinthians 10:13 NCV). Those words don't just cover temptations to misuse sex, do drugs, or graffiti the school grounds. They also fight urges to despair, throw pity parties, and give up.

When you wipe out skiing, getting that ski tip up signals for help. It tells everyone else on the lake to steer clear. Sometimes you crash and can't even muster that, and your head bobbing among the waves can be tough to see. The good news? In the big lake of life, God watches over you perfectly and continually. He's always ready to swing the boat around and pick you up.

You can face anything if you face it with God. When you know God is always with you, you're willing to try hard stuff.

God has said, "Never will I leave you; never will I forsake you." So we say with confidence, "The Lord is my helper; I will not be afraid."

Hebrews 13:5–6

Day 111
Wax Worship

Josiah ran to his house, flew to the family room, dug for the TV remote, and flipped on a sports channel.

It's true.

For the past half season, Charles Denton—everyone's all-time favorite wide receiver—had crumpled to defenders like a little kid. He dropped passes Josiah's dog could have caught. And without Denton's usual stellar performance, his team plummeted in the standings.

And now the TV screen was splashed with video of a dozen squad cars pulling up at Denton's home and police taking Josiah's hero into custody. Denton admitted to everything from drug addiction to fixing games.

Later that evening, Josiah ripped down all the Charles Denton posters in his room and shredded them into tiny pieces. Except for one—which he kept for a dart board.

Read 2 Timothy 3:10–14

How do you pick someone to model your life after?

Big and powerful people can make you do what they say. You might not like the president, but you listen. Sometimes you have to follow, even if you're no fan.

Other people don't need to force you to follow. They make you laugh. Or they inspire you, like they're the next best thing to masked superheroes. Or you picture yourself doing what they do—singing, shooting hoops, skiing, skating—just like they do. They're so cool you can't contain your enthusiasm.

You probably don't sit down and consciously decide who your heroes will be. Maybe you should. The apostle Paul listed all the reasons why Timothy should imitate him and heed what he said. Among the reasons: He knew Paul up close. The apostle was real. Through victories and catastrophes, his coolness lasted a lifetime.

Many pop heroes turn out to be wax figures who melt in the heat. It's usually the heroes close by—like parents, grandparents, or teachers—who endure.

> But as for you, continue in what you have learned and have become convinced of, because you know those from whom you learned it.
>
> *2 Timothy 3:14*

Day 112

Shortcut to Disaster

On his thirteenth birthday, Marc's parents gave him the keys to a rebuilt classic Mustang. It was his ticket to immediate uber-coolness. Sure, it had to sit in the garage until he got his driver's license, but how many other thirteen-year-olds had a car title tucked in their underwear drawer?

Not that Marc waited to drive. Sometimes when his parents were gone, he backed the car out to the driveway. When that became a bore, he spun around the neighborhood. The illegality fueled the thrill—if he got caught driving underage, he woulnd't get a license until he was eighteen.

By the time Marc graduated from high school, his Mustang was as hot as ever, and so was he. He had the right car, the right friends, the right look—the total package. But he wasn't around to enjoy it for long. Just after graduation, he was killed in an accident.

Read Psalm 73:27–28

How do you feel when bad people get to their goals before you do?

Some people get all the good stuff sooner than you do. A few get it by working hard and doing what's right. Others get it by taking shortcuts: They slam others to score friends. They impress others with stuff anyone can get in a store. They give away their body.

They're cool. They know it. The whole world knows it.

When all goes well for them, you feel jealous. You want what they've got. You think, *Why can't that be me?* You wonder if you're wasting your time following God. You start to plot your own shortcuts.

That reasoning makes sense until you realize one thing: Success gained by doing wrong doesn't last. God promises that people wrongdoers will lose control and crack up, like a driver skidding off a cliff. One moment the cool ones cruise, the next they crash.

Having everything doesn't mean you have it made. That comes from enjoying God and what he gives you, when and how he chooses.

> Those who are far from you will perish; you destroy all who
> are unfaithful to you. But as for me, it is good to be near
> God. I have made the Sovereign Lord my refuge.
>
> *Psalm 73:27–28*

Day 113

Don't Just Stand There!

You rushed through a shower, swallowed a hard-boiled egg whole, and ran out the door wearing mismatched socks. Now you're standing in the cold waiting for the school bus with still-wet hair freezing into icicles. Could you help it you slept late? Well, yeah—but it's your parents' fault you had to get to the bus stop pronto. They said they wouldn't drive you to school if you missed the bus again. They called it "taking responsibility for yourself," or something like that.

You're especially perturbed because you're not thrilled about getting to school anyway. If the bus doesn't show up, you can goof off all day. But you know that the bus will arrive sooner or later, so you wait. And wait.

Read Titus 2:11–14

What big event are Christians waiting for? What should you do in the meantime?

As Christians, we're waiting for Jesus to come and transport us to God's kingdom. Jesus died so we could serve and worship God, be adopted into his family, be transformed into new people, and spend eternity as friends. In heaven, God will be King, and we will be his.

Sometimes that feels like waiting for a slow school bus. It seems a long way off (2 Peter 3:3–14). But it isn't. God's reign as King begins *now* for those who know him. Instead of killing time at the bus stop and wishing we were back home in bed, we can spend our every moment getting ready for eternity—getting better at loving God and other people. When Jesus shows up, we'll be dressed and ready to go, a pure people belonging wholly to God (Ephesians 4:22–24).

You have to make the choice to get to the bus stop—to become a Christian—for yourself. You also have to make the choice to do something worthwhile—to keep growing up spiritually, instead of wasting time—for yourself.

Don't let God's bus leave without you. And don't just wait around doing nothing.

> We wait for the blessed hope—the glorious appearing
> of our great God and Savior, Jesus Christ.
>
> *Titus 2:13*

Day 114
Dream Vacation

The tour brochure looked so pretty.

Pictures lie.

Okay, not everything about your family's vacation was awful. Your bargain flight took off on time—2:38 a.m. They served a meal in-flight. Well, more of a snack. Maybe the pilot's leftovers from the airport lounge. Your creaky rental car from Bob's Borrow-a-Bomb was smart protection from carjackings. Your family was in no danger of looking like wealthy tourists.

Then again, your mom had to clean the hotel bathtub before you could use it, and all week long you had to sleep on suitcases piled on top of the bed—to avoid infectious diseases. And on the one day nice enough to hit the beach, the only place to lay your towel was downwind from the Porta-Potties.

All week long, a question whined inside: *Why is this happening?*

Read Psalm 22:1–11

Do you wonder if God is worth trusting when things go wrong?
Why—or why not?

Be honest. As we skip through life hand in hand with God, we expect first-class accommodations—posh hotels, nice cars, and discount tickets to all the big attractions. We trust our all-knowing, all-perfect God to make the weather sunny and lines short.

When things go wrong, we feel as if our Father above booked us on a nightmare trip with a fourth-class travel agency.

Psalm 22 records David's wonderings about the Lord's travel arrangements: *I've heard all sorts of stories, God, about how great you are. So where are you? Haven't you heard me? My enemies surround me. People think I'm cracked to trust you. I've trusted you my whole life, but I'm not feeling the love. Please help soon!*

When trouble hits, even the best of believers sometimes wonder where God is.

Nope, your trip through life won't be trouble-free, because the world you travel in is no paradise. The sooner you learn a big truth, the better you'll cope: No matter what you face, God hangs tight with you all the way.

My God, my God, why have you forsaken me? Why are you so far
from saving me, so far from the words of my cries of anguish?

Psalm 22:1

Day 115
Whipped Potatoes

The food brawl was well underway before Mrs. Hoffmeister ambled toward the student cafeteria for her daily turn as lunch supervisor. But when she entered the lunchroom, the fight escalated into war, with Mrs. Hoffmeister instantly becoming the room's sole target. Mashed potatoes whizzed and whirled from every direction, pelting her from head to toe. Students hated Mrs. Hoffmeister. Still, she could whip any kid in the school—and most teachers. No one dared to exit when she bellowed, "ENOUGH!" and made everyone sit utterly still until the dean showed up.

Michael was innocent, having downed all his ammunition before the food fight broke out. When he argued that he didn't deserve to stay after school, no one cared. Give the guy a pea, and he would have been right in the mix.

Read Psalm 36:1–9

Why is the world such a mess?

Food fights. Funny? Sure. A mean mess we expect someone else to clean up? Usually. Wasteful? Probably. Still fun? Of course. Nothing beats flinging mashed potatoes.

Human-on-human battles might be okay if they stopped there. But they get far worse. We envy, bash, and kill one another. We destroy dignity. We think violence and deceit are normal.

God intended the world to be a place where we believe in him enough to do right—not only because we respect his power, but because we trust his wisdom. We were meant to bask in his love, swim in his goodness, rest in the shade of his protection, feast at his beachside barbecue sloshing down cold sodas. Life was to be a summer vacation.

But humanity chooses to live in the lunchroom throwing food—scorning God, cooking up more ammunition, and high-fiving each other every time a target takes a hit.

We've spoiled paradise.

> Your love, Lord, reaches to the heavens, your faithfulness to the skies. Your righteousness is like the highest mountains, your justice like the great deep.
>
> *Psalm 36:5–6*

Day 116
Quit Gawking

Ooooooo . . . lights swirl as you lie on the floor. "He was on his way to Sunday school when he slipped on a banana peel," says a peer. "He hit his head pretty hard. He's so stupid."

"Hormones," mumbles a doctor. "He's at that awkward age."

"God did this to you," smirks your youth pastor. "Payback for putting cereal in my sleeping bag on our last retreat."

A parent grabs the youth pastor by the ear and complains about "all the wild young people at church." An elder lays one hand on the banana peel and points the other toward heaven and casts out a demon. Then a lawyer walks by and whispers in your ear, "I'll help you sue the church—for waxing the floor."

Read John 9:1–12

Who's to blame when bad things happen to people?

Face it: You're responsible for much of what you suffer. You cut class, so you flunk. You don't hustle, so the other team scores. You flip the banana peel, and it flips you. Peers and parents and hormones exert influence, but they don't make your choices. You do. And you live with the consequences.

At other times, you're clobbered by a situation you can't control. You catch the flu. Your parents divorce. You're beaten up or abused. You discover you're dyslexic. You're not to blame, although you still decide how you respond.

Jesus' disciples accepted popular opinion about the man born blind:

Someone sinned. The question was *who*—the man (before birth, they claimed) or his parents.

Jesus rejected both storylines. And his disciples missed the main point: What would God do?

That's still the point. When bad things happen, God wants to help the hurting through *us*. He can move through the *miraculous*—his extraordinary displays of power. And he's even glorified by the *tenacious*—people who rely on his strength to triumph in awful situations. To Jesus, the blind man wasn't a puzzle to solve. He was a person to help.

This happened so that the works of God might be displayed in him.

John 9:3

Day 117
Pumping Hearts

How could God let this happen? If God really loved Tyler, he wouldn't be lying in a coma. If God really cared, he would have kept that truck from plowing into Tyler's car.

Jasmine was convinced that God could work wonders and put her brother back together. She just didn't know if he would.

Read Acts 20:17–24

Can you expect God to do miracles? How come?

People have no shortage of agonizing problems—broken friendships, twisted minds, imploding families, failing bodies. Even as our outsides fall apart, an even deadlier problem lurks inside: We don't know God well. Our hearts have stopped beating for him.

The apostle Paul saw that God used every experience of his life, good and bad, to address that one problem. God wanted Paul to know him well and for others to know him too. So the apostle focused his whole life on God's rescue plan—staying close to God and completing the job God gave him, obeying even when God's plans led to pain. Being part of God's rescue squad mattered more than any pain he suffered (2 Corinthians 6:3–12).

From God's perspective, our need for him is the biggest emergency of life. God wants to jump-start our hearts. When we become friends with God through Jesus, our hearts pump anew. When we help others become his friends, even more hearts pump. We want God to fix our circumstances. God wants to fix us.

That doesn't mean God leaves us twisting in pain. We pray for what we believe is best—to have a brother back, for a friendship to heal, for parents to stick together. We act where we can and ask God to act where we can't. God does what he sees best to jump-start hearts and to accomplish all of his other plans and purposes for us.

Sometimes God works unbelievable miracles for our outsides. When we let him, he always works miracles on our insides.

> I consider my life worth nothing to me; my only aim is to finish
> the race and complete the task the Lord Jesus has given me—
> the task of testifying to the good news of God's grace.
>
> *Acts 20:24*

Day 118

Your Mama

Willy was walking to school, minding his own business, when Logan and company jumped him for his lunch cash. Logan sat on Willy's chest and knuckled his forehead until he coughed up the money.

Suddenly a screech from the end of the block distracts Logan. One of Logan's buddies yells, "Mother on a rampage! RUN!"

Logan and friends fall over each other trying to escape as Willy's mom steams toward them in fatigues, face paint, and whomping black boots. She heaves the bullies over fences into their own backyards, but not before threatening to push their noses to the back of their heads the next time they touch Willy.

Willy gets up. "Thanks, Mom."

"No problem," says Willy's mom. "Anything for my baby."

Read Psalm 144:1-8

Does needing God's help make you weak? Why—or why not?

You would probably rather go home with a black eye than be rescued by your mom. But there are some battles you can't fight yourself.

Even David—the fierce warrior who wrote Psalm 144—admitted he needed God. Without God, he was nothing—a "breath," a "fleeting shadow." He begged God not to stand by. He asked God to split the sky, roast the mountains, and light up his enemies. David needed God to rescue him.

Sometimes God dashes down the block to save you. But he also arms you to defend yourself.

As king of Israel, a political country ruled by God, David saw foreign nations who served other gods as enemies. *Your* biggest enemies aren't people. They're spiritual. And they don't want your lunch money. They want to bully you out of your faith. God gives you weapons to strike back: truth, righteousness, the good news of Christ, faith, prayer, sureness that you belong to God, and the Bible (Ephesians 6:10–18). God's weapons all defend and strengthen your trust in God.

Needing God doesn't make you a mama's boy—or girl. You never outgrow your need for God.

He is my loving God and my fortress, my stronghold and my deliverer,
my shield, in whom I take refuge, who subdues peoples under me.

Psalm 144:2

Day 119
Next Time I'll Floss

Gzzzzzzzzer goes the drill. "Does that hurt?" your dentist inquires.

Hurt? Would it hurt if I twisted a pencil in your eye at six thousand RPM? "Just a little," you respond politely. "Maybe I need something for the pain." When a long snort of laughing gas does nothing for your agony, you stop thinking how much money you'll get when you sue your dentist and start wishing you had paid more attention to your mom's childbirth stories. *How did she breathe? Hoo-hoo-hee?*

Your bleary mind tries to make a deal. *Stop it! Stop it! Next time I'll floss!* Your dentist pauses—to let the filling dry—then heads out the door. *Why does he keep bobbing in to check on me? To see if I'm dead?*

Read Isaiah 40:27–31

How do you know God hears you when you ask for help?

You just want a little something to take the edge off your pain. You would settle for way less than a miracle. You make God a generous offer to become a missionary to Ukarumpa in exchange for a wee bit of help, and you wonder why he doesn't respond.

You think God has said, "Forget it, slimewad. Chew dirt!" You feel aggravated. You're crying out, *Hello, God! Can't you see I'm hurting? Quit ignoring me. Why won't you answer me?*

He has. Be assured that God doesn't sleep or go to lunch. And he doesn't put a price on his services. He doesn't hear you because of *your* promises to him but because of *his* promise to you: You belong to him. He sees your problems and hears your prayers.

But he answers prayers the way he knows is best (1 John 5:14–15).

When God doesn't say "Yes," he's not necessarily saying "No." Sometimes he says "Wait" or "I'll answer, but not the way you think." When you trust God, he renews your strength—to walk, to run, to fly. And to defy life's drills.

> But those who hope in the Lord will renew their strength. They will soar on wings like eagles; they will run and not grow weary, they will walk and not be faint.
>
> *Isaiah 40:31*

Day 120
Out of Cash

Mia's mom sat at the kitchen table, tablet open to a spreadsheet, carefully calculating how much money would remain after each bill was paid.

"I'm sorry, honey," she told Mia when she finished. "There's not much left. Enough for a pair of pants when school starts and a shirt at the end of next month."

Only one pair of pants? Mia thought. Good thing her mom hadn't noticed the hole in the bottom of Mia's shoes, or that's what she'd get. A hole she could hide from the kids at school—at least until it rained and her feet got wet and stunk. Worn-out clothes she couldn't mask.

Mia knew that her mom was doing her best to provide, but she still felt sick. *I look like a troll crawling out from under a bridge. I'll be the only one not wearing new stuff!*

Read Psalm 31:1–5

Where is God when you suffer?

Whenever you struggle—whatever your struggle—questions often pour in: Why won't God fix my problem *now*? When will God punish people who hurt me? Why do bad things happen to me? Where is God when I hurt?

When you ache, you're convinced you're a loser—that you're the only one in the world who doesn't measure up. You're the only one who botched the test. Or whose parents fight or work too much. Or whose clothes are less than fresh-off-the-rack.

When you suffer, you feel alone.

You're not.

When God doesn't insert his powerful hand into your situation and immediately fix your problems, you might conclude he's left you to fend for yourself. He hasn't. You belong to him. And for the sake of his name—his reputation and truthfulness—he will lead and guide you. He's your rock to hide behind, your bulked-up protection from all enemies. Whatever misery you face is an opportunity to cry out, "Protect me, God. I'm yours!"

Turn your ear to me, come quickly to my rescue; be my
rock of refuge, a strong fortress to save me.

Psalm 31:2

Day 121
Okay to Hurt

Amelia sat against the back wall of the funeral home. She couldn't drag herself to the front, up to her best friend's open casket. Alexis was gone, and now Amelia was dying on the inside. People said Alexis was in heaven. All Amelia knew was that she wasn't here anymore.

What bugged Amelia most was how hardly anyone talked about Alexis. Adults chatted about the weather and how tough it is to be a kid these days. Kids gabbed about school and mean teachers and stupid homework. It was like Alexis never existed. Even her locker was already cleaned out.

Amelia was screaming inside to talk about *all* of it. No one else wanted to talk about *any* of it. When it came to tragedy and pain, her crowd had one rule: Get over it.

Amelia's mom suggested she tell God how she was hurting.

"Why God?" Amelia said. "He doesn't have a clue."

Read Matthew 5:4

What good is God when you're hurting?

You're probably good at faking tough. You learned to act strong when you fell and ripped up your leg and forced yourself to stop crying. You got to practice toughness when you got a good scab going and someone came by and kicked your shin.

God doesn't make you fake toughness. When you cry to him, he comforts. When you wail to him, he listens. He's your always-present help in times of trouble (Psalm 46:1).

Your Lord understands loss. He's watched his best creation—human beings—turn away from friendship with him and turn on each other. He witnessed the death of his Son, Jesus, for all the evil of the world.

God has hurt figured out.

While God won't shut down your sadness, he also won't let you wallow in it. He heals you, then invites you to help others. Whenever God comforts you, he wants you to pass that care on to others facing tough problems (2 Corinthians 1:3–4). He heals you—and makes you his agent of healing in the lives of others.

Blessed are those who mourn, for they will be comforted.

Matthew 5:4

Day 122

Angry Too

You and your dad were so delirious after watching your favorite team clinch a playoff spot that it seemed obvious you should hit your favorite burger joint to inhale some midnight sliders and wind down.

Halfway through your feeding frenzy, two guys with nylons over their heads burst into the restaurant waving shotguns. They herded everyone into the store freezer and made you lie on boxes of food with your hands behind your head. They jabbed your dad in the back with the shotgun and threatened to blow away anyone who moved.

A few minutes later, they were gone. The men had left. But they were never far from your mind. When your best friend came over with a nylon stretched over his face, you slammed the door and crumpled. Screaming in the middle of the night or shivering when you recall the freezer and the masked men is not so humorous. You want to punch walls knowing the men got away. You can't understand why God hasn't put them on ice for good.

Read Habakkuk 3:3–16

When will God punish people who do wrong?

God is the one Being in the universe who is totally holy—powerful, wise, and good in everything he thinks, says, and does. He can't tolerate sin. Habakkuk's prayer recalls what God did to the Egyptians, Israel's slave masters, until that nation finally let Israel go. Gory stuff.

God isn't just irate about Egyptians. He threatens eternal separation from himself and everything good for all who continually battle against him. The Bible pictures their place of punishment as unstoppable fire (Revelation 21:8), everlasting chains (Jude 6), and utter darkness (Matthew 8:12). People who do evil will get what they deserve, even if they don't get caught on earth.

Honestly, we all deserve separation from God. But he doesn't wish judgment on anyone (2 Peter 3:9). He waits for people to admit their sin and accept his forgiveness.

That's why God doesn't always ice enemies now. When he seems slow to punish people who do wrong, be glad he isn't quick to punish you.

In anger you threshed the nations.

Habakkuk 3:12

Day 123

Get Real

"You gotta get over it." Branden tried to knock sense into Malik. "I know what you're thinking—that you can get your parents back together and make everything the way it used to be. Forget it, Malik. Stuff won't ever be the same. I should know. It's been six years since my parents divorced. They treat me like a movie rental. They borrow me for a few days and give me back when they've seen enough."

Branden didn't hold back. "You learn to survive on your own," he said. "Hey—if you're smart, you can take advantage of this whole thing. My dad tries to buy my love, because he knows Mom can't afford to keep up. I keep upping the price. I get something new every weekend. You'll make it if you just remember one thing: When they trash you, you trash them back."

Read Romans 4:18–21

How did Abraham react when God promised to help him?

Back at the start of the Bible, God told Abraham he would be the father of a great nation, God's chosen people. But Abraham couldn't start a nation without first fathering a family, and he and Sarah had no kids. When Sarah heard God's promise, she snorted (Genesis 18:10–15). *Hey God!* she thought. *Aren't you a few decades late?*

Abraham wasn't stupid. He knew as well as Sarah that their bodies were out of fire. Practically ready to expire. He didn't ignore the problem. He faced facts with faith. He was sure God would do what he had sworn.

Here's reality: Life hurts. Here's a bigger reality: God keeps promises.

It's a fact: You're starting at a new school and you're totally alone. But *God says he will never leave you* (Hebrews 13:5–6). It's a fact: You want to rip the eyebrows off people who wound you. But *God promises to punish those who hurt you* (Romans 12:19). It's a fact: Life at home or school is falling apart, and you don't think you can cope. But *God promises to work through even bad things to bring good to your life* (Romans 8:28).

What you see and feel in your real world can make God's promises sound crazy. But he always keeps his word.

[Abraham] did not waver through unbelief regarding the promise of God.

Romans 4:20

Day 124
Waiting

Angel towels off the steamy bathroom mirror, looking close to gently comb the few strands of hair left after her chemotherapy treatments. Her doctors are hopeful the drugs have killed her cancer, but everyone still sighed with relief that she lived to see today, her birthday.

As Angel gets ready for her party, she mulls over whether to wear her wig or to go with the hip bald look her friends want her to try. *A year ago, I worried about bad-hair days,* she thinks. *Now it's no-hair days.*

The mirror refogs. Angel wipes it again, this time to stare into her own eyes. *I wonder if I'll be alive in another year.*

Read Romans 8:18–27

Why don't problems go away?

Life isn't a sitcom where every difficulty ends in hugs, smiles, and high-fives within twenty-two minutes. The future is a foggy mirror.

But God promises an eternity in heaven where you'll face not danger, death, disease, discomfort, nor displeasure (Revelation 21:1–8).

Life here and now still churns with problems. Believers groan as we wait for a perfect world. Creation itself—everything God made—moans like a woman in labor, looking for the birth of a renewed, perfected planet. Even God's Holy Spirit groans as he prays ("intercedes") through us for God's perfect will for us.

That's all foggy. What we do see, however, is that the world is out of whack. Life at its best is less than perfect. People sin, and creation produces mosquitoes, hurricanes, and cancer. Life at its worst is ghastly. And our best efforts to fix things are just wigs. They cover up a problem but don't grow new hair.

Our problems won't be solved completely until our "adoption as sons" (and daughters) at the end of time when God shakes the world, when he eliminates evil and perfects everything that belongs to him. That's what we hope for. That's what God promises us.

And so we wait.

I consider that our present sufferings are not worth
comparing with the glory that will be revealed in us.

Romans 8:18

Day 125

In the Meantime

Kaylee and her pastor sat in the rec room of a mental health unit.

"They've got me locked up like I tried to kill someone!" Kaylee blurted.

"You *did*. You tried to hurt yourself. We won't let you do that."

"Well, this place is humiliating. They took away my shoelaces and my belt and anything else they think I can use to hurt myself. I can't use the phone. You're the first person I've seen other than Mom. It's like jail." She calmed. "They did let me go for a supervised walk outside today. That was nice. I haven't gone for a walk in a long time. Dad and I used to walk together. You never met him, did you?"

"He died before I moved here, remember? Kaylee—your dad—is his death what this is about?"

Kaylee started to cry. "I don't know—it's about my dad and my mom and my sister and my friends! I just wanted to get away."

Read Habakkuk 3:17–19

What do you do when hurts don't go away?

Some tactics for dealing with pain are like prying the protective cage off a fan and inserting your face. People who make those choices—to rebel, drink, inhale, misuse sex, hide, weld headphones to their head, or quit life altogether—miss out on fingers and foreheads and noses. Or on life.

But there are other choices that refresh, like plopping in front of a fan on a hot day. *You can choose to deal with your problem*: Change what you can. Talk with people who can find solutions—parents, teachers, counselors, and pastors. Memorize Bible passages that encourage you. *You can choose to keep busy:* Join a club. Exercise. Play sports. Goof off with your friends. Do homework. Help around the house. Find a hobby. Most of all, *you can choose to keep trusting God*: When everything goes wrong (when "the fig tree doesn't bud" or "the fields produce no food"), God is still Lord. He still watches over you. He's still Savior. Even when everything else goes wrong, he is right there with you.

Though the fig tree does not bud and there are no grapes on the vines
. . . yet I will rejoice in the Lord, I will be joyful in God my Savior.

Habakkuk 3:17–18

Day 126
Hanging In

Almost a foot shorter than anyone else in his grade, Lucas lives with a long and ugly *can't-do-that* list.

I can't reach the pull-up bar.

I can't spike a volleyball.

I can't look a classmate in the eye.

I can't see the screen unless I sit in the front row.

I can't stand getting bullied in the locker room.

Trapped in the body of a lot-younger kid, Lucas can't make himself grow. He can't change his situation. But he can choose to conquer it.

Read 1 Peter 1:3–9

What keeps life's rough stuff from being a waste?

People beat their bodies in weight rooms or do waddle-till-they-wheeze marathons to stay fit. Adultish-types pull all-nighters to survive college, work graveyard shifts to save for a house, stay glued together in nasty marriages to try to jump-start love, or give up money to help people they've never met.

Painful Truth 1: You can choose pain to gain huge prizes.

Painful Truth 2: You can find gain even in pain you don't pick.

No circumstance you'll ever face can outsmart God's control. With a flick of his finger, he can you rearrange pain or remove it. But if God doesn't take away the troubles trampling through your life, consider those troubles part of his training to make your faith strong.

Pain only works its wonders in you if you submit to its training. Hardships strike out of nowhere and slap you upside the head. But God turns them into something useful. They're like a workout to make you righteous and peaceful. They prove your real devotion to God. And your faithfulness brings glory to God.

If you try to wiggle free from God's gym, however, the circumstance that can bring a spiritual benefit becomes a waste—it wastes *you*, that is. It becomes stupid suffering instead of a sweet workout for your soul.

You may have had to suffer grief in all kinds of trials. These have come so that
the proven genuineness of your faith . . . may result in praise, glory and honor.

1 Peter 1:6–7

Day 127
You Understand

Ms. Hernandez wanted Aaron out of her class. Funny kid, but his defiance was contagious. Only one discipline tactic remained, something she reserved for uncontrollable kids: a dose of embarrassment. Hoping to force Aaron to shape up, she sent him across the street to the elementary school—slamming the seventh grader back to second grade.

She thought it was punishment. Aaron loved it.

From his big desk in the back of the room, Aaron noticed a little guy named Sam. He acted just like Aaron—bouncing off the walls, zero focus.

One day Sam asked Aaron for help, and the seventh grader discovered he could explain the answer. The pair became study buddies. And when Aaron watched Sam's teacher trying hard to help Sam, he realized how miserably he had treated Ms. Hernandez.

Read 2 Corinthians 1:3–11

How does God make good come out of bad?

The last thing you want to hear when you hurt is that your experience will make you strong and wise.

But it's true. You learn from tough stuff.

We're not exactly sure what the apostle Paul suffered in Asia, but whatever it was, it caused intense despair. He was as terrified as if he were shackled to an electric chair and someone was about to flip the switch. His confidence in himself was shattered, yet he found that God was "the God of all comfort." And he shared that comfort with the Corinthians.

Rough times teach you trust—confidence that God accepts you, cares for you, and ultimately will bring you to an eternity with himself in paradise (Romans 5:3–4). You learn to rely not on yourself but on God.

God doesn't plan for bad things to happen in your world. But like a shapeless lump of clay, God can spin your life into something good. He heals your hurt and uses you to heal the hurts of others. Your pain isn't a waste.

[God] comforts us in all our troubles, so that we can comfort those
in any trouble with the comfort we ourselves receive from God.

2 Corinthians 1:4

Day 128
Heading Home

Gia slouched in her chair, staring at her desk, convinced that everyone around her was staring at *her*.

The night before, after the final performance of the school play, Gia went to the cast party with instructions from her parents to be at the front door for her ride home at ten thirty—an exceedingly generous school-night curfew, they said. When Gia didn't exit the party on time, her dad strolled to the front door, rang the doorbell, and bellowed inside. There she was—Gia Lee, star of the school play, deserting the party right after it started, exiting hours earlier than anyone else.

In the car, Gia protested that she wasn't tired at all. A minute later, she zonked out. Her dad had to carry her into the house.

The next day at school, all her friends could talk about was how she—and her dad—pooped on the party.

Read Hebrews 11:13–16

How did believers of the past feel about their home on planet earth?

Most people in this world have chosen to run from God. So if you're trying to run *toward* him, you're going to bang heads with lots of folks going the other way. Big things, little things—you'll clash. You won't always fit with your peers.

You might assume the problem is your parents—but they just want what's best for you. The issue isn't God—his commands are always good. It isn't you—provided you're trying to do right. It isn't even the people around you—it's bigger than that.

The real problem is that this planet isn't your home. As a Christian, you're a citizen of heaven (Philippians 3:20). And that makes you an "alien" and "stranger" for as long as you live here.

When you follow God, you'll always ache for something better. But it isn't until heaven that you receive *all* that God has promised: total happiness and utter protection.

Heaven is where you belong. It's a long walk before you get there. But it's the one place where you'll feel totally at home.

> They said they were like visitors and strangers on earth. . . . They
> were waiting for a better country—a heavenly country.
>
> *Hebrews 11:13, 16 NCV*

Day 129

Jesus Goes to Your School

Suppose you decide to invite Jesus to your school for a day. Big experiment. Maybe you even post an event alert to let everyone know.

Everyone warns you that Jesus will act weird and humiliate you. So when he meets you at the bus stop, you're relieved he's not in a robe. His signature sandals look pretty hip, in fact.

After English, Jesus agrees with you that Mr. Johnson indeed ranks among the driest teachers in the universe—and he's heard them all.

Classmates notice Jesus squished into a desk next to you, but you don't introduce him to anyone. Jesus looks hurt. One time you dart off, leaving Jesus hanging. Then you run back. He's right where you left him, waiting patiently. You promise not to do that again.

By the end of the day, you figure you've hit it off with Jesus. You ask him to come back tomorrow and follow you around again.

Jesus leans over and whispers in your ear.

"Huh?" You're bewildered. "You want *me* to follow *you?*"

Read Psalm 97:1–6

What would life be like if Jesus showed up at your school?

You might like school. You might hate it. However you feel, by the time you graduate from high school, you'll spend more than a million minutes in classrooms. Not counting homework. And time doesn't fly when you're not having fun.

So what would happen if you invited Jesus to tag along for those million minutes?

While it's nice to ask Jesus to come to school with you, it's a little backwards. His job isn't to follow you around. It's your job to follow him.

Jesus calls you to go wherever he leads. Right now, that includes school. But when Jesus shows up, he isn't going to slink around out of sight, taking a last-row seat and leaving a spot of hair product on the back wall. Jesus is Lord of all. He owns every minute of life. And his goal is to show you his way to do school.

The mountains melt like wax before the Lord, before the Lord of all the earth.

Psalm 97:5

Day 130

Great Expectations

The night before Diego graduated up to a bigger school, he tossed so much he tore the sheets off his bed. "NO! NOT THERE!" he screamed as his old teachers dragged him to the gaping mouth of a raging monster. At the monster's mouth stood Diego's parents, propping open the front doors. Diego's mom had that sympathetic look she got when he was little and had to drop his shorts at the doctor's for a shot. His dad shouted encouragement as Diego's teachers tossed him in: "This hurts us more than it hurts you!"

The doors snapped shut behind Diego. Like a gargantuan tongue, the crowds inside swished him this way and that. He felt as if he were being chewed to bits by overgrown molars.

Diego couldn't wait for the final bell so the school would spit him out.

Read Joshua 1:1–11

What does God promise to do for you when you head to school?

God was nudging his people to enter the incredible land he had promised them. The Israelites had known for a long time that their leader, Moses, wouldn't go with them. But they all feared that with Moses gone, their lives would never be the same. Not that the mighty leader was always their favorite. Things just seemed normal—safe—when he was around.

The Israelites had nothing to fear. God had promised success, provided they stuck close to him. It didn't matter that they didn't know where they were going. They knew their Lord. They knew his commands. And three times God reminded Joshua and all the people: "Be strong! Be strong! BE STRONG!"

When you grow into a new school, you leave your old place behind. And it's gone—except for a head full of facts and fun memories of favorite classes, like recess. What made your life "normal" is dead.

Yet God says you have nothing to fear. He doesn't toss you into the next stage of life all alone. He swears to stay by your side and teach you *his* way to do school. He'll show you how to conquer the monster.

Have I not commanded you? Be strong and courageous. Do not be afraid; do not be discouraged, for the Lord your God will be with you wherever you go.

Joshua 1:9

Day 131
Crawling the Walls

"Class, I'm going to step down to the office for twenty minutes," your social studies teacher says to you and your cohorts. "I want you to stay at your desks, studying pages 643 to 678 of your textbook."

Party! everyone thinks. *She didn't just say she was leaving. We know where she's going and how long she'll be gone!* As your teacher takes off down the hall, lookouts scramble. *She's gone!* Chips and energy drinks appear from nowhere. Guys break out cards. Girls dance on desks.

As paper airplanes and footballs fly overhead, you obediently start reading your assignment. You pass page 678 and zoom toward page 700, until the rest of the class notices you. Then they pelt you with garbage.

Read Colossians 3:22–24

You're not supposed to crawl the walls at school. Why not?

Your classmates probably wouldn't riot if your teacher left the room. Or maybe they would. But if they did, you probably wouldn't be the only one not goofing off. Or maybe you would. Or maybe—just maybe—you would lead the revolt.

The choice you make all starts with one question: Is school pointless—or not?

The slaves to whom the apostle Paul wrote seldom suffered as badly as slaves living in pre–Civil War America. In major Roman cities, more than half the population were slaves, including most teachers and doctors. Still, the slaves were property controlled by owners. They could do little about their bondage except alter their attitude.

Kind of like you at school. You can choose to *want* to do what you *have* to do anyway. You can make up your mind that you're working for God, your Master.

You don't do school for teachers. You do it for your future. And God is a big reason you can embrace homework, listen in class, and stay clear of trouble. Doing school God's way starts with doing school for him.

> Slaves, obey your earthly masters in everything; and do it,
> not only when their eye is on you and to curry their favor, but
> with sincerity of heart and reverence for the Lord.
>
> *Colossians 3:22*

Day 132
Blowin' in the Wind

They had a deal. Cameron, Ethan, and Wyatt ate together. Always. Then none of them would look stupid eating alone.

At the opposite end of the lunchroom from where they usually sat was a zone that oozed cool, a table full of girls and guys whose every awesome move made others gawk in admiration.

One day when Cameron approached the cool table, its occupants gave him the stink eye. They might forgive him this once if he immediately crawled back to where he belonged. Then they saw he was with one of their own. They let Cameron in—for today, anyway.

Ethan and Wyatt stood up to watch Cameron and Kate find seats. As Cameron eased into coolness, they almost applauded. They waited for his signal inviting them over. But when Cameron pulled out his lunch and started to eat, they figured it out. They'd been dumped.

Read Romans 15:5–7

How do friends stay friends—and make more friends?

When you lack friends, you blow through school like tumbleweed. Barely part of the landscape, you feel dried up and ugly. Occasionally you get burned to keep other people warm.

With friends, you don't feel alone. You feel okay. Valued. Like you fit.

Making new friends is great. Except when new relationships kill other friendships. In the chapter before the passage you read, the apostle Paul hints that the best way to make friends and stay friends (a "spirit of unity") is to pull people together instead of pushing them apart.

Paul says your goal is nothing less than to accept other people like God accepts you, welcoming them into your group, into your space, treating them the way you want to be treated (Matthew 7:12). Dumping your old friends and grabbing cool new ones isn't how you get to the top. You do that by hanging close to God. He wants everyone in his friend group (2 Peter 3:9), and he never forms a ring so tight there isn't room for more.

Accept one another, then, just as Christ accepted
you, in order to bring praise to God.

Romans 15:7

Day 133

Top Dog

Emily glanced at her score, cracked a wicked smile, and nosed around to see what her classmates got on the test. Everyone hid their papers. They knew she did better. She always did.

Emily snatched Dylan's test. He was so nice—but so slow at school. "Give it back!" Dylan begged, looking like he was going die of embarrassment.

Emily snorted. "Maybe you should sit in the back with the other idiots," she advised. "They could tutor you. Maybe you'd pass."

Read Psalm 26:1–2

How do you know when you've truly done well at something?

If you bust the curve, you might think you did your best. But grades don't tell the whole story, like whether you mastered anything that will stay in your brain long-term.

If your sibling always catches the blame for everything bad, you might think you're the good child. But dodging your parents' discipline might just mean you're good at hiding your shenanigans.

If you know less about the Bible than your Christian friends, you might conclude you're a spiritual slug. But feeling less mature than your friends might leave out the important fact that you're getting to know God.

If you determine what you think or feel about yourself by how you seem to stack up against others, you're using a yardstick that's never the same length twice, and you'll either crush people with your bloated head or feel tiny and worthless.

When you measure yourself with the yardsticks you find in the Bible, you'll notice that all of us fall short of God's perfection (Romans 3:23). You can also hear God's applause when you do well (Matthew 25:21). And you can see what you're shooting for and be assured that God promises to remake you (Romans 14:4).

Then you don't have to make others look bad to make yourself look good.

Test me, Lord, and try me, examine my heart and my mind.

Psalm 26:2

Day 134
Waiting for the Candy

I've read this a bazillion times. With her head in her hands, Kendra peeked through her fingers at her math book. *I still don't get it.*

She knocked her book onto the floor. *Math is so stupid.* What worried her most, however, was that *she* might be the problem. Working with a math aide three days a week had helped Kendra keep up—until this year. She toiled away. She wanted to do well. Other subjects were tough, but math was the worst. Every study session was like starting over, as if each night someone poked a syringe in her skull and sucked out her brains.

Kendra mulled her choices: Pretend school doesn't matter. Pack a shopping cart full of makeup and hope she succeeds as a model. Plan on bagging groceries for the rest of her life.

God, Kendra prayed, *you said you would be with me wherever I went. So where are you? Why is this so hard?*

Read Isaiah 41:8–16

If God is with you, why doesn't he make homework easier?

Worms. They spend their lives digging dirt only to get squashed on the sidewalk. Or bit in half by a bird. Or stuck with a fishhook. Or shrivel up when the rain-soaked ground dries up.

You're not a worm. God made you glorious (Psalm 8:3–9). But that doesn't mean you never feel a little slimy.

God is with you when school goes well—and when things go awful and you feel wormish. Whatever you face, God stays with you because you belong to him. He's promised you his total help.

You feel tense, however, in the gap between when your problem hits and when God provides, between your hurt and God's help. The Lord isn't a candy machine you can rock until the good stuff drops. He also doesn't swallow your money and leave you empty-handed. He gives you what you need when you need it most.

Problems now. Provision in God's time. In the meantime? *Trust.*

So do not fear, for I am with you; do not be dismayed, for I am your God. I will strengthen you and help you; I will uphold you with my righteous right hand.

Isaiah 41:10

Day 135

The Art of Endurance

Morning after morning, you shut off your alarm, crawl from bed, trudge to school, and take your seat in your first-hour art class.

You once clocked your teacher saying "Um" forty-eight times in six minutes. At forty-nine you fell into a coma and lost count. After you regained consciousness, you killed time by plucking out your eyebrow hairs.

The way you see it, the system is taunting you. You feel you have no choice but to go deviant. While the class makes metal stick figures, you manufacture a miniature spring-loaded catapult to launch notes to a friend at another table. When the class builds a life-size log cabin out of tongue depressors to commemorate Abraham Lincoln's birthday, you hang sticks from your nose. And one day when you're especially bored, you rewire the pottery wheel to make it spin in hyperdrive.

Your clay flies. It *thwonks* your teacher on the head. You get detention. More excitement.

Read Galatians 6:7–8

How do you cope when school bores you?

Some school days make you feel like you could have unscrewed your brain and left it at home, you didn't need it. Or a teacher doesn't care about what he's teaching, so neither do you. Or you can't see what school has to do with real life because you have more important things occupying your mind, so you tune out.

Peers try a million different tactics to bust the boredom—from talking when it's time to shut up to arriving at school high. What will *you* do?

Doing well in school or anywhere else can be boring—until you see the reward. Doing what's right is like putting seed in the ground. Sooner or later, plants sprout. It might take a while, but you'll reap peace that God is right and satisfaction that you did right (Hebrews 12:11). And that's never boring.

> You will always harvest what you plant. Those who live only to satisfy
> their own sinful nature will harvest decay and death. . . . But those
> who live to please the spirit will harvest everlasting life. . . .
>
> *Galatians 6:7–8 NLT*

Day 136
Spit Out the Bones

Girls look up to her. Guys just stare at her. So when the seventeen-year-old Olympic hopeful stepped up to speak at the school assembly, everyone hushed.

"When I sprint, I imagine myself flying through the air," she told them. "In my mind, my feet barely touch the ground."

You have the same power inside you to unlock all that you can be. What's the key? Believe in yourself. If you believe hard enough, you make things happen. You can change what you become.

You can picture your way to beating the person running next to you. You can think your way to straight A's. You can make yourself a millionaire by visualizing it in your mind. You can even stop your little sister from being a brat. Just imagine it and you have it.

Read Proverbs 3:5–8

Can you be strong—or smart—without God?

There are times you're not totally sure of yourself. You need a boost to keep you from crumbling.

Mentally rehearsing the situation might help. But it doesn't alter reality. If you could imagine your way to success, by now you would be high-jumping fifty-three feet, pulling straight A's, and racing a Ferrari.

Through God, you can have great confidence: "With your help I can advance against a troop; with my God I can scale a wall" (Psalm 18:29). Even so, God gently reminds you of this: "Without Me you can do nothing" (John 15:5 NKJV). Your brain is never as big as you think. You're not as strong or wise as you tell yourself. God is what powers your life.

No matter where you go to school, you can't swallow whole everything you hear and see: "Depend on yourself." "Just accept what I say. Trust me." "The Bible is full of myths." "Ignore your parents. Make your own decisions." God gave you the Bible to help you separate truth from lies (2 Timothy 3:14–16).

When you eat fish, you eat the meat and leave the bones. You can swallow a few tiny bones and live to tell about it. But if you don't strain out the big ones, you'll gag. Or choke and die.

Trust in the Lord with all your heart and lean not on your own understanding.

Proverbs 3:5

Day 137
School Smarts

While Anthony's classmates spent five weeks in the library writing a paper that counted for half their grade, he perused back issues of *Sports Illustrated* and *MAD* magazine. He snickered when the class genius inquired how his research on the feeding habits of Galápagos tortoises was coming along. He roared with laughter when kids dug into piles of obscure sources. "You don't have to do all that," he informed them. "The teacher's just trying to scare us."

The night before the paper was due, Anthony spotted a movie he wanted to watch. He popped a huge bucket of popcorn and quaffed four cans of Mountain Dew, glad his parents didn't know he had a report due. The next day, his classmates turned in twenty-page reports with the required forty footnotes. Anthony turned in two pages scribbled in pencil off the top of his head.

Read Proverbs 4:5–13

What's the easiest way to get through school?

You might have nightmares about school for the rest of your life. Like forgetting to go to class—all semester. Or losing your locker combination. Or misplacing your schedule and no one will give you a new one.

School can be scary. So how do you survive the nightmare right now?

Start by staying awake. You won't have to study so hard on your own if you pay attention and take notes in class. Listen to teachers. Laugh back at peers who mock you for studying hard. Do your own work and remind yourself that most of the time hard work still pays off.

Getting smart doesn't mean memorizing Wikipedia, devouring dictionaries, or kissing up to teachers. It's knowing what your goal is and how to avoid the traps between you and your destination. It's figuring out the best way to get things done—following God's rules, staying within his boundaries of right and wrong and his guidelines of good, better, and best.

Those are the things you're supposed to do. They also happen to be the smart things to do. They're the easy way to get through school.

Do not forsake wisdom, and she will protect you.

Proverbs 4:6

Day 138
Your Life in Pictures

You flip open your yearbook and spot your face on twenty-two of thirty-six pages. *You were magnificent.* You captained three teams, climbed your way to first-chair violin, and captured Student of the Year honors for your 4.0 grade-point average.

Or maybe you've been bad—*really bad*—and you're splattered on just as many pages. Surprise! You were voted "Wild Child of the Year" and "Most Likely to Live in a Home for Juvenile Delinquents."

Or you struggled along in the middle of the pack and no one knows you were even there. You didn't get voted "Best Dressed" or "Best Personality" or "Class Brainiac." It takes three passes through the book to find a single tiny picture of you. Page thirty-one, bottom inside corner, it's you with the flu. Even in black-and-white, you look green.

Read 2 Corinthians 3:18

*Why do you go to school? What will you be
remembered for? What will you accomplish?*

There are more efficient ways to do school if your sole reason for being there is to absorb facts. The computer teacher could hardwire you into a virtual reality system and give you a limitless brain. Or for a low-cost, low-tech education, teachers could lock you in solitary confinement with a textbook and feed you only after you choked down algebra.

You need to learn school stuff so you don't spend your life refilling the burrito bar at Taco Tim's. And you pick up other skills at school too, like how to get along with friends—and enemies—and frenemies; how to work with teachers—your bosses; and how to keep going when you'd rather quit.

God sends you to school for one more reason: to use the experience to remake you to look like Jesus, who knew God the Father totally (John 17:25–26), obeyed God willingly (John 6:38), and loved other people completely (John 15:13). People saw God's glory—God's greatness—reflected in Jesus, just like they can see it in you.

You may not rate a ton of pictures in the yearbook. But hopefully your classmates will always remember *who* you looked like.

We . . . are being transformed into his likeness with ever-increasing glory.

2 Corinthians 3:18

Day 139
No Lie

Isaiah rounded the corner just as Hammer's fist pounded Tyler's stomach. Isaiah tried to backpedal, but Hammer—a muscled kid who spoke little and showered less—hoisted Isaiah a foot off the ground and shoved him against a wall.

"Didn't see nuthin', did ya?" Hammer grunted. Isaiah's feet tap-danced against the wall. Isaiah shook his head *no*. "Tell anyone and you'll be next. Understand?" Tyler was doubled over and holding his stomach, wheezing. Isaiah nodded his head *yes*.

A teacher asked Isaiah if he knew who hurt Tyler. Isaiah said he didn't and moved on to blend in with a crowd of students.

God could choose to act just like Hammer. He could be a knuckle-dragging brute, scaring us into believing *his* version of the story, no matter what we had seen with our own eyes. Or he could be a deceiving charmer, winning our love one moment only to drop us with a *splat* the next.

Read Isaiah 45:18–19

How do you know that God tells you the truth?

God is bigger and smarter than any of us. He could outmaneuver, out-argue, and outwit us, making us believe lies. But he doesn't.

We don't always want the truth. Unlike us, God swears to be honest in everything he says: (1) He speaks openly, for everyone to hear; (2) he doesn't tease—when he tells his people ("Jacob's descendants") that they can know him, he means it; (3) he speaks not just truth but *the* truth; and (4) he—and no one else—knows perfectly what is right.

Massive promises. And we can be certain they're not massive lies. If God was into busting faces or breaking hearts, we would be stupid to trust God. But he's not. His honest words are backed by kind actions.

God's ultimate promise is to be God for everyone who trusts him: "There is no God apart from me, a righteous God and a Savior" (Isaiah 45:21). And when God sent Jesus, he gave you the ultimate proof that he means what he says.

Listen up.

I am the Lord, and there is no other. I have not spoken in secret.
. . . I, the Lord, speak the truth; I declare what is right.

Isaiah 45:18–19

Day 140
Bewildered No More

This is so stupid. One bright, shining Sunday morning, while all of Abril's friends romped at the beach, she rotted in church. Abril's mom had split from her dad three years ago because he drank and beat up the family, and a few months back the divorce was finalized. About the time of the divorce, Abril's mom started going to church. She had found God, and he was helping to put her life back together.

Good for her, Abril thought. *But why drag me with? I've got better things to do. Besides, God is like Dad—useless.*

Abril had never seen God, but she sees her friends. She knows she can count on them. God? She wasn't so sure.

Read John 4:19–26

(The passage picks up in the middle of a conversation between Jesus and a woman getting water at a well.) How do you know what God is like?

Abril isn't the only one perplexed about God. Plenty of people think that God is a figment of your imagination. To many, the cross is just jewelry.

Confusion about God isn't new. A long time ago, Jesus told a woman at the well that she needed to get her facts straight. When she tried to draw him into an argument over the best place to worship God, Jesus said she was missing the point. Ceremonies and services and holy places are dusty religion if you don't "worship in spirit and truth," that is, if your heart doesn't respond to God.

Jesus revealed to the woman that he wasn't merely a prophet—someone who speaks *on behalf* of God—but the Messiah—God come as a human to speak *for himself* with the human race—and, even more than that, to save it.

Jesus came because God wanted to prove his power and trustworthiness to us. He wants us to understand clearly what he is like (John 1:14; Colossians 1:15). He wants us to see that he's the One worth listening to.

> The woman said, "I know that Messiah" (called Christ) "is coming. When he comes, he will explain everything to us." Then Jesus declared, "I, the one speaking to you—I am he."
>
> *John 4:25–26*

Day 141
Pop-Tarts

You awoke to waves tickling your toes. You remembered a boat . . . a storm . . . being tossed overboard . . . but nada more. As your foggy brain starts to clear, you realize you're ashore and alone on a tropical island. You soon begin to wonder about the least-fun way to go: *shriveling from starvation, or being mauled by wild animals?*

Then you see it, a few yards up the beach: a boxcar-size crate of Pop-Tarts.

"There is a God!" you shout. Sure, you're still shipwrecked, but you're the sole owner of an unlimited supply of your favorite food. For the next couple days, you tan on the beach waiting to be rescued, humming reggae jams and tossing down Pop-Tarts. But when a rescue party doesn't show up, a crucial truth dawns on you: You can't live on Pop-Tarts alone.

Read John 6:30–40

What's the one thing that will sustain you for life?

Chowing down a Pop-Tart or two—okay, maybe three or four—is a delectable snack. But you can't rely on them meal after meal. Sooner or later, you need real food.

Just before uttering the words in this passage, Jesus fed five thousand people with a few loaves and fish. Some who witnessed the miracle promised to believe in him if he could produce another sign—*Hey Jesus, could you do burgers and fries this time?* Perceiving that the crowd just wanted to satisfy their physical hunger, Jesus taught them about deeper pangs.

Jesus said they needed more than the first convenient crate of Pop-Tarts. If the crowd would just look around, they would see a limitless feast awaiting them in the jungle. Jesus declared, "I am the bread of life." He's not a snack. He's the feast of life. He alone can permanently satisfy people's deepest hunger and thirst.

Jesus didn't just want to take the crowd to lunch. He wanted to give them eternal life. But for anyone to accept his gift, they needed to want more than a meal. They needed to want him.

> Then Jesus declared, "I am the bread of life. He who comes to me will never go hungry, and whoever believes in me will never be thirsty."
>
> *John 6:35*

Day 142
Give Me the Light

Caleb hadn't noticed the rain pelting the roof or the wind tearing at the curtains on his open bedroom window until weather sirens blasted him awake. The storm had knocked out power, so he bumped through the dark to his parents' room. His older sister was holding his sobbing younger sister. Socks landed at his feet as his dad ransacked a dresser drawer to find a flashlight.

Just as Caleb's mom shooed everyone downstairs to shelter, lightning exploded a tree in the backyard. Even Caleb's dad bolted down the stairs—minus a flashlight to light the way. With no light to tame the darkness, all the family could do was huddle in the blackness and wonder what more the storm could bring.

Read John 8:12

How does Jesus light up your life?

When the lights flicker out on a stormy night, you bump your way around your home. Sure, you can cope. But if the lights stay off and the storm keeps on, life gets confusing and scary. You wish for real sight.

Jesus came to shine in a world where sin blocks out God's light (John 1:4–5). In the shadows of spiritual darkness, wrong looks right and good seems bad.

But Jesus shines into the darkness with a light that keeps you from getting lost. His life and words shine on the difference between right and wrong. The closer you stick to him, the better you see.

After a while of stumbling around in the dark, your eyes adjust to the lack of light. You get along better than before . . . but when the lights come back on, you realize how little you could actually see.

In the midst of darkness, you might get used to the lack of spiritual light. You start to think you can see pretty well. But when Jesus shows up, you realize the shapes you saw in the darkness weren't what you thought.

The light is the place you want to live. In Jesus' light, every move doesn't result in a bump and bruise. In him, you have light for life.

> I am the light of the world. Whoever follows me will never
> walk in darkness, but will have the light of life.
>
> *John 8:12*

Day 143
Not That Dumb

Adriana smelled trouble smoldering as soon as she walked in the door. As she tiptoed toward her bedroom, her mom stopped her short. She held out a small plastic bag and asked Adriana what was in it.

"It's parsley." Adriana shrugged. "I chew it for my breath. All the kids do. It just dried out."

Her mom wasn't *that* stupid. "Don't play games, Adriana. It's not dried parsley. It's weed. What are you doing with drugs in your backpack?"

"You were in my backpack? You have no right to go through my things."

"I was looking for the makeup you borrowed and didn't return. Adriana, I can't believe you'd do this. I'm too angry to talk now. You go to your room until your dad gets home."

Read John 8:21–30

What did Jesus mean when he said, "I am from above"?

Members of the Flat Earth Society want you to believe—surprise—that the earth is flat. From observations you make in everyday life, it's tough to disagree. One glance outside should cause you to say, "Yup. Flat like a pancake." But as soon as you get a bigger view—like photos of earth taken from space—you're forced to say, "Nope. Round like a ball."

No one messing around with drugs wants to admit that parents or teachers or doctors have a better, bigger view of the danger of abusing drugs. No one likes to be criticized, questioned, or condemned. But we have to admit that we don't have the ultimate understanding of ourselves and our world.

Above all else, it's God who has the big picture, a view of all people and all events for all time.

Jesus said his teaching wasn't something he made up. He spoke as God's Son, come "from above," from the Father in heaven. He echoed what he heard from his Father. He warned us for our own good.

Confusing? The crowds around Jesus thought so. But the point is that Jesus didn't speak as an ordinary human. He saw more than us. And he knows more than us.

If you do not believe that I am he, you will indeed die in your sins.

John 8:24

Day 144

Pink Bunny Sheets

You stroll to school wrapped in the only bedsheets left in the linen closet—your little sister's pink bunny sheets. You would have preferred plain white, but whatever. You step into traffic, protected only by a raised hand, and tires screech as cars skid to a stop. You raise your hand again to bless a neighbor's labradoodle.

When you get to homeroom, you walk to the front and command silence. "I have an announcement," you say. Your peers pause to listen only because you look so demented. "I will be running class from now on. You see, I am God."

You're serious. But the roaring laughter of your classmates echoes in your ears as your teacher escorts you to the principal.

Read John 8:48–59

Why did the crowd want to kill Jesus?

If you announced to all your friends that you're God, they would point you to a padded room—once the hilarity died down. Yet for many people back in Bible times, it was just as preposterous when *Jesus* announced he was God. He was their neighbor, the son of their local carpenter (John 6:42).

To us, the crowd's reaction to Jesus seems overdone. He says, "Before Abraham was born, I am!" and they pick up rocks to hurl at him. What did Jesus say that got them mad enough to kill him?

Whenever Jesus used the phrase "I am _____" ("the Messiah," "the Bread of Life," and so on), he echoed the name God had given himself in the Old Testament, "I am who I am" (Exodus 3:14). It was a name so revered that the Jews didn't dare speak it aloud. In Jewish law, for a man to apply that name to himself was a crime deserving death. Jesus' simple "I am" was a blunt claim to be the God who existed before time began.

Some people argue that Jesus was merely a good man, a teacher like Confucius or Thomas Jefferson. But other great teachers didn't claim to be God. Jesus did. And he was willing to die for his claim.

> Jesus answered, "I tell you the truth, before Abraham was even born, I am!" At that point they picked up stones to throw at him.
>
> John 8:58–59 NLT

Day 145

The Voice

Four-year-old Henry peeked an eye around the chips and dips on the store endcap. *Not here.* He looked around another corner. *Not there.*

Lost in a supermarket filled with strangers, Henry pulled his jacket hood tight to hide his crying eyes and quivering lip. He shook with lostness. He'd lost his daddy.

Henry ran down aisle after aisle, farther from his dad. His dad, however, was already searching for him. Eventually his dad caught up to Henry and picked him up, holding him tight. Henry buried his face in his dad's hugs. "I'm here, Henry," he whispered. "It's okay. Daddy's here."

Read John 10:1–11

How do you recognize Jesus' voice?

A well-trained watchdog is wary of any stranger who comes near its family. Nothing distracts it—not biscuits, not cooing "Here, doggie, doggie," not yelling "SHUT UP, YOU DUMB DOG" while waving your arms like a lunatic. You can't trick a good watchdog. If you're not its master, it won't be your friend.

A child loves the voice of Dad and Mom, and a watchdog jumps when it hears its owner. As believers—like sheep—we recognize our Shepherd's voice.

A shepherd gives each sheep a name. He provides food by day, shelter at night. He stands at the gate of the pen to check the sheep one by one. Because the sheep know their shepherd's unique call, they scatter at the sound of anyone else's voice.

The sheep have experienced the shepherd's kindness firsthand, so they know he isn't like others who might sneak into the pen and hurt them. The shepherd's only concern is the good of the sheep in his care.

Once you know that Jesus wants to lead you into the best life God has in mind for you, then you won't be fooled by violent or stealthy voices that want to turn you into a lamb chop. They don't sound like Jesus. His voice is kind. Jesus is your Good Shepherd.

> The thief comes only to steal and kill and destroy; I have come
> that they may have life, and have it to the full. I am the good
> shepherd. The good shepherd lays down his life for the sheep.
>
> *John 10:10–11*

Day 146

Don't They Get It?

Sweat beads on Parker's lip. He glances left, then right. Just like last time, they come at him from all directions. All at once a guy built like a walk-in freezer flies through the air and jumps him.

Parker screams, wakes up, and sits up in bed.

It was only a dream—this time. He would have to think twice about ever again busting the curve on a biology test.

Sometimes doing the right thing makes other people mad.

Read John 10:31–39

What would you do if people chased you with rocks?

It was the same scene all over again. The religious leaders wanted to kill Jesus, this time because he called himself "the Son of God." Jesus didn't mean that God had given him birth. Calling himself "the Son of God" meant (1) that Jesus was God and (2) that Jesus had a unique relationship with the Father. They were separate yet one (verses 30 and 38).

Jesus didn't roll over and let his critics pelt him. He tried to persuade them with Scripture. If they could accept that God honored mere human rulers with the title "gods" or "sons of the Most High" (Psalm 82:6), then his claim to be the Son of God was no crime. He was, after all, God's special representative to the world.

And he offered his life as proof: *The works I do*—healing disease, casting out demons, calming storms, feeding multitudes, raising the dead—*show that what I say is true. The miracles I do are what my Father does. I am who I claim to be.* Jesus' claims and the good he did go hand in hand. He argued that his actions alone are proof enough to believe.

Jesus wants you to be sure about one thing, and he can't make it any clearer without slapping your face: *When you look at me, you're looking at God. If you reject me, you reject God. If you don't follow me, don't claim that you're God's child.*

Believe me, Jesus argued. Some didn't. *You can't kill me for doing what's right.* One day they would.

> Even though you do not believe me, believe the works, that you may
> know and understand that the Father is in me, and I in the Father.
>
> John 10:38

Day 147
After the Funeral

When Ellie's grandma got cancer, she was living two thousand miles away in Florida. Ellie's parents said they wanted Grandma to die at home, with family surrounding her. At a family meeting to decide whether Grandma should come to live with them, Ellie voted yes.

That sounded great a year ago.

Now it hurt. Ellie hardly knew her grandma before she moved in. If Grandma had died halfway across the country, her death wouldn't have mattered so much. Ellie would have missed Grandma at Christmas and birthdays, but that was about it. Now Ellie knew her really well. Now she missed her.

After the funeral, Ellie cried herself to sleep. Her parents said they would all see Grandma again someday. But to Ellie, that sounded like a fairy tale.

Read John 11:17–26

What happens to believers when they die?

Time-warp yourself sixty or seventy years into the future. You're at a funeral, but no one notices you're there. The old photos of the dearly departed in the back of the church look familiar, like pictures of a long-lost childhood friend. To take your mind off the organ music warbling in the background, you line up to view the body.

When you look into the casket, you see *you*—drained of life, caked in makeup, laid out in your best clothes. All around you, family and friends are crying.

If you could be a guest at your own funeral, what would you say?

For Christians, saying "We'll see Grandma in heaven" isn't a sweet fib we suck on at funerals to make ourselves feel better. Death is a consequence of sin (Romans 6:23), but Jesus took the punishment for sin for all who believe in him. Believers die physically, but death can't keep us down. Jesus is the Resurrection and the Life, and what Jesus did for Lazarus temporarily—check out verses 38 through 44—he will do for us permanently (John 3:16).

"I know you miss me," you would say if you could speak. "But don't cry forever. I followed Jesus. I'll be in heaven. I hope you'll be there too."

Jesus said to her, "I am the resurrection and the life. The one
who believes in me will live, even though they die."

John 11:25

Day 148

Stinky Feet

"Look out!" a voice from the bench yelled at Noah, the team's star batter. "Jayden's behind you!"

Too late. Jayden lay on the ground wondering what planet he was on, walloped in the forehead by a wild warm-up swing. The bench emptied and everyone crowded around the Panthers' bat boy.

"You weren't warming up where you were supposed to!" Jayden's older brother yelled at Noah.

"So?" Noah shrugged and glanced at Jayden moaning on the ground. "He's okay. Don't worry about it." He kicked at Jayden. "Hey, kid. Get me some water."

Read John 13:1–5, 12–15

Why did Jesus wash his disciples' feet?

Jesus chose an outlandish way to show strength. Politicians often stay on top by digging muck and spewing lies. Gangs show who's boss by tagging turf and leaving bodies as reminders. Teachers sometimes resort to threats of detention, suspension, and expulsion.

Jesus is Master of the universe. All things are under his power. But you wouldn't have known that when he knelt to wash his disciples' feet. Rather than commanding honor and making his disciples bow to him, Jesus stepped into the role of the lowest household servant. He peeled off his shirt, wrapped a towel around his waist, then unlaced the sandals and washed the feet of a dozen burly guys who had spent the day tromping down dirt roads. Sweat, dust, and leather—imagine the stench.

Jesus' disciples should have washed *his* feet. He washed theirs.

He didn't use his power to knock his disciples down. He lifted them up.

To us, Jesus might look like a bat boy flattened by a blow to the head. But don't mistake his servanthood for weakness or stupidity. He's really the King.

> You call me "Teacher" and "Lord," and rightly so, for that is
> what I am. Now that I, your Lord and Teacher, have washed
> your feet, you also should wash one another's feet.
>
> *John 13:13–14*

Day 149
Kitty Kitty

With paws blistered from scurrying down miles of backcountry gravel roads, you hurt. What an awful vacation! You're a thousand miles from home, and after a week you've seen no trace of your owners, whom you misplaced when you ditched your kitty carrier to search for mice. Bad call.

No one understands your lonely *meow*, so you can't ask directions. No one knows who you are or where you belong, but maybe if you keep searching you'll find your owners again.

Fat chance.

Stories of pets sniffing their way home across thousands of miles make for great tearjerker movies. But face facts: It almost always takes an owner to track a pet down to bring it home.

Read John 14:1–7

Where does Jesus plan to take his followers someday?

As human beings we're lost—but not because our Owner decided he was tired of caring for us. We weren't flung out of a moving car in the middle of nowhere. We wandered away from God (Isaiah 53:6). And we're a long ways from home.

Asking people for directions isn't much help. They're lost too. *Look for the god inside yourself,* they say. *Work hard to be good enough for God. Trust data and nothing else. Accept fate. Make up your own beliefs. Look to spirits and stars. Pummel your body to perfection. Get rid of desire—care about nothing.*

Human thinking can't lead you home to an eternity of paradise with God. Its destinations are confused. Its routes are dead ends.

Jesus knows where to take you and how to get there. He's tracked you down. He says, "I'm the way and the truth and the life. Want to come home?" Jesus alone is the Way—he died for you and opened the gate back to God. Only Jesus is the Truth—he gives a perfect picture of God. Jesus is the one real Life—he conquers death so you can live eternally.

He's the road back to where you belong.

> Jesus answered, "I am the way and the truth and the life.
> No one comes to the Father except through me."
>
> *John 14:6*

Day 150

Resolutions

The clock struck midnight. Everyone cheered, but Elizabeth faked a smile. She thought about the past year—*what a disaster!* She had spent most of the year in her room, grounded from the phone and screen time and from getting together with friends. She had fought with her parents so much that they had threatened to ship her to boarding school.

Elizabeth was even more depressed because she knew deep down that the strain was her fault, brought on by her own stubbornness. She had told them she wanted to make her own mistakes. And she did.

In the first hours of the new year, Elizabeth resolved to obey her parents. She closed her eyes and made her promise. She smiled as she opened her eyes, convinced things would be better.

They weren't.

Read John 15:4–5

What's up with Jesus calling himself a "vine"?

If happy resolutions were enough to make us better people, the world would already be a paradise. Or at least nail-biting would be extinct.

Jesus came to make it clear that it wasn't human promises but a divine Person—Jesus himself—who would make us new people. It's through *him* and everything he does for us that we grow up spiritually.

Horticulture lesson: Fruit doesn't pop up in a grocery store out of nowhere. It starts on a vine, tree, or bush.

Jesus said that he's the one True Vine. We're branches. If we want to bear good fruit—if we want to mature spiritually—we have to "abide" or "remain in" or "stay connected" to him.

Fruit won't grow on a branch disconnected from the vine. So our human promises—the ones we make without tapping into his power—mean little. Trying on our own to be good—without Jesus' help—gets us nowhere. We wear out.

What matters is relying on God to forgive us, live in us, teach us, and encourage us—and to be close to us as we stay close to him.

> I am the vine; you are the branches. If you remain in me and I in you,
> you will bear much fruit; apart from me you can do nothing.
>
> *John 15:5*

Day 151
Promise or Threat?

It was a little like getting a fortune cookie written by Mom for every breakfast. Whenever Ryan's mom went on business trips, she left a stack of dated envelopes on the kitchen table, each with a note inside for Ryan to read while she was gone.

Sometimes there were lists of things for Ryan to do. A few notes were warnings—like nudging Ryan to study ahead for an upcoming test. Some envelopes held a wad of cash to treat the family to pizza or a movie.

The notes reminded Ryan that his mom cared about him. They also made it impossible for Ryan to forget that his mom had high expectations of how he would act, even when she was away.

Read Revelation 22:12–16

After Jesus ascended to heaven, he appeared to his disciple John to reveal "what must soon take place" (Revelation 1:1). What did he promise?

Three times in the last chapter of the Bible, Jesus said that he would return to earth (22:7, 12, 20). That's a threat. It's also a promise.

When your parents leave you home alone and you pull stunts you shouldn't, you might dupe them into thinking everything went swell—that you did your homework, that you didn't blast your music loud enough to rattle the dishes or invite friends over when they said not to.

Jesus can't be fooled like that. That's the threat.

But the promise is that Jesus is coming to remake the world the way he wants it to be—with God on the throne and no death or crying or pain (Revelation 21:1–5). Those who "wash their robes"—who accept forgiveness and new life in Christ—will spend eternity with God in paradise.

Sometimes you might feel like God is far away. Yet through the Bible he's written you notes to read each day—warnings, things to do, words meant to remind you of his love and to encourage you to do what's right until he comes back.

Do you believe his notes? Is he the One you listen to?

Look, I am coming soon! . . . I am the Alpha and the Omega,
the First and the Last, the Beginning and the End.

Revelation 22:12–13

Day 152

Who Do You Listen To?

Flash forward through your day. . . .

A teacher pats you on the head and says your history essay was outstanding. She says you're way smarter than your peers.

A friend pulls on your sleeve and urges you to ditch class.

Your sweetie begs you to meet after school, even though your parents want you to cool your relationship.

Your aunt smothers you with hugs and says your war with the neighbor kid couldn't possibly be your fault, because you never do anything wrong.

Your dad rips into you for the B you got in math. When he was your age, he always got A's.

A commercial flickers on. Beauteous guys and girls leap and dive in a game of beach volleyball. Everyone breaks to throw back a cold beer.

Battered by the noise, you collapse onto the floor.

Read Psalm 25:1–6

Who do you count on to always tell you the truth?

You can't escape hearing dozens of voices—family, school, friends, media, even your own crazed body and brain—telling you every day what to do.

You're surrounded. Maybe even crumpled on the ground in confusion.

With so many voices shouting at you, which ones do you believe? How do you know who's wrong—or who's right? Which voices speak truth? Which spout lies? Who should you listen to?

The easy fix is to give up and follow whichever voice is the loudest. But that isn't the only way forward. God wants to lift you up, look you eyeball-to-eyeball, de-wax your ears, and utter pure truth. He invites you to tune in to his voice and follow him. He promises to help you sort through the other voices, distinguishing truth from lies, good from bad, real from fake.

God's voice isn't the loudest, because he respects you too much to scream at you. But listen up. He's got life-altering words for you.

Show me your ways, Lord, teach me your paths; guide me in your truth and
teach me, for you are God my Savior, and my hope is in you all day long.

Psalm 25:4–5

Truth in a Toilet

Ten seconds ago, the couple on the screen was staring deep into each others' eyes—sappy but harmless. All of a sudden they're sucking face like a car wash during the scrub cycle—and then their clothes come off. Your contact lenses fog. You didn't see that coming.

What do you do? Your choices: (a) cover your eyes—but peek through your fingers, (b) take notes, (c) stomp out of the room and never watch another movie, or (d) make excuses for watching something you know you shouldn't.

No good answers. Better question: Why are you watching the movie? What are you looking for?

Read Proverbs 2:1–15

How can you get wisdom?

God's wisdom helps you "live in safety and be at ease, without fear of harm" (Proverbs 1:33). That sounds a lot like the chilling relaxation you want. Sometimes a movie or music dishes up what you're looking for. It expresses what you feel or states a truth about life. But it might not speak the ultimate truth and reality that satisfies. Only God's wisdom does that unfailingly.

Be honest. You often have to sift through a heap of bad to get a tiny bit of good. Trying to find wisdom in some places is like looking for lost change in a toilet. It might be there, but it's not worth the dig.

Disgusting? Yep. So is the swirl of waste served up online, not to mention in, at, and on TV, videos, music, concerts, magazines, books, comics, and computer games—not just skin, sex, violence, and out-of-control wildness, but sarcasm, selfishness, and general stupidity.

If you're looking for authentic wisdom—for the truth and reality that leads to life—there's a better place to look.

Wisdom is treasure worth searching for. It's worth crying out for. And God is *the* place to get it. Don't bother digging for gold in a Porta-Potty.

> If you call out for insight and cry aloud for understanding, and if you look for it as for silver and search for it as for hidden treasure, then you will understand the fear of the Lord and find the knowledge of God. For the Lord gives wisdom.
>
> *Proverbs 2:3–6*

Day 154

Buena Contesta

You hate that smug I'm-older-than-you, I-know-it-all look your big brother sometimes flashes. "I'm worried about you," he says as he sits you down on the couch. "I've done some dumb stuff that I don't want you to get into." You wonder what stupid thing he just did to make him feel the need to straighten you out. *We knew all along you were dumb. What's your point?*

"Some of those kids you hang around are trouble," he advises. You squirm. He's right. Then your brother gets an odd look. A tear bubbles in the corner of his eye. That's never happened before. "I know I've treated you like a dirtbag," he apologizes. "But I really care about you. You need to be smart. I hope you'll listen to what I say."

Read 1 Kings 3:5–15

Why did Solomon ask God to make him wise?

God appears to you in a dream, offering to grant one amazing request. You suddenly feel phenomenal cosmic power right at your fingertips.

What would you ask for? The ability to run a hundred yards in 3.6 seconds? A chance to captain a real-life starship *Enterprise*? For your worst enemy to die in a freak accident? How about sole ownership of Apple, Microsoft, and Google?

Think bigger.

Asking for wisdom is more wiley than wishing for more wishes. Wisdom unlocks every part of total devotion—being close to God, steadfast, thoughtful, strong, loyal, unselfish, forgiving, honest, dependent on God, and free from peer fear.

Okay, okay. Wisdom is best. But who should you ask to help you get wise?

Some grown-ups aren't smart enough to ever say "no." Some siblings can let you down. You might know friends as cool as you, but surely none as bright.

How about starting with God? He's the one Being in the universe who knows everything.

Good answer.

I will give you a wise and discerning heart.

1 Kings 3:12

Day 155
Wise Guy

Pen and narrow-ruled notebook at the ready, you lean forward in your seat and strain to look as smart as the other students in your first college class. Your professor strolls in, easy to spot with his hipster jeans, man bun, and $E=mc^2$ tattoo. His accent reveals that he was born on the distant island of Academia.

As your professor explains requirements for you to earn an A, B, or C, a guy in the front row waves his hand wildly. "Is this going to be on the test?" he asks. The professor sneers, and students likewise look down their noses. "Leave now," your professor warns, "if you're not planning on *working* to earn a C. You will work, or you won't pass.

"You will succeed," he continues, "if you remember that *I* am here because I know more than you. *You* are here to benefit from my wisdom."

You cringe. But you know he's right.

Read Proverbs 1:1–7

Who teaches you to get smart?

Life is a string of events in which others do for you what you can't do—and teach you what you don't know—until you grow capable yourself.

Admit it: Sometimes, in some situations, you're helpless and dumb.

Don't feel bad. So is everyone else. We all need what God wants to teach: "wisdom" (knowing how to live skillfully), "discipline" (training in obeying God), "discretion" (choosing rightly between two ideas or two actions), and "prudence" (thinking through actions before you do them). God's wisdom rescues you from being simple or immature, all with the goal of acting well toward yourself and others.

The incredible thing is that the all-knowing God never treats you like an idiot. He isn't a professor looking to parade his vastly superior knowledge.

One caution: *God can only teach you as much as you want to know.* You get smart only when you "fear God," that is, when you respectfully submit to his teaching because you know that you need him to figure out life.

You'll always need to learn from the Father who knows best.

The proverbs of Solomon son of David, king of Israel . . . for giving
prudence to the simple, knowledge and discretion to the young.

Proverbs 1:1, 4

Day 156
Trippin'

Your social studies teacher is fresh out of college, but she looks as if she found all her clothes in the attic of an old-time hippie. She has a real name, but you can't help but call her Moonmuffin.

A chia pet on Moonmuffin's desk daily bestows fresh sprouts for her tofu sandwich. *Gotta love chia,* you think, *and hemp.* Scattered around her desk are crystals she says keep her from sickness and all sorts of mayhem. You say they're pretty. She says they're powerful.

When your class studies the Salem witch trials, she offers to read palms and brings in a white witch to speak. "She's wonderful," Moonmuffin gushes. "She harnesses the power of nature to do good."

Yeah, right, you think. *She tries to harness the power of rabid dogs and bat fangs and killer sharks. This is our role model?*

Read Proverbs 1:20–33
What happens to people who refuse to wise up?

This is one section of Proverbs where you don't want to recognize yourself. You don't want to be *simple*—dimwitted, too stupid to watch where you're going. You don't want to be a *mocker*—sharp-tongued, too proud to accept advice. And you definitely don't want to be *foolish*—stubborn, too headstrong to be corrected, apt to repeat your mistakes like a dog that dines on its own vomit (Proverbs 26:11).

The simple, mockers, and foolish have a few things in common. They like themselves just the way they are. They live as if God doesn't exist. And because they continually reject wisdom, catastrophe will do them in.

Not smart.

You won't straighten out every person in the world who rejects God. But it's your job to not be duped when they try to sell you a different god—or no God—or new rules of right and wrong. Understand what they say. But understand too where they go wrong. After all, you can be so open-minded that your brain falls out.

For the waywardness of the simple will kill them . . . but whoever listens
to me will live in safety and be at ease, without fear of harm.

Proverbs 1:32–33

Day 157
Dig It?

Bruno had heard so much about high school being tough that he panicked his freshman and sophomore years. He studied hard, pulling better grades than anyone expected. Then halfway to graduation, he decided to slack.

His school counselor called him in. "At this rate, you won't graduate on time," his counselor warned. "You understand that, don't you? What are you going to do about it?"

Bruno promised to dig in, but his promises got to be a joke. He goofed around in class and study halls and after school. *I'm just doing what my friends are doing,* he told himself. And when spring semester of his senior year rolled around, he was short on credits he needed to graduate.

Oops.

Read Ecclesiastes 7:23–25

Will you get smart if you just wait long enough?

Suppose you don't quite hear your elderly neighbor when she leans over the fence to whisper in your ear. But you think she said there was gold buried in your backyard. Your response wouldn't be, "Did you say something?" or "Were you talking to me?" or "Excuse me, I didn't quite catch that. Would you be so kind as to repeat what you said a moment ago?" You would say, "Did you say GOLD? WHERE?" If you didn't catch the message the first time, you would scream for clarity. And then you would scoop, shovel, excavate, and detonate until you found gold.

It's not enough to *want* wisdom. You have to *search* for it. Just like graduation doesn't simply happen—you don't get smart without studying—wisdom doesn't just drop into your lap.

Attaining wisdom might feel as far-off and far-out as graduating from high school or college. True, not every nugget of wisdom you get from God is applicable that instant. That makes it tempting to slacken your search or give up altogether. But the only way to get wise is to keep at it, storing up wisdom so you have it when you need it.

So I turned my mind to understand, to investigate and to search
out wisdom and the scheme of things and to understand the
stupidity of wickedness and the madness of folly.

Ecclesiastes 7:25

Day 158
If You're So Smart

Laura grimaced at the poster Adrianne and Paul were making for their youth group's Christmas musical. To be honest, the head on Adrianne's shepherd looked as if it had been crushed in an accident, and Paul had run out of space writing the date, time, and place.

"Can you make it any uglier?" Laura asked. "Are you *trying* to keep people away? Anyone who looks at that would rather stay home with a freezer full of Christmas cookies and eat themselves into a sugar overdose. Of course, most of you aren't worthy of attention anyway. You sound awful. None of you can act. You should have seen our school musical. That's a real group. We had tryouts and I was the directors' first choice. We didn't take just anyone, of course."

"Of course," Paul mimicked. "Anything else, Your Greatness?"

"You don't have to have an attitude. I just don't want anyone to think that this musical is all the better I can do."

Read James 3:13–18

What's the difference between real smarts and fake smarts?

Imagine a relay race with millions of runners on the track at one time, each caught up in catching and passing a gigantic baton. Runners can enter the race at any time. Here's the really bizarre part: No one races against anyone else. The goal is to get everyone to the finish line in good time.

That's what following Jesus is like. We're all in the race. We work together. James says that if you have real smarts you help others along in the race. You do good with humility, deliberately accepting people who are less mature, skilled, or brainy than you. You don't simply look out for yourself. You show gentleness not because you're weak but because you're strong.

When you have fake smarts, you rush to beat out others. You cheat. You loosen other runners' cleats and trip them up midstride. You wallop people to get to the front of the pack.

James says not to pretend you're trying to do good. You're just out to look good.

> Who is wise and understanding among you? Let them show it by their good life, by deeds done in the humility that comes from wisdom.
>
> *James 3:13*

Day 159
Nowhere to Go

Older guys surrounded Landon and his friends as they strolled home from school. The biggest guy grabbed Landon. "I saw you sneaking around. You stay out of my face."

"Out of your face? I was just walking home. I wasn't anywhere near you." The thug hit Landon with a punch, a slap, and a full-on wallop. Landon's head snapped to the side and his lip gushed blood.

Landon lived with his parents in a city apartment in a rough neighborhood. They never made enough money to move away. When he bussed to a school in the 'burbs, the natives mocked and harassed him.

Landon wanted a place where he fit. Someplace safe. He didn't know where it was. He for sure didn't know how to get there.

Read 2 Chronicles 14:11

What does it mean to really trust God?

Some problems—school, home, friends, health—loom so big that you can't budge them. It's like you're a junk car stuck in a trash smasher. The walls close in. No escape. You know you're supposed to trust God. But how?

The verse you read picks up mid-description of how King Asa and his troops squared off against a vast army of Cushites. Asa's actions show what to do when there's not much you can do. He prayed. And obeyed. That's trust.

Asa reminded God and himself that there was no one as powerful as God, and that he alone was their hope. Then King Asa led Israel into battle, confident the Lord was with them. God crushed the Cushites.

The end of the story is less happy. Late in life, Asa refused to depend on God and do what he knew was right. He bought help from an evil army and sought healing from wicked doctors. Even when a prophet reminded Asa that "the eyes of the Lord range throughout the earth to strengthen those whose hearts are fully committed to him" (2 Chronicles 16:9), Asa refused to trust in God.

Asa's nation remained at war. His illness got worse. The king had something even better than *somewhere* safe to go. He had *Someone*. But he forgot.

Help us, Lord our God, for we rely on you.

2 Chronicles 14:11

Day 160

Walk on the Wild Side

"I understand that this wristband will let you track me wherever I go," David says. "But what if a bear eats me? Will the band keep beeping inside its stomach? What if the bear only eats my arm? How will you find the rest of me?"

"Trust me!" his scoutmaster replied. "You have your map and compass and know how to use them. You have two days to travel to our pick-up."

David was still alarmed. "This map. Is it right?"

"Of course. I picked your route carefully."

"Did you double-check this compass?"

"Yes, that's my best one."

"One more thing," David pleaded. "I've never been to where I'm going."

"That's the whole point," his scoutmaster explained. "Now git!"

Read Genesis 12:1–5

Is trusting God stupid? Why—or why not?

God told Abram—later called Abraham—to head to a land of extreme blessing. God's command was like a treasure map Abram trusted enough to leave a comfortable life in Ur and go where God had pointed.

The Lord also wants to lead you to places you've never dreamed of. He's given you a map and compass—his Word. It's your totally accurate guide to getting along, growing up, and making the most of life.

Trouble is, even if a map is perfect and the path it charts exotically exciting, you'll never move from point A to point B if you don't trust the map. You won't ever wholeheartedly follow God if you don't rely on the wisdom of your outfitter.

You could concoct all sorts of reasons *not* to go where God wants: "I'd act more like a Christian—if I had more Christian friends." "If I had a deadly illness—then I'd trust God." "Believing God would be easy—if I had more time to read my Bible." "I wouldn't do stupid stuff—if my friends didn't ride me so hard."

That's like making up scary bear stories. God doesn't pass out incorrect maps. He doesn't deal in broken compasses. So be daring. If you believe God, you'll walk on the wild side.

So Abram went, as the Lord had told him.

Genesis 12:4

Day 161

Is God a Wuss?

Avery didn't mean to be nosy, but there weren't many books in the locker across from hers, considering three people were using it. It looked like the most popular spot at school. There was never a crowd, but someone was *always* there—before school, after school, between classes. The locker was a puzzle. It didn't bother Avery . . . except that sometimes she felt left out. Whatever was going on, she wasn't part of it.

Then one day she saw an argument at the locker. Faces tensed, pills spilled, a knife flashed. The dispute ended quietly, but that didn't calm Avery. Now she felt unsafe. And she felt stupid because she instantly understood why the locker was so busy.

Most of all, Avery was angry at her school. The people in charge either didn't know what was going on or didn't care. She wasn't sure which was worse.

Read Isaiah 46:3–13

Is God really powerful? If he is, why is the world a mess?

The Bible claims God is all-knowing and all-powerful, big enough to direct the galaxies yet near enough to spin every atom of his creation. He guides his people from birth through old age. He creates, carries, and rescues. He predicts the end from the beginning. He accomplishes all his goals. No one compares to him. He's God, and there is no other. He's in charge.

The world, however, doesn't always look that way. If God is so powerful and so loving, how can his world be so full of sickness, misery, hatred, racism, injustice, and genocide? It's no surprise when people conclude that God is distant, stupid, powerless, or uncaring. Or all of those things.

Here's the catch: God designed the world to be a place of righteousness where people accept his love and live together in peace. Yet he also gives people freedom to follow or disobey his commands.

God says that when everyone listens to him and trusts his authority, life will be heavenly.

Unfortunately, not everyone agrees.

I am God, and there is no other; I am God, and there is none like me.

Isaiah 46:9

Day 162
The Jester

Gloomy clouds gathering over the kingdom fit the sour mood that had afflicted the king's subjects since they heard a rumor of a country with no king. In that imaginary country, no one told the people what to do—or what not to do. With everyone having the freedom to do as they pleased, people there, it was said, were exceedingly wise and happy.

Although the king's subjects had been wholeheartedly happy with the king's rule, they grumbled that their lives should belong to themselves, not to the king. Yet no one thought to do anything about their discontent until the king's jester busted out a rhyme:

> "The king is bad and you are sad . . . Of course he is to blame.
> Just follow me and you will see . . . Your lives won't be so tame."

From that day forward, the people decided to live as if they had no king, shutting out his provision and ignoring his commands.

Read Isaiah 14:12–14

What did the being Isaiah describes do wrong?

A human being who rules with total control is called an "absolute monarch" or a "dictator." No person has the ability or right to handle that much power.

But God does. He isn't one of us. He *is* ruler of all. He made everything and has complete authority over it (Psalm 24:1–2). That would be unbearable if God's love for us weren't perfect. God's total love, total knowledge, and total power make him worthy of our total devotion.

But not everyone agrees. The Bible talks in a hazy way about the beginning of a rebellion against God. Satan, whom God had made the most beautiful of all created beings (Ezekiel 28:12–19), decided *he* should be in charge. He believed he was wiser than God.

Satan is the jester who puts our fears into words. He spends his time trying to persuade the world that *he*, not God, is the one worth listening to.

> You said in your heart, "I will ascend to heaven; I will raise my throne above the stars of God. . . . I will make myself like the Most High."
>
> *Isaiah 14:13–14*

Day 163
Red Tights

Luke pulled out a huge Mercedes-Benz hood ornament strung on a long chain inside his shirt. "Cool, huh?!"

Gabriel was shocked. He was certain that Luke hadn't found his latest fashion statement on the ground or ordered it online.

"No big deal," Luke spouted. "That's why people have insurance. Besides, people who drive cars like that have plenty of money to fix them. A couple hundred bucks to them is like buying bubble gum. You want one?"

"My parents would kill me if—" Gabriel tried to protest.

Luke just rolled his eyes with an expression that said, *Don't be a dork*. "No one's gonna find out."

Read Genesis 3:1–7

How did Satan make rebelling against God look good?

This scene seems to be the only instance where Satan suited up in a snakeskin to get human beings to pay attention to him. But he's still devious. He twists thoughts, making good seem bad and bad seem good.

In his conversation with Eve ("the woman" in the passage), Satan questioned whether God had indeed mentioned eating fruit. He wanted Eve to conclude that specifics about right and wrong didn't matter much, even to the Lord.

Satan and Eve both made God's rule even tougher than God had. (Check Genesis 2:16–17, where God only forbade eating the fruit of one tree.) Then Satan told Eve the consequence she feared was a lie. God said she would die, but that wasn't true. Satan finally lured Eve in with one last morsel: God had laid down the law just to deprive her of something wonderful.

Satan's tactics haven't changed. His biggest ploy is widespread, everyday deceit. His voice hisses all around us: "You can run your own life." "Nothing will happen." "God just wants to wreck your life."

Don't expect Satan to pounce at you from behind a corner, sporting red tights and a tail, shouting, "Hey, you! Wanna sin?" Satan still slithers like a snake.

"You will not certainly die," the serpent said to the woman.

Genesis 3:4

Day 164

The Art of Self-Defense

Chase rams the controller. His weapons display blinks. WEAPONS LOCKED ON ENEMY TARGET. He fires. Oh yeah! Four choppers and eight tanks blown to microbits. MISSION ACCOMPLISHED. Nothing beats zinging around in a helicopter gunboat shooting rockets and laser-guided missiles.

When Chase's parents told him they were divorcing, he felt as if he had been shot—except this was no game. When people ask how he's doing, Chase always says he's okay. He tells himself the same thing. But he spends most of his time alone, shooting up digital enemies.

The rules are simple—kill or be killed. There's nothing to figure out. Vaporizing his enemy means he wins. Chase hits the Play button again.

Read Ephesians 6:17

How can you defend yourself when your trust in God is under attack?

It's easy to believe when things go well. You're convinced: *God is good. Powerful. Right. He loves me. He tells the truth.*

It's not so easy to believe when life explodes.

You're in a fight to the finish. Tough circumstances make you wonder why people treat you badly, why your family fights, why school is so hard. When you can't figure out why God doesn't step in and fix it all, you might be tempted to think differently about him: *God is evil. Weak. Mistaken. He doesn't care. He's trying to trick me.*

Even Jesus reached a point where he was tempted to stop believing and obeying his Father. When he was hard pressed by Satan in the wilderness, he fought back with Scripture. Point by point he countered the devil's bait with verses from the Old Testament (from Deuteronomy 8:3; 6:16; and 6:13). He applied Scripture to his life, and Satan fled.

You can't shoot laser missiles at your thoughts. But God's Word is a potent weapon. You gain ammunition every time you study your Bible, and you access that power when you apply those truths to life. You fire when you say, "Hey, brain. Ignore that lie. It's not true. God says . . ."

That's the only way you'll win.

Take the sword of the Spirit, which is the word of God.

Ephesians 6:17

Day 165

Rock Your World

You struggle to keep your footing on the steep steps. With a canoe perched on your shoulders swaying forward and back and side to side, each step tests your balance and tortures your weary muscles. You paddled eighteen miles and portaged overland four more. But climbing Stairway Portage was the worst—a hundred yards straight up. Once you carry the canoe to the top, you climb down and up twice more to get all your other gear.

When you collapse in camp that night, you and your fellow paddlers open your packs. You find more than food and clothing. Your packs are full of rocks. Large rocks. Many large rocks.

You've been sacked. Your supposed friends back at base camp snuck in and loaded your packs with countless extra pounds.

Read Matthew 11:28–30

What does Jesus ask you to carry when you follow him?

If doing life as a Christian were a canoe trip, you wouldn't be exempt from ridiculous portages, strong headwinds, and crazed mosquitoes up your nose. Obstacles and opposition are part of the trip no one can escape. Life is often a toil. Following Jesus doesn't mean someone else will paddle your canoe while you kick back and duff.

But as a Christian, your Outfitter won't load your backpack with back-busting rocks. The One who maps your trip and packs your load wouldn't do that to you. The burden he expects you to carry is light. His authority over you is kind and fair (Psalm 145:17). His love for you never ceases (Lamentations 3:22). He knows exactly how much you can lift (1 Corinthians 10:13). And he unburdens you when the weight becomes too much (1 Peter 5:7).

Contrast Jesus with the jokesters who load your bags with boulders. Whether they aim to be funny or mean, you carry stuff you don't need to—heavy expectations, useless maps, bug repellent that doesn't repel, and sunblock that doesn't block. That's what can happen whenever you let anyone but Jesus pack your sack and guide you through life.

Come to me, all you who are weary and burdened, and I will give
you rest. . . . For my yoke is easy and my burden is light.

Matthew 11:28, 30

Day 166
In a Coffin

After spending her entire summer serving at a Christian camp for needy children, Kiara hoped for a little more enthusiasm from her friends. They flipped quickly through her summer photos. They looked bored even when they saw kids' faces of every age and color. They stared into space when she shared her intense excitement for teaching kids about Jesus. No one even perked up when she talked about doing a ropes course with the camp staff—and how she'd hung upside down fifty feet off the ground.

One day, after yet another apathetic reaction from a good friend, Kiara ran home to her room and thought horrible thoughts about her summer of service. She thought about hitting delete on all her pictures. She wished she could trash the whole experience.

Read John 12:23–28

What do you think it means to "fall into the ground and die"?

When Jesus said we should "hate life" and "die" like kernels of wheat, he spoke wildly to make a point, as in "Don't have a cow" or "You eat like a pig." Jesus doesn't want you to walk in front of a truck or toss yourself off a cliff. To "hate your life" or "to die" is to be totally devoted to him. To boldly trust and obey him in every situation of life. To continually choose him as your absolute Lord.

Doing all of that can cause you a heap of agony. As you break sinful habits, let go of selfish ambition, or feel rejected for following Jesus—that discomfort is what Jesus means by "death."

The pain that can come from obeying God, however, is only half the story. After death comes life. A seed sitting on a shelf in a shrink-wrapped package can't grow. Only when a seed is dropped into the ground does the soil's scratchiness and cold wetness force a plant to spring up.

In the midst of death, God grows new life in you and in others. Suffering for following Jesus—that experience of falling into the ground and dying—feels as fun as lying trapped in a coffin. But remind yourself of this truth: God promises to come and lift you out.

Very truly I tell you, unless a kernel of wheat falls to the ground and dies,
it remains only a single seed. But if it dies, it produces many seeds.

John 12:24

Day 167

Wave Walking

Jesus instructed his followers to row across the lake, promising to meet them on the far side. To a bunch of professional fishermen, the plan sounded easy enough. But as Jesus' disciples battled fierce winds, they must have wished they were back on land. With oars flexing and the hull groaning, the boat drifted backward almost as much as it lurched forward.

And then in the middle of the night, they spotted someone coming toward them. Without a boat. On *top* of the water. And not on a Jet Ski. It was Jesus. But they didn't know that. Before their fright sent them overboard, Jesus urged calm. "Take courage," he said. "It's me. Don't be afraid."

Read Matthew 14:22–33

What did Jesus' disciples learn in the storm?

Jesus' stroll on the roiling sea encouraged his disciples. He knew they were straining to follow his command, and he wouldn't let them struggle alone. He met them in the storm and overpowered it. He even invited Peter to walk on the waves with him. When Peter's doubts caused him to sink, Jesus caught the disciple's hand and challenged him to trust his powerful care.

Being a Christian doesn't drop you into a calm sea tickled by a gentle breeze. It might stir up storms. And Jesus' daring invitation sounds even crazier than rowing across a stormy lake or walking on water: "Know me," he says. "Live for me."

But Jesus never leaves you to face the winds alone.

When darkness upsets your sense of direction, when winds scream, when spray pokes your eyes, Jesus comes to you and says, "I'm not a figment of your imagination. I'm not too good to be true. I'm real. Don't be afraid! It's me! I'm here!" He cares for you, lifting you up through his Holy Spirit, his Word, and other followers.

Do you want to hang tight with God? He feels closest when you're with him on the waves, practicing prayer, courage, and action out in the wind, gaining a daring faith that transforms you into a wave walker. He's worth your total devotion.

Immediately Jesus reached out his hand and caught him.
"You of little faith," he said, "why did you doubt?"

Matthew 14:31

Day 168
Scruffy

"Swank, huh?" Papa Scruffy says to his family as they spy the mansion high on the hill. "Toldja it'd be great." Pops maneuvers the family's rusted purple school bus past the front gate and brings the vehicle to a loud screech on the front lawn. Out pile Pops, Mama, and fourteen little ones.

The greasy horde follows the hundreds of candles lighting the way up the driveway to the house, bursting into a ballroom of long-gowned ladies and tuxedoed gentlemen. Grabbing fistfuls of elegant cocktail wienies, they flop on a couch in front of a wall-filling TV. As they claw for the remote control, it drops and shatters, with the tube locked on *WWE WrestleMania 67*.

"Poyfect!" Pops exclaims. He kicks his shoes off onto a glass coffee table. "Hey yous," he yells to the host. "Hows about a foot rub?"

Read Psalm 15:1–5

What does God expect of you if you want to live close to him?

Pick your part at the party: As a follower of Jesus, you are (a) the valet who gets run down, (b) a well-scrubbed partygoer, or (c) a member of the family Scruff.

Perhaps surprisingly, the right pick is c. We're all an unholy mess before we get to know God.

But also b. Because we don't stay scruffy for long.

Getting to know God is like showing up at a party filthy and hideously underdressed. Because each of us sins, none of us is good enough to approach God on our own—to live on God's "holy hill." Yet he loved us while we were grimy with sin (Romans 5:8). God makes us good enough to be in his utterly pure presence, making us right with himself through Christ's death, rolling open the gates and inviting us in (Hebrews 10:19–23).

God and his partygoers welcome the unwelcomable. Yet it isn't right to stay messy, to spew on God's kindness. We're now aware of our sin. It's fitting that those who live on the hill learn to act like the one who owns the house. We learn to stop running over people and insulting our Host. If we keep on being rude and crude we won't enjoy God's party.

Lord, who may dwell in your sacred tent? Who may live on
your holy mountain? He whose walk is blameless . . .

Psalm 15:1–2

Day 169
Zero Tolerance

Adam sat outside the school office while the principal talked to his mom. An hour earlier, he had been pulled from class by the school dean—the person who dished out discipline. The dean said that someone reported a knife in Adam's backpack.

The dean said he had it. Adam said he didn't. He turned his backpack upside down and there it was, a small pocketknife. It wasn't his.

Adam went pale and started to explain, but he knew the dean wouldn't believe him. "Zero Tolerance" meant she didn't care who the knife belonged to or how it got there. She wouldn't even try to find out. A weapon meant a three-month suspension. No exceptions.

Read Psalm 26:1–12

Who knows you're right when everyone says you're wrong?

You've *fwopped* your little sibling on the head countless times. For once you were actually being nice, but that's not what your parents think. They ground you.

Your protests of innocence sound hollow. Get over it.

There's another kind of false accusation that's harder to swallow. You walk into a clothing store and the manager's ugly glance says that your age makes you instantly guilty of shoplifting. Or you overhear a funny story at school, only to figure out it's about you—and not true. Or you choose to hang out with one friend, and another suddenly thinks you're evil by association.

In the Bible, being "blameless" goes beyond being able to say you didn't do wrong—*this* time. It's being absolutely sure that your one goal has been to live tight with God, doing his will, obeying in the power of his truth and love. You can justly say you didn't join those plotting to do wrong. You did your best to do right.

David was sure of his innocence. No one but God believed him. He knows the truth.

Vindicate me, Lord, for I have led a blameless life; I have
trusted in the Lord and have not faltered.

Psalm 26:1

Day 170
Can't Hide

Preston awoke at the light of a laptop flicking on. "What are you doing?" he asked, tangled in his sleeping bag. "What time is it?"

"*Shhh,*" Cal hushed. "I brought some entertainment."

By now the four other guys sleeping over in Preston's basement were also awake.

"What is it?" Kyle asked.

"Just wait," Cal replied. "This is the nastiest clip ever. You gotta see this to believe it."

Moving flesh flashed onscreen. "My parents—!" was all Preston could blurt out.

Read Psalm 32:1–11

What happens when you try to hide wrongdoing?

You know the feeling of that sickening knot in your stomach followed by an urge to crawl into a corner. You're embarrassed because you did something idiotic. You're maybe even ashamed for doing something wrong (what this psalm labels "sins" and "transgressions" and "iniquity"). You don't want anyone to know. Not your friends, not your parents, not even God.

You can't live like that.

When you've done wrong and you haven't made it right with God, part of the pain you feel comes from him. It pushes you back to him. You could wallow in your badness or ignore your conscience, but God wants you to let him help you.

You can't rescue yourself. You can't remake yourself. God can.

It's freaky that God can see everything about you. You can't hide. Then again, you don't have to. God knows you inside and out. It's good to be known for who you are. No better, no worse, just the real you.

God hates when you suffer by yourself. Hanging tight with God means you hide *in* him, not *from* him.

When I kept silent, my bones wasted away through my groaning all day long.
. . . Then I acknowledged my sin to you and did not cover up my iniquity.

Psalm 32:3, 5

Day 171

Between Disasters

Katie's hair mostly hid the huge scar high on her forehead. She knew that the jagged mark wasn't pretty, but it reminded her what she had survived.

Two years earlier, she had been riding shotgun in an old pickup with her dad down a country highway when another driver slid through a stop sign. Her dad braked, but their truck slammed the car so hard that Katie went through the windshield.

At first, Katie was so drugged she hardly knew who she was. When the doctors weaned her off pain meds, she had to fight back screams.

Strange—Katie almost wished she could go back to that time. God felt so close. People constantly prayed for her and with her. When she got weary of headaches and surgeries and shots, God was tough for her. She promised God that if she got well, her whole life would belong to him.

Looking back, Katie wasn't sure how well she had kept her promise.

Read Psalm 40:1–10

How do you stay close to God when your life goes great?

Some days, you can hardly see God through your pain. You can't wait for him to rescue you from a tough situation, and you think that obeying God will get easier once everything is okay. Yet the moment that life begins to go better, you wonder if it takes mishaps and tragedy to feel close to God.

When life sends you flying, you land quite naturally on God's lap. It's not hard to understand why you need him.

Between disasters, however, it's tempting to run off and ignore God. Yet there's still lots you can do to stay close to him when life goes great: Thank God today for what he did yesterday. Take time to better understand his "will," how he wants you to live. Help people who now need you. Encourage other believers ("the great assembly") when they struggle. Tell others what God has done and what he keeps on doing.

With each experience God pulls you through, he puts a "new song in your mouth." But your best lyrics don't always have to tell how he plucked you out of a slimy, gator-infested pit. You can sing about calm times too.

He put a new song in my mouth, a hymn of praise to our God.

Psalm 40:3

Day 172
Spout Off

"Why don't you look where you're going?" Julia spewed. She had enough to worry about without Tadd running into her and knocking her books and papers to the floor. She stooped down to pick up her things.

"Look where *I'm* going?" Tadd sassed. "Why don't you go where *you're* looking?"

Very original, Julia thought. *And I know—I'd look better if I wore a hat on my butt and walked backward.* With her crossed eyes wandering all over, no one could tell where Julia was looking. Besides that, she walked a bit sideways, like a crab.

At home in her room that night, Julia read her Bible the only way she could—a couple inches from her face. She broke down and cried. Then she did something she had never done before. She screamed at God: "WHY DON'T YOU FIX ME?"

Shocked at what had slipped out, Julia covered her mouth. And waited for lightning to strike.

Read Psalm 13:1-6

Is it okay to yell at God?

How long until you show up? David prayed. *Remember me? Or have you forgotten who I am and what I need?* Those are harsh words from a guy the Bible applauds as "a man after [God's] own heart" (1 Samuel 13:14).

David spoke his mind and lived to tell about it.

Big feelings simmer inside you when you have confused thoughts or painful emotions or a hurting body. Harsh words sometimes boil over onto yourself, people around you, even God—*especially* God, the one with ultimate power and complete control.

When you hurt, you don't have to hide your pain. David wasn't afraid to tell God about his hurts. They were real. But he always came around to ponder a bigger reality, that God's love never quits.

David didn't stop at speaking his mind and his heart. He spouted off until he was able to praise God again.

> How long, Lord? Will you forget me forever? How
> long will you hide your face from me?
>
> *Psalm 13:1*

Day 173
Not So Fast

Judd had skipped enough grades to enter high school as a weaselly little eleven-year-old. He was smarter than almost everyone at school—teachers included. He never got anything wrong on anything. He tutored calculus. And he had won a nationwide writing contest for his science-fiction novel—what reviewers called "a page-turning romp of aliens rampaging the galaxy."

Everyone hated Judd.

Judd wished the kids in his neighborhood would be nicer. Every day after school he dashed home, scurried into his backyard tree house, yanked up the rope ladder, and hid. Neighborhood kids would stand below and threaten to pound his head in. So he threw rocks at them until they went away.

No one ever came to Judd's rescue.

Read Psalm 35:1–10

Will God ever deal with your enemies?

It's weird. Think something nasty about an enemy and it's a *bad attitude*. Say it to someone else and it's *gossip*. Shout it at your enemy and it's *picking a fight*. Tell it to God and suddenly it's *prayer*.

How can you get away with that?

Because prayer is about pouring out all your thoughts and feelings to God. It's asking *God* to do his thing, not dispensing justice with your own hands. It's pleading for *him* to halt evil and give evildoers the punishment they deserve.

Old Testament believers were a bit hazy about life after death, so their prayers against enemies usually scream "Crush them NOW, God. Don't miss your chance!" The New Testament is clear, however, that much of the payback for evil—God's judgment, or his "vengeance"—won't happen until the end of time (Revelation 19:11–21).

And that's okay. God gives even awful people a chance to respond to his kindness. His concern for now is to reach them (2 Peter 3:7–9).

Contend, Lord, with those who contend with me;
fight against those who fight against me.

Psalm 35:1

Day 174
How It Ends

You sit alone in your dimly lit family room, deeply engrossed in the final six minutes of your all-time favorite show. This week's supervillian just fired up a chainsaw to hack your hero to pieces.

Your heart stops. *Thumpa Thumpa. Thump.* The chainsaw growls inches from your hero's head. You sweat. Your stomach curls.

"BOO!" your dad bursts in. "Scared you, didn't I? What's on? Oh—a rerun. In just a second his sidekick is going to—"

"Don't tell me!" you scream.

You hate when someone tells you the end.

Don't be ridiculous. You already know.

Read Psalm 18:1–15

*How do you feel while waiting for God to
save you from a tough situation?*

Think about it. Shows can't kill off their main character. But episode after episode, they're masters at making you wonder. They get you nervous. They let you hang through commercials. Worse yet, just when the clock tells you danger has to end, they flash "To be continued . . ."

Real-life suspense isn't nearly as entertaining.

You're ill—and you wonder when you'll get well. Your parents have decided to divorce—and you grow weak waiting for court dates that drag on forever. Or you're anticipating a killer test, an important game, a big recital or concert or play—and you melt into a queasy goo.

The instant before your frustration is relieved—the moment relief is right around the corner—can torture you into hopelessness.

And then it's over. You're okay. God comes through for you.

He *always* does. Not always how you expect. Not always when you want. But in his way, he always does. So stay loose. You know how your show will end.

I called to the Lord, who is worthy of praise,
and I have been saved from my enemies.

Psalm 18:3

Day 175
Waiting for the Pumpkin

Sophie flashes a smile at the finish of her balance beam routine. She nailed it. Her scores flip up—her brain does quick math—first place!

Her coach sweeps her up in a huge hug. "Incredible!" her coach cries. Sophie's teammates crowd around her, proud of their star.

The next day at school, everyone knew that Sophie won the state junior title. Her classmates spend the morning chatting about her chances of making the Olympics someday.

What a year. Six months earlier, Sophie had moved to the area. She was miserable. Now she could see what God had done—a new school, a new coach, and better friends than ever before.

Then Sophie got a letter awarding her a full scholarship to an elite gymnastics camp. She felt weirdly anxious. *This all feels too good to be true.*

Read Psalm 118:1–16

How are you supposed to react when everything goes well?

When life seems surprisingly good, you might feel like Cinderella. You're having a ball, but you worry your carriage will turn back into a pumpkin.

Jesus warned that following him would be tough at times. "In this world you will have trouble," he said (John 16:33). Paul reminded readers that suffering is part of being a Christian (Philippians 1:29). And James explained that bad times transform us into strong believers (James 1:2–4).

But when things go well—big things, little things, or everything—don't spoil your fun by convincing yourself it will all blow apart! And don't spoil yourself by thinking your success is all because of you. Every good gift comes from God (James 1:17). So celebrate good times, good things, and good friends by thanking him.

If saying thanks doesn't come easily, think hard about three things: *Your past*—when life wasn't so sweet. *Your present*—how God's help got you to a better place. And *your future*—that God will always be your refuge. And then say thanks.

Give thanks to the Lord, for he is good; his love endures forever.

Psalm 118:1

Day 176

Remember When

Twice a year, Luke and his dad drove to the country to visit the gravesite of Luke's mom. This time his new stepmom went with them. Luke wondered what his mom would have thought of Denise. He liked her.

"You'd be just as tall as Mom now," Luke's dad told him. "She'd still beat you at arm wrestling."

"But I would crush her at hoops," Luke shot back. "Her jump shot was feeble."

Luke and his dad talked for a long time, while his stepmom mostly listened. It helped to pause to remember the past. Before Luke's mom died of cancer four years ago, she always said that God would take care of him.

Looking back, Luke could see that he had.

Read Psalm 77:1–20

What keeps your heart attached to God?

Your favorite plushy chair has never let you down, so you drop into it without thinking. A friend is a proven secret-keeper, so you don't hesitate to spill your guts. A restaurant has never dropped your burger on the floor or spit in your soda—not that you know, anyway—so you're a raving fan.

Trust. It's built on past reliability.

You count on God best when you remember what he's done for you.

Some days you'll wonder where God has gone. *Doesn't he love me anymore? Where are the friends he promised me? Did I do something to make him mad?*

When Asaph, the author of Psalm 77, worried that God had forgotten him, he gained courage from recalling God's past acts. God blew apart the Red Sea to let Israel escape slavery. God led his people to freedom. God filled their lives with kind and powerful deeds.

God has acted with kindness and power for *you* too. The same God you read about in your Bible is *your* master and friend. He sent Jesus to die and to rise again for you. He energizes your heart through his Holy Spirit. He's always with you, helping you conquer your circumstances.

Remember that. And trust.

I will remember the deeds of the Lord.

Psalm 77:11

Day 177

All You Have—All You Need

With a couple intense Christian friends close by, Jonathan had it made. Jonathan, Joshua, and Josiah went to the same church, the same school, and even lived on the same block.

But then Joshua moved away. A few months later, Josiah started making excuses for not showing up at church. Then he started dodging Jonathan altogether. When Jonathan called to go skate, Josiah's sister claimed he wasn't home. The last time they sort-of talked, Josiah answered the phone himself. When he recognized Jonathan on the other end—*click*.

Jonathan heard that Josiah's dad thought it was stupid to be a Christian. After a while, Josiah thought it was stupid too.

Jonathan was stuck by himself. He knew it wasn't supposed to be that way—but that's how it was.

Read Psalm 142:1–7

What do you do when you feel alone?

You're alone—the only Christian your age you can spot. Or your Christian friends have other teachers or attend other schools. Or maybe the Christian friends have faded away.

Sooner or later, your Christian friends let you down. Those friendships are supposed to be your shelter. But sometimes you get left out in the rain.

That's your cue to find your way to God, who sometimes lets you feel alone so you learn to hide in him.

The intro to Psalm 142 says that David penned the psalm in a cave, possibly when Israel's King Saul had literally gone insane and wanted to do David in (1 Samuel 22:1–2).

What exactly did David do in the cave? Hid. Prayed. Learned to trust. Got to know the God who over and over says, "I will never leave you nor forsake you" (Joshua 1:5; Hebrews 13:5). David became better friends with the God who sticks close when no one else does.

Then an odd thing happened. When David hid in the cave—in God—his family came and supported him. And so did a bunch of friends.

I cry to you, Lord; I say, "You are my refuge."

Psalm 142:5

Day 178

Open-Door Policy

"Remember what you said back in lockup?" Kaylee quietly asked her youth pastor. "It was right after my attempt. I said, 'How come I'm locked up? They're treating me like I'm a murderer.' You said it was because I tried to hurt myself."

"You didn't understand me then, did you?" he remembered.

"No. I didn't care about myself. I didn't know who I was or why I shouldn't hurt myself. It's taken a while, but I get what you meant. I don't want to hurt myself ever again. But I'm still stuck on something. I know I'm a Christian. And I know you keep telling me, 'God is *always* there for you, Kaylee.' But how can God forgive me for how I treated myself—and what I did to my family? I'm afraid God doesn't want me anywhere near him."

Read Psalm 103:9–12

Will God ever get so mad at you that he shuts you out?

Picture this. You never get mail, but one day you've got a FedEx envelope at your door. Inside? Membership documents for the poshest club in town—good for a lifetime, all expenses paid. You can't wait! You're gonna golf, swim, smash a racquetball, and twirl in a whirlpool, all on the first day.

You're supposed to get free entry at the front gate. But what if the promise isn't true? What if the club votes you out? What if they're just teasing—and plan to laugh at you the moment you show your face?

Most free gifts are scams. But God's offer of friendship is real.

You might not feel acceptable to God. But he hasn't shut you out. Through Jesus, God has fully dealt with your sin—past, present, and future. He's flung your sin farther than the ends of the universe.

Remember? When Jesus died for your sins, he opened the way for you back to God. If you've said, "Yes, God, I've sinned and need your gift of forgiveness," then you're forgiven, fit to hang with the King of the universe.

If God didn't want you close to himself, he wouldn't have sent his Son to open the door and invite you in. But he did. Walk on in.

As far as the east is from the west, so far has he
removed our transgressions from us.

Psalm 103:12

Day 179

God Is the Crust

If life were a pizza, God would be the crust.

You toss a lot of toppings on your pizza—school, sports, clothes, sleeping, relaxing, shopping, lessons, clubs, parties, and more. God isn't just another topping on the menu you can pick or ignore. Nor can you ask for God on one part of the pizza and leave him off the rest. You can't slice up your life and say, "These are the pieces without God, and these are the pieces with God—church and youth group."

If Jesus is your Savior and Lord, he's a part of everything you do. He gives your life its shape and determines what fits on top and what doesn't. Without the crust, everything slides off.

Read Mark 1:35

How did Jesus focus his attention on God?

Pizza crusts are always in danger of being ignored, because the toppings are so obvious. Because you *can't* see God, it's easy to forget him amidst all the things you *can* see.

When you eat pizza, you need to slow down and savor the crust. As you go through your week, you need to slow down and focus on God.

You can spend time with God two ways: in a group or on your own. You need both.

In a group, the strong faith and support of other Christians give you encouragement. Groups allow you to get recharged and celebrate your friendship with God.

Being alone with God helps you get to know him personally; you need one-on-one time to understand what someone is really like. Jesus did that. Even he needed time to talk with his Father alone.

Reading your Bible is part of that. Spending time reading Scripture is how God speaks to you. Learning to talk *to* God—learning to pray—is the other part of spending time with God. God doesn't want to talk *at* you but *with* you.

Very early in the morning, while it was still dark, Jesus got up, left
the house and went off to a solitary place, where he prayed.

Mark 1:35

Day 180
Auto Show

You've never laid eyes on such a sea of sculpted metal and glass. When your parents veer left into SUV- and family-sedan land, you dart right in search of monster pickups.

Suddenly, smack in front of you, is your all-time favorite ride. Unoccupied.

All mine—for a minute. You settle into the seat, adjust the mirrors, and lean your noggin on the headrest. You wrap your hands around the leather wheel, close your eyes, and dream of thundering a hundred miles an hour down a dirt road. *Wake me up when I've got my license. This is better than any racing game. This is the real thing.*

Well, sort of. You can't test-drive a vehicle at an auto show.

Read Psalm 34:8–22

What good does it do you to follow God?

Life is no car show. It's a speedway. A road rally. A demolition derby.

Good news: God doesn't just look hot on the show floor. He tests best in the real race of life. "Check me out," he says. "Take me for a spin. See how I do." Drive with him once and you'll never settle for anything less than his closeness and care—and his pedal-to-the-floor, hold-on-to-your-seat blessings.

Following Jesus has what car salesfolk call "the intangible benefits of ownership." Believe it or don't, hanging with him as leader of your life can bring you friendship when you least expect it—and for deeper reasons than why people flock to a beautiful car.

Here's why: When you get on the path of following Jesus, you find others traveling the same direction (Psalm 119:63). As you do his will, you deepen friendships and help others (Ecclesiastes 4:10). As you share God's friendship, you add new friends (Matthew 11:19). And by soaking in God's love, you're strengthened to spread his care (1 John 4:19).

Jesus is worth following. If you let him, he makes you into a great friend. And like your parents say: If you want friends, then be a friend worth having.

Taste and see that the Lord is good. Oh, the joys of those who take refuge in him!

Psalm 34:8 NLT

Day 181

Popularity Bubbles

You bounce down the hall, joyful to be at school. Well, you don't actually skip. And you're not quite gleeful. You just mind your own business, shuffling from class to class, gliding along with a clump of classmates.

Suddenly you feel a hand on each elbow—and another hand around each bicep—and your feet lift off the floor as your back slams against the wall. You hang against lockers, feet dangling.

You're held up by a blockheaded brute, the human equivalent of a prehistoric coelacanth fish thought to have gone extinct a jillion years ago. On the right is Blockhead's thin twin. He's wiry. Beady-eyed. With a few hairs on his upper lip he's trying to pass off as a mustache. You could do better with a marker.

"We're here to get rid of you," Blockhead informs you. "Everyone just voted, and you're gone."

Read John 12:42–43

Whose vote counts when it comes to being popular?

Even at the meanest of schools, students don't literally take a vote to decide who's in and who's out. Or maybe they do.

It's like this. You're minding your own business when life suddenly morphs into a popularity contest. Vote after vote, only a handful kids come out on top. Maybe it's you. Maybe it's not. The winners get to tell everyone else how to think, feel, and act.

That's the role the Pharisees grabbed for themselves. As the religious leaders of Jesus' day, they pressured people to reject Jesus. They made others crumple in fear, threatening to kick them out of the synagogue—their place of worship—for following Jesus. How come? "They were more concerned about what people thought of them than about what God thought of them" (John 12:43 GW).

It's natural to care what others think of you. It's even normal to campaign for votes. But if you have to choose between being loved by the masses or pleasing your Master, there's only one vote that really counts.

They loved the praise of men more than praise of God.

John 12:43 NKJV

Day 182
Blah Blah

Jimmy leans over to pop the question everyone wants you to answer: "So," says the talk-show host, "what's it like being the most popular young person in the world?"

"Tough." You wink. "Been working at it for years. It's like climbing Mount Everest. I knew if I wanted to scramble to the top, I needed the right stuff.

"I've got everything I need right here." You dig in your book bag. "Look— my IQ test—140. Genius, you know. Plus, I've got sculpted muscles swathed in just-right percentage of body fat. And flawless clothes, hair, teeth . . . Oh—and I always keep a few ugly admirers next to me so I look good."

You rummage at the bottom. "But here's my coolest tool, Jimmy. It's an attitude I can't survive without: I'll do *anything* to be liked by everybody."

Read Matthew 21:1–11

How did Jesus react to the crowd's admiration?

People probably don't lay palm fronds in your path and shout "Hosanna! You the King!" Then again, you probably don't expect the royal treatment Jesus got on Palm Sunday.

Still, you know what it takes to survive the high winds, frigid cold, and lack of oxygen as you scramble to the top of Mount Popularity. The crowd makes it know that peaked biceps or the right bra size or bowing to the everyone's wishes will make you likable.

Those things won't take you upward. And they won't keep you on top. What you don't see in the Bible passage you read is how quickly the fans who crowned Jesus "Mr. Jerusalem" changed their minds. Five days later, the people who liked Jesus became a school of piranhas. They begged for him to be killed on a cross (Matthew 27:22–23).

Jesus knew that popularity scatters like snow flurries in the wind. He refused to play to the crowd, and made obeying his Father his ultimate aim (John 4:34). Jesus didn't pack for the popularity climb; he picked a path to please God.

The crowds that went ahead of him and those that followed
shouted, "Hosanna to the Son of David!"

Matthew 21:9

A Dog Ate My Arm

"We get voted 'Cutest Couple' at the fall party," Mira fumes, "and then he dumps me! He says he likes Nikita better. And he tells the whole school I'm a psycho. I'll show him psycho!"

"Ugh," adds Britney.

"And then he thinks I should go out with him again after *he* gets dumped," Mira laughs. "Well, now *he* looks pitiful. Why should I care?"

"You're too right," Britney chimes. "Too bad."

"He's such a dog!" Mira wails.

"Such a dog!" Britney agrees.

"He might as well have bit off my arm," Mira sneers. "He ran off with it dangling from his mouth. He's been curled up gnawing on the bloody stump—and now he wants to shake my hand."

Read Galatians 5:14–15

What happens when people battle for popularity?

When you get caught up in *who-likes-who* and *who-won-what* and *who-is-better-than-who*, sooner or later you get clawed. A few especially bad players will chomp off your arms if you aren't careful. Once they're done with your arms, they'll attack you again and gnaw off your legs.

Lots of people approach life as a popularity contest. But in God's way of doing things, love is the way.

You're stupid if you don't realize some people are out to bite you as they claw their way to the top. It's foolish not to notice that some are so dangerous that you best scamper away when you see them coming (2 Timothy 3:2–5).

But to love one another—that's God's goal.

Being kinder and gentler might feel weird. Then again, what's truly weird is gnawing off arms and legs.

When people fight to be popular, both sides wind up bitten. And they devour each other down to the last bite.

> If you bite and devour each other, watch out or
> you will be destroyed by each other.
>
> *Galatians 5:15*

Day 184

Bottom-Feeders

Kane jumps up and down on the soccer field, pretending to warm up. Actually, he's checking out his fan club. A clump of girls on the sideline wave and blow kisses. *This is so sweet,* he thinks. *I've got groupies.*

Last season Kane was an awful player. Then he grew six inches. As Kane and team thrashed his school's archenemies, he grew a fan club.

Kane tells himself the girls know quality when they see it. After all, they all play too, and they can appreciate his skill. Moreover, he isn't the only guy with a cheerleading section. And hey, Kane is no sexist pig. The guys cheer girls on too.

Kane's parents are less than thrilled with his new friends, not just the girls but the guys. They're all good students, and they smell drug-free. But they constantly slam anyone not in their group. Kane's parents want him to spend time with his old church friends. But who needs those losers when half the girls' team is chasing him?

Read Proverbs 13:20

Why hang out with wise guys—and gals?

Whole species of fish have figured out there's always plenty of food if you're willing to eat the muck found on lake bottoms. Likewise, you'll always have lots of friends if you settle.

The Bible shows two kinds of wise guys and gals. James says that *real wise people* are "pure; then peace-loving, considerate, submissive, full of mercy and good fruit, impartial and sincere." They live a "good life" full of "deeds done in the humility that comes from wisdom."

The scoop on *fake wise people* is scary. James says that when people are full of "bitter envy and selfish ambition," life is full of "disorder and every evil practice." Even a tiny bit of fake wisdom gets hugely nasty: it's "earthly, unspiritual, of the devil" (James 3:13–17).

You can be a bottom-feeder and bloat yourself on cruddy friends. Or you can look for the best friends. And remember: You are what you eat.

Walk with the wise and become wise,
for a companion of fools suffers harm.

Proverbs 13:20

Day 185

Scrape Away

"Dang!" Cody moans. "Paint chips in my eye again!"

"Where are your goggles?" Micah asks.

"They steam up and I can't see," Cody retorts. "Besides, I've got flecks of old paint stuck to my arms and face and everywhere. Look at my hair. This job is just stupid. What's the point of fixing this piece-of-garbage house?"

Abby rolls her eyes. "Well, Cody, we're here to help."

"Yeah," Micah adds. "You knew it would be like this."

"Whatever we fix," Cody argues, "is going to fall apart again anyway. The people who live here can clean it up themselves. Why should we help?"

Abby answers. "Because the job is too big. It takes all of us."

"I quit," Cody says as he walks away. "I'm on a team with a bunch of nerds doing a hopeless job for people too lazy to do it themselves. What a waste."

Read Matthew 27:27–31

How did Jesus get messy to help people?

Jesus was totally God. But he never acted like he was above helping. Born a baby and trained as a carpenter, he grew up and did good wherever he went—healing, feeding, making miracles, feeling people's joys and pains. In return, Jesus was beaten, bloodied, and killed. Even when he died for us, he never grumbled that his life was being wasted like a kicked-over bucket of paint.

When you're too good to help certain people—anyone, anywhere—you're claiming a superiority that God's Son scorned. Jesus didn't deny his greatness. Instead, he made the most of his amazing goodness to help people.

You can choose to look out for more than your own interests. To serve people who need your help more than you need it yourself.

Just like Jesus did.

> They spit on him, and took the staff and struck him on the head again and again. After they had mocked him, they took off the robe and put his own clothes on him. Then they led him away to crucify him.
>
> *Matthew 27:30–31*

Day 186

Did Her Head Just Pop?

"It's *kabloom*, sing!" Mr. Edstrom yelled at Marsella. "You hear the explosion stage right, then you burst into song. Can't make it easier! Got it?" The play's director whirled around and walked off. "Everyone—take ten!"

Marsella was aghast. She *never* got yelled at.

With opening night a week away, cast and crew were biting nails. An angry cast swarmed around Marsella. "Looks like Ms. Everybody-Loves-Me froze up again," Jake mocked. "What's your problem?"

"I . . . I . . ." Marsella stammered.

"If you hadn't been worrying about your hair holding up under the stage lights, you wouldn't have missed your cue."

Marsella started to bawl.

"Poor baby," Jake taunted. "Hey, everyone," he grinned. "Was that a balloon, or did her big head just pop?"

Read 1 Samuel 16:1–13

How does God judge popularity?

Imagine Jesse's sons showing off for God's prophet. Son Eliab thinks, *I'm the biggest.* Abinadab hums, *I'm the baddest.* Shammah goes, *I'm the brainiest.* Four additional sons get scrutinized. God whispers to Samuel, "Don't be impressed by their outsides. I examine a person's insides."

Samuel nixes all seven sons. Then in walks David, baby of the family. "Pick him!" God shouts. So Samuel pours oil on David's head as a signal of God's blessing.

David was working hard outside every day, so he was ripped and tanned. It wasn't long before he'd whup Goliath, so he clearly was no wuss. And in time he'd run a country, so he was no dunce. But what counted to God was David's innards: David was "a man after [God's] own heart" (1 Samuel 13:14).

It's not your job to deflate others. But it *is* your job to poke a pin in popularity bubbles by valuing what really counts. Beauty, brains, and brawn don't impress God. It's things on the inside that are worth a wow.

The Lord doesn't see things the way you see them. People judge
by outward appearance, but the Lord looks at the heart.

1 Samuel 16:7 NLT

Day 187
Shoe Licker

"Sign my yearbook?" Akemi asked sweetly. "And can I sign yours?"

Me? Huh? Ian blinked. *She wants what?* For two years, Ian sat next to Akemi in math, slogging together through tough problems. But Akemi had evolved into the babe of the grade. Now she never noticed him.

"Here. Thanks!" Akemi handed back Ian's yearbook. "Gotta go. See ya!"

She just wanted all the signatures she could get, Ian thought. But she filled his whole back cover with stuff like "Your friendship means a lot to me" and "You're a special guy. Stay that way." Her "Call me!" and "Love, Akemi" almost made Ian pucker. Her phone number at the bottom about made him puke with excitement.

Maybe she writes that in everyone's yearbook. But why her phone number? A week into summer, Ian had to find out. He called. Out fumbled "Helloit'sIan yougavemeyournumberandsaidtocallhowsyoursummergoing?"

"Ian? Ian who?" she quizzed. "I don't know any Ians." *Click.*

Read Galatians 3:26–28

What's it matter that we're all "one in Christ"?

Some people make you climb a mountain to lick dirt off their shoes.

True, God puts people in positions of leadership—as parents, teachers, bosses, police, and presidents. Someday it will be your turn to lead. In fact, leadership holds the world together (Romans 13:1). But God tells powerful people never to use their God-given authority to harm others (Matthew 20:25–28; Ephesians 6:4).

The fact that God grants some people authority doesn't alter this huge truth: God made all people equal. Being "one in Christ Jesus" means that whatever might make us special—as in privileged, stuck-up, and snotty—really means nothing. We're all equal before him—and nothing like race, gender, status, money, looks, or power decides how much we're worth or what treatment we deserve.

Jesus makes us a community (people hanging together) of equality (where everyone is valuable). You don't have to lick anyone's shoes.

> There is neither Jew nor Gentile, neither slave nor free, nor is there male and female, for you are all one in Christ Jesus.
>
> *Galatians 3:28*

Day 188

Lettuce Head

Owen stabbed the air to make his point. "I'm gonna be the next class president. Everybody knows this is my year." Complete with bow tie and floopy hair, Owen looked like a half-sized clown. "I'll make a bunch of ridiculous promises," Owen declared. "I'm a shoo-in with all the students who think I can actually shorten the school day. And Samantha—she's gonna be dust in the wind."

"Don't be so sure," Samantha snarled. "You shouldn't hold your strategy sessions in the hall. And keep up that look. I'll beat you for sure."

"Well," Owen laughed, "you're as stylin' as a school librarian."

"You're goin' down, Owen," Samantha stomped.

"Prepare to be buried, little librarian."

Read 1 Corinthians 9:24–27

What's the prize that matters most in life?

The apostle Paul and the recipients of his letter knew that athletes preparing for the Isthmian Games—a huge competition held in Corinth that rivaled the Olympics—went into brutal training. Athletes did it all to win a wreath of laurel or—believe it or don't—celery. Paul is saying, "I fight as hard as those athletes." But Paul competed for a different prize. Above all, he sought to live the message he taught about Jesus.

Paul's biggest competition wasn't other people. He aimed his hardest shots at himself. He was like ancient fighters who boxed with leather straps tied to their knuckles, except he beat his own selfishness black-and-blue.

Ancient athletes won prizes that wilted only slightly more quickly than supermodels get ugly, the rich and famous get out-pizzazzed, or presidents get replaced. Someone who's prettier, richer, or more popular always comes along.

Being your best for God is the one contest where winning lasts forever. Hanging tight with God always beats wearing lettuce on your head.

Everyone who competes in the games goes into strict training. They do it to get a crown that will not last, but we do it to get a crown that will last forever.

1 Corinthians 9:25

Day 189

Belly Itches

Your letter to the ultrapowerful owner of the world's most ultracool software company was so ultrabrilliant he flew you to his ultraluxury compound to critique his ultrasecret next release.

Upon arrival, you're surrounded by a pack of guard dogs. "Oh my," you smile. "What big teeth you have." But the dogs heel like well-trained pups. You scratch their bellies. You feed them treats. They fetch. You can't believe they're killers.

"It all depends which side of the fence you're on," your host explains. "I'll show you." You walk out the compound entrance, where metal gates clang shut behind you. "Try to reach inside," he instructs. All those darling puppies suddenly bare fangs, barking and springing wildly into the air. "See what I mean?" he says. "Inside, they're your friends. But try to get in from the outside uninvited, and they'll maul you."

Read 1 John 3:18

When is it okay to snarl at people not in your group?

Cliques are like packs of guard dogs. Inside their fence? They cuddle. Outside? They're vicious. Depending on what the pack thinks of you, they morph from fang to friend or vice versa.

You might think that no group you belong to deserves to be called a "clique." But think hard: What do people have to do to fit with you and your people? What do you do to shut others out? What fences do you put up? Exactly who don't you let in? And what fangs do you flash?

There are a million reasons to bare your teeth. But know that God flashes a welcoming smile at people unlikely to be welcomed into anyone's club. God focuses his care on shut-out people like widows, orphans, and aliens (Zechariah 7:10). And his love reaches to left-out people all around you.

Inviting into your group the very people that others lock out is a sure sign of your total devotion to God (James 1:27).

Dear children, let us not love with words or speech but with actions and in truth.

1 John 3:18

Day 198

Pass the Oxygen, Please

Alec heard basketballs pounding in the church gym, each splat and slam echoing in his under-the-staircase cave. As people shot hoops after youth group, Alec heard someone yell, "Where's Alec? We need another player!" He smiled. *They'll never find me.* He had sprinted away after youth group and ducked into his hiding spot. A few minutes longer, and he'll dart outside and his parents will pick him up, getting away unseen.

Alec thought back to what his pastor had said about "belonging to the body of Christ." *I don't think I can count on anyone here. No one cares about me. I don't feel welcome.*

Then a thought occurred to him: *Maybe I'm not trying.*

Read 1 Kings 19:9–18

Why did Elijah feel all alone? What could he do about it?

Life is a lot like hanging out underwater. Christian friends are your hose to the surface—not just for a whiff of fresh air, but for the oxygen you need to survive.

Elijah—one of God's key prophets—added up his friends and got zero. He was hated by Queen Jezebel, for instance, and hunted by her armies. To get away, he hiked for forty days and then crawled into a cave.

God heard Elijah's lonely cries. But then he asked why Elijah was hiding.

Elijah thought someone evil was standing on his air hose. Truth was, he was suffocating because he had distanced himself from God's people. In reality, Elijah had a whole horde of friends he could count on, people who also respected the Lord (1 Kings 19:18).

There's no such thing as a scuba tank that lets you frolic forever through the deep waters of life all by your lonesome. You need a lifeline, the air hose of friendship. That hose can kink, so you need to tend it carefully.

When you feel alone, tell God that you trust him to help you find Christian friends. Then get your backside out of whatever cave you've crawled into—and search for his answer!

I am the only one left.

1 Kings 19:10

Day 191
Back on the Bus

Soon after Audrey's family moved to a developing nation for her dad's job, she spotted signs on the traffic light poles: "Pedestrians should huddle together and cross the street quickly." Audrey appreciated the heads-up, but she didn't have anyone to huddle with on the way to school. And where were the signs warning cars not to drive on the sidewalk?

Audrey got used to dodging through the city in taxis. But taxis were pricey. A few classmates had motor scooters. But after one skidded across her toes and slid under a truck, she stayed off them. Audrey settled on taking the city bus to school—a bus with a big tough shell and bunches of fellow riders. Sometimes buses bashed into storefronts. She sat in the back and felt safer, because buses don't back into buildings.

But that didn't begin to deal with all her challenges *inside* the bus. . . .

Read Isaiah 43:1–3

Who rescues you when your crowd lets you down?

You would like to think that moving with a huddle protects you. But sometimes your safe spot—a team, a youth group, a pod of dependable friends—is more like a bad bus ride. You're caged with strangers. You have to watch where you sit. Who you talk to. The people who might pick your pockets or weird you out.

And that's still not the worst of what can happen when your huddle of so-called friends hurts you. Sometimes the friendship bus crashes and burns.

What happens to you then?

You have a Friend who's able to jump into the flames to rescue you. God isn't a sidewalk bystander who *might* dash to your aid. "Redeemer" means God owns the bus—plus the people and packages and everything else on board (Exodus 6:6–8).

When you're riding along and your crowd blows up on you, God is there. He's promised to rush in, pack you up in his arms, and wrap you in a fireproof blanket of love.

You belong to God. He won't leave you alone on the bus, *especially* when the bus goes up in flames.

I will be with you.

Isaiah 43:2

Day 192

Total Toughness

What was supposed to be a tame all-girl sleepover for Laura's birthday was going hyper, obnoxious—and worse. Kaelyn and Jordan hadn't planned to sleep much, but this exceeded their foggiest expectations.

Kaelyn and Jordan had become suspicious that a frothy pink birthday punch was causing the craziness when a dozen guys from school walked in. The two girls glanced at each other. Without a word, they knew it was time to exit. So at three in the morning, they dialed a parent. Jordan's dad groaned like a bear wakened from hibernation, but as soon as Jordan whispered "alcohol" and "boys," he was right there.

Everyone stared as Kaelyn and Jordan rolled up their sleeping bags and headed for the door. They stood outside in the cold, their best friends inside laughing at them—their ex-best friends, probably.

Read 2 Timothy 1:7

You know you're supposed to resist peer fear. But how?

Nothing is scarier than facing a roomful of people who think you're a dork. You might want to be friends, but something about you makes them haters. They might not like what you do. They might not like *you*.

You could talk like them, act like them, mistreat people like them, smoke or drink or inhale like them—all to keep from looking stupid and feeling alone. You could suck up and give in. You could give up and let people control you.

Or you can stick with the Friend who sticks with you and let him make you strong.

God promises that the same power that raised Christ from the dead lives inside you (Romans 8:11). His Holy Spirit remakes you to want and to be able to do what's right. That's a "spirit of power" and a "spirit of self-discipline." But he also promises to equip you to face others with a "spirit of love." It's what made Jesus' first followers fearless and forgiving even when others hated them (Acts 6:8–8:2).

Following God doesn't make you timid. It makes you tough.

For the Spirit God gave us does not make us timid, but gives us power, love and self-discipline.

2 Timothy 1:7

Day 193
Don't Dump Your Deodorant

You couldn't wait to see your classmates again after summer vacation. You were busting with excitement to unveil your new self-confidence.

The kid at the next locker backs away. "What happened to *you*?" he asks.

"Hiiiiiyaaaa," you breathe. He backs up farther. "So you noticed? I've decided to ignore peer pressure. I no longer care what other people think."

"Well, you smell like you live in the basement of an outhouse."

"I'm happy to let you form your own opinion about me," you say. "It won't change how I act. I haven't showered since June. Soap, shampoo, deodorant, toothbrush, toothpaste—I threw them all away. And I've taken up public burping. Did you know that in many cultures a hearty belch is appropriate appreciation for a tasty meal?"

Read 1 Timothy 4:12

What's the upside of peer pressure?

Peer fear. Teachers lecture you. Parents shield you. Anti-drug, anti-smoking, anti-drinking, and anti-bullying campaigns try to scare you. But not all peer pressure is beer pressure.

Everyone needs *good* peer pressure—a healthy dread of what others think. Good peer pressure is the deodorant of life. It stops life's little stinks.

Still, there's an even better peer pressure that accomplishes more than keeping a lid on your public belching. The *best* peer pressure helps you choose God and his ways (2 Timothy 2:22).

In fact, you don't have to simply put up with being pressured. You can initiate the pushing. Not by becoming a drug dealer or going deodorant-free, but by modeling what a totally devoted Christian looks like—in how you talk, love, and hang tight to God and his commands.

No matter your age, your faith can influence people around you. The world wants you to cave to peer fear. It's time you start pushing the other way.

> Don't let anyone look down on you because you are young, but set an example for the believers in conduct, in life, in love, in faith and in purity.
>
> *1 Timothy 4:12*

Day 194
Cannibal Lunch

I thought they were my friends. But now they're fixin' to have *fillet of me.* You're bound and gagged, suspended over a boiling caldron.

You try to buy time. You beg them to slow down. All you want is a chance to wiggle free—and run away. But there's no chance of escape.

You try to remind them of all the times they said or did something you didn't like—and how you let them off the hook.

You can't convince them to have a conversation.

They dip your toe in so you can feel the burn.

Then they get a hotter idea.

They don't even bother to cook you.

They eat you raw.

Read 1 Peter 4:12–19

What can you do when people pick on you?

Bullies and other bad people come and go. And come again. It's a fact of life that when one drifts away, another one shows up who's just as bothersome. The fact that people pester you is unending (John 16:33). Some may even hate you (1 John 3:13). And even best friends sometimes hang you over a hot pot (Psalm 41:9).

The apostle Peter distinguishes between the peer-eat-peer of daily life and actual suffering for Jesus.

Peter says this: When you get boiled for putting a fork in people—anything ranging from unkind words to murder—or for putting your nose in other people's business—as in meddling—don't blame your suffering on anyone but yourself.

But when you don't deserve the pain you're enduring—you get boiled for doing right—there's a bigger reason for your suffering. You're taking one because you're on the Jesus team.

That's when you would really like God to help you wiggle free. But it's also when God lays before you a huge choice: Will you try to boil those who boil you? Or will you continue following God and doing good?

So then, those who suffer according to God's will should commit themselves to their faithful Creator and continue to do good.

1 Peter 4:19

Day 195
Leftovers

Leftover tuna hot dish stared back at Megan from the refrigerator shelf—a heaping bowl of over-boiled noodles and oily tuna mixed in with a mound of mushy peas. *Blechhhhh. Not a chance.*

Nothing against her dad's cooking—and she didn't want to be ungrateful for food—but anything worth eating wouldn't be hiding in the fridge in such massive quantities.

The unidentifiable food behind the tuna had sprouted legs and was plotting to escape. So Megan reached for stuff to make her trusty bestie—a peanut butter sandwich. But the kitchen was bare of bread.

With her parents out at a movie and her older brother gone with friends, Megan threw herself a pity party. *Just me and my tuna,* Megan pouted. She stabbed at her food with a fork. *This stuff's just like me. I'm a leftover.*

Read Psalm 84:10

How do you cope when life leaves you all alone?

Some days you feel like you've been tossed off a skyscraper. You're hanging by your fingernails like an over-the-ledge cartoon character. You're alone. Hurting. Screaming for help. You wonder if a rescue squad will ever arrive.

Even though fear has stabbed you through-and-through, you're smart enough to be on guard against people who just pretend to help. You won't let yourself be fooled by people who enjoy watching you suffer.

When genuine help arrives, however, you cling to it. You're grateful for a rope from above. You loop it around your waist and tie in tight.

God promises to be there to meet your needs (Philippians 4:19). He promises—in his perfect way, in his perfect time—to come to your rescue (Psalm 72:12–14). Most of all, he promises to be with you no matter what (Hebrews 13:5).

When you're lonely, grab hold of God. Holding tight to him is the best place you could ever be.

Better is one day in your courts than a thousand elsewhere; I would rather be a doorkeeper in the house of my God than dwell in the tents of the wicked.

Psalm 84:10

Day 196

Rip Your Buns Off

The name "Crusher" should have been a clue. But the guy who emerged in a splash of fireworks as the next wrestler looked scary even from your seat up in the nosebleeds.

The voice of the master of ceremonies reverberates through the arena. "The next match-*atch-atch*," he roars, "involves audience-*ence-ence* participation-*tion-tion*." You wonder how anyone would be fool enough to go to the mat with that human monstrosity. But you're about to be the fool. As the crowd chants, "YOU! YOU! YOU!" you're bodysurfed to the front and heaved into the ring.

"I'm going to tear you to pieces," Crusher growls as he circles you. "And when I'm done, kid, I'm gonna rip your buns off and make me some earmuffs."

Read Matthew 10:28–31

Who's the most fearsome guy in the universe?

Immediately prior to the Bible chunk you just read, Jesus told his disciples what to expect when they headed out to spread the word about him. Some folks would welcome them warmly. Others would try to do them in.

Yet if the world is tough, God is even tougher. If you think peers can power-bomb you, wait until you see what God can do to his enemies. If you're not on God's side, you've picked a reserved seat in a hideous place where his Son never shines.

While these are some of the Bible's most straight-talking words (verse 28), they're tag-teamed with some of its most tender (verses 29–31). God knows the flight plan of every sparrow on earth, yet those tiny speckled birds are sold in ancient markets for next to nothing—two for a penny.

God watches over you infinitely more closely. He knows the smallest details about you. He cares about your frailest parts. His goal is never to shred you.

> Do not be afraid of those who kill the body but cannot kill the soul. Rather, be afraid of the One who can destroy both soul and body in hell.
>
> *Matthew 10:28*

Woof

"She's still a dog," Arianna laughed. "At least we taught her to heel. Woof!" Arianna and her cabinmates laughed loudly.

The girls had vowed to "woof proof" Rachel by the end of their week at summer camp. So they showed her how to shave her legs. They did her hair. They slathered on makeup. They donated shirts and shorts. And they coached her in maximum boy appeal. By the time they finished, Rachel looked like a show poodle.

Then Rachel stood in the cabin door. She had shaken out her hair and washed off the makeup. She was back to her own clothes. And she looked like the same old Rachel. "I appreciate what you did," she stammered. "But I liked myself the way I was. I'm nothing fancy, but I'm me."

Read Genesis 1:31

Who likes you no matter what other people think?

Name a quality that makes you unique, and chances are good that people have poked fun at it. You're picked on for *temporary flaws*: You dropped the ball, tanked the test, or put your foot in your mouth and chewed vigorously. Or you get teased about *things that might never go away*: If you're big like a truck, they say you beep when you back up. If you're bony like boards jutting from the back of a pickup, they tell you to tie a red flag to your backside.

God knows you inside and out. After all, he made you. And he loves what he sees. All the ways you think and feel and look and act—he can't get enough of those.

And Genesis tells you exactly what he thinks when he looks at you. When the Lord looked down at creation, he said it was "good." When he made humans, he proclaimed it "very good." One Bible translation puts it like this: "Then God looked over all he had made, and he saw that it was very good!" (Genesis 1:31 NLT). That verdict includes you—all of you—and every unique quality that God built into you.

You're no dog. A little quirky? Maybe. Your own person? Definitely. And in his eyes? Wonderful. Undoubtedly.

God saw all that he had made, and it was very good.

Genesis 1:31

Day 198

One Coach

The pitcher's mother screams from the stands: "Come on! Blow it right by!" The catcher tries his hardest to tip you off balance: "Hey, *battah battah battah,* suh-wing, *battah battah battah.*" The pitcher gives you a stink eye and hurls a tough one. Even the ball seems to laugh at you as it flies over the plate. And as the pitcher readies another throw, some stranger yells from behind the backstop, mere feet away. His words reverberate in your helmet: "Look at me when I'm talking to you!"

You refuse to be distracted. You glance at your bench. Your coach watches you calmly. Nods encouragement. Claps hands to tell you, *Keep at it. Eyes on the ball.*

Backstop guy speaks again: "I said *look at me when I'm talking to you!*" This time you spin in your cleats to look. He stares you straight in the eyes. *Huh? Who's he? And why's he yelling at me?*

Read Acts 4:13–21

What did Peter and John say when religious leaders told them to shut up about Jesus?

If a stranger hanging around the backstop says your stance is too wide or you need to square-up to the plate, he's maybe hollering advice worth taking. But if he tells you to swing blindfolded or slide into home plate on your face, he's clearly not rooting for you.

There's a bigger point. When you play ball, you answer to *one* voice: your coach. The water boy can't signal you to steal second. Your best friend can't tell you to swing for a home run. Bystanders aren't your boss.

Peter and John had just healed a man who couldn't walk (Acts 3:1–10). They openly gave credit to Jesus, and the same religious leaders who sent Jesus to the cross wanted them to shut up. Their order clearly contradicted God's command to speak up about faith (Acts 1:8), and God's guys had one response: "We've got *one* coach. We obey *his* voice" (see both Acts 4:19 and 5:29).

Jesus is the clear, calm voice calling to you above the roar of the crowd. And when you listen to him, you'll win.

But Peter and John replied, "Which is right in God's eyes:
to listen to you, or to him? You be the judges!"

Acts 4:19

Day 199
No Fear

"The Dwarfs" got their nickname when they started playing basketball together in elementary school. By the end of middle school, they were best friends and the core of the best team around, sure to power their small high school to a state title.

The name stuck because they *hi-ho-hi-ho*ed everywhere together, on or off court. They dressed, talked, and did their hair alike. Whoever they liked was popular. Anyone they disliked would die a painful social death.

The group broke apart when two girls became Christians. "That isn't what we do," the other five told Kelli and Alexis. "We're not into God." That tipped off a tough game of five-on-two. On court, the other girls pushed Kelli and Alexis out of plays. Off court, they turned their backs and walked off.

That was a game Kelli and Alexis saw no way to win.

Read Numbers 14:1–9

How did Joshua and Caleb stand up to the crowd?

When peers try to force you to follow their rules, they usually don't toss you an exploding basketball. They don't press a gun to your head and shout, "Cheat! Cut people down! Slack off! Scream at your parents!"

They play mind games (Romans 12:2). They make you think your world will fall apart without them. And peers get power over you because you give it to them. They don't *force* you to follow—you *choose* to do what they want because you believe two lies: (1) doing wrong to please them is more important than doing right to please yourself, and (2) making them happy matters more than making God happy.

The people of Israel declared that God was mean and his followers idiots. They feared they would be slaughtered by giants in the promised land. Joshua and Caleb hit back with truth—that the God of might would do them right. They refused to rebel against God. They also refused to fear the crowd.

Because Joshua and Caleb dared to be different, God blessed them (Numbers 14:30). They turned out to be the real giants.

Only do not rebel against the Lord. And do not be afraid of
the people of the land, because we will devour them.

Numbers 14:9

Day 200

Lemmings

Mama Lemming had it marked on the family calendar. *March 20*. First day of spring. Annual Lemming Migration.

Like all the other good Lemmings, the family loaded up their Lemmingmobile and headed to the sea. Why the sea? They didn't know. Everyone was going.

A minute out of the driveway, the Lemming children grew impatient.

"Are we there yet?" sister cried.

"How much farther?" brother whined.

Other Lemmingmobiles clogged the interstate. "Oh, this is just great." Papa Lemming banged the steering wheel. "Now we'll never get there."

When the Lemming family finally arrived at the ocean, they leapt from the car and ran with all the other Lemmings into the water, where not one of them lived happily ever after.

Read 1 Peter 5:8–11

Would you rather be a Lemming or a Lert?

Lemmings are tough ratlike rodents native to northern Europe. When their colonies get too crowded, millions of lemmings leave home in spectacular mass migrations. They sometimes run into the ocean. Not one bothers to answer the question that really matters: Is this a good idea?

It's not. Lemmings can't swim.

Lemmings don't intend to drown themselves. They're just looking for a less crowded place to live. They think they're about to cross a river when they wind up over their heads. Lemmings are stupid.

Lerts, on the other hand, ask smart questions. If someone tries to talk a Lert into doing something that sounds hinky, a Lert learns more: Who's in charge? Where are we going? Is this a good idea?

Lerts have learned to tell the difference between truth and lies. Unlike lemmings. Don't be a lemming. Be alert.

> Stay alert! Watch out for your great enemy, the devil. He prowls
> around like a roaring lion, looking for someone to devour.
>
> *1 Peter 5:8 NLT*

Day 201

Thugs Are Us

"Here it is." Savannah poked at the movie listings on her phone. "It's showing at nine o'clock. Let's go."

Bailey moaned. "My parents said to be home at nine thirty."

"So?" Laila practically told her parents when *they* should be home.

"Do the math," Bailey shot back. "The movie is two hours long. I'd be a little late."

"Since when do you listen to your parents?" Laila inquired.

Savannah had an idea. "Can't you call your parents and tell them you'll be late?"

"They'll say no. We're leaving early in the morning for my grandparents' to—"

Savannah cut her off. "We're going. You can go home if you want."

"You know what your problem is?" Laila asked. "You're not any fun."

Read James 4:1–2

How do you spot a thug?

The thugs you know probably look nice. They dress like you. Talk like you. Want what you want. Go to your school and live in your neighborhood.

They probably don't burgle homes or lie in ambush for innocent pedestrians. But these thugs still take from others to enrich themselves—to look good, feel big, be popular, set the rules, and get what they want. They move in cliques and pick easy targets. Even without weapons, they leave a trash trail of busted feelings, broken promises, stolen property, disappointed parents, wounded bodies, and stabbed hearts.

You know enough to run from thugs who whisper at you from alleys. It's the thugs nearby that you have to beware of—the ones who stop messaging, stop saying hello, and stop being your friend when you don't join them.

There's also a thug lurking inside you that you have to guard against. It's the part of you that wants to take by force or by stealth what isn't yours.

Thugs aren't always strangers on the street. Sometimes the thugs are us.

> You desire but do not have, so you kill. You covet but you cannot get what you want, so you quarrel and fight. You do not have because you do not ask God.
>
> *James 4:2*

Day 202
Stupid

Tyler knew to step aside.

He simply wanted to get to his assigned school assembly seat in the auditorium. But as he trudged upward, he saw the Mob—the six most popular guys in middle school, plus their girls. They rushed up from below, like they were going to run him over. Tyler scampered out of the aisle and stood in a row of seats to let them pass. But the Mob stopped at the same spot.

"Hey, stupid," they said. "Those are our seats."

That they were. And the Mob wasn't moving. So Tyler took the only way out—a long detour to the other end of the row, climbing over another mob of yelping classmates already in their seats.

He lived.

But half the auditorium saw his crawl of shame.

Read Matthew 5:5

What's it mean to be meek?

Don't take it personally when people pick on you. Mean people are like a mosquito pack that wants to tank up on your blood. You might feel like a particularly plump target. Truth is, they suck blood anywhere they can get it.

Sometimes you can stand up for your rights. Like by speaking truth (Ephesians 4:15), relying on the authorities God put in place to make things right (Romans 13:1–5), or running for help when you can't solve a problem yourself (Matthew 18:15–17).

Other times there's no escape. You get stomped on your way to the cheap seats.

The meekness Jesus talks about isn't weakness. It's gentle, self-controlled strength. It means being better than the bullies who thrash the world. God is on the side of the gentle, and Jesus hints at who will *not* win the ultimate popularity and power contest—the proud, strong, aggressive, harsh, and tyrannical who suck life from others.

Inheriting the earth means God gives a prize—someday, some way—for every pint of blood you give up. So it's clear who the real losers are.

Blessed are the meek, for they will inherit the earth.

Matthew 5:5

Day 203
Thonk

In celebration of Jayne's big brother graduating from high school, friends and family from near and far crammed their house and yard for a congratulatory cookout.

Mom said it was only polite to invite the new neighbors, and on the big day, little Conner showed up with the rest of his clan. He didn't come alone, however. Along with him came his drone, which he was piloting to hover high overhead. Ever since Conner had moved in, Jayne had seen it buzzing the area. "I'm getting this all on camera," the little guy says. "I'll upload the video so you all can watch it!"

"Aww," says Jayne's mom. "That's so sweet."

What a dweeb, thinks Jayne. *Couldn't he leave his toy at home?* Jayne's thought was interrupted when Conner's drone malfunctioned and dropped from the sky, thonking her head, slicing it open, and sending her to the ER for stitches.

Read 1 John 4:19–21

What gives us the power to love people we don't like?

Annoying little neighbors who drop drones on your head aren't the only people you know who make you spurt blood. You're surrounded by foes and even friends who can be challenging to love.

Our perfect God would have every reason to find us annoying and wish us away. Despite our failures and limitations, God sees something amazingly special about each of us. Including you.

After all, he made you (Psalm 100:3).

Nothing can separate you from his love (Romans 8:38–39), which reaches to the heavens (Psalm 36:5).

And don't forget this: God's colossal love for you and your fellow earthlings is why he sent his Son, Jesus, to live and die (John 3:16).

If God had wanted you to make pets of the less-than-likable people around you, they would have been born with collars. Seeing none, it's obvious he wants you to do more than collect nerds. He wants you to love them with the love he lavishes on you.

We love because he first loved us.

1 John 4:19

Day 204
Human Puck

Ching-thwipp. Another shot off the post and into the net behind Justin.

"Sorry," Justin apologized—again.

There was no ice where Justin grew up. When his family moved north, he found his new friends more or less came out of the womb wearing hockey skates. Putting Justin in the goal kept him out of their way, but even his baby steps in the net sent him skidding like a human hockey puck.

Most days no one cared. But this time his friends got mad. Justin came home with a cut-up lip and a blood-soaked jacket. They'd shoved him, and he landed face-first on the ice.

"Justin, what are you trying to prove?" his older sister reasoned. "You're good at English. You're pretty great at chess. You thrash those guys at basketball and—"

"But nobody cares about any of that," Justin moaned. "All that matters is that I can't play hockey."

Read Romans 12:3–8

Why would God want you to understand what you're good at?

You can go back to back with your friends to see who's taller. You could compare test scores to see who's brainier. But the real measurement of who you are is all the good gifts God built inside you.

You might still be figuring out what makes you unique. That's okay. But know that God made you good at something. For sure.

You might recognize yourself in the list of "spiritual gifts" the apostle Paul inserted here (or in 1 Corinthians 12:7–10 and Ephesians 4:11–12). Or you may have other talents. You might be the person who tutors math. Or someone with a shoulder soaked with the tears of hurting friends. You could be the tightest writer your classmates have ever read. Or you may be a rock-steady influence on one close friend. Celebrate that!

You can't quit everything you're no good at. No one gets out of serving or supporting others. No one gets a free pass out of school. But it's okay to boldly put your unique talents to use. What you're good at may not make you popular, but it's your amazing gift to this world.

We have different gifts, according to the grace given us.

Romans 12:6

Day 205
Better Than Buff

"Try it again, Bekka. Like this." Natalie stepped into the blocks. At the sound of an imaginary starting gun, Natalie exploded. She screamed past Bekka and soared over three hurdles before jogging back.

"I can't do that!" Bekka moaned. "You look like a gazelle."

"A gazelle? Gazelles smell. Besides, I think they get stalked and eaten," Natalie protested. "But thanks. By the way, you do great too."

"By the way, I do *not*." Bekka got quiet. "Natalie, that's why I'm going to tell Coach you should take my spot as team captain. You're way better than I am. You're maybe best in the whole state. You never put anyone down, you listen to everyone, and you're great at helping people. Before you came over here, I was so frustrated I was ready to wrap a hurdle around someone's head."

"I'm glad I could help," Natalie said, "because I like to help. But it's God who makes me run fast. You're making too big a deal of me."

Read 1 Corinthians 4:7

Where do you get all your great gifts?

You invite a new friend to your house. You'd be totally rude if: (a) you drag her over the dog to see your best-ever report card—the one your mom blew up as big as the fridge, (b) you wildly arm-wrestle her until your superior musculature rips her rotator cuff, (c) you mercilessly beat her on your billion-bit video game system, or (d) all of the above.

Brainiacs are bright. Body builders are buff. Millionaires are marvelous. But every ounce of our knowledge, might, and money—everything else we are or own—comes from God alone.

When you feel like bursting out in a song of praise, don't yodel about yourself. Sing to God, who is absolutely kind, fair, and right. His faithfulness clears hurdles higher than the sky. His bright shining glory races around the earth (Psalm 108:3–5). You may be a big deal, but God is way bigger.

> Who says you are better than others? What do you have
> that was not given to you? And if it was given to you, why
> do you brag as if you did not receive it as a gift?
>
> *1 Corinthians 4:7 NCV*

Day 206
Slick Slob

I *can't believe Jeremiah pays attention to them*, Caleb fumed. *They're wrecking everything.* Caleb stared at his youth pastor as he talked to the newcomers in his youth group. They goofed off. They stunk of smoke. They looked like they crawled out from under the drum set at a metal concert.

A little later, Jeremiah pulled Caleb aside, looking like he'd read Caleb's mind. "They aren't going to get fixed all at once. God's working on them. Did you clean up right away when you got serious about following God?"

Caleb remembered how long it took for him to break a bunch of bad habits. "Caleb," Jeremiah pointed out, "most of these kids have gotten kicked around bad. Think how you can help them up, not push them down."

Read Galatians 6:4–5

How do you handle being good at something?

You might be embarrassed by your report card. You might hide when someone says, "Let's play volleyball!" You might cringe when people eye your less-than-stylin' clothes. Yet someday you'll discover something where you're slick—and most everyone else is a slob.

Take your faith, for example. If you pay attention in Sunday school, you might think you're a saint. Truth is, you are. But not because of anything *you* did. Because of Jesus' death for you, you truly are holy (Colossians 1:12). Because of his life in you, you've got gifts to help you change the world (1 Peter 4:10). Yet apart from God, we're all spiritual slobs. And we're to use our spiritual strength to pull people out of sin.

Whatever good things we have and are, God gave to us (1 Corinthians 4:7). You can always find someone bad—and feel better. You can always find someone better—and feel bad. What really matters is what's going on with you. And how are you maximizing your gifts to help others?

When you do better than others, thank God for how he's helped you. And figure out who *you* can help next.

> Each one should test their own actions. Then they can take pride in
> themselves alone, without comparing themselves to someone else. . . .
>
> *Galatians 6:4–5*

Day 207
Up Front

"You belong up front," Sara's mother gushes. "You deserve it. If you're ever going to win the Teenage Miss contest, you *have* to be in the front. Do you think the judges will pick a girl content to stand in the back?"

The next day at her gymnastics team photo, Sara and eleven girls waited for instructions. *This'll be in the paper*, Sara thinks. *And the yearbook. And plastered in the school showcase by the trophies. And I'll include it in my entry. I've got to get to the front!*

Sara inches forward. She pushes past her teammates and drops into the splits. *Idiots. They just stand there. They don't know what really matters.*

Sara's coach shakes her head. "Sara, I want Camila in front. Move to the back.

"No!" Sara protests. "Me! Me! Me! I *have* to be in *front*!"

Read Mark 9:33–37

What does someone who possesses "humility" look like?

"What were you arguing about?" Jesus asks politely.

He knows. But he asks anyway.

"Nothing," they blush. "It's not important."

Jesus had just told his disciples he would soon be killed. Not that he was getting a star in Hollywood. Not that he had been invited to all the hot talk shows. Not that he was playing to packed stadiums on a sold-out world tour.

He said he would soon be crucified.

You would think the disciples would have asked Jesus how he felt about dying. Or exclaimed that they suddenly understood that being the world's Savior—or his follower—wasn't glamorous. But they didn't.

Jesus declared that following him isn't about pushing yourself to the front of the crowd. To be first is to be last. To be like him is to welcome those who others laugh at and label. To imitate him is to serve—even suffer—to bring others life (Matthew 20:26–28).

Jesus was God himself (John 1:14). But even he didn't push his way to the front.

Sitting down, Jesus called the Twelve and said, "Anyone who wants to be first must be the very last, and the servant of all."

Mark 9:35

Day 208

Not My Sister

Megan cringed when Mrs. Nguyen's eyebrow arched. She recognized that look. "Megan?" her teacher had said cheerily as she called roll on the first day of class. Then Mrs. Nguyen spotted Megan. When she got a good look at Megan, she glanced down her class list. "Megan *Ronson?*" And the raised eyebrow said it all: *You look like Morgan. You'd better not act like her.*

"She knows your sister, Megan," someone teased. "She thinks you're Morgan."

There wasn't a kid in school who hadn't heard of Megan's older sister. No one would ever forget that three years ago Morgan was expelled for selling drugs and then tried to torch the school.

I'm not my sister! Megan wanted to say. *Give me a chance!*

Read Psalm 139:1

Who knows the real you—and who you can be?

They don't see you. They see what they *think* you are. You remind them of an older brother who was so bad that you'll never get your own chance to be good. Or they remember your sister who was so smart and sugary that you can't ever compete. Even people who don't compare you to siblings want to label you and stuff you in a box. They recall every time you've embarrassed yourself from third grade on—and won't let you escape. They never forget your mishaps—and don't let you change.

The crowd wants to define you. If you let them tell you who you are and who you can be, you're trapped. Kicked to the curb.

They don't understand you like God does. He's searched you and knows you—every thought, word, and action. He saw you before you were born (Psalm 139:15–16). And he wants you to live without comparing yourself—or letting yourself be compared—to others (Galatians 6:4).

You figure out who you are not by listening to people who box you in but by seeing yourself through the eyes of the One who knows you best. God blows the tops off their containers. He sets you loose to follow him and become everything he made you to be.

You have searched me, Lord, and you know me.

Psalm 139:1

Day 209
Made for Friendship

Birth was scary, wasn't it? As you lay in a basket in the middle of a whizzing intersection, trucks coughed smoke into your little face and jolted you up and down. A speeding car nicked your basket, spinning it topsy-turvy. After a few hours in the intersection, you crawled through traffic to search for food by the side of the road.

Your birth probably didn't happen that way.

You weren't assembled in a mad scientist's underground laboratory and popped into the world through a sewer lid, left to fend for yourself on the street. God had a better plan. You were given life by an act of love and snuggled tight in a mother's womb. When you were born you were caught by someone's caring arms, fed, clothed, and protected.

Read Genesis 2:18–25

Who were the world's first friends?

When God made the world's first man, Adam was alone with the animals and the rest of creation. But not just alone—*lonely*, without a friend. God saw that being alone was about as fun as being born into a traffic jam. So for Adam he created a friend—Eve. Adam and Eve were "flesh of flesh" and "bone of bone" and exactly what the other one needed. Man and woman lived as perfect friends in paradise, the Garden of Eden.

God didn't stop there. He wanted human beings to know their Creator. So he made them in his image (Genesis 1:27), able to relate to God in a way a rock or a raccoon never could. God and people knew each other up close. God is pictured as "walking" in the Garden and talking directly with Adam and Eve (Genesis 1–3). God's purpose was not only for people to know each other but to know him.

God had a big plan. Adam and Eve were just the start. God designed his world to be a paradise of relationships. Everyone would get along. No one would get hurt. Everyone would worship God and respect neighbors. God, men, women, girls, guys, parents, children, even animals and plants had a role.

That was the plan, anyway.

> The Lord God said, "It is not good for the man to be
> alone. I will make a helper suitable for him."
>
> *Genesis 2:18*

Day 210

Drop-Kicked

"I'm not talking to Charlotte ever again," Jaqi said, her face burning red. "She said she could keep a secret, but she told the whole school what I said. I took all my things out of our locker and moved in with Lucy. I left Charlottes's locker door hanging open. I hope someone steals her stuff."

God intended relationships to spin like a top, with everything in smooth balance. But it's obvious something went wrong. God made friendships and family, love and unselfishness, but instead we live with fights, cliques, divorce, racism, and hatred.

What happened?

Adam and Eve were the world's first friends. They were also the world's first enemies.

Read Genesis 3:1–13

What did Adam and Eve do wrong? What was the result?

God had put Adam and Eve in paradise, the Garden of Eden, and told them to take care of the Garden. He made one rule: "Don't eat fruit from the tree of the knowledge of good and evil." God said eating the fruit from this tree would cause them to die (Genesis 2:17). When the serpent said it would make them wise like God, they chose their own way rather than God's. They picked what they *thought* was good rather than trusting what God—who will never lie—had *said* was true.

By breaking God's command, Adam and Eve drop-kicked the top that God had set whirring in perfect balance. They threw the first family feud. Then, knowing they had sinned against God and each other, they were ashamed of themselves and covered up with fig leaves. Adam and Eve blamed everyone but themselves. Even worse, they fought against God. Their actions said, "God, we don't need you." They hid from God, who sent them away from his presence in the Garden (Genesis 3:21–24). The friendships between Adam and Eve and God now wobbled and bobbed like a sputtering top.

God, though, didn't give up on the people he had created for friendships. He determined to get the top spinning right again.

They hid from the Lord God among the trees of the garden.

Genesis 3:8

Day 211
Wipers

Snoozing in the dark in the backseat of the car, you hadn't bothered to open your eyes until the noise on the roof told you rain was bucketing down. Feeling the car slow down, you leaned forward from the backseat to try to see ahead. You could tell your dad was having a hard time seeing the road, but after a scary while you made it home.

Without windshield wipers and headlights, you wouldn't have made it home through the storm.

After Adam and Eve (and Noah and others at the start of the Bible), the human race crashed. Evil turned the world into a dark, stormy night. All people saw of God was a smeary blob—like the view through a rain-splattered windshield with broken wipers—and they had veered into a spiritual ditch without even knowing it. They were upside down with the gas pedal floored and the wheels whizzing, but they weren't getting anywhere.

Read Genesis 17:1–8

What did God promise Abraham?

Even though the human race had raced away from God, he came up with a plan to get us home safely to himself. But God didn't wait for people to come to him. Even at our worst, he made the first move to be our friend and to help us understand him again (Romans 5:8). Abraham's story marks the beginning of God working to show himself again to a race who had forgotten him.

So God "covenanted" (promised) to build a new nation—Israel—starting from the descendants of Abraham, a man who believed in and obeyed God. He promised to be the God of that people and to give them a new land to live in. He would rule them fairly, and they were to worship him and love one another.

Evil wasn't going away. God wouldn't blow away the storm and force everything to be good and right, because he wants people to have freedom to choose for or against him. But by showing himself to Abraham, God flipped on the wipers and headlights so that we could see him through the storm. He was starting to show us the one road back to himself.

I will establish my covenant as an everlasting covenant . . . to be your God.

Genesis 17:7

Day 212

Name That Car

Your head snaps as a convertible blows by. Sweet! What was it?

If you want to tell one car from the next, you study the shape of the hood, the outline of headlights and taillights, the slope of the roof. More than that, car brands have marks—logos, grille emblems, or similar names for different models. Once you know what to look for, all it takes is a glance to tell a Ford from a Chevy or a Porsche from a Ferrari.

Read Exodus 3:1–10

How can you know you've seen God?

If you saw a burning bush, would you figure it was God? Maybe. But if that's the only way you could recognize God, you might have to look a long time. After all, when was the last time you heard God's voice while herding sheep? When was the last time a shrub caught fire in your backyard?

God did reveal himself in a burning bush. Once. At the bush, however, he waved a hood ornament in our faces to show how he would later reveal himself *many* times—to his people in Israel, through Christ, even to you.

The first wave: Moses knew immediately who it was when God said that he was the God who loved Abraham. Remember? This is the God who founded a new people and acted in real ways. God repeated his promise to bring his people into a good land.

The second wave: God felt his people's suffering and rescued them from slavery. He even used the blood of a lamb painted over a door to protect his people from his judgment on the Egyptians (Exodus 12:21–30).

In time, Jesus would die a bloody death so that we could be spared from God's anger and freed from sin and become God's friends forever. But God prepared the way for that event. He didn't want us to wonder what car just cruised by or to mistake anyone else for the only true God. He wants us to recognize him when he comes to us.

> There the angel of the Lord appeared to him in flames of fire from within a bush. Moses saw that though the bush was on fire it did not burn up.
>
> *Exodus 3:2*

Day 213
Suited Up

Football would be tough to follow if both teams wore the same clothes. Uniforms show who's on which side. Besides that, uniforms and the insignia on them describe what the team is supposed to be like. The Chargers—faster than a crazed linebacker. The Giants—able to squash the opposition in a single down. The Packers—guys who grind up enemy players and shove them into sausage skins.

Uniforms also tell what a team is trying to do. A football player, you've probably noticed, doesn't wear a baseball uniform or running gear. A baseball glove isn't much good for catching footballs, and a tank top and shorts don't protect from tackles.

Read Exodus 20:1–17

What does God want his people to look like?

The uniform of God's team isn't something they wear, like nice Sunday clothes, Jesus pins, or Christian T-shirts. It's their thoughts, words, and actions toward God and toward one another. God owns the team and designs the uniform: He's the Lord their God. He's our Savior.

God gave ten commands that describe what his team looks like when we're totally devoted to him. The first few ensure everyone understands that God alone is God. Nothing is more all-important or trustworthy than him—not an old hunk of wood or stone, or modern idols like music, clothes, sports, grades, or popularity. Even God's name deserves respect. It's not something to say in anger or surprise but with awe. God's team also sets aside time to rest and worship him.

The other part of the uniform covers how players treat one another. Rebellion, murder, unfaithfulness, lying, or wanting stuff that belongs to someone else—those things dirty the uniform.

Jesus said that these commands and all the other do's and don'ts in the Bible could be summed up this way: Love God and love your neighbors (Matthew 22:35–39). That's the uniform that shows whose team we're on—and what game we're trying to win.

I am the Lord your God. . . . You shall have no other gods before me.

Exodus 20:2–3

Day 214
Build-Your-Own Burritos

"Why does it matter? It's a church." Paige was mad that her parents wouldn't let her go to church with Peyton, a Mormon friend. Paige didn't see any difference between her own church or Peyton's. "Besides, the kids are more into it there. Everyone talks. They don't just sit there, and they really know what they believe. Can't I go? Peyton's really nice."

Read Deuteronomy 12:1–7

Why is God so picky about what people believe?

Nice is nice, but it doesn't make beliefs true.

Even when the human race angered God, he never gave us the silent treatment. He never stomped to his room to pout, leaving us to wonder who he was, what he was thinking, or what he wanted from us. Just as you want people to understand and accept the real you, God doesn't want you to misunderstand him.

Think of it this way: God is no build-your-own burrito bar. You can't pick the guacamole but flick the onions, or choose the cheese but lose the beans, making God fit your taste. While you're free to build a burrito to *ooh* and *aah* over, it's not okay to make God into what you think is best—not on your own or with groups that create gods and religions different than what the true God has revealed in the Bible.

God wants you to know him exactly as he is.

God also determines the what, when, where, and how of following him. When it came to worship, for example, he told his people what to get rid of, where and how to build a temple, what to eat, and how to sacrifice animals—in so much detail that it makes you want to tell God to chill. Yet the rules helped God's people stand out from their neighbors and understand that God wants pure, obedient, disciplined followers.

And God made a big point: He's the one who determines what's important and what's not, what's right and what's wrong, what's real faith and what's fake.

He's in charge. He's God.

You must not worship the Lord your God in their way.

Deuteronomy 12:4

Day 215
In Living Color

Sammy's parents had warned their little guy to stay clear of the street. But nothing seemed to stop him from edging nearer and nearer the curb to watch traffic, or even from chasing balls into the street.

Then a car hit his dog. Sammy saw his pet flattened on the road, and he ran bawling into the house. After that, Sammy seldom forgot to look both ways. Blood taught Sammy what his parents' words could not. Now he understood the danger.

Just because God had told Israel how to act didn't mean they always obeyed. In fact, his people often did the exact opposite. Because they didn't trust God's intelligence or goodness, they didn't like his rules or believe his warnings. They treated their evil—their sin—like it didn't matter.

Read Leviticus 16:15–17, 20–22

How did God help his people understand the awfulness of sin?

God told his Old Testament people to offer sacrifices that would make peace for (or "atone" for) their sin. On behalf of the people, priests killed bulls, goats, and sheep and spread the animals' blood on special tables in the temple to display in living color the seriousness of sin: Death is the penalty for breaking God's commands (Genesis 2:17; Romans 6:23).

Once a year a special ritual, called the "Day of Atonement," showed the two sides to God's view of sin. First, *God judges our sin.* It isn't right for wrong-doing to go unpunished, so God required a goat be killed for the people's sins, instead of putting the people to death. Second, *God wants to forgive.* So he told the priests to send a second goat—a "scapegoat"—into the wilderness, symbolizing how God removes and forgets our guilt (Psalm 103:12). Year by year, these sacrifices reminded Israel of the horror of sin.

Sound awful? Disobeying God is even worse. Even the death of an animal couldn't fully show the badness or fix what was really wrong. An animal can't pay the penalty for anyone's sin, just as a lawbreaker today can't send a pet to take his place in the electric chair.

The penalty for human sin must be paid by a human being. Someone had to die for the sins of the human race for us to be friends with God again.

[The priest] shall then slaughter the goat for the sin offering for the people.

Leviticus 16:15

Day 216
Time Out

"You can't tell me what I can't do," John hissed at his principal. "My parents won't believe anything you say." Sure enough, when John's mom arrived she looked ready to slug Mr. Phillips.

"Mrs. Jones, you're well aware of the problems we've had with John," Mr. Phillips started. "This morning he hot-wired a custodian's utility cart and skidded around the basement of the school. Security cameras filmed everything."

"Not my Johnny!" John's mom shrieked.

"The custodians chased him to the elevator," Mr. Phillips continued.

"I didn't do it, Mom," John protested. "They just don't like me."

Mr. Phillips got to the point. "I'm sorry you don't want to admit what you did, John. But you've shown us over and over that you're not interested in being in class. You've endangered yourself and others. After a three-week suspension, you'll be transferred to another school."

Read Jeremiah 16:10–15

What does God do when his people won't stop doing wrong?

Like a parent who gives a child a time-out or a principal who dishes out detentions, God disciplines his people to teach them right from wrong—not to be mean, but to make sure they learn what's best for them.

As time passed, Israel became so rebellious that they couldn't see the wrong they were doing. They wanted anything and everything but God. The Lord's only option was to give them what they wanted. He allowed them to be dragged from the land he had given them to a distant country that followed other gods. Yet God promised to bring an end to the punishment they brought on themselves, just as he saved them from slavery in Egypt.

God disciplines his people not to demolish us but to shake us awake. God sets consequences for sin not because he hates us but because of his incredible love (Hebrews 12:5–6).

> See how all of you are following the stubbornness
> of your evil hearts instead of obeying me.
>
> *Jeremiah 16:12*

Day 217

The Heart of the Matter

It's the first day of school, and you've already heard the lecture four times. Now it's Mrs. Robinson's turn to read the class rules she's posted in the front of the room. As each rule is pronounced, your mind becomes more devious:

"Speak only when called upon." *Okay, I won't talk—at least not while she's looking. But notes—she didn't say anything about not passing notes.*

"Remain in your seats." *Ha! I'll do what I did last year. I'll forge a note from my doctor saying I have a bladder problem so I can leave whenever I want to.*

"And no food, drinks, gum, pets, weapons, hats, electronic games or gadgets, or drugs—over-the-counter or prescription—in class." *Anything else?! I'll show her—I won't bring my brain to class either.*

Read Jeremiah 31:31–34

How does God change the way we react to rules?

Knowing a rule doesn't guarantee you won't break it. Even if the rule is good and right, when someone posts a rule, we itch to rip it down. Rules, we feel, are made to be broken. One fact is certain: Rules aren't enough to rein us in. Something inside us needs to change.

From the giving of the Ten Commandments to the warnings of the prophets, God read rules to Israel for hundreds of years. Like rattling off rules at the beginning of a school year, it helped for a while. Then Israel returned to their normal behavior, or worse. After times of following God closely, the people went back to worshiping hunks of stone and hating one another.

Through the prophet Jeremiah, God promised a better time, when his people would no longer wander off. His people would get beyond plotting to escape rules and live under a new agreement with their God.

God promised that this new covenant would re-create a fresh, tight friendship that would begin with forgiveness and result in a new heart. God would write rules on the inside—on people's hearts, not on a screen or a stone tablet. Love would build from the inside out, so that his people would follow because their hearts were totally devoted to him.

> I will put my law in their minds and write it on their hearts.
> I will be their God, and they will be my people.
>
> Jeremiah 31:33

Day 218
The Ultimate Faceplant

It took you a while to figure out where you were. Miles back you had ditched your group to pound your mountain bike to the top of a remote bluff. There you howled like a caveman, flung your skid lid into the bushes—*who needs a helmet?*—and broke off the trail.

Riding close to the bluff's lip, you threaded downward through rocks and underbrush. But halfway down, your front tire caught and stopped. You flew over your handlebars, airborne until your face hit a tree. *Thud.*

Whamming the tree was good. It kept you from going over the cliff.

After you came to, you struggled to stand. Then you stumbled. Something was wrong with your leg.

Bike broken, you can't walk, and now it's getting dark. Not good.

Read Isaiah 42:1–9

How did God promise to help his hurting people?

If you were lying half-conscious in the middle of a wilderness, you wouldn't need a pamphlet on bike safety. Instructions for skidding down a steep, twisting single-track wouldn't do you much good either. You'd need a paramedic in a flight-for-life helicopter. Someone who could save your life.

By the end of the Old Testament, God's people and the rest of the human race had done the all-time end-over-end, a total faceplant. They were spiritually broken, imprisoned in spiritual darkness. God promised help. But not more rules or rituals. Instead, a Rescuer.

The Rescuer who God would send would heal the broken and give sight to the blind, setting people free from sin's guilt and power the same way God had saved his people from slavery in Egypt. His mission was to help not just Israel ("the people") but all of humanity ("the Gentiles").

God could have left the human race alone. After all, we made the mess all by ourselves, and God had done all he could for us (Isaiah 5:1–7). But God wouldn't give up. The Rescuer was his last-ditch effort to save us and bring us back to himself.

I will keep you and will make you to be a covenant for
the people and a light for the Gentiles. . . .

Isaiah 42:6

Day 219
Mummified

What a year! Six months post-faceplant you're still in a body cast. Being plastered and bandaged and tractioned like a mummy hasn't been a party, although it's given you time to binge-watch every episode of three dozen shows. What's made your experience incredibly worse, though, has been the weird behavior of your best friend.

She's sent everything ever made for a sick person—sappy sympathy cards, shiny balloons, stuffed animals, smelly flowers. But here's the strange part: It's been six months and she's never come to visit. You decide that your best friend is now an ex-friend when you get a postcard scribbled from Disneyland: *How are you? I am fine. Wish you were here.*

Read Luke 2:4–12

Why was Jesus born?

Prophecies and promises once fuzzy in the Old Testament quickly become clear in the New Testament. God's Son was on his way.

One second, the Son of God was ruling the universe with the Father and Holy Spirit in the dazzling brightness of heaven. The next second, he was born on earth—still totally God, but now also fully human. Angels proclaimed who he was: Savior, Messiah, Lord. He was called Emmanuel ("God with us") and Jesus ("the Lord saves") (Matthew 1:21–23). Think of it! God came to visit his creation. God knew that real friends don't just send sympathy cards. They come in person.

God saw that his critically injured world needed help. He didn't just gaze at us from a distance, where problems get lost in a haze. He came as a friend—up close and personal, right here.

And when he came to visit, he did more than sit in a chair next to our bed and pity us. By leaving his glory and coming to earth, it was like he too climbed into a body cast, so we could be certain he knows what we go through (Hebrews 4:14–16). He felt the same temptations and limitations we do. He felt the craziness of itching where you can't scratch, beneath a cast.

He didn't leave us suffering alone.

I bring you good news that will cause great joy for all the people. Today in the town of David a Savior has been born to you; he is the Messiah, the Lord.

Luke 2:10–11

Day 220
Jesus in Nap Land

Cameron's parents said he had to go to church this morning. *I wonder if Grandma and Grandpa know I haven't been to church since they visited last summer.* When they arrived, Cameron looked around. *Same as last time; no one my age.* By the middle of the service, the music had made him drowsy. Then the sermon threatened to push him over the edge into nap land. *I know my parents mean well, but this isn't for me.*

It's hard to know what a Christian your age should look like—or even whether it's possible to utter "young" and "Christian" in the same breath. Most kids, like Cameron, think going to church is buying a ticket to snoredom. It's slouching, snoozing, counting bricks. All 4,672 of them. One by one. By one. By one. Is that the best you can expect?

Or church may mean the opposite—messy games, riotous outings, running from ride to ride at amusement parks. The leaders gave up doing Bible studies because no one listens. Their goal is to entertain the kids and keep them from trashing the church. Is that all there is?

Read Luke 2:46–47

What was Jesus like at your age?

Jesus was the Son of God, but he was no abnormal, mutant teenager. He faced the same challenges you do, including the temptation to think that faith is only for parents and freaks (Hebrews 4:14–16). But he chased neither snoredom nor youth-group silliness. He chose growth.

The adults Jesus talked with didn't beg him to listen. Instead, he amazed them by asking hard questions and grappling with real answers. He prioritized learning at the temple, to the point that he didn't even notice his parents had left for home. The result? Jesus matured in a way that impressed both God and people.

You probably suspect that there's more to being young and Christian than sleeper sermons or youth-group lock-ins. Even if no one else your age is showing you what you can be, Jesus demonstrates what you're capable of. He's with you now to help you (John 15:5). Don't settle for anything less.

Everyone who heard him was amazed at his understanding and his answers.

Luke 2:47

Day 221

Upside-Down World

Pull out your school yearbook or a magazine and flip it upside down. Now stare into the eyes of all those upside-down faces.

After a while, foreheads become chins, and chins turn into pointy coneheads. Most girls have bushier beards than most guys. Kids are bald and bald men don't have beards.

Smiles look like frowns, and you can see down everyone's nose.

Notice anything else?

After a while, these grotesque, upside-down faces begin to look normal.

Read Matthew 5:1–12

How can Jesus' words be true when they seem wildly off the wall?

The world is like an upside-down yearbook. Things that should look bizarre start to look normal. Actions we should recognize as evil begin to look more than fine: Bullies take over the playground, cheaters pull good grades, and sleazy girls get cute guys. The rebels—instead of God's friends—look like the ones who are happy.

Jesus' teaching aimed to turn things right side up, to display how God sees the world. The people who show mercy (not bullies) will be happy, because God will show them kindness. Those who want to do right (not those looking to do wrong) should be happy, because God will satisfy them. The pure (not the impure or mean) will know God. Even if this world is upside down in the worst way—with people insulting you, hurting you, and lying behind your back—God's way is best. Sooner or later, he'll make things right side up.

Fortunately for your yearbook, you know that heads go up, feet go down. When you knock some sense into your head, right side up looks right once again.

The teachings of Jesus—the whole Bible, in fact—show what life looks like right side up (2 Timothy 3:16). They define what *normal* actually is. No confusion—up is up and down is down.

> Blessed are those who hunger and thirst for righteousness, for they will
> be filled. . . . blessed are the pure in heart, for they will see God.
>
> *Matthew 5:6, 8*

Day 222
This Man Is No Loser

As Sean floats past the girls scrunched against the gym wall at the school dance, he thinks he's a love potion in motion—that is, until the girls snarl at him and tell him to quit blocking their view of the real men. Yet even the girls feel a flash of pity for Sean when he trips over his shoelaces and he flops to the floor with an *ooof*. Then the captain of the football team hunks past, and the girls forget all about Sean.

God is looking for friends. But don't mistake God for the school loser, a guy desperate for a dance, someone to feel sorry for. He's more like a cosmic Prince Charming thundering through space on a war horse (Revelation 19:11–16). He's the only one who can save the princess. And there's nothing wrong with the Prince. It's his love who is frozen in a coma.

Read Luke 23:32–46

Why did Jesus die?

God put Adam and Eve in paradise and told them to live happily ever after with him as Lord and each other as friends. But Adam and Eve stopped serving God and others and began serving themselves. Their sin shattered their friendship with God.

So God started over. He created Israel as a new people and saved them from slavery. Yet despite God explaining his rules again and again, his people battled back, even when God reminded them that the penalty for their hatred toward him was death. All humanity rebelled, and all were sentenced to die (Romans 3:23).

God's Son suffered that sentence. At the cross, however, one of the thieves dying next to Jesus noticed something: Jesus hadn't done anything wrong. He wasn't being punished for *his* sins. He was being punished for *our* sins. An Old Testament prophecy explains: "But he was wounded for the wrong we did; he was crushed for the evil we did" (Isaiah 53:5 NCV).

God sent his Son to die for our sins because no one else could. Only Jesus was perfect and sinless, the only human being never deserving death, and the only one who could take our sins upon himself.

Jesus was no loser. He just loved us enough to come to die in our place.

But this man has done nothing wrong.

Luke 23:41

Day 223
Part of the Family

"So what do you think, Audrey?" The Sutton family and Audrey's social worker all turned and smiled at her. Audrey's smile lit up her face.

Until last year, Audrey's life had felt like a bad game of basketball. She was juggled between foster families like a loose ball thrown from team to team, slipping through fingers and skittering out-of-bounds. Things got better when she went to live with the Suttons, the first caring family she'd ever had.

Now she was about to *swish* through the hoop in a game-saving three-point long shot. The Suttons wanted to adopt her.

Read John 1:10–13

The "he" in the passage is Jesus. Who does God adopt into his family?

Most kids grow up with the parents who gave them birth, maybe with step-parents added in. Or they're adopted as babies. Either way, it's easy to take parents for granted—except when they divorce or die, or when you think they're mean and wish you could trade them in for a new set.

Kids adopted when they're older get a unique view of family life. They get a choice to accept or reject a set of parents, to join a family or not. In effect, they have to say to their new parents, "I need you. I'll accept your love. I want to be part of your family." They have to say yes to cement the relationship.

God promises to adopt all who say yes to him. Jesus' death and resurrection is God's offer to adopt you. And the offer is free, no strings attached. Our sins made us God's enemies, but Jesus' death made it possible for us to be his friends (Colossians 1:21–23).

Whether we've never been a part of God's family or have grown up taking our heavenly Father for granted, we need to say to God, "Because I've done wrong, I need you. I believe that Jesus died for my sins. I accept your forgiving love. I want to be your child." That's how you become a Christian. That's how you become one of his people.

In God's family, *everyone* is adopted. It's the only way in.

Yet to all who did receive [Jesus], to those who believed in his
name, he gave the right to become children of God.

John 1:12

Day 224
Is This for Real?

"You're so stupid! How can you believe that stuff?"

Maria invited Emil to a Friday night Bible study; she didn't expect him to attack her.

"Corpses don't come back to life."

"I know." Maria didn't know what else to say.

"Then how can you believe in Jesus? Why go to church at all? It's all fake. I'd rather go to Elena's party than your Bible study."

Emil was right—sort of. Without the Resurrection, Jesus would be just another dead person to read about and forget.

Read 1 Corinthians 15:1–8

What's so important about Jesus rising from the dead?

If we think Christ is stuck in a grave somewhere, our faith crumbles. The fact that Jesus rose is like the bottom piece in a stack of blocks. Pull it out, and everything crashes. The truth is, however, that it's harder to believe that Jesus *didn't* rise from the dead. After he'd been buried for three days, five hundred people saw Jesus alive—walking and talking—and his disciples risked death to spread that good news. There's no better explanation for the empty tomb than Jesus' rising from the dead. Jesus isn't a dead dude from history class. He is the risen Son of God, the world's Savior and Master.

The Resurrection is God's proof to us that Christ's death paid in full the penalty we deserved for our sins (Romans 4:25). Jesus' resurrection is also God's promise that he will raise *all* believers to eternal life. And when you know eternity will be a party for you, you won't feel so pulled to the wrong parties here on earth. Your faith will seem worthless if you think only about the grief you get now for being a Christian and not about the great stuff God has planned for later (1 Corinthians 15:19, 32).

But you don't have to wait for all the good stuff. God wants the friendships he has planned for eternity to start now.

> For what I received I passed on to you as of first importance: that
> Christ . . . was raised on the third day according to the Scriptures.
>
> *1 Corinthians 15:3–4*

Day 225
More Than a Party

Eric and Kora collapsed with a couple of cold sodas after a long, hot day of work. In a few days their short-term missions team would split up and return home.

"I can't go home," Eric complained. "My friends at home aren't like the team at all. They say they're Christians, but everything bad I've ever learned, I learned from them. People here are energized. They read their Bibles without being nagged. They try hard to be good to one another. Everyone wants to get closer to God."

"There's no one like that at home?"

"My parents are okay. But that's not the same. At school there's a few religious freaks. There *is* a church, though, that I've visited a couple of times. The kids seem better there."

"Maybe your parents will let you go to a Bible study there or something."

"Maybe. I just don't want to go backward. I'm going to miss this."

Read Acts 2:42–47

How did the first Christians grow together?

A baseball team doesn't result from a mass of players colliding in a field to toss gloves into the air, run, and slide in the outfield, or pitch and hit and spit at random. Players have to commit to the team and its goals, learn the game, and practice together.

You may have glimpsed at church or camp or on a retreat what can happen when Christians all live for God. The incredible friendship in Acts—what the Bible calls "fellowship"—doesn't happen by accident. You have to pursue it by joining a team and sticking together to pray, study, worship, share, and care together. No one rides the bench. Everyone plays.

The Christians around you might not be your first choices for teammates. You might dislike their clothes, music, hair, or humor. They may go to the wrong school. All of that is less important than the fact that you all belong to God's family. Fellowship isn't just good friends getting together to party. It's God's friends getting together to grow.

They devoted themselves to the apostles' teaching and to the fellowship,
to the breaking of bread and to prayer. Everyone was filled with awe.

Acts 2:42–43

Day 226
Keepers Weepers

You're walking with friends when you spot it. *Is that a . . . ?* A small piece of greenish-white paper by the curb waves in the breeze. *It's gotta be a piece of a magazine or something.* A few steps nearer. *Well . . . it might be.*

You get close and you're sure. *Jackpot!* Money just meant to be yours. What happens next? You don't announce your find to your friends. Instead, you artfully distract them. Slyly pulling coins from your pocket, you toss them behind you. Your friends hear an unmistakable *kerjink, kerjink* and whip around to search the road for the fallen coins. You dash to the cash, pick it up, and slip it into your pocket. Finders keepers.

Read Acts 1:1–8

Why not hog God all for yourself?

Before Jesus was taken up into heaven, he didn't just promise to text once in a while. He said he would stick with believers through his Spirit *living in us.* The Holy Spirit comforts and teaches us (John 14:16), enables us to obey God (Romans 8:11), and as Acts 1:8 says, gives us power to tell others about him.

Why tell others? Because God doesn't adopt anyone into his family to be an only child.

God wants a huge family, with people from all over the world (Revelation 5:9). He assigns us a crucial role in enlarging the family. We pass along to outsiders the same love and friendship God gives us as members of his family. We explain that Jesus died to fix their relationship with God, and we tell them how they can be adopted into the family.

If you're worried people might laugh at your faith, it's tempting to throw pennies to distract them from what you really possess—changing a conversation away from God, hiding the fact that you go to church, acting like whoever you're with. Yet meeting God as Savior and Lord is like unearthing a limitless, eternal treasure. You've found a Mount Everest of gold. Don't be stingy about sharing it with your friends.

> But you will receive power when the Holy Spirit comes on you; and you will be my witnesses in Jerusalem, and in all Judea and Samaria, and to the ends of the earth.
>
> *Acts 1:8*

Day 227
Babycakes

You don't need warning stickers to tell you not to drink drain cleaner. When you feed your face at school, no one brings you a booster seat and spoon-feeds you cafeteria goo. Your parents don't keep you on a stretchy leash at the mall, nor do they call a baby-sitter every time they leave you at home.

All of that would be weird. You started out as a baby, but you didn't stay that way. It would be just as strange to stay a spiritual baby.

Read Ephesians 4:11–16

How do Christians grow up?

You didn't get past diaper disasters and drool all by yourself. You won't grow up spiritually without other people either. And they won't grow without you.

Adults might think of you or your peers trying to help others grow—ministering to others—like you're newborns trying to run the hospital. But that isn't how God sees you. Through his Holy Spirit, he's given you gifts to help the body (the whole church, the believers that make up God's family all across the world).

You might not see yourself in the list of gifts in Ephesians (or in 1 Corinthians 12:7–11 or Romans 12:6–8). But here are a few more specific starters: God might have gifted you to work with younger kids, to use drama or music to tell people about Christ, or to teach from the Bible. You might be good at leading worship, serving food, encouraging friends, welcoming strangers, or building houses for the poor. You might be a role model for other students or even to older people at church. Having a gift doesn't mean you're the best at something, only that you do your best for God.

When all believers put their gifts into action, everyone knows God better and thinks, feels, and acts more like Jesus. When they don't, we're like babies bobbing on the raging seas, tossed to and fro by wrong values and ideas. You can guess the outcome of that—babies sink. You have to grow up to swim.

> Then we will no longer be infants, tossed back and forth by the waves.
> . . . Instead, speaking the truth in love, we will grow to become in every respect the mature body of him who is the head, that is, Christ.
>
> *Ephesians 4:14–15*

Day 228

Final Exam

Your English teacher smiles and claps her hands together. "Class, you all possess a *fa-a-abulous* thirst to learn." She says this so fabulously that you almost believe her. "Because you're mature enough to monitor your own work," she pauses and says the next part slowly, "you won't be graded this quarter. Isn't that *fa-a-abulous*?" She bobs her head up and down as if your brain-dead class couldn't answer even *that* question without help. "And as a further sign of our *fa-a-abulous* faith in you, we won't grade your behavior or report to your parents."

With that, half the class bolts. You decide to stick with it, but as weeks pass, you become bored. You can't tell if you're learning anything. Besides, class isn't fair. Classmates who never show up get the same credit you do. When you have a group project, no one else does any work. Then again, neither do you. But hey—at least you feel bad about it.

Read Matthew 25:31–41

How would you act if there were no heaven or hell?

Be honest. You wouldn't study for long in a class with no grades. When good isn't rewarded and bad isn't punished, you figure out quick enough that it doesn't matter what you do. So you do what you want, not what you should. You do what *feels* good, not what *is* good.

God promises that your friendship with him won't be a waste. One day—the Bible doesn't say exactly when—Jesus will come again, and everyone on earth will take a final exam with one question: *Were you God's friend?* Those who become God's friends through Jesus' death will stand before God without a flaw, totally forgiven (Colossians 1:22), and live eternally with God. Those who fail the test will be judged guilty and receive unending punishment (Matthew 25:46).

God says this final exam is simple to grade because his friends are easy to spot. Because they trust Jesus, they love the same way God loves, caring for the hungry, for strangers, for the needy, sick, and imprisoned. They're surprised they get a reward, since they know it was God's love, forgiveness, and power that changed them. God made them everything they are.

Come, you who are blessed by my Father; take your inheritance,
the kingdom prepared for you since the creation of the world.
Matthew 25:34

Day 229

Harpbeat

The line to get through the gate piled up behind two men clobbering each other with politeness: "You first." "No, you." "Really, I insist." "Thank you, but you first." It went on and on and on. *Whatever*, you tell yourself. After all, you have all of eternity to wait.

The unisex white robe you receive once inside is exactly like everyone else's—a slap to your individuality—though you can't complain about the spring-fresh fabric softener and lack of static cling. Getting a heavenly body is a bit better. You like the pearly white teeth and flawlessly clear skin, although getting hair like an evangelist caught you by surprise.

It took you a few centuries to figure out this was supposed to be heaven. All in all, it was probably hardest to get used to broccoli at every meal and a gazillion screens with nothing playing but religious talk shows.

Read Revelation 21:1–8

What will heaven really be like?

If you're anything close to normal, you can think of better things to do with your eternity than squat on a cloud and strum a harp. Fortunately, God has better stuff planned for us.

The good things we've had here will be like baby mush compared to the unending feast of heaven. What we've enjoyed of God's creation—music, nature, color, beauty—will be given to us in abundance, with boggling intensity. We can expect incredible surprises, because our dreams now are warped by sin. Whatever we find in heaven will totally satisfy.

Even better than the place will be the people. God's friends will live in his peace—no enemies, no popularity contests, no prejudice or jealousy, no ugly names or biting words. But the real life of this eternal party will be God himself. He'll live with us the way he's wanted to since he created this world—with no doubt, fear, or sin separating us from him. We'll begin to know God as well as he knows us, and celebrate him for giving us an eternity of friendship with himself and his people.

They will be his people, and God himself will be with them and be their God.

Revelation 21:3

Day 230
The Big Ditch

"Mom!" Erin howled. "You said I could pick my own clothes!"

"I'm not just going to watch you empty my purse," Erin's mom countered. Of course she couldn't just walk in and pay. She had to help pick everything—down to socks. Worse yet, Mom wouldn't dream of leaving Erin's dad and brothers at home. Erin's shopping trip had turned into family night at the mall.

For a while, Erin's family didn't notice her walking faster and faster, always at least twenty steps in front of them. No one, that is, until Erin's brother gave her away. "Why won't she walk with us?" he whined.

"What's wrong?" her dad bellowed. "Don't you want to be seen with us?"

Read Proverbs 6:20-22

Why does God stick us in families?

In the beginning is Dad and Mom. They bring a baby home from the hospital, maybe from a foster home. It's cute—love, marriage, baby carriage. But families are more than cute. There's no better place to teach a drooly new human how to grow up.

Deep down inside, you probably love your family. Some days you even like them. But growing up means you're in the process of leaving them.

That's where the problem starts. It's part of God's plan for you to have a family to guide you. But it's also part of God's plan for you to grow up, to learn to make your own choices, to live on your own—but most of all, to hang on to him and follow him for yourself. Your family has been there to care for you, but you're learning to care for yourself.

You're caught in the middle—you still depend on your family, but your family isn't always around. Already you have to fend for yourself with friends, with strangers, at school, out and about. You're not a baby anymore.

But your family isn't always so sure. And unless you want them to treat you like you're still stuck in a stroller, you need to figure out how to get along at home—and on your own.

My son, keep your father's commands and do
not forsake your mother's teaching.

Proverbs 6:20

Day 231
Squid Sauce

Marcus gags as he spoons a glop of creamed corn onto his plate. "Nate doesn't have to eat this stuff at his house," he moans. Marcus neglects to mention that he once ate Brussels sprouts in squid sauce at Nate's house—and liked it.

Dad glares. "You're being rude."

Marcus snaps. "I always have to do what you say!"

"You just need to eat what we cook," Dad responds calmly. "Unless, of course, you want to cook instead. You could always use your allowance to call for pizza."

Marcus slumps in his chair and stirs his creamed corn with his fork. *I always have to do what they say.*

Read Ephesians 6:1–3

How does it benefit you to "honor your father and mother"?

Being good to your parents doesn't just mean keeping your food reviews to yourself when you think supper is gross—although that's a start. It means even *more* than swallowing hard through what you know you're supposed to do. Honoring your parents means *respecting them* and *obeying them willingly*.

When Paul wrote this passage to the Ephesians, he repeated one of the Ten Commandments, the laws God had given his followers hundreds of years before. God was never dumb about how hard obeying can be. He didn't assume that parents are always right or worthy of respect. After all, God knew that the first parents he created—Adam and Eve—rebelled against him. Their home wasn't happy—one of their sons murdered the other (Genesis 3:1–4:16). Still, God clearly said how it's supposed to go: We're to obey our parents.

That's blunt. But God doesn't say that listening to your parents will merely steer you clear of unhealthy food and bad table manners. As you obey your parents, he promises to guard your life. Parents aren't God, but the Lord's caring hands reach out to you through them.

Honoring your parents is right. It's also smart.

"Honor your father and mother"–which is the first
commandment with a promise–"that it may go well with
you and that you may enjoy long life on the earth."

Ephesians 6:2–3

Day 232
Grounding Your Parents

"She'd be cute if it weren't for her ears," Allison's dad teased.

Allison's friends laughed. That just egged her dad on. "Did you know that when you call Allison you have to pick which ear you want to talk to? Her ears are so big they're in different area codes."

They all laughed again. Allison didn't. But Dad was on a roll. "We're thinking of taking up windsurfing," he grinned. "We won't need sails."

Why does he always have to joke about my ears?

Allison faked a smile and got up to refill her glass, then hid in the kitchen popping popcorn. She finally told her friends she had homework to do and exited to hide in her room. Allison wished her dad would shut up. Instead *she* did.

Read 1 Timothy 5:1

What can you do when your parents get way out of line?

God commands us to obey our parents. But his list of commands for parents is even longer. It's your parents' job to guide, discipline, and encourage you—to direct you without driving you crazy.

Sooner or later parents goof. They love you but don't know how to show it. Or they know what to do but do it imperfectly. They say hurtful things. They pile on rules and demands but don't raise a finger to help. They snoop too much and listen too little. They cut you down instead of building you up. And so the Bible warns parents not to push their kids to anger: "Do not nag your children. If you are too hard to please, they may want to stop trying" (Colossians 3:21 NCV).

You wish you could ground your parents—but you can't. It won't help to spit back or act up or scream at your parents—especially if you're explaining what God expects of them. But you can talk. Instead of backing off or sassing back, tell them how you feel and what you need. This is your chance to gently persuade them, to talk to them the way you want to be talked to—with respect.

Your parents can't change if they don't know what hurts or annoys you. If you don't learn to speak up, your only choice is to put up.

> Never speak harshly to an older man, but appeal to him
> respectfully as though he were your own father.
>
> *1 Timothy 5:1 NLT*

Day 233

Butting Heads

Tyler did well at school. But he didn't want to.

When his friends bragged about their bad grades—how low their quiz scores could go—Tyler plotted. For as long as he could remember, he had studied hard. He figured he deserved time off for good behavior. So he decided that at the start of the next semester he would slack off. He would show up for school but leave his brain at home.

For nine weeks, Tyler lounged like a sloth. Then mid-semester notices went home, and his parents discovered he was flunking math.

Pick Tyler's parents' most likely choice: (a) applaud his desire to fail and get him ready for life on the streets by letting him camp in a refrigerator box in the backyard, (b) feed his need to relax by jetting him to a lush South Pacific island, or (c) ground him until he's thirty or until his grades improve, whichever comes first.

Easy pick.

Read Proverbs 3:12

Why do your parents discipline you?

You know how it turns out when you butt heads with your parents. You act or think or feel one way. They want you to act or think or feel another way. They endeavor to restrain your outsides and reshape your insides.

So does their discipline ooze from an evil plot to ruin your life? Hebrews says it comes from a wish to make you the best you can be. You're hurting yourself, so your parents stop you. You're doing less than your best, so they push you to reach higher. You're committing wrong, so they help you do what's right. Parents may differ about how and when to step in, but they're programmed at the factory to do discipline.

Their care reflects *God's* care.

Discipline hurts. Training is work. No athlete enjoys every rule or instruction breathed by a coach. But a coach isn't a coach if he or she doesn't drill his team. And parents aren't parents if they don't train their kids.

The Lord disciplines those he loves, as a father the son he delights in.

Proverbs 3:12

Day 234

Horsing Around

"But you said I could go," Li protested.

Li's mom stood firm. "Li, if you had finished your chores, you could go. But you didn't. And so you can't."

"I did my chores. I mowed the lawn."

"You mowed down two new shrubs because you were in a hurry. Then you ran out of gas and left half of the backyard undone. Remember? And you didn't Weedwack."

"I'll get it done," Li seethed. "Can't I decide when I'll do it? You always treat me like I'm a little kid."

"Well, right now you're acting like one."

Read Psalm 32:9

When will your parents treat you like you're grown up?

Horses are beautiful, but they're no match for your brains. Horses don't read maps. They can't follow directions. When you want a horse to go somewhere unfamiliar, you put a bit in its mouth, hop on its back, and *steer.*

Sometimes your parents think they have to steer *you.*

Not long ago, you needed your parents to feed, wipe, burp, and bathe you. You learned to walk, but it took a long time before you could cross the street by yourself. You learned to talk, but it was quite a wait before you made much sense.

Changes came gradually. Trust built slowly. The point? You can't fake maturity. You can't pry control away. To get freedom, you have to prove yourself. Your parents may loosen the reins a bit if you conform on the outside—if you do what you're told. But you'll get even more freedom when your parents sense something good happening inside—when you *want* to do what's right. Playing the part of the perfect child isn't enough. Parents want to know you have a strong mind—good judgment. They need to see you have a pure heart—good character.

Your parents will always think of you as their baby. But if you don't act like one, you up the chance they won't treat you like one.

Do not be like the horse or the mule, which have no understanding but
must be controlled by bit and bridle or they will not come to you.

Psalm 32:9

Day 235
Real Family

Halfway through their youth group's winter retreat, Simon decided to show Miranda how much he liked her. He howled like a wolf as he roared down the icy sledding run—straight at Miranda. He hit. She flew. She body-slammed into the hard ground. What love.

Simon and Chelsea and some other friends carried a sore, dazed Miranda back to the chalet, propped her in front of a fireplace, and brought her pizza.

Late that evening around a blazing fire, Miranda bragged to the whole group about her shatterproof skull. She said her friends on the retreat were her real family. Friends were cool and home was horrible. Lots of kids nodded.

As Chelsea listened to other kids tell their stories and hint that *all* parents and brothers and sisters were awful, she felt like jumping up and yelling, "No! My family isn't like that!" Chelsea liked her family. Home was safe. Home was good. But she wondered if anyone would believe her.

Read Ephesians 4:29–5:2

How can a family be friends?

Some people assert that every family is a mess. Here's the truth: Some families get along most of the time. Many get along at least some of the time.

You might not live in one of those families. You may live with divorce, violence, or alcohol or drug abuse. Your parents may work too much. You might even have been hit or sexually abused—if that's you, find a counselor, pastor, or teacher to talk to.

Whatever kind of family you live in, you can still control how *you* act. It's easy to be nice to friends (Luke 6:31–35). But you no doubt let yourself do things to your parents and brothers and sisters you would never do to your friends.

It doesn't have to be that way. The apostle Paul says that the love and forgiveness God has for you is something you can pass on to the world around you—including your family. You don't have to sass, spew, or hit and turn your family into enemies. As far as it depends on you, you can be a friend (Romans 12:18). You aren't weird if you get along with your family. You're weird if you don't try.

Be kind and compassionate to one another, forgiving each other, just as in Christ God forgave you.

Ephesians 4:32

Day 236
Watch Your Head

Your eight-year-old body lies on an emergency-room gurney. You gaze up through a sterile white sheet at the bright lights above you. Through a slit in the sheet, a doctor sews your scalp back together. The doctor asks how you cracked your head open. Technically, *you* didn't. Your six-year-old brother did it for you. He rammed your head into the corner of a chimney.

"What kind of kid would do that?" the doctor squawks. You wonder too. You're no psychologist, but you think it maybe had something to do with what you did to him a month earlier. At your grandparents' farm, you swung open an old-fashioned garage door, caught your brother's mouth, and knocked out eight front teeth. *I should have said I was sorry. Nah. It was an accident. Did anyone* make *him put his mouth there? Besides, they were baby teeth. They were going to fall out anyway.*

Maybe he was mad about that.

Read Ephesians 4:26–27

What's the best way to keep your family cool?

You can't help but get hot living in a family. You live close, share chores, hog each other's space, and "borrow" each other's stuff. Living as a family always ignites strong feelings. That's normal.

The real problem is when you overheat.

Ephesians tells how to hose down the flames. "Don't let the sun go down while you're still angry" doesn't mean "Get even before it gets dark" or "Dish it out before dusk." It means this: Talk. Listen. Forgive. Forget. Before you go to bed. While problems are little. Before the flames flare up again.

Don't wait to fix things with your family. And don't forget that a few verses later Paul tells *how* you can get the guts to get over hurt: You can forgive others because God forgave us.

If you gash your hand, you don't wait days to clean it out and stitch it up. Ignore the wound for a while and you'll get a vicious infection. Take a year and it will kill off your arm. Wait a few years longer and it will eat away your head.

Do not let the sun go down while you are still angry,
and do not give the devil a foothold.

Ephesians 4:26–27

Day 237
Barf Once, Dine Twice

As Kara time-warps through the wormhole, her cheeks and the corners of her eyes and mouth all slide toward her ears, peeled back like a too-tight face-lift. Twenty-some years into the past, she jolts to a stop. Suddenly Kara is watching her mom's life in fast forward.

She sees her mom flirt. She smokes and is acting cool, laughs—drinks, drank, drunk. Kara waves her hand in the face of her teenage mom. Her mom is startled. Kara speaks before her mother can. "See, you had your fun!" Kara accuses. "Now I want mine."

The wormhole begins to unravel, pulling Kara back to her own time. "You're not seeing all of me," her mom calls out as Kara blasts away. "You're not seeing what I really thought and felt. You can't see the pain!"

Read Proverbs 26:11-12

Why do as your parents say—and not as they maybe did?

When you were little, your parents could say, "That's a stove. It's hot. It will burn you." You might have said, "No, it's not" and "No, it won't." But you were short enough that they had no problem putting you in your place to protect you.

Guess what? You're not small anymore. And your parents' ability to keep your hands away from flames is almost gone.

Still, you've mastered the stove lesson. Your parents probably don't have to beat you back to keep you from broiling your fingers for breakfast. Why? At some point, you decided your parents aren't completely stupid. Sometimes you don't know best.

Adults have all done things they regret. What seemed fun at the time—and what might sound fun to you—doesn't look so good to them now. Like a whopper sunburn, the damage didn't show up until later. But they still got burned. And maybe it caused a deadly case of cancer.

Your parents and other adults want you to learn from your mistakes—and from theirs. To do anything less is to be like a toddler too dumb to stay away from the stove—or like a dog that barfs once and eats twice. He goes back for seconds of what already made him sick, mistaking it for another meal.

As a dog returns to its vomit, so fools repeats their folly.

Proverbs 26:11

Day 238

Noseprints

An hour after your parents were supposed to pick you up at the movie theater, you're pressing your nose against a lobby window, staring into the distance, watching for their car. You sit down. You get up to look. You pace. You try every cell number you can think of. No answer. You pace some more.

Your friends are long gone. The ushers stare at you half-sorry, as if you're an orphan. Then you start to wonder if you are—if your parents are dead in a car crash somewhere. You push away that thought. *What could they be doing that's more important than picking me up?*

When they finally pull up, you crawl into the car and slam the door. Your parents can't wait to tell you about the deal they found on a new home entertainment system. They brag that it will shake the walls.

At the moment you're unimpressed.

Read Isaiah 49:13–16

How can you be sure God doesn't forget about you?

Some parents are messed up and hardly know who you are. Others have checked out, or they spend time on anything but their kids.

Most parents are just plain busy. Someone at home has to make money. Not only that, but you share your parents' attention with siblings, grandparents, and more. Parents have to sleep and eat and collapse like everyone else.

Sometimes the reasons parents are unavailable are understandable. Sometimes they aren't. Either way, you can feel lost and alone.

When God's people worried he didn't care about them, he reminded them that no mother could fail to care for her child. But even if she did, God wouldn't forget his people. Their names are written on his hands, just as you jot yourself reminders, only better. The forgotten are "engraved." *Very* noticeable. *Very* permanent.

When you feel your parents aren't there, God is. He hasn't, won't, and can't forget you.

> Can a mother forget the baby at her breast and have no compassion
> on the child she has borne? Though she may forget, I will not forget
> you! See, I have engraved you on the palms of my hands.
>
> *Isaiah 49:15–16*

Day 239
Up on the Rooftop

Alexandra's parents stood in the driveway studying the snow on their garage roof. "They're not footprints," her dad said. "It's just the wind."

"It's strange how the wind makes little marks from Alexandra's window to the edge of the roof closest to the fence," her mom observed, "and knocks the snow off that one spot on the fence—and makes more of the little marks from the fence to the driveway."

"Well, maybe they are footprints. But they're not hers," her dad argued. "I asked her. She said she doesn't sneak out."

"Then how in the world do you think they got there?"

"I don't know."

"So we're not going to do anything about her sneaking out?"

"No."

Read 1 Samuel 2:12–17, 22–25

Who loses when your parents play stupid?

Eli's sons did unbelievable evil—the equivalent of skimming cash from the offering plate and sexually abusing women in the church. They got away with sin at least in part because their father knew what they were doing and refused to correct them. He was too foolish to believe what others told him—or at least too slow to stop them, even when God warned him.

Some days you can outwit your parents with half your brain tied behind your back. But taking advantage of their temporary denseness is like jumping at a chance to drink toilet cleaner. If a two-year-old's parents didn't childproof their house, you wouldn't cheer—you'd feel sad and scared. Freedom from sane boundaries isn't freedom at all.

You're no two-year-old. Ultimately *you* are in charge of yourself. When you choose to do wrong, it hurts your parents. It hurts others. But it hurts *you* worst. If your parents won't stop you, stop yourself. If they won't confront you when you head out a window, find someone who will.

Eli and his sons, by the way, didn't live happily ever after. They ignored God and died for their sins (1 Samuel 4:11–18).

This sin of the young men was very great in the Lord's sight.

1 Samuel 2:17

Day 240
Start Your Engines

Michael's brother Jared had been away at college for almost three months before he made his first trip home at Thanksgiving. Long after their parents had gone to bed, Michael and Jared were still awake talking. What began as a conversation about disgusting cafeteria food, enormous classes, and stunning college women got serious.

"Mikey," Jared said, "there's a lot of drinking there. You can pray that I find friends. It's not like here. I had friends who didn't drink. Now I live in a dorm wing with twenty-nine other guys. Some of them party every night of the week."

"So what are you going to do?" asked his wise younger bro.

Jared mentioned starting at a Bible study on campus. "Good people there," he said. "Remember what Dad used to tell us when we were little and he went on business trips? 'Be strong and courageous, because God is with you.' That's helping me survive. So many things are new."

Read James 1:2–4

What do you need to be ready to survive on your own?

There's only one road to maturity, and it's full of potholes.

Imagine a world where your parents don't stand ready to whip out the wallet. Where you decide *when* you study or *if* you study—or *when* you go to bed or *if* you go to bed. Where you can choose your friends, your enemies, your roomies, and your church—or none of the above. Where you can bake brownies for breakfast or inhale tater tots three times a day. Where $5 is a fortune and you have to decide if your clothes will survive a spin in the washer if you mix colors with whites—or maybe you decide never to wash them at all.

Welcome to life on your own.

You'll grow up fast then. But you're getting ready now. How you spend the next few years determines whether you're prepared—or scared—to live on your own. Every rough spot in the road is a test. And every pothole you learn to steer around now is one less that can blow a tire later.

Let perseverance finish its work so that you may be
mature and complete, not lacking anything.

James 1:4

Day 241
Missing Mom and Dad

Your teammates nearly flatten you as they bound out of the locker room. Coach is sick, the assistant out of town. Practice canceled.

Your parents don't expect you home for two hours, so they'll never know what you're up to. You have total freedom to slip away—to go anywhere, to do anything. Big question: What to do?

Bigger question: Who are you when your parents aren't around?

You spend a lot of your existence out of your parents' sight. But you're never out of their minds. They relax only when they know where you're going, what you're doing, and when you'll be home—and even then they're nervous. When you step out of their sight, you leap into another dimension: the danger zone.

You probably don't see it that way. You don't bow and scrape and thank your parents for the privileges of freedom. You just bolt. Being off on your own is no big deal.

Think again. It is.

Read Luke 2:42–52

How did Jesus act when he misplaced his parents?

When Jesus' parents headed home from Jerusalem, they traveled with a caravan of relatives. They assumed he was somewhere among the group.

Wrong. After three days, Jesus no doubt had noticed Mary and Joseph had left without him. But Jesus didn't exactly worry himself sick or pull down a cell phone from heaven or issue an Amber Alert for his missing Mom and Dad. He sat tight. In a good place. Doing the right thing. Even when his parents weren't around.

Whenever you step out, it's *your* job to look after yourself—where you're going and what you're doing. Part of that job is keeping your parents informed so they don't implode from anxiety. The even bigger part is watching out for their number one concern: you.

None of us is brilliant enough to always make wise choices. None of us is upstanding enough to always make good choices. But God is both wise and good. And he's promised to lead the way (Proverbs 3:5–7).

> "Why were you searching for me?" he asked. "Didn't
> you know I had to be in my Father's house?"
>
> *Luke 2:49*

Once Upon a Tractor

Dane sat in the tractor's enclosed cab, howling with his music. But when he finished plowing the back forty of the family farm, he quieted down and watched the sun set over the rich black fields. *Maybe farming is okay.*

For his upcoming eighth-grade graduation, Dane had to give a speech describing what he would be doing ten years from now. He knew exactly what he was *supposed* to do—work the farm. But he had other ideas. He was afraid everyone would laugh if he shared his real dreams. Besides that, Dane didn't want a blowup like the one his sister and her husband set off when they left the farm. He'd never seen Dad so mad and hurt.

It's just a stupid speech. Maybe he could make up a story about being a farmer. *It's not really a lie. I can't talk about being a youth pastor. Dad will kill me.*

Read Psalm 139:13–16

Who decides the direction of your life?

Your parents hold you to a routine meant to make you an Olympic swimmer, but you dream of being an artist. You want to transplant brains, but your family tells you you're stupid. Your dad expects you to be his clone, but you'd sooner haul garbage. They laugh, they scold, and you get the message: Conform or face the consequences.

Conformity can be good. Without parental pressure, you would ditch school, make armpit noises during sermons, and whine like a baby when you don't get your way.

It would be wrong to obey your parents if they ever told you to do obvious evil (Acts 5:29). And it's wrong to disobey them when they tell you to do what's definitely right and good. But the solutions to some quarrels aren't that clear. Quiz yourself: Why do you want to break the mold? Who do you want to please?

Your goal isn't to unnerve your parents but to run to what God wants. You're to listen to parents faithfully. And you're to obey God completely—chasing hard what he designed you to be. Your parents gave you birth, but God made you. You're his.

All the days ordained for me were written in your
book before one of them came to be.

Psalm 139:16

Been There, Done That

"Discussion ended," Paul's dad announced. Paul crossed his arms and glared straight ahead.

As Paul's dad pulled the car to a stop at a red light, Paul undid his seat belt and climbed out of the car.

"What are you doing?" his dad demanded. "Where do you think you're going?"

"I can't stand this. I'll walk home—if I decide to come home." The traffic light turned green. Cars honked. Paul's dad flipped on his hazard lights. Angry cars sped around.

"You don't understand me!" Paul shouted above the traffic noise as he walked away. "You don't know what I face!"

Read Ecclesiastes 1:9–10

*How is your world different from what your
parents faced when they were your age?*

Your dad dies a quick digital death whenever he tries to play video games. You're mom can't work the Wi-Fi printer. And you're still giving them both lessons on the fundamentals of the home entertainment system.

So when your parents tell you how to dress, what to listen to, who to hang out with, where to go, and when to be home, you're less than confident they know what they're talking about.

It's true that your parents don't go to your school. But you can be sure that if they've lived on earth as long as you have, they understand at least a bit of your world.

Even if your parents actually *were* born in the Stone Age, they still understand trials and temptations. When they were young, they just got in trouble for different things—like not cleaning the cave, driving the dinosaur too fast, cutting their hair too short, or not piercing their nose.

There have always been opportunities to rebel. Everyone faces choices between right and wrong. There's nothing new under the sun.

There is nothing new under the sun. Is there anything of
which one can say, "Look! This is something new"?

Ecclesiastes 1:9–10

Day 244
You Ain't Seen Nothin'

"These are the happiest times of your life," people say.

You hope not. In fact, you wish you could blank out the past year. It started with you growing four inches so none of your clothes fit right. It finished with your orthodontist saying you had to get braces, unless you wanted teeth growing out of your nose. Merry Christmas.

Speaking of your face, it doesn't look like it used to. You stare in the mirror, worried that one eye is lower than the other. Maybe it's your head that's crooked. Then there's that beachball-sized zit on your chin.

If this is as good as life gets, then you dread what's ahead.

Read Psalm 84:1–7

How do you keep your life carefree—right here, right now?

Ancient Israelites went to the temple in Jerusalem—the "house of the Lord"—to feel close to God. But they never had an easy walk. To stand in the splendor of God's dwelling, they endured a trek of dust and scorching heat.

Growing up is a trudge through the desert. God wants to grow your body, brain, and heart to look like him (2 Corinthians 3:18). But you get annoyed. You face new challenges. You struggle with always-changing relationships.

You may like being your age. You may hate it. Either way, two things are true: It won't last long, and God helps you get along.

When the Israelites "set their hearts on pilgrimage," when they chose to live close to God, even the Valley of Baca (the valley of "weeping" or "thirst") became a well-watered oasis of palm trees and ponds. But the best was always yet to come. When the Israelites reached the temple, they couldn't imagine a better place to be.

When you're totally devoted to Jesus, a trudge through the desert becomes a stroll in the sun.

Blessed are those whose strength is in you, who have
set their hearts on pilgrimage. As they pass through the
Valley of Baca, they make it a place of springs.

Psalm 84:5–6

Day 245

Nightmare

You should stay away from the news before you go to bed. Or maybe all day long. You feel besieged near and far:

Double murder-suicide down the block. Opioid abuse. Kidnappers crawling through windows. Exploding healthcare costs. Political protests. Rampant racism, hatred, and division. Terrorists, drones, and soldiers in harm's way. Politicians bought by big business. Unchecked climate change. Drought, floods, and monster storms. Disappearing icecaps. Melting permafrost. Mass extinctions. Manmade earthquakes and assorted environmental catastrophes. Immigrant raids. Political oppression. Global flu epidemics. Ethnic genocide. Children starving.

Solutions?

Read Proverbs 2:12–22

What dangers in life are worth worrying about?

Humans have always faced obvious threats. From woolly mammoths to the risk of global thermonuclear war, history hasn't been kind. Life has definitely been worse at times, but the world could surely be better. You want a long and happy life—emphasis on "long" and "happy." You expect circumstances to improve as you age. But maybe you worry that by the time you grow up there won't be anything left to enjoy.

Danger can feel like it's on your doorstep. Media thrusts you into terror attacks, wars, murder investigations, and drug busts, and it drops dying children on your family room floor. You see the world's problems, but you might become blind to the dangers most likely to do *you* in.

Get this: *You* are the biggest threat to you. The main factor in the safety and success of your future is how well *you* follow God's pattern for life. A thug crawling in your window is probably less of a threat than *you* crawling out at night.

Growing up won't get easier. Yet when you trust in God, you're like a well-watered tree that doesn't fear heat (Jeremiah 17:8). You not only survive, but you thrive—and get a chance to fix your planet's problems.

Wisdom will save you from the ways of wicked men.

Proverbs 2:12

Day 246
Caleb Meets Chloe

"I guess we're lab partners. My name is Chloe."

I know who you are. Every guy in the grade thinks you're hot.

"Hi. I'm Caleb."

Everyone says you're easy and that your boyfriend deals drugs from his locker. I don't know if any of that's true. I just know you're the most beautiful girl I've ever seen.

One day during lab, Caleb needed Chloe's attention. When he tapped her arm, he swore he could feel her hotness. Her arm was the softest thing ever. And one time she grabbed his hand. "I'd be failing if it weren't for you" she said. "Thanks. You're really nice."

I'll be a corpse by morning if your boyfriend catches me looking twice at you. But I want a girlfriend just like you.

Read Proverbs 6:23–29

Why do we get lured into doing wrong?

The toughest temptations you face nearly always have a *face*.

You usually aren't tempted by a flea-infested drug dealer driving a beat-up car. The people who tempt you have *amazing* faces. They have *caring* faces. They laugh at your jokes. They think you're smart. They understand how you think and feel. They like spending time with you.

In order to stay friends, you're tempted to do whatever they want—throwing out God's commands by flipping out on the class dork, joining whatever's going on at the party, dating a non-Christian, blowing off school, or battling with your parents. The more you like those people, the more it feels right to do wrong.

But *amazing* isn't just having a flawless complexion or clothes or a car. And *caring* isn't about making you feel good when you do bad. Pimps care for prostitutes and people care for their dogs. That doesn't mean you want to be a hooker or a hound.

Who's truly amazing and caring? People who guide you into wisdom, watch out to protect you, and remind you to stay on God's paths.

> When you walk, they will guide you; when you sleep, they will watch over you; when you awake, they will speak to you. For this command is a lamp.
>
> Proverbs 6:22–23

Day 247

Grumpy Burgers

"It's so unfair," Ellie complained. "I was done with my exam. I was just looking at a text."

Caught using her phone during class, Ellie found out she had messed with the wrong teacher. Sure, Mr. Holeen said he had a "no cell phone" policy in class, but how was she supposed to know he was for real?

Ellie did her best to lay out her side of the story to her parents. They were key to ever seeing her phone again, because until they picked it up at the school office, she couldn't get it back. "I don't know why the rule applies to after a test," she argued. "I mean—I was just sitting there. Everyone else was still working and I was already done. What was I supposed to do—dig in my nose?"

Read Romans 13:1–2

Why do what people in charge say you should?

If a teacher goes demented, you could break every rule and work hard to make him or her look like a fool. Or if you work for a jerk, you could drop burgers on the floor, spit in the soda, and blow your nose in the fries. Or if a cop gets in your face, you might decide to mouth off.

Think twice. Teachers give grades. Bosses hire and fire. Police have handcuffs, tear gas, and jail cells. Acting up can land you on the wrong side of a principal, a boss, or the law.

Dodging the punishment that authorities dispense is only half of why the Bible says you should submit to them—why you should obey them. Here's the other half: Authority is God's idea. He designed a world where teachers have principals, bosses have bosses, police have chiefs . . . Without leaders containing us, we clobber each other.

Sometimes authorities go ballistic for bad reasons. But the only thing worse than living in a world where everyone seems to boss you around would be living in a world where no one does.

Consequently, whoever rebels against the authority is rebelling against what God has instituted, and those who do so will bring judgment on themselves.

Romans 13:2

Day 248
Time Warped

Fast forward your life twenty-five years.

You stare at a screen, reviewing your monthly family finances. It looked simpler when you were little and your parents took care of everything.

"Honey, I don't know how we can do this!" you vent. "The mortgage, the car payment, and Maya's orthodontist bill are due at the same time. We can either live on the street or go hungry. Which would you prefer?" For the next three hours, you and your spouse discuss new ways to increase income and cut expenses.

What's the moral of the story? That you should move into a tent, ride bikes, and throw back any children with crooked teeth?

Nope. It's that no one is going to pay your bills for you.

Read Proverbs 6:6–11

Why work hard?

Whenever you try to slide by, you always fall behind. You might think you can take shortcuts on your schoolwork, for example, flipping to the back of the book to find the right answer. But your brain will hit the fan when you take a test.

No, the Harvard admissions office won't ask how you did in eighth-grade math. But they'll be able to guess. What you study now prepares you for high school, which outfits you for even bigger moves. If you waste away in middle school, you'll be years behind students who decided not to dangle on the edge of disaster.

Whenever God gives you school, chores, or other jobs to do, learn to work *now* "with all your heart, as working for the Lord, not for human masters, since you know that you will receive an inheritance from the Lord as a reward. It is the Lord Christ you are serving" (Colossians 3:23–24).

It will be a while before you have to manage cars, kids, braces, bosses, bills, houses, or other adult-sized hassles.

But you're in training.

> Go to the ant, you sluggard; consider its ways and be wise! It has no
> commander, no overseer or ruler, yet it stores its provisions.
>
> *Proverbs 6:6–8*

Day 249
First Things First

"Anyone else do their homework?" Silence.

Jason is cool, Taylor thought. Her Sunday school teacher never blew up at the class, even though no one except two kids in the front row ever handed in the short homework he assigned each week.

Taylor shyly held up her paper. "Mine's done." She slumped in her seat. *I'm not a church nerd,* she reassured herself. *Then again, maybe I'm turning into one. Or maybe the nerds aren't so nerdy.* All Taylor knew for sure was that she felt better when she read her Bible and talked to God, like Jason taught in class.

Sadie interrogated her after class. "I can't believe you actually did the homework. What's wrong with you? Don't you have anything better to do?"

"I don't know. I've done the last few. I might as well turn them in."

Then it occurred to Taylor that maybe she wasn't the one with a problem. "Don't *you* ever think about God?" she asked Sadie.

Read Luke 10:38–42

What does Jesus say you need more than anything else?

You've seen the symptoms of terminal adulthood: sleepy reflexes, saggy clothes, not to mention petrification—brains as dense as rock—or putrefaction—moldy attitudes.

The middle part of *adult,* you note, is *dull.* No one wants that.

Mary—along with countless other women and men in the Bible—shows how to mature without getting musty. Her approach to stillness won't age you prematurely.

If you want to get to know a friend, there's no substitute for slowing down—chatting over coffee or lounging next to a glassy lake or flopping on your bed with your phone.

Jesus wants you to be like Mary, to slow down and spend time with him. By reading his Word—the Bible—you "sit at his feet" and hear *from* him. By praying—by telling him what you think and feel, what you like about him, asking for his help—you can talk *to* him.

It's one kind of sitting still that doesn't mean you're dull.

She had a sister called Mary, who sat at the Lord's feet listening to what he said.

Luke 10:39

Day 250
Don't Waste Yourself

Even if they didn't ask, Brandon made sure everyone knew what he wanted for Christmas: No socks or underwear. Just cash. *I should tell them to put the money they save on wrapping paper and bows into the card.* He built a spreadsheet of what he expected from each relative and friend. A card from Aunt Cynthia. *Cash!* Another from his grandparents. *Cash! Cash!* And another from his parents. *Cash! Cash! Cash!*

In the end, Brandon amassed more money than he dreamed, a tad more than the $309.50 he needed for a processor to supercharge his gaming system. But when he went online to order the chip, he got bushwhacked.

As Brandon mindlessly wandered to his favorite shopping site, he clicked to buy a bunch of items that had been sitting in his cart forever. While he was there, he prepaid for a game that wouldn't release for months. And when he finally got to his favorite computer store, his eye was caught by an LED upgrade that would light his gaming tower in lime green inside and out.

Brandon was broke. And not too bright.

Read Proverbs 2:6–11

What good is God's wisdom?

If you go shopping without a plan for what you're going to buy, you might as well wear a button that says, "Rob me. I'm stupid." Choose on the fly, and later you'll regret it. Get distracted, and you'll be disappointed. Better to think, pray, decide, and attack.

You also have something to spend even more valuable than a holiday hoard or a summer of cash from mowing lawns or sitting babies. God wants you to spend all of your time and talents well. And he'll show you how. If you cry out for understanding, he'll give you all you need: "wisdom" (an ability to live skillfully), "knowledge" (brain capacity and insight into right and wrong), and "discretion" (being able to pick rightly between two actions or ideas). He'll keep you from wasting your life.

For the Lord gives wisdom, and from his mouth come knowledge
and understanding. He holds victory in store for the upright,
he is a shield to those whose walk is blameless.

Proverbs 2:6–7

Day 251
Your Hand Looks Dead

The last time Lauren raised her hand in class, her science teacher said her hand resembled a corpse he had dissected in college. Lauren quickly slipped her hands under her desk. When everyone had finished roaring at Mr. Cooper's remark, she peeked at her hands, flip-flopping them in her lap. They looked plenty alive to her.

Mr. Cooper had been mean to Lauren ever since she missed a week of school because of the flu. She was still a test behind the rest of the class. Mr. Cooper was treating her like some sort of delinquent. *What's up with that? I'm trying my hardest.*

Now Lauren needed help again. She couldn't decide whether to risk another rude remark or to keep her mouth shut and maybe fail.

Read James 1:5

How does God respond when you ask for his help?

No one wants to look stupid, helpless, or needy. You would rather leave class bewildered than admit you're confused and ask a teacher to explain the same point for the sixth time. You would prefer to bake your phone in an oven than admit at a party that you don't know how to dance. And you would sooner get your head pounded inside out than let your mom fend off a bully on your behalf.

Admitting to yourself that you need help takes guts. Actually asking for it is even harder.

Once you get up the courage, you don't need people making you feel like a bonehead—as in a teacher who treats you like a moron to motivate you to work harder. Or like a parent who roughs you up to make you tough enough for the real world. Or like an employer who perpetually reminds employees who's boss.

God has the answers you need. If you need to know right from wrong, good from bad, or truth from lies, you can go to him.

But knowing God is available does you no good if you fear he'll mock you. God doesn't laugh. He doesn't scold. He simply helps.

If any of you lacks wisdom, you should ask God, who gives generously
to all without finding fault, and it will be given to him.

James 1:5

Day 252
Just in Case

Garrett could have asked God months ago for stamina to study for Ms. Weston's fearsome history class. He instead waited until the end of his twelve-minute end-of-the-semester cram session before finally whipping out a prayer: "God, I need a good grade tomorrow. You don't want me to flunk and develop poor self-esteem and spend my life sleeping under a bridge, so please work on Mrs. Weston so I get an A."

Garrett was sure God would come through for him.

Well, not totally sure. By the time Garrett sat down to the test the next day, he had devised a foolproof path to an A, in case God didn't deliver. He scribbled an encyclopedia of American history on his arm, and he arranged to sit within eyeball distance of the smartest kid in class. Between God, cheats, and the son of Einstein, Garrett had things covered.

Read James 1:6–8

Why is being "double-minded" so bad?

If you constantly ask a super smart friend for the best methods to study—then never crack a book—and constantly whine about failing—your friend would stop trying to help you. Likewise, God knows that unless you're ready to listen and obey, it's useless to show you truth.

The Lord enthusiastically gives wisdom to anyone who asks (James 1:5). He requires you to trust his desire and ability to answer your request. He expects you to rely on him enough that you act on the truth he shows you—following his directions, walking in his way, doing what he says.

Faith trusts. Doubt hatches backup plans. Double-mindedness picks and chooses. Part of you wants God's truth, part of you doesn't. Part of you wants to obey, part of you won't.

Don't assume you need flawless faith before God will answer you. No human being trusts perfectly. What God wants is a trust that shouts, "I do believe! Help me to believe more!" (Mark 9:24 NCV).

> The one who doubts is like a wave of the sea, blown and tossed by the wind. That person should not expect to receive anything from the Lord. Such a person is double-minded and unstable.
>
> *James 1:6–8*

Day 253
Wasted Waiting

Andrew inspected his list: Three months of clean socks and underwear. *Check.* Extra toothpaste. *Check.* Razor and shaving cream—just in case his facial hair decides to sprout. *Check, check.* Skip the deodorant. *Uncheck.* He'd be alone on his quest.

It would be a long wait. But he was ready.

Andrew set out early one Saturday at the start of summer vacation. He felt like he should climb a mountain, but he lived in the southern Minnesota flatlands. He did the best he could, finding a barely detectable three-foot rise in a nearby cornfield and setting up camp. After pitching his tent, he carefully arranged cornstalks to spell "HELP!" when seen from above.

Andrew wasn't hoping to be spotted by a search plane. He just wanted God to show up—in a lightning bolt, a jabbering bush, a vision, a dream. He didn't care. He just wanted God to speak and tell him the secret of life.

Finding God's truth isn't that hard.

Read Psalm 119:9–16

Where do you go to hear God's voice?

You can locate truth in lots of places. God lets you learn from parents whose heads aren't empty, and from grandparents and other older people whose lives have been full. He allows you to study history so you don't repeat others' mistakes, and science and the arts so you aren't ignorant about your world.

The Bible's truth is unique. It's "inspired by God" (literally "God-breathed," says 2 Timothy 3:16). The flawless truth of the Bible measures everything else that claims to be true—a web page, a friend's words, a musician's lyrics, an author's ideas, or a screenwriter's view of life. It points out when you're wrong and applauds when you're right.

God intends for you to read and apply the Bible along with other followers so you can better understand him, yourself, and your world. Scripture is God's perfect, reliable, written word. It's the first test of who to listen to.

I have hidden your word in my heart that I might not sin against you.

Psalm 119:11

Day 254

He Said He Loves Me

Wendy curled up on the living room couch to watch out the front window, jumping at every passing car and telling herself that the snowy weather made her father late. But he was already two hours overdue, and a dark thought crept into her head: *He's not coming.*

A few days earlier, Wendy had received a letter from her biological father apologizing for running out on her and her mom ten years before. He promised to spend time with his daughter. Wendy's mom warned her not to expect much from the man who had deserted them both, but Wendy's hopes ran wild. She was going to see her father!

Now she stared out the window, blinking away tears. *But he said he was sorry,* she told herself. *He said he loves me.*

Wendy fell asleep waiting for her father, who never showed up.

Read 1 Corinthians 13:1–3

What does love have to do with truth?

It's hard not to give the benefit of the doubt to a parent who wants to come home and make things right. Anytime *anyone* promises you something you really want, it's hard not to believe them.

But that can be wishful thinking. Words aren't trustworthy if they aren't backed up by deeds. In fact, from the Bible's point of view, truth is more than promises, bare facts, or correct thoughts. Truth is *lived.* Like 1 John 3:18 says, "Dear children, let's not merely say that we love each other; let us show the truth by our actions" (NLT).

Truth without love is like poison in a Popsicle: sweet but deadly.

Scripture is the first test of truth.

Love is the second. People worth trusting don't necessarily know the most. People you can count on combine knowledge with real-life love. You know they've grasped truth if they love as God loves.

You can't escape people whose words outdo their deeds, but you can avoid being duped by them. Beware: Without love, talk is worthless.

> If I have the gift of prophecy and can fathom all mysteries and
> all knowledge . . . but do not have love, I am nothing.
>
> *1 Corinthians 13:2*

Day 255
Barf Bag Parachute

You settle into your seat and the flight attendant begins to rattle off safety instructions. *Spare me,* you think. *Let's get this bird in the air.* Just as she starts, however, you interrupt and ask why the plane is taking off late.

"Oh," she says, "we had an itsy bit of trouble getting a door shut. I think I fixed it." *THE DOOR?* your head explodes. *YOU THINK YOU FIXED IT?!* A few days earlier the same kind of plane dropped a door midflight and sixteen passengers were sucked out of the plane.

You snap to focus as the flight attendant discusses sudden loss of cabin pressure and using your seat cushion as a flotation device. When she points to the plane's exits, you take that as a message from God. Better to deplane now than to fall from forty thousand feet using a barf bag as a parachute.

Read Matthew 7:15–20

How can you spot a good person?

When you walk onto a plane and buckle in, you assume the aircraft has been tested, retested, and reretested by an expert. Unfortunately, few people rigorously test spoken and written words for truthfulness. That's a problem: Anyone can fake truthfulness—for a while.

So Jesus suggests another test of truth. *Scripture* is your first test. *Love* is the second. *Consistency* is the third.

Jesus says people are like trees. What people produce over time reveals their real nature. An athlete's approach to life, for example, can seem fast and cool until he beats his wife. Time makes clear he's not what he seems to be. His skill on the field doesn't make him someone you want to act, talk, think, or smell like.

You wouldn't board a plane if you thought it would crash. Why take death-defying risks with who you listen to? A plane ride lasts a few hours. Who you listen to affects your whole life.

You're safest with people probably already around you—youth leaders, Christian friends, parents—people who have *proven* in word and deed that they love you like God does.

> By their fruit you will recognize them. . . . Every good tree
> bears good fruit, but a bad tree bears bad fruit.
>
> *Matthew 7:16–17*

Day 256

Stargazing

Like she did every morning, Isabelle refreshed her favorite website to discover what her day would hold. A stop to read her horoscope was an essential start to her day. Most days it read like the notes her mom tucked in her lunch box when she was little: *You'll have a happy day if you're nice to everyone.* But Isabelle relied on her 'scope to guide her life.

A speaker had told her youth group that horoscopes had dark spiritual connections—and were out of bounds for believers—but Isabelle kept reading them religiously. As long as they didn't make her foam at the mouth or cause her to kill her family with an ax, she didn't see anything wrong with them.

Read Acts 19:13–20

What did the early believers do about their occult habits?

You could make a lot of touchdowns if you hid the football in a sack, snuck out of bounds, climbed through the stands, and dashed into the end zone. Taking shortcuts to truth can be just as tempting. It might even work. But it wouldn't be wise if the stands were full of enemy fans ready to rip your head off.

God has ruled certain sources of knowledge a danger zone, out of bounds for his followers. The reason is obvious. As the seven sons of Sceva discovered, the evil spirits sitting in the stands are nothing to mess with.

Horoscopes—like divination (foretelling future events), witchcraft, spells, psychics, tarot cards, palm readers, contacting the dead, and channeling spirits—attempt to tap into special supernatural power and knowledge that's hidden ("occult") from normal human senses (Deuteronomy 18:10–12).

The early believers admitted to God that they had stepped way out of bounds, then trashed many millions of dollars of occult materials.

Some occult practices are simply scams. Others purport to call on dangerous spirits. What's most wrong with the occult is that it seeks advice and help from the wrong source. That's pointless. God never hides truth from his friends.

A number who had practiced sorcery brought their scrolls together
and burned them publicly. When they calculated the value of
the scrolls, the total came to fifty thousand drachmas.

Acts 19:19

Day 257
Get Smart

Justin dreaded seventh-grade gym class—mostly the part about having to use the locker room. After a few weeks, however, he decided the locker room wasn't so bad—especially when the topic turned to girls, which was most of the time.

Justin had never had a girlfriend, but he bragged like he had ample experience. The talk didn't stop in the locker room. Instead of just talking *about* girls, Justin started talking that way *to* girls. He told them what he wanted to do with them. The more he talked, the more he wanted. And the more he wanted, the more he tried to get it.

Read 1 Kings 11:1–11

Why did ultrawise Solomon lose his love for God?

News sites are packed with stories that make you think *I'm not that stupid.* Flood victims perched on housetops because they ignored rising waters. Charred bodies of people who didn't think a forest fire would reach them. Mangled drivers who laughed off the risk of alcohol.

They misjudged the danger. You would never do that. Or would you?

If anyone had a right to say, "I'm not that stupid," it was Solomon, the world's wisest man (1 Kings 3:12) and son of Israel's most godly king. Yet Solomon let his foreign wives draw him into religious practices he knew were wrong. He built temples to foreign gods who were worshiped through ritual prostitution and child sacrifice. Even Solomon wasn't smart enough to escape the lies, and he lost his love for God.

You're surrounded by lies that try to pull you from God and his ways: *Adults are stupid. Money equals happiness. Hip clothes and a perfect body make you supreme. Sex is a recreational sport without rules. Treating people like trash doesn't stink.*

You'd like to think you're wise enough to outwit those voices. But the instant you think you're that smart, you're likely to discover how stupid you can be (1 Corinthians 10:12).

As Solomon grew old, his wives turned his heart after other gods,
and his heart was not fully devoted to the Lord his God.

1 Kings 11:4

Day 258
Morning Breath

You wouldn't think of facing your friends without scrutinizing yourself in a mirror.

You inspect your hair (*is today a hat day?*).

You search for facial fuzz and contemplate whether to keep it or shave it (*or should I scream?*).

You conduct a pimple census (*should I wear a mask?*).

For the rest of the day, the image you see in the mirror each morning—good, bad, or utterly ugly—is seared in your brain.

Studying yourself in the mirror is a serious endeavor. And you do more than gawk. When your breath creates a green fog, you make friends with your toothbrush. When light glares off your shiny nose, you get chummy with the soap. When your hair looks like your mom's high-school graduation photo, you break out the heavy equipment and commence reconstruction.

Basically, you (1) see something and (2) do something.

Read James 1:22–25

How can you really pay attention to God's words?

Listening to God by reading the Bible is like peering into a mirror that perfectly reflects everything you need to see about yourself and your world—what's great, what's good, and what needs to go. God's Word lets you see yourself and everything else as God sees it: truthfully.

But *hearing* is only the first part of listening to God. *Doing* is the second part.

Paying attention to God means not just looking into the mirror of God's Word but responding to what you see. When you *listen* and *do* you will "be blessed." You'll find safety and freedom as you stay close to God.

God is the one Being in the universe who is totally powerful, totally smart, and totally loving. He's the One you can trust to be totally honest with you.

He's the One to listen to. And he's the One to obey.

Do not merely listen to the word, and so deceive yourselves. Do what it says.

James 1:22

Day 259
So Gullible

Mateo saw the four-foot stuffed animal hanging in the carnival booth and knew that dog would win him Amber's love, at least for a day. All he had to do was pop balloons with a BB gun. What could be easier?

"Everyone wins a prize!" hollered the woman in the booth. Mateo unwadded a dollar bill and picked up a gun. His older brother knuckled him on the head.

"You're so gullible," Daniel lectured. "It's a rip-off. Watch how you get three shots and then get a different gun. If you hit too many balloons, they give you a gun that doesn't shoot straight."

The woman running the game saw Daniel whispering and pointing. "Hey, kid!" she yelled as they wandered to other games. "You chicken? If you're so good, get over here and show everyone."

You don't need a knuckle on your noggin to know that carnies don't run their games purely for your enjoyment. They want your money. They'll say whatever it takes to get you to play their games. But it's an unnerving thought to realize a carnival isn't the only place you have to sort truth from lies.

Read Isaiah 59:1–11

What are people like when they don't listen to and obey God?

Truth can be hard to find. Peers fib behind your back and to your face. Stars inflate their images to sell you the goods. Politicians distort, deceive, and mislead. And if you hadn't noticed, even people trying hard to be honest make mistakes. There's one fact you can be sure of: People don't always tell the truth.

Without God changing our minds and words, people naturally follow the "ruler of the kingdom of the air" (Ephesians 2:2), who is the "father of lies" (John 8:44). Truth gets lost and life becomes a shadowy darkness, a confusing carnival, a sticky web of lies.

It would be nice to think you could accept as true anything that people tell you. But don't plunk down your money until you understand how the game is played.

Your lips have spoken falsely, and your tongue mutters wicked things.

Isaiah 59:3–4

Day 260

School Pictures

Alana opened her packet of school pictures and gasped. Her face looked as if she had smashed it against the camera.

Her friend Leah pretended to hide her own packet. Alana grabbed it, hoping someone else's picture looked just as bad.

"Promise not to laugh, okay?" Leah begged Alana. "I look awful!" *Um, okay.* Leah's photo shimmered like a model's, and Leah knew it.

Leah pulled out Alana's picture. "Ooooh. Alana, Alana," she said sadly. She handed the packet back. "I'm so sorry. Bad day, huh?"

That night in her room, Alana studied her face in a mirror, worried to death over one point: *Do I really look like my school picture?*

Read Psalm 139:23–24

How do you get an accurate picture of yourself?

If you actually looked like most school pictures, there would be a law forcing you to wear a paper sack over your head. And some days you might feel like you could be the president of Uglies Anonymous.

Yet if you can't trust a photograph, how do you discover what you really look like on the outside—or more importantly, on the inside?

People's opinions can be deadly accurate—or wildly wrong. An enemy won't paint a nice picture: "Whadja do to your hair?" or "Nobody likes you" or "You wuss." The portrait friends paint of you can be just the opposite—too pretty, like an airbrushed photo with all the imperfections gone: "It wasn't your fault at all" or "You're a perfect friend" or "Don't ever change."

The writer of Psalm 139 knew that only God sees us the way we really are. The Lord knows us inside and out, even better than we know ourselves. So the psalmist asked God to examine his words, attitudes, and actions and reveal the ugly parts of his life. Then God could make those parts better.

Being happy with yourself means being willing to let God beautify your unpretty parts. And that starts when you see yourself honestly.

Get it? It's God's view of you that's true.

Search me, God, and know my heart; test me and know my anxious thoughts.
See if there is any offensive way in me, and lead me in the way everlasting.

Psalm 139:23–24

Day 261

Doggy Bags

Sheena growled inside as she watched the kids at the park pick teams. *Those kids make me so mad! They always leave out the little ones.* When Sheena was small, she always got picked last. When she got bigger, she didn't get picked at all.

But now she could do something about it. What Sheena loved about her summer job was helping the shy and small kids who got stomped on like she always did. She still wasn't much good at playing ball—especially not with kids almost her age—but she did know how to take the bunch who felt unwelcome and start a whompin' good game of kickball.

Sheena glanced at the ball diamond, then at her little kickballers. They weren't leftovers. And neither was she.

Read 1 Corinthians 12:14–21

We're all different—is that good or bad?

You might think you're in a league by yourself. You're the first, the best, the greatest, the latest. *Too vain.* Or you might lean to the other extreme, thinking you're a wretched slime. *Too down.* But whatever you are, the world needs you.

Your body wouldn't work if every part were the same. An ear can't see. An eye can't hear. You don't walk on your hands or eat with your feet. No part is better. None is a spare.

God put his followers together as the "body of Christ." We can't function without the gifts God puts into each of us—gifts of serving, teaching, leading, encouraging, and a bundle of other abilities. (Ephesians 4:11–16 and Romans 12:3–8 list even more gifts.) And gifts don't work just in church. The qualities and skills God has built into you show up at home, school, when you work, and with friends.

Criticizing others because they lack your particular gifts is like lopping off your hand. And hiding who *you* are is like lashing your other hand behind your back. Neither is smart—unless you like to eat with your feet.

> Even so the body is not made up of one part but of many. Now if the foot should say, "Because I am not a hand, I do not belong to the body," it would not for that reason stop being part of the body.
>
> *1 Corinthians 12:14–15*

Day 262
Masterpiece

"Brandon! Jeremiah! Tadd! Andrew!" The cabin leader jarred his campers awake. "Get dressed, gentlemen. We're going for a hike." At first, the guys wondered why Jason was rousing them at three in the morning on the last night of camp. Then they worried about what he might have planned to retaliate for their obnoxiousness that week.

The four boys stumbled through the forest behind Jason until they stopped at the shore of a lake. The sky exploded with stars.

Jaws dropped. Jason told them to sit down and enjoy the view. It was the first time all week they shut up. "Makes you feel small, doesn't it?" Jason asked after a few minutes. The guys stayed quiet. Jason waited a bit before he said more. "God painted an incredible sky, didn't he? But it's nothing compared to what God made when he sculpted you. You guys need to stop acting like dirtballs. You're more than that."

Read Psalm 8:1–9

What does God think of the people he made?

Bragging is pointless. God owns everything. He's the best at everything. And we don't have anything good that didn't come from him (1 Corinthians 4:7). Compared to God, the Maker and Master of everything, we're practically mudsplats.

That, however, isn't how God thinks about us. He created us to reflect his greatness the way the moon—which makes no light of its own—reflects the light of the sun. He gave each of us the privilege of knowing and worshiping him, the God of the universe. He made us responsible for ruling our world.

Those aren't jobs you haphazardly give to mudsplats.

You probably look at things you craft—like an art class clay pot, a napkin holder from shop, a report for English—and think it's stupid. But God was incredibly pleased when he made you (Genesis 1:31).

You're so much more than mud. You're God's masterpiece.

When I consider your heavens, the work of your fingers, the moon and the stars, which you have set in place, what is man that you are mindful of him?

Psalm 8:3–4

Day 263
Nowhere to Hide

No. Your stomach knots. *They didn't.* You were only gone a minute. *No! They couldn't have.* They did. *They left without me!*

A bunch of your classmates had loaded up a bus for a day trip of skiing and snowboarding, but you figured you had time for a quick pit stop. By the time you came back out, the bus had left. No one missed you.

What do I do now? Call home and congratulate Dad and Mom on being the proud parents of a loser? Maybe there's a bumper sticker they can plaster on the van to tell everyone. No—wait. I could roll in the snow, hide in the bathroom for the next six hours, and come out just as they get back. If I play it right, I can make everyone believe I went with them. Yeah, that's the plan.

Read Psalm 139:1–10

Where can you go to hide from God when you feel dumb and dumpy?

God always has his eye on you.

Sometimes you don't want to be seen. You might be terrified that God knows everything, hears everything, and sees everything. You could feel like a criminal suspect—bugged, followed, and photographed by the FBI—or like a convict tracked by a radio anklet. Nowhere to hide.

It doesn't have to feel that way.

God knows trivial facts like the weight of the lint in your belly button and the progress of the pimple you're tracking. He knows enormous things like all your problems, hurts, and needs.

Because God knows you completely, he can guide you with perfect wisdom. Since God is everywhere, you can rest in his protection. He doesn't track your every move to catch you slipping up. He isn't making a list and checking it twice. God doesn't spy. He cares. He says that you matter, especially to him.

God is the best friend who's always at your side. He'll never drive off without you.

You know when I sit and when I rise; you perceive my thoughts from afar. You discern my going out and my lying down; you are familiar with all my ways.

Psalm 139:2–3

Day 264

Major Goal

Through thin walls, Brianna heard what she wasn't supposed to. The school counselor told her dad that if her work didn't improve by year end, she would have to repeat the grade.

Her dad's response burned. "I realize she's had problems," he apologized. "She's a little slow."

Slow? Brianna thought. *Why doesn't he just call me stupid?*

At that moment—and forevermore—Brianna pledged she would never again let anyone say she was dumb. She started studying with a flashlight under her blankets late at night and setting her alarm to wake her before the crack of dawn. She wanted the highest grade in every class. A 95 wasn't good enough; she hammered herself until she got 100.

Read John 4:34

What's your biggest goal?

You like being laughed at: *You wear that shirt all the time. Your answer was stupid. You waddle when you run. You sweat when you talk in front of class.*
Probably not.

Nothing is wrong with wanting to dress hipper, score higher, run faster, or speak sweeter. There's a problem, however, if you think that winning the race, making your hair look perfect, or never wearing the same outfit twice makes you valuable and acceptable to yourself, to others, or to God.

Jesus knew he had one overarching goal in life—and if he kept that purpose in mind, everything else would fall into place. His biggest aim was to do exactly what his Father wanted, his "will." Jesus set his heart on nothing else. And the same goes for us. Ranking anything above doing God's will is settling for less-than-best.

When you think that brains, bucks, and beauty are the most important things you could ever possess, you know you've caught an attitude that doesn't come from God.

> "My food," said Jesus, "is to do the will of him
> who sent me and to finish his work."
>
> John 4:34

Day 265
The Sign

A cold night rain pelts the rebel encampment outside the king's palace. You and a dozen other guerrillas warm yourselves near a fire, waiting for your only meal of the day—tree bark soup.

Endless fighting has made you tough and tired. Through the palace gates you see bright lights and hear what sounds like a party. A sign on the gate reads WELCOME. LEAVE YOUR WEAPONS OUTSIDE. ROYAL FEAST AT MIDNIGHT. COME EARLY.

"What do you think the sign means?" you wonder out loud.

"It's exactly what we're fighting against," your commander hisses. "The sign is a lie! The king hates us. Why else would we be out here starving?"

"So why aren't the gates locked?" you ask.

"It's a trick. A trap." Your commander's bitterness makes you shiver. "You're not starting to believe the sign, are you?" He swings his automatic rifle around and shreds the sign with a spray of bullets. "Tomorrow we'll try again to storm the palace."

Read Psalm 5:4–8

What does God think of people who rebel against him?

Some enemies of God are easy to spot, as though they carry bazookas. Their wrongdoing—their sin—is obvious: They fight, kill, lie, or steal. They disobey parents and disrespect siblings. They misuse sex. Or they harm their own bodies by drinking or abusing drugs.

Other people's sins are harder to see. Even people with nice outsides can have rotting insides, says the Bible. They might refuse to bow before God's greatness or applaud his absolute goodness. They hatch their life plans and mistrust God's wisdom. By that standard, God says that *all* human beings have messed up and sinned—including you. We're all rebels (Romans 3:23).

God can't stand evil. As rebels, we've been kicked out of the palace (Genesis 3:22–24). But God doesn't hate us. He wants us close. And it's our own fault if we stay out in the cold, because the King has created a way to welcome us back in.

Drop your weapons and come inside for the party.

You are not a God who is pleased with wickedness.

Psalm 5:4

Day 266
Inside the Palace

Outside the king's palace, you glance again at the sign your commander shot up during the night: *WELCOME. LEAVE YOUR WEAPONS OUTSIDE. ROYAL FEAST AT MIDNIGHT.* It's freshly painted, bullet holes gone. Then you see the king walking the palace gardens, tools in hand. *The king himself fixed the sign.*

You instantly know the rebels are wrong. You slip off your weapons and ammo and run through the gate toward the king.

Countless times you had been told that land mines would kill anyone who dared step inside the king's gate, but when you reach the king, you realize you haven't been blown apart.

"Welcome," the king says. "I've been waiting for you."

Read Colossians 1:21–23

How can you stop being a rebel against God?

You probably don't work hard to befriend your enemies. But that's what God has done. The human race wasn't interested in a truce, yet God flung open a gate back to himself through Jesus (Romans 5:8).

We've all made ourselves God's enemies, deserving death—total separation from God—for our sins (Romans 6:23). Yet God sent Jesus as the welcome sign, your invitation to enter the palace of King God, and the gate back to God. You accept that invitation by putting down your weapons, by admitting to him your sinfulness and need for his forgiveness: "God, you're King of the universe. I've rebelled against you by what I think, say, and do. My rebellion deserves death, but I know now that Christ died in my place."

That's how you bolt through the gate back to the King. That's the beginning of being a Christian.

That's when God welcomes you back in his palace as his son or daughter. You've been "reconciled," made friends again. Your friendship with God and other believers starts now—and lasts forever in heaven.

The sign is true. It's up to you to respond. Are you still a rebel, or have you gone through the gate and become a child of the King?

Once you were alienated from God and were enemies in your minds
because of your evil behavior. But now he has reconciled you.

Colossians 1:21–22

Day 267

At Our Ugliest

Dirk Stetson became quarterback when his coach discovered the seventh-grader didn't need an offensive line. He was three years ahead of his time—so much bigger and better than other boys in his grade that he could fend off opponents with one hand while bulleting rib-busting passes with the other.

Dirk was the most popular person in school. Boys imitated his uber-cool stance at the restroom mirror. Girls spun around quickly when he looked their way so he wouldn't catch them staring.

Then Dirk's face erupted into a million red, oozing acne volcanoes. Girls turned away. Boys found other friends. Coach replaced Dirk with someone bigger and better. And one day Dirk stopped looking in mirrors. Even he couldn't stand looking at himself.

Read Romans 5:6–8

What can you do to make God look away and stop loving you?

Sometimes you feel like a blemish the size of a third eye has erupted in the middle of your forehead. It's oozy and ugly, as big and bumpy as a golf ball. You think your flaw makes you unlovable.

That flaw might be something about how you look. Or how you do at school—or don't. It might be an embarrassing family situation. It might be a dark secret you hardly admit to yourself.

You might try to hide your flaws from yourself, your friends, and your family, but you can't hide anything from God. He sees everything. And he still likes you.

He proved it. Not many people would die for a religious snob (a "righteous" person in Romans 5:7 probably means someone with right actions but a cold heart). A few might give their life to save a good friend. No one would consider dying for a flawed, sinful person, yet God did. He proved his love for us by sending Christ to die for us when we were at our worst—not when we were perfect, but at "just the right time."

God doesn't look away. Ever.

> But God demonstrates his own love for us in this: While we were still sinners, Christ died for us.
>
> *Romans 5:8*

The Ultimate Coach

Bat in hand, the coach flips a baseball into the air and hammers it into right field. Robert backpedals as fast as he can, but the ball still soars over his head and hits the ground.

"GET IN HERE!" the coach bellows, and Robert runs to home plate. "Bobby, who's going to get the ball if you don't?"

"No one, sir."

"Give me fifty. NOW!" Robert does fifty push-ups and runs back to right field. He misses a short pop-up, and a grounder skips between his legs.

It isn't a great practice. Lots of mistakes. Lots of push-ups.

Read Romans 12:2

How does God change you for the better?

Every Christian starts out like a baseball player who needs to learn basic skills. In fact, we need a *lot* of help.

Minus Jesus, it's like our caps are pulled over our eyes. We stumble around, unable to track the ball of God's truth. We're out of shape—more or less dead—and we've forgotten how great it feels to jog along with God. We don't really understand the game we're playing—we think that evil will make us outrageously happy, and we crave worse and worse things more and more.

God says things have to change.

When we begin to follow Jesus, we put off evil thoughts and actions like a grimy, sweaty uniform and get dressed in a new life created by God. That process starts when we become Christians and keeps on until we reach heaven.

God isn't a mean coach waiting for you to mess up so he can scream at you, punish you with push-ups, or kick you off the team. He works by changing how you think and feel.

The Lord kindly remakes you from the inside out, teaching you that living in sin never makes you, him, or the rest of the world happy—at least not in the final score. When you know that, you can live for God out of love, not fear.

Do not conform to the pattern of this world, but be
transformed by the renewing of your mind.

Romans 12:2

Day 269

Superhero

When the bus pulled into the tiny border town, Tiffany flew down the steps. She and twenty other supercharged junior-highers were about to battle the forces of darkness, building houses as a way of demonstrating God's love.

Tiffany felt like a hero—that is, until her feet hit the ground. Then she didn't feel heroic at all. She wore jeans instead of blue tights, and a T-shirt instead of a cape. Her heart pounded with panic, and she remembered she couldn't speak the local language. One whiff reminded her she was far from home. What was she thinking when she signed up for this?

Read Ephesians 2:8–10

*What does God plan for you as his follower
once you've accepted his forgiveness?*

Sinning isn't like flicking a firecracker that pops on the ground. It's more like tossing a match at a truckload of dynamite, then sticking around to watch. You don't walk away in one piece. Some explosions—selfishness, jealousy, greed, anger—shred hearts one at a time. Others—adultery, abuse, prejudice, injustice, war, hunger—maim whole crowds.

Trusting in Jesus' death for you makes you God's son or daughter. His forgiveness—the unmerited favor the Bible calls "grace"—is a pure gift. But the King doesn't plan for his children to lounge around the palace.

God doesn't expect you to be a superhero; he wants you on the bomb squad.

Your first mission is to let God help you love the people you see every day, defusing explosives in your own life. Then you can start to befriend kids struggling at school, help older people in your neighborhood, teach kids at church, serve the city, or undertake a short-term mission trip. God will use you to prevent explosions and repair the damage sin has done to the world, by doing the things HE plans for you.

You don't need special orders from headquarters. All believers are on the bomb squad. Just look around and get started.

*For we are God's handiwork, created in Christ Jesus to do good
works, which God prepared in advance for us to do.*

Ephesians 2:10

Day 270

He Has Plans for You

"Mom, I want to go hiking with Callie's youth group," Jad said quietly. "It's right after school gets out. It's not very much money, and a bunch of people are going."

"You want to sign up for *what*?" Jad's mom mocked. "Let me see that." She grabbed the brochure. "How far? In the mountains?"

"I know," Jad pleaded. "I know it will be hard, but I want to try."

"Get that idea out of your head," her mom spat. "You'd die out there. Who will lug your body back?" When her mom finished laughing, she spewed some more. "This is just another one of your stupid ideas. You're useless. Maybe collapsing out in the woods would prove that to you. You'll *never* amount to anything."

Read Jeremiah 29:11

How great is your future when you know God?

It's awful to be declared worthless. Tossed away. After all, even trash gets recycled. Even garbage has a future.

If you face life with no hope, you'll seek relief however you can find it—even in ways that bury you alive. Or you'll seek revenge—to show everyone how bad you can be.

When God's people were at their lowest low—taken as prisoners to a faraway land—God gave hope to people who felt like forgotten garbage. They thought they were goners, but he had their future in mind. God had plans to make them flourish.

God doesn't promise to make you a bazillionaire or to snatch you from every sickness or hardship. Yet even when your faith in God leads to tough times, a future with God is worth anticipating. Proverbs 3:5–6 puts it like this: "Trust in the Lord with all your heart and lean not on your own understanding; in all your ways submit to him, and he will make your paths straight."

You don't have to wait for God to fix your life. Your bright future starts now if you hang tight with him.

"For I know the plans I have for you," declares the Lord, "plans to prosper you and not to harm you, plans to give you hope and a future."

Jeremiah 29:11

Day 271

She's a Cutie

"Don't look." Mitch nudges Ryan. "She's after you again."

Ryan knows exactly who "she" is. Grace. Wherever Ryan goes, Grace is there grinning.

"She wants to marry you," Mitch says. Ryan slugs him.

Grace does stare at Ryan a lot. Ryan doesn't mind. Until everyone starts saying Ryan likes Grace. *That* Ryan does mind. "You have to ditch her," Mitch warns. "No one else likes her, so you can't."

One day when Grace trails Ryan on his way to class, he yells. "Quit following me!" Grace runs away crying. She never looks at Ryan anymore.

But Ryan still thinks she's cute.

Read Proverbs 30:18–19

Why do guys and girls fall in total love?

The girls used to run from the boys. Now they chase them. Guys were afraid of girl germs. Now they want to get sick. True, some girls are still uninterested in boys, and some guys still wipe boogers on girls. That's okay. A trickle of curiosity sooner or later turns into a flood of fascination. How do you handle that?

Love is easy to appreciate but hard to understand. It's like the hottest restaurant around, yet where everyone picks a different dish. Why people are attracted to each other is as baffling as an eagle floating through the sky, a snake slithering across a rock, or a ship navigating the sea.

You never totally figure it out.

It's time to start trying. God has definite plans for how he wants you to get along.

God isn't shy. The Bible is blunt. And the parts of the Bible that talk about how girls and guys should get along weren't scribbled in by monks stuck at a monastery without a date. They were composed by the One who comprehends love best (1 John 4:7–8).

> There are four things that are too mysterious for me to understand:
> an eagle flying in the sky, a snake moving on a rock, a ship finding
> its way over the sea, and a man and a woman falling in love.
>
> *Proverbs 30:18–19 TEV*

Day 272

Teased at the Table

"Calvin and Cassie sitting in a tree, K-I-S-S-I-N-G. . . ." sasses Zoe across the supper table. "I saw them holding hands at the park."

"Dad, make her stop," Cassandra begs. "I said it nice. I didn't say 'Shut up!'"

"What's this?" her mother smirks as she pulls out a crumpled note. "I have some evidence I found in Cassie's jeans. It says here, 'I love you, Calvin.' With a big heart at the bottom. It sounds like *real* love to me."

Does she think this is cute? Cassandra wants to crawl under the table—and out the door and into the street and under a truck.

Cassandra can't say what she really feels: *I'm not a little kid, Mom. Don't make fun of me. Calvin is nice. I like him.* She can predict her mom's response. *"Sure you do, dear. That's so sweet."*

Read 1 Corinthians 13:4–8

What does true love look like?

You like someone. You decide to go together. You hold hands to show you're a thing. You share a locker. You text, message, and talk. People expect you to hang on each other. Some say you should hunt for tonsils with your tongues or go on a groping expedition.

So what is love? How do you show it? How do you accept it?

Love is partly *feelings*. But a relationship won't last on tingles. Love is partly *physical*. But most of that is out-of-bounds until you're married. Real love is more than either of those. *Love is a commitment in attitudes and actions to always do the best you can for another person.*

Still, it's harder to say what love *is* than what it looks like. People who love each other learn to be patient and kind. They avoid envy or boasting. They teach each other how to consider the other's feelings and to seek the other's best. They work to be slow to anger and to forget wrongs. People in real love obey God. They protect, trust, and stick by each other.

Sound grown-up? Not exactly. It's the way all people should always act. And it's something you can practice now (Galatians 5:22–23).

[Love] always protects, always trusts, always hopes,
always perseveres. Love never fails.

1 Corinthians 13:7–8

Day 273

Bag the Best

Liam did his best to get noticed.

In seventh grade, Liam was into rough-and-smelly. He slugged girls he liked. Or tickled them mercilessly. If she giggled—how could she help it?—he thought she wanted more. When nothing else worked, his mastery of body noises were sure to score him attention.

In eighth grade, Liam upped his sophistication. He quoted geometric proofs and chemical equations and obscure dates from Roman history. The girls thought he was dumb.

In ninth grade, Liam tried cool. He showered in his dad's cologne, undid the top three buttons on his shirt, hung a gold chain around his neck, and said "Hey, baby" a lot.

Liam smelled better, but he was more annoying than ever.

Read Proverbs 3:1–4

How can you get noticed by someone you like?

You won't sprain your brain coming up with *bad* ways to get attention.

If you're a guy: Challenge a girl to a belching contest. Ask a girl if she wants her makeup to look like that or if a dog licked her. Mess with her hair. Tell a dirty joke. Walk around with your neck muscles at maximum flex.

Or if you're a girl: Get mad at a guy and make him guess why. Send messages through friends. Wear a skirt so tight you have to hop. Be a tease. Tell a guy you want to be "just friends" and never speak to him again.

What's the alternative?

You might doubt God knows how to bag a boy or get a girl. So you worry. *If I do what's right, I'll be a nerd. If I'm nice, they won't notice me. If I act like myself, people won't like me. If I tell them I'm a Christian, they'll think I'm weird.*

So what exactly does God say to try? Act loving and reliable toward everyone. You'll be seen as secure, confident, loyal, and kind.

Sounds awful, doesn't it? Sounds like someone *you* would want to know. Others will too.

> Let love and faithfulness never leave you. . . . Then you will win
> favor and a good name in the sight of God and man.
>
> *Proverbs 3:3–4*

Day 274
Friends First

"We're not 'a thing,'" Aaron protested to his buddies. "We're friends."

Jessica was first-chair trumpet—and Aaron second, a total humiliation to his guyhood until she started helping him become a better player. He realized that it didn't matter to her who was better; he liked that she didn't let him beat her and take first chair just because he was a dude.

Jessica had some explaining to do with her friends too. *He hasn't asked you to go anywhere? He hasn't bought you anything? Why exactly do you hang out with him?*

Read 2 Corinthians 6:14

What's the most important part of a relationship?

When you're a prisoner to love, you worry about what you say, what you wear, how you look. If you talk to another guy or girl, your cellmate goes nuclear. When you get labeled "boyfriend" or "girlfriend," you're best pals with some people and an instant enemy to others. And a guy-girl relationship feels like prison for another reason: When your sentence is up, you're out. Your friendship usually ends.

Few people are worth that. When you look back, you wish you had a long-term friendship instead of a short-term relationship. So before you lock yourself up and eat the key, take a step back, go slow, and be friends first.

If you work at being friends instead of "going together," what's left?

Talking. Learning to not blab what the other person shares. Discovering hobbies. Surviving school together. Figuring out how to get along with his or her parents. Cheering at games and concerts and recitals. Befriending lots of people, not just one. And following Jesus together.

If friendship is the most important part of a guy-girl relationship, Jesus is the most important part of the most important part.

God says never to "yoke" yourself—to go together, date, marry, or even cling tight as best friends—to someone who doesn't follow Jesus. You'd be like animals clamped together that plow in different directions. Your goal is to find a friend plowing toward Jesus just as fast and hard as you.

Do not be yoked together with unbelievers. . . .

2 Corinthians 6:14

Day 275
Sheer Delight

As the guys wait to take their annual physical fitness test, Mark congratulates himself.

This is perfect. Mark knows he can do more pull-ups than any other guy in his gym class. Or in his grade. And a girls' class is testing just a few feet away. *Jayla can see me. She'll think I'm hot.*

"Mark!" the gym teacher hollers. "You're next!"

Tad, the class thug, boosts Mark up to the bar. "Hey, Markie-poo!" Tad snorts. "Jayla's watching. Make her proud."

Jayla turns when she hears her name. Mark does a pull-up. A second. A third. The guys begin to chant. "FOUR! FIVE! SIX! SEVEN!"

Then Tad yanks Mark's gym shorts.

Mark is finished.

Read Isaiah 62:1–5

Does God ever think you're a reject?

Guys don't usually dream of their wedding day, getting dressed in white from head to toe, stepping down the aisle to "Here Comes the Bride," their beauty inspiring *ooh*s and *aah*s.

Yet guys can still grasp the meaning of that image of a stunning bride. God cherishes you—girl or guy—as a groom cherishes his bride. No groom stands up front and says, "She's so ugly." No groom says, "Crawl back in the swamp and fix your face." No groom stands at the altar and offers to trade his bride for someone else in the congregation.

God's people—ancient Israel, called "Zion" and "Jerusalem" here—were labeled "lonely" and "unlovely" by their enemies. God renamed his people "the delightful one" and "my bride."

God promises that when you're mocked or dumped or rejected, you still reflect his blazing glory. You're "a royal diadem [crown] in the hand of your God." And he promises that one day everyone will see you the way he does.

> For the Lord will take delight in you. . . . As a bridegroom
> rejoices over his bride, so will your God rejoice over you.
>
> *Isaiah 62:4–5*

Day 276

Cut-Out Cuties

A voice whispers inside Jennica's head. *Shouldn't you be studying?*

"I suppose," Jennica replies. "This is so much more interesting."

What's more interesting than math?

"Cutting out cuties for my wall. Admiring their God-given qualities."

What do you think of boys when all they care about is how girls look?

"They're so shallow. I'm not like them."

How do you think the guys in the picture feel about you staring at them?

"They like to be looked at. I want them. And they're all mine."

Read 1 Thessalonians 4:1–8

What's it mean to "learn to control your own body"?

You don't run through a supermarket tasting all the soda and squeezing all the fruit. You don't open a box of cereal, take a bite, and spill the rest on the floor.

Anyone knows that isn't the proper way to shop. You don't take, taste, or waste what doesn't belong to you. The Thessalonians, however, thought that when it came to sex they could plunder the supermarket, try before they buy, and taste-test sexual love before marriage (called "fornication") or outside of marriage ("adultery").

The apostle Paul told them to control themselves. A footnote in many Bibles explains that he commanded them to "learn how to acquire a wife" in a way that pleases God. Anything less hurts not only the couple who disobeys God but their future spouses (what Paul calls "wronging a brother").

To hunt for hotties in a holy and honorable way means you don't treat anyone as an object (Job 31:1). You speak about them with respect (Ephesians 5:3–4). And you back off when guys want to grab and girls want to hold.

You probably don't realize you're already shopping for your future spouse. But you're maturing—which means you've been flung into the supermarket.

It's a long time until checkout. Be careful how you treat the merchandise.

It is God's will . . . that you should avoid sexual immorality.

1 Thessalonians 4:3

Day 277
Nuke-Powered Toaster

The sweetie you met on the second day of summer camp makes you sweat. You hold hands at the campfire, and as the fire crackles you sneak an arm around each other. You decide you want to burn lips at the basketball court, the camp's after-dark spot. You want your first real kiss. Really bad. Your new friend hesitates, then says no.

What do you do? Multiple choice: (a) beg the next nearest available person of the opposite sex to head with you to the basketball court, (b) pretend that kissing bores you, (c) hang out in the craft shop and make yourself a friendship bracelet, or (d) spit at the feet of the person who rejected you.

Read Hebrews 13:4

God made sex great. How great?

If you rate human experience from zero to ten, taking a bath with your hair dryer scores a definite zero—painful, scorching, and deadly. God intends sex to be *waaaaay* at the other end of the scale. But sex is only that great for those who wait.

To "honor the marriage bed" means to keep sexual intercourse—and the intense physical affection that precedes it—for marriage. Sex is God's wedding present to a man and a woman who seal their love through a public promise to stay together for life.

God's gift is hotter than a nuclear-powered toaster.

You don't want to power up now. Physical affection starts a chain reaction God designed to end in an awesome explosion. If you feed fuel to the reactor now—in your thoughts, by what you watch and hear, by heated kissing, by goals you set—you'll start a meltdown that you won't stop.

The fire and fallout from breaking God's command are deadly. You worry about *conception*—creating a baby. You risk *infection*. You face *rejection* when the relationship ends. And you won't escape *detection*. You strain your most important relationship—your friendship with God.

So what's your choice? Another option: (e) Ask yourself some questions: Why do you want to get to the basketball court? What game are you playing?

Don't try so hard for your first kiss. Wait for the best.

Marriage should be honored by all, and the marriage bed kept pure.

Hebrews 13:4

Day 278

Dental Floss

Paige dashes from the changing house to a boulder along the beach—one not quite big enough to hide behind. That rock is just like her new bikini—not big enough to hide behind.

Paige thinks: *I can't believe I bought this. Too late now.*

Guys think: *No need to hide. We think you look great!*

Girls think: *She's so sleazy. Why does she get all the attention? Maybe I should get one of those.*

Read 1 Timothy 2:9–10

Why bother to be modest?

When you were little, your parents taught you not to let people touch your "private parts." Big news: Your private parts are still private. You're the proud owner of a God-designed, getting-grown-up body.

Your goal is *not* to give away as much as you can (Proverbs 5:15–23).

Girls: When Paul wrote that women should "dress modestly," he wasn't picking on females. He knew that people—*especially* guys—are drawn in by what they see. When you choose a swimsuit spun from a single spool of dental floss—or some other skimpy item—it can be interpreted as an invitation. Dressing with "decency" doesn't mean you have to wear a trash bag. You should be proud of every bit of your body. Yet when you bait boys with your outward appearance, you're asking them to see less than the real you.

Guys: That's NO excuse for you to grab with your eyes or your hands what isn't yours. When you start to want what you can't have, stare somewhere else (Matthew 5:27–30). Shut the browser. Stop the clip. Hang up the phone. Run away. Beg your girlfriend to cover up or find yourself a new one.

Back to both of you: When you buy a present for a friend, you don't wrap it up and then kick it down the street or hurl it around a crowd. You would never hand a friend a torn and dirty gift. And a half-unwrapped present spoils the surprise.

You're the gift. Your spouse is the recipient. Take care of the present.

I also want the women to dress modestly, with decency and propriety.

1 Timothy 2:9

Day 279

Tale of an Idiot

So-called scientists in snazzy white lab coats brief you before the experiment. "We're testing a new brand of stay-fresh sandwich bags," they inform you. "We've constructed a bag big enough for you to crawl into. We'll zip you inside, lower you into a cage with a person-eating tiger, and watch what happens. Rest assured, *nothing* will happen. You'll be absolutely safe. Our new bag is totally airtight, so the tiger won't catch a whiff of you. And tigers won't eat what tigers can't smell.

"Any questions?" they ask.

Just one.

Are you that stupid? Would you trust your life to a sandwich bag?

Read Romans 16:17–20

What did Paul warn the Romans to watch out for?

They say you can trust your health and life to a condom. Ads, friends, media—even some doctors, teachers, pastors, and parents—advise you to accept less than God's best.

They're like the folks that the apostle Paul warned the Romans against. They don't want what's best for *you*. They want to drag you into their disobedience, into following evil appetites instead of God, who is totally wise (Psalm 139:1–12) and totally loving (Psalm 145:17–18).

Paul says to flee from people intent on feeding you to a tiger. But sometimes you don't even know you're being caged.

Remember God's best: God designed sex to be shared by a husband and wife in order to be physically and emotionally united (Genesis 2:22–24).

Run away from the rest: Sex isn't for people not married to each other. Sex isn't a party game. Sex isn't a dare or a contest to get as much as you can. The sex God invented isn't selfish, hurtful, violent, or controlling. Sex isn't something adults or teens do to children. Sex isn't a spectator event—a sport you ogle on a screen.

God's kind of sex is never dirty. It's private, but never something you have to keep secret or be embarrassed to talk about with an adult you trust.

Don't be stupid. Don't let anyone toss you to a tiger.

For such people are not serving our Lord Christ, but their own appetites.

Romans 16:18

Day 280

This Means War

"Where are you and Syd going after the game?" Austin's mom asks.

"I don't know." Austin shrugs. "We'll figure that out later."

Austin's parents look at each other. *Say something,* they both silently say.

"Are you planning to go out with anyone else?" Austin's dad tries to sound calm.

"I don't know yet."

"We don't think it's a good idea to leave your evening unplanned. We need to know where to find you," Austin's dad reasons. "Why don't you text her now and ask what she wants to do?"

Read James 4:7–10

*Why is it smart to plan—to decide ahead of time
what you're doing and where you're going?*

When you shoot rapids, you don't shut your eyes and trust your raft to go where it should. You declare war on the river. You jam your paddle into the water, pull and push, and work as a team with other rafters.

When parents ask your plans, they aren't prying into your privacy. They need to know you'll be okay. More than that, they want *you* to know where you're going. They don't want you to drift wherever currents drag you.

The same lesson fits all of life. You have to *choose* not to drift, and to fight to stay upright. And you need to decide while the river is calm, before hormones swamp you and peers push and spin your raft.

When you "submit to God," you give him your will. You say, "God, I want what *you* want." You declare that you're done drifting: You reject sin and get rid of "double-mindedness," halfhearted paddling.

Growing up is one of the wildest rivers you'll ever run. God wants you to decide *now* to follow him completely and, specifically, to stay pure sexually. You can write yourself a reminder of what you decide at the bottom of this page. Date it. Sign it. Celebrate it. And stick with it.

If you don't decide, then you've chosen to drift. And maybe drown.

Submit yourselves, then, to God.

James 4:7

Day 281

Their Pain, Your Gain

"You're going to do *what?* Why?"

"I don't know. I'm curious," your friend explains.

"Don't you think it's wrong?"

"I don't think God would let me get hurt. He wants me to fit in, doesn't he?"

How do I answer that one? Maybe she's right.

"Besides, I know my mom did it when she was my age. She's always saying it was wrong. That's easy for her to say. She had her fun. She wants to spoil mine."

Read 1 Corinthians 10:1–12

How can you avoid making stupid sexual mistakes?

As a friend climbs into a car, he slams his hand in the door.

One bash is an accident. Two bashes is a coincidence. Three bashes should make even a melonhead ponder what he's doing wrong. And after watching your friend's mishaps, how many times would you have to crush your own hand in a car door before deciding to be more careful?

The people of Israel had awesome experiences of God. He rescued them from slavery in Egypt and led them to freedom in a cloud and pillar of fire. He gave them Moses' leadership and fed them with bread from heaven. Yet they turned away from what they knew. They chased evil instead of the Lord, constructing fake gods (Exodus 32:1–6), sinning sexually (Numbers 25:1–9), and grumbling against their God (Numbers 21:4–6).

You don't have to experiment with sin to know that it's wrong—and that sooner or later it hurts. You can believe the Bible and your parents and other followers of Jesus when they say sin isn't the fun it's cracked up to be.

Experience is a great teacher—especially someone else's difficult education. You're smart to learn from your own mistakes. You're brilliant to learn from the blunders of others.

Their pain, your gain.

These things happened to them as examples and
were written down as warnings for us. . . .

1 Corinthians 10:11

Day 282

His Way or the Highway

"Would you rather stay here or run in with me?" your dad asks.

"Here. Just leave me the keys."

As soon as your dad is out of sight, you crawl over the driver's seat, move the mirrors, and tilt the wheel. Best of all, you get to pick the music. You settle back on your throne. It's a moment of paradise in your neighborhood Kwik-E-Mart parking lot.

In eight months and eleven days, you'll take revenge on the world for being held back in kindergarten, getting your driver's license a year before any of your friends. It's a long wait, but you need the time to convince your parents to dump the family roadster and procure a car more suitable to your style.

Driving is your dream. So where ya gonna go?

Read Psalm 16:11

What does God promise when you travel his road?

You've got transportation. What's your destination? You've got freedom. Where do you want to wind up?

Maybe you want to blast your car a hundred miles an hour down sketchy back roads. That *would* be a blast—if you like to soar ditchward.

God has a better path for you. Suppose you trust in the Lord with all your heart—unlike people who aren't sure what they want (James 4:8). You choose to not rely solely by your own brainpower. You seek guidance from the Ultimate Smart One. The result? God powers you far and fast.

Another way of looking at it: You acknowledge that compared to God, you're not all that wise. You respect his assessment of good and evil. You choose his path. Once again—the result? Going God's way does you good.

God's way isn't bump free. Sometimes God jars your attention to keep your eyes on his road, but it's still smoother than ramping off-road.

You can choose to drive in a ditch. But when you pick God's way over your way, you find the path of life.

> You have made known to me the path of life; you will fill me with joy in your presence, with eternal pleasures at your right hand.
>
> *Psalm 16:11*

Day 283
Slam the Lid

Every day after school, Colin climbs into a garbage dumpster. He's constantly amazed by what's there for his enjoyment. He wallows in moldy leftovers and slimes he can't identify. He rolls in trays of used kitty litter and bags full of dog poop. He peers at items gross beyond imagination. Who knew such riches were free and so easy to get?

Garbage is everywhere, all there for the taking. Oozing from the internet, TV, videos, music, computer games, magazines, books—it's a lot like row after row of open dumpsters, inviting you to dive in and play.

Some filth is obvious and out-of-bounds, the stuff that make you think, *I don't want my mother to see this.*

Other filth is the I-don't-think-it's-so-bad stuff we continue to wallow in even after its stench suffocates us. It's swimsuit issues and shows that warp our view of love and sex. Or the stars who make us feel subnormal if we don't imitate them. Or the glimpses of the rich and famous that give us an unscratchable itch to acquire more stuff. Or anything that makes rage and violence seem like good ways to get things done.

Notice that all these things seem to say life is happier with God out of the picture. When was the last time you saw God in a dumpster?

Read Philippians 4:8

What good stuff should you fill your mind with?

No sane person spends his day playing in a real dumpster. Lots of people, though, play in mental garbage. It takes courage to slam the dumpster lid shut and go play somewhere else—to surf to a better site, switch channels, pick a different group, watch a different video—but that's what the Bible urges you to do.

Anything good, praiseworthy, true, honorable, right, pure, beautiful, and respected—that's what should fill your mind. How much of what you read, listen to, and think about passes those tests? What are you doing to slam the lid shut on things that don't—and to focus on things that do?

Are you a dumpster diver? What can you do to shut the lid?

> Whatever is true . . . noble . . . right . . . pure . . . lovely . . . admirable—if
> anything is excellent or praiseworthy—think about such things.
>
> *Philippians 4:8*

Day 284

The Llamgod

Shhhh—listen to the drumbeat: BOOM-boom-boomp. BOOM-boom-boomp. Fiery lights flash from the Temple of the Llamgod as worshipers travel well-worn paths crisscrossing the dark jungle.

Worshipers devote hour after hour to accumulating sacrificial offerings before entering the temple gates. Without a sacrifice, worshipers can only wander the edges of the temple, adoring the temple riches from a distance and longing for the day they can charge into the frenzy at the Temple of the Llamgod. The temple attracts many young worshipers, who often slave in the kitchens of the Temple of the Llamgod to prepare lavish offerings.

At the temple, worshipers lay their offerings on ceremonial tables where their gifts are recorded. In return, worshipers receive gaudy trinkets as proof of their sacrifice. Oddly, the trinkets often lose their luster once removed from the temple grounds.

Read 1 Timothy 6:6–10, 17–19

What should you think about money?

If a mall belched smoke or had an idol in the food court, it would be easier to see that it can be a temple to a deceptive god: money.

A mall's lights, colors, music, food, friends, and fun stuff are like the market-places in Bible times where people mingled and Jesus and other kids no doubt played. That's good—not bad. And shopping online brings part of the excitement home 24/7 from anyplace on earth.

Shopping has a shadow side that can swallow you in darkness and devotion to a fake god. When spending controls your time, affection, and energy, then your favorite shopping venue has stolen your heart away from God and other important things. They've become a temple for enlarging your greed—not a place where you shop to meet your needs. Ask God to show you if the things you buy fit his best plans for you—or if you're standing in line to sacrifice to the Llamgod.

But if we have food and clothing, we will be content with that. Those who want to get rich fall into temptation and a trap and into many foolish and harmful desires that plunge people into ruin and destruction.

1 Timothy 6:8–9

Day 285
Mess Up Their Minds

Michael and Trevor had caddied through fourteen holes when they reached a dogleg where they had to walk a couple hundred yards ahead on the fairway to spot balls as they flew off the tee.

The boys despised the guys they were caddying for. When the men missed a shot, they cussed at Michael and Trevor. But Michael had a way to get even.

Michael and Trevor stepped behind some trees while they waited for their golfers to hit. Michael teed up half a dozen golf balls from his golfer's bag and pulled out a big wood to hit them.

"What are you doing?" Trevor whispered.

"What does it look like I'm doing?" Michael turned to concentrate on his stance. "I . . ." *whack* . . . "hate . . ." *whack* . . . "this . . ." *whack* . . . "guy . . ." *whack* . . . "so bad . . ." *whack whack*. The balls flew off. Then Michael pulled a spare pair of golf gloves out of the bag and tucked them into his pockets. "That's because he tips bad."

Read Romans 12:17–21

What do you do when you crave revenge?

If you crave revenge because you think it will put an end to a bad situation, think again. Revenge only prolongs and intensifies your fights. You slam. They slam. You have no choice but to slam slam. Or slam slam slam.

When someone mistreats you—hits you or pranks you or smears you behind your back—your first job is to "do what is right" and "live at peace with everyone." Rather than getting even, attempt to fix the situation peacefully. Granted, the person you battle might make peace impossible, but the problem shouldn't be you. And if things don't change, then leave revenge to God. He promises to repay wrong better than you ever can.

"The best way to get rid of an enemy," an old proverb says, "is to turn him into a friend." If you really want to mess up your enemies' minds, love them. It's your only real way of disarming them and getting them on your side.

"If your enemy is hungry, feed him; if he is thirsty, give him something to drink. In doing this, you will heap burning coals on his head." Do not be overcome by evil, but overcome evil with good.

Romans 12:20–21

Roadkill

There's a natural phenomenon you've no doubt studied in science class: When it's time for animals to die, they instinctively do an astonishing thing. Whether furry woodland creatures or city squirrels or bunnies, they mosey quietly to the side of a road, lie down, peacefully take their final breath, and expire.

Wrong. Those animals wander onto the road and get hit by cars. They're roadkill. Street pizza. Unhappy meals at the curbside café.

The sight of a cuddly animal on the side of a road is sickening.

Just as sad is seeing someone flattened by mean words.

Read Ephesians 4:29

How do you know what's okay to say and what's not?

Roadkill occurs when drivers move so fast that they hit an animal before they can stop. Words kill when we don't even bother to hit the brakes.

We often we speak without thinking—that's like not knowing where the brakes are. Other times, we rev our brains ahead of time, thinking up ugly things to say—that's as bad as gunning the engine.

If we deliberately ran down animals, a judge would yank our driver's license. Unfortunately, no one will intervene over our tongues and lips. We have to learn self-control. All we can do is practice being "quick to listen, slow to speak" (James 1:19).

So what words do you need to filter? Try these: Words should be helpful—not harmful—so if you say something negative, make sure it's to build up, not tear down. Laugh with people, not at them. Dirty jokes always disrespect someone. If you've got a problem, talk straight to the person, not behind his or her back. Complaining says you don't like what God has given you, so give thanks instead. Saying "God" as a cuss word means you don't take him seriously.

Just because an animal walks across the road doesn't mean you can hit it. Just because something is true doesn't mean you should say it. Slow down and let someone live.

Do not let any unwholesome talk come out of your mouths,
but only what is helpful for building others up according to
their needs, that it may benefit those who listen.

Ephesians 4:29

Day 287
It's Your Decision

Samantha felt uncomfortable wearing a long skirt to her first debate. Sam never wore "girl clothes." But it felt good to dress up. She got to fire the first shots in a debate over protecting endangered species.

Sam had tried running cross-country. She wheezed. She made cheerleading, but the girls just trailed boys they thought were cute and cut down girls who didn't make the squad. Sam didn't think there were any other Christians on the debate team, but the advisors and other students were fun. She got to stretch her brain. Finally she fit.

Once, after making an opposing team whimper and bawl, Sam was asked to join a weekend tournament team. Stupendous—until Sam realized she couldn't make church for a few months. Sam's mom said she had to make her own decision. Suddenly it was Sam who felt like crying.

Read 1 Corinthians 10:13

How do you choose to do right when you're all alone?

You don't live in a bubble. Your world, you might have noticed, isn't into Jesus. Your Christian friends aren't always around. And you aren't fitted with a pressurized space suit to keep you safe when you venture alone into spiritual nothingness.

Like every other follower of Jesus, you'll face temptations to do wrong. But temptation doesn't always hit you as scary offers of sex and drugs. The biggest enticement you'll likely face is this: to stop paying attention to God. To do well without him. To ease him out of your life. To be the fool who says, "There is no God" (Psalm 14:1). The fool doesn't mean that God doesn't exist. He means that God doesn't matter.

Often it's you, God, and a temptation—no one looking, no Jesus-loving friends to pull you back. In those moments, the decision to obey God—to make him matter—is yours alone.

God always provides a way to choose for him. You might not see it at first. But choosing to hunt for his way out is the first step in making him matter. And it's a big part of total devotion.

When you are tempted, he will also provide a way
out so that you can stand up under it.

1 Corinthians 10:13

Day 288
Keep-Away with the Truth

Dad eyeballs you and your sister as you all stare each other down at a family meeting called after he discovered empty beer bottles in the trash. Both of you deny knowing anything.

One of you is lying. Your dad has to figure out who.

Telling a lie is like playing keep-away with a friend's shoe. She needs her shoe, but you hide it behind your back or toss it over her head, around her side, anywhere out of reach. You're having fun, but after a while your friend stops laughing. She gets frustrated. Then angry. And with good reason. It's tough to limp along with only one shoe.

Read Ephesians 4:25

Why is telling the truth important?

Lies never seem so bad when you're the one telling them. After all, liars can escape consequences (if you lie to parents or teachers), skip studying (if you cheat on a test), or avoid paying (if you shoplift or steal songs or software).

But the supposed benefits of lying are themselves deceitful. When people play games with truth, the world grinds to a halt, even worse than when you can't get a shoe back. When people lie to you, you don't know what to believe or who to trust, who's a winner or who's a loser, who deserves a reward or who deserves punishment, what's good or what's bad, who your friends are or who wants to hurt you.

It's hard to live in a world full of liars. You badly need the shoe of truth, but it keeps flying over and around you, out of reach.

If you don't like being lied to, then don't lie to others. That's what Ephesians means when it says, "Speak truthfully . . . for we are all members of one body." Truth is so important to the way God designed the world to work that he lumps lying together with sins most people would never commit, like murder, sexual immorality, satanism, and idolatry (Revelation 22:15).

Playing keep-away with the truth never wins.

> Therefore each of you must put off falsehood and speak truthfully
> to his neighbor, for we are all members of one body.
>
> *Ephesians 4:25*

Day 289

Nerd Magnet

Sally knows she's a nerd magnet. Wherever she goes, she attracts a crowd of unusual people. Misfits and social outcasts somehow know Sally won't push them away like other people do. You might squirm a bit when you see someone like Sally act with uncompromising kindness to everyone she meets. She puts a disturbing question right in your face: Do you really have to be nice to everyone?

Read James 2:1–9

What's so awful about playing favorites?

What the Bible calls "favoritism" (better known as "playing favorites") is judging others and being nice or mean to them based on prejudgments and outward appearance.

The rich guy in James 2 got polite words and a cushy seat, while the poor man got gruff orders to sit on the floor or stand in the back. That was more than a social gaffe. James writes, "What are you doing? You are making some people more important than others, and with evil thoughts you are deciding that one person is better. . . . You are guilty of breaking God's law" (verses 4, 9 NCV).

It's foolish to favor the popular while insulting everyone else.

The world is like a tree. The branches up top are filled with the most popular, wealthy, athletic, best-looking, and best-dressed people, while everyone else clings to branches at the bottom. If you try to climb higher, the folks at the top beat you down. They drop sticks on your head, stomp on your fingers, and giggle when you slip and plummet toward the ground.

The people in the bottom branches are special to God. Because they have less wealth or popularity or looks, they're often more hungry for God.

People known as "nerds" can make great friends. They like you and let you be yourself. They're *people*. And they're not any weirder than you.

Jesus-like love respects everyone, not just a few favorites. Love recognizes the full equality of every person on earth.

It isn't wrong to show kindness to people who dazzle you, but it's sin if you don't show kindness to those who don't.

My brothers and sisters, believers in our glorious Lord
Jesus Christ must not show favoritism.

James 2:1

Day 290
Lumberjacks on Ice

You and your friend look like lumberjacks-turned-surfer-dudes as you trudge across the street in your flannel-and-baggies outfits, headed for the neighborhood hill.

With snowboards swung across your backs, you're a little slow. Too tardy for the guy in the Corvette waiting at a light to make a right turn. He honks. *What's his problem?* He guns the engine and edges forward. As he turns behind you he nicks your friend's board and breezes your leg.

You pick up a hunk of ice and wing it at the Vette's back end.

Chink! Ice connects with window. No damage. But driver skids to stop. Driver blasts into reverse. Grinds to stop. Exits car. Chases snowboarders. Cop sees chase. Cop prevents your premature deaths. *Good thing.* Cop totally blames hip kids. *Bad thing.*

You find yourself in the backseat of a police car on the way home. The officer phones ahead. Your parents greet you at the door.

Read Psalm 33:12–19

Why be honest?

You blew it. You were caught in the act. Or you're at least the prime suspect. What's your first reaction to being accused?

Your gut no doubt tells you to sneak away like a prisoner who sees the guards snoozing. Or you blow a hole in the prison wall by telling a bold, bald lie. Or you point out the evil done by someone else and cover your own bad acts, like raging about the psycho driver but subtracting from your story the ice hunk you flung.

None of us likes to be wrong. It's easy to tell less than the whole truth. But God wants to lead you into *worship* toward him, *humility* toward yourself, *love* toward others, *commitment* to do right in all circumstances, and *honesty* when you've sinned—it's what keeps you stuck tight with him. Dodging truth leaves you dead toward God (1 Thessalonians 2:10).

God knows the whole story—what you've done and what you haven't. If you ask him, he'll help you be honest with him, yourself, and other people. He'll help you admit your part—no more, no less.

From heaven the Lord looks down and sees all mankind.

Psalm 33:13

Day 291
One Good Reason

In the dirt. *Ball one*. Into the bleachers. *Ball two*. Monica launches the softball toward home plate, and it barely misses the batter's back. *Ball three*. Bekah—the batter—hurls back a threat: "One more pitch like that, girl, and I'll push the ball in one of your ears and make a new hole to pull it out." Monica again sends the ball toward home plate—this time brushing the back end of Bekah's ponytail. *Ball four*.

In an instant, Bekah is at the mound, and with one swift shove, Monica is flat on the ground, Bekah pinning her down, arm cocked to punch.

"Give me one good reason why I shouldn't pound you."

Unfortunately, Monica isn't a fast thinker.

Read Matthew 5:7

Why be merciful?

Jesus told a story about a servant who owed his master a monster stash of cash. When the servant heard that he, his wife, and his children were to be jailed for the debt, he begged for mercy. In response, the master forgave the servant's debt and set him free. One day, however, the forgiven servant bumped into a man who owed him a relatively tiny amount of money. When that man couldn't cough it up, the servant had him tossed in prison. The master, on hearing this, understandably went bonkers. He tossed his servant in prison after all.

"This," Jesus said, "is how my heavenly Father will treat each of you unless you forgive your brother or sister from your heart" (Matthew 18:35).

You—and I—and everyone else on the planet—have done wrong. Sinned. Piled up a big, unpaybackable bill. Jesus, however, paid the penalty—death—that God decreed for your debt of sin (Romans 6:23). And forgiveness of your sin is free for the asking. John wrote, "If we confess our sins, he is faithful and just and will forgive us our sins" (1 John 1:9).

That's God's good news. But it's ludicrous to say you believe in your need for forgiveness and have said "Yes!" to God's mercy if you can't show mercy to others.

You'll get back what you dish out.

Blessed are the merciful, for they will be shown mercy.

Matthew 5:7

Day 292

Chessheads

Luke dared join the chess club because it met so early before school that no one would ever know—no one who mattered, anyway. Each morning he ducked out of the club meetings a few minutes early, snuck out the school's back entrance, and strode back in the front door. Perfect—until Ms. Kalu, the chess club sponsor, decided to take the club to after-school tournaments. Problem? That's when Luke played on the school soccer team.

The soccer team was good. They knew it. And next to soccer, their favorite sport was kicking kids they didn't like—like anyone in the chess club. When Luke was with his soccer friends, he set the team record for rude remarks about the chessheads.

And then one day after school, two buses sat in the school driveway, both full of people hanging out the windows screaming at each other, both waiting for Luke to board.

Read Proverbs 6:12–14

What price do you pay when you change to fit your surroundings?

Before you go to battle in the desert, you slip into sand-colored clothes and coil a rubber rattlesnake around your head. If you fight in the Arctic, you dress in blizzard white and hang icicles from your nose. And for combat in the jungle, you wear green and black fatigues complemented by face paint and twigs in your hair. It's simple survival.

If camouflage is good for the Marines, it's good for you, right?

You'll change a lot more than your clothes if your only social survival strategy is doing whatever it takes to fit . . . to belong . . . to blend in. You pretend to like stuff you hate and detest stuff you love. You talk behind people's backs and out of both sides of your mouth. You get talked *into* and *out of*. And you devour anyone you think resides lower on the food chain. With winks, nods, and inside jokes, you're two-faced. Deceitful. A fraud.

At least two people know the truth. You. And God. When you hide the real you, no one can mock you. Nor can anyone truly like you.

A troublemaker and villain, who goes about with a corrupt mouth . . .
who plots evil with deceit in his heart—he always stirs up conflict.

Proverbs 6:12, 14

Butchered Haircuts

"I guess it means that if I'm going to tell people I follow Jesus, I should act like it," Mark told his youth group. Toward the end of the semester, Mark cut a class he hated. His teacher found out and reminded Mark that earlier in the year he had protested having to read a book that seemed anti-Christian. "I really blew it," Mark said. "Mr. Wallace called me a hypocrite to my face, and he's totally right. I can't stand up for Jesus one day and act as if I don't know him the next."

Ironic. Mark didn't respect someone in authority, and it was that same person who pointed out an inconsistency in his life, a place where he needed to grow up spiritually and get tighter with Jesus.

Read Romans 13:3–4

What good is authority?

The apostle Paul bluntly says that those who rebel against earthly authority in fact rebel against God—and that God will judge them. He also explains why.

Paul doesn't claim that parents, teachers, coaches, police, bosses, pastors, youth group leaders, and other authorities are perfect or their judgments are flawless. He does say that God uses authorities to help you, and because of that, he expects you to obey them.

God gives authorities power over you to keep you in line and to shape your character—even the police officer who pulls you over for speeding, the coach who benches you for sassing back, or the teacher who gives you a bad grade when you don't study. They teach you to respect others' rights, to work as a team, and to discipline yourself.

Submitting to authority hurts, but it produces results. Hebrews 12:11 says that "no discipline seems pleasant at the time, but painful. Later on, however, it produces a harvest of righteousness and peace for those who have been trained by it."

Do you want to be free from fear of the one in authority?
Then do what is right and you will be commended. For the
one in authority is God's servant for your good.

Romans 13:3–4

Day 294
Mother's Day

With his mouth full of food, Isaac outlined his afternoon plans. His mom glared at him coldly. "Aren't you forgetting something? Shouldn't we do something *I* want to do?"

"How come?" Isaac asked and kept eating the lunch his mom had fixed.

"Here's a clue. It's Mother's Day today. You haven't even said 'Happy Mother's Day.'"

"Does that mean I can't go to a movie with my friends this afternoon?"

Isaac's mom gave up. "Fine. Forget about me. Go do what you want."

At supper, Isaac flung a small bag into his mom's lap. "Here's your present. Happy Mother's Day." His mom pulled out the unwrapped present. It was a black coffee mug that read, *I'M NOT FAT. I'M JUST SHORT FOR MY WEIGHT.*

Isaac grinned. "Funny, huh?" Mom wasn't laughing. Isaac backpedaled. "All the other ones said stuff like 'I love you.' What did you expect?"

Read Exodus 20:12

Why should you honor your parents?

Honoring your parents means more than being nice to them on parental holidays. It means respecting, communicating with, and obeying them all day, every day. It means treating them the way you hope to be treated. Your parents deserve honor for giving you life and caring for you.

You might not be impressed by their parenting skills. At times, you may even wonder why they gave you life. But God doesn't instruct you to listen to and obey only parents you think deserve respect.

God told his Old Testament people that he would give them an incredible place to live, the "promised land." He said that by obeying his commands, they would live long and prosper. His presence and care would be part of their daily lives. God specifically promised to bless those who trusted *him* to guide them and shape them *through* their parents—even though parents aren't perfect. And the same principle works now.

Honor your father and your mother, so that you may live
long in the land the Lord your God is giving you.

Exodus 20:12

Day 295

Almost Human

Bad timing. You exit a store and right in your face is the school librarian. Earlier today you made her nostrils flare. Your latest little game is to ever-so-slowly tip your chair onto its back legs until she yells to put it down. Today you made her so furious she almost knocked you off your chair herself. And now there's nowhere to run—she's spotted you.

She's holding hands with some guy. *A husband? The monster's married?* And two girls are with them. *Daughters? She's reproduced?* You imagine her daughters as freaks bred to inflict pain on another generation of students. Then you blink. They're about your age, and they look normal enough.

"Hi!" the monster waves. *Strange—she sounds friendly.* She introduces her family and then pulls you aside. She says she hopes she hasn't been too hard on you. She doesn't want you to get hurt, and she explains that the custodians are always getting after her for broken chairs.

As she walks away with her family, the library lady looks a little different to you. Almost human.

Read 1 Timothy 2:1–2

What can you do to get along with people in authority?

God is King, but we don't just answer to God. At times, he puts us under human authority—parents, teachers, police, employers, the government—with the power to punish evil and reward good (1 Peter 2:14). At other times, God places people under our leadership. If everyone does his or her part, the world runs smoothly.

If you want leaders to be an asset to you, help them however you can.

If you need them to do their job better, pray. Start by praying that they'll lead wisely. Ask God for them to make it possible for you to live your faith fully. Pray for all the leaders in your life to be responsive to God's leadership.

Do you disagree with an authority? At the right time, you can respectfully share your point of view.

Whatever you do, treat authorities as people. Even if you're convinced they're not.

I urge, then, first of all, that requests, prayers, intercession and thanksgiving
be made for all people—for kings and all those in authority.
1 Timothy 2:1–2

Day 296

Rule Busters

Minutes after hearing that six more teachers would be laid off because of budget cuts, students hatched a plan. When the bell rang for third hour, students walked out and planted themselves on the school's front lawn. Signs unfurled. Students chanted, "NO MORE CUTS!"

Students who refused their principal's plea to return to class were suspended. Those who protested looked down on students who chose to stay in class. Parents whose kids were suspended complained rights to free speech were being ignored. Administrators said the walkout disrupted school.

Read Acts 4:13–22

Why did Peter and John decide to disobey authority?

Retaliating when a person or group in authority does something you don't like is a natural reflex. But is it right? When can you disobey someone you're supposed to obey?

Disobeying isn't okay just because you don't like the rules. It's an option when God's commands are directly challenged—and when all other methods fail. Peter tried reasoning before he threatened disobedience, and *then* he continued to preach because stopping would mean breaking God's clear command.

Most Christians agree there are instances we should oppose authorities in the wrong. Europeans hid Jews from the Nazis. American blacks broke laws that abused them for the color of their skin. People today rightly stand up for a multitude of civil rights and against all kinds of injustices.

If you choose to break a rule, or engage in "civil disobedience," be willing to suffer the consequences. Daniel went to the lions' den for praying (Daniel 6). Shadrach, Meshach, and Abednego went to the furnace for refusing to bow to an idol (Daniel 3:16–18). Their actions against ungodly laws pointed out the wickedness of the rules and invited God to display his power. At the same time, their acceptance of punishment demonstrated respect for the authorities God had established (Romans 13:1–5).

If you're going to be a rule buster, be ready to get busted.

But Peter and John replied, "Which is right in God's eyes:
to listen to you, or to him? You be the judges!"

Acts 4:19

Day 297

Escape the Little Table

A swarm of relatives crowds your home for Thanksgiving dinner—and you wonder where to sit. "Over there," says your mom.

"Over there" is a plastic play table reserved for the kiddies. It's been years since you could squeeze your knees underneath. *Why am I always stuck at the little table?*

The moment the crowd says "Amen," you see the flash of a spud-loaded spoon. "Incoming!" A tableful of little tykes lets potatoes fly. At you.

Splat. Potatoes in your hair. Stuck to your eyebrows. Up your nose. All over your shirt. And since you're the oldest, you can't retaliate.

You want to break loose from the little table. When your mom finally invites you to the big table, you find it's almost worse. The grown-ups debate the merits of vehicles—purchasing versus leasing. *Who cares?* They ooh and aah over the asparagus—and swap recipes. *Get a life. All of you!*

You ask to be excused. You wish you could go back to the little table.

Read Ecclesiastes 11:5

Little table—big table—which do you prefer?

The massive adolescent metamorphosis happening in your mind, heart, and body is as untraceable as the wind. What God is making you into is a mystery. You're dangling in that long season of life between diapers and dentures—more precisely, you're caught between childhood and adulthood. You're stuck between tables.

If you goof off like a little kid, people shake their finger: "You're not a three-year-old, you know. Act your age!" If you try to act grown-up, they panic: "You're not ready for that. Act your age!"

God knows exactly what's going on. He knows you're not a baby, and he also understands if the big table looks like a total bore.

God knew you well when you were a kid. He counts on being close to you when you're grown. Wherever you're at in life, he wants you to hang tight with him. His love for you is unstoppable. And he has loads to tell you.

> As you do not know the path of the wind, or how the body
> is formed in a mother's womb, so you cannot understand
> the work of God, the Maker of all things.
>
> *Ecclesiastes 11:5*

Day 298

Your Underwear Flying High

Your teacher waved a pair of underwear high overhead. "Class, do these belong to anyone?"

Your fourth-grade class was field-tripping to the middle school pool, and you were terrified—of the locker rooms, showers, changing in front of other kids. But you stuck to your plan. You wore your swimsuit to school under your clothes and hid your underwear—along with an enormous towel to change underneath—in a duffel. You had everything covered.

So when you saw the underwear flying in the breeze, you snickered. *Who would drop a pair of underwear in front of the whole class?* Ms. Burzloff kept waving the underwear, as if to flag down the owner. *What's she going to do next? Wear them on her head?*

Then you recognized them. You checked your duffel. They were yours.

Read Psalm 139:13–14

You look in the mirror and hardly recognize yourself. What's going on?

You might still wish you could change in a locker. What you feel, how you think, or who you see in the mirror may be bewildering or embarrassing or confusing.

You're like a video image morphing from one creature into another. You know who you used to be. Right now you can only glimpse yourself in midmorph motion.

The biggest unknown is what you're turning into. A werewolf? A beluga whale? A not-so-jolly giant? Or maybe someone is playing a cruel joke on you—and you're never going to grow up.

Your Designer isn't worried or confused. He made you unique. Exactly the way he wanted. God crafted your "inward being," your brain and feelings. He "knit together" your body as a cover and carrier for everything inside. You're "fearful" and "wonderful." Not *scary*. Awestriking and incredible!

God has been caring for you since he put you together in your mama's womb. He has your present and future brain, heart, and body all figured out. And what he plans for you is good.

For you created my inmost being; you knit me together in
my mother's womb. I praise you because I am fearfully
and wonderfully made; your works are wonderful.

Psalm 139:13–14

Day 299
No Crime

They might as well have demolished the store. The hangout was gone.

Old Mr. White owned a bodega next to school. He always said he liked kids, which to him meant anyone under forty.

But students were his favorites. He knew most of them, even the ones who tried to rip him off before they became a fan. When kids had problems—with whatever—they stuck around to sort them out with Mr. White.

One day Mr. White told his friends he was retiring and selling the store. Things changed fast. To the new owner, "student" meant "guilty." Attempting to guard the cash register and the candy aisle at the same time flustered the new owner, so he hung a sign on the door: *Only one student in the store at a time.* When kids kept gathering on the sidewalk in front of the store, he blasted elevator music to push them away. So they left.

Read Mark 10:13–16

If Jesus owned a store, would he chase students away?

Seeing Jesus was like getting a megastar autograph, only better. Parents brought their children to Jesus for him to "bless" them, to put his hands on their heads and proclaim God's kindness and love for them. Some of the kids swarming Jesus were small enough for him to pick up, but not all. The word Mark wrote here for "children" is used in Luke 8:42 to mean a twelve-year-old.

The toddlers, kids, and young teens closing in on Jesus didn't even get close. Jesus' friends—his disciples—blasted them away: "Don't waste his time," or "He has things to do. People to see. All more important than *you.*"

Jesus stopped his disciples and blasted *them.* The young crowd was exactly who he wanted to see—not because kids are always cute or nice or because they always do what God wants, but because they demonstrate how to depend on him. Everyone needs to count on the Lord's love the way a young daughter or son looks up to a parent.

Thinking like a kid is the only way to make sense of God.

Let the children come to me, for the Kingdom of God
belongs to such as they. Don't send them away!

Mark 10:14 TLB

Day 300
Size Twelve

"*Yowww-eeeeeee!*" Jason's golfer bellows. "Look at that! Never seen anything like it."

The foursome of caddies and their golfers all whistle through their teeth at the sight of the third hole. Rain had turned the whole fairway into a water hazard. Everyone mumbled about skipping to the next hole, but Jason's golfer teed up and settled in to whack the ball.

"Don't worry about it," Jason heard him say. "Have you seen the size of my caddie's feet? Hey, kid—what size shoe do you wear?"

"Twelve," Jason answered.

"Canoes! Just what I guessed. You can float out to fetch golf balls."

Read 2 Chronicles 16:9

What matters most about a person?

Some days it feels like the only thing anyone notices is how you look on the outside. Guys flex their biceps and wonder if the girls think they're manly. Girls flex their legs so their thighs *splurge* a quarter inch less.

God cares about more than that.

Recall how God sent Samuel to find a king? Samuel was hunting for that kingly look—maybe a male supermodel. God told him, "I don't look at the outside. I check out the inside. I want to see a heart that is good, one totally devoted to me." God picked David, the youngest brother, as the nation's next king. God announced that he was the one guy who was "the kind of man I want. He will do all I want him to do" (Acts 13:22 NCV).

You're at your best not when you're toned and tanned on the outside but when your insides are super-developed. When you're self-controlled, honest, unselfish, thoughtful, and discerning. When you respect God, yourself, and others.

There's a promise for you when you give yourself completely to God. Your Lord is searching for people who totally belong to him. He's going to make you strong beyond your wildest imagination.

> The Lord searches all the earth for people who have given themselves
> completely to him. He wants to make them strong.
>
> *2 Chronicles 16:9 NCV*

Day 301
Burst That Bubble

Ever since Alana had gotten her driver's license, her head had blown up into a monster snotbubble.

"Please?" Caitlyn begged. "You're already going to the mall! And it's just me and Chloe."

"Not with us! Ride your bikes. We're not having little sisters tagging along."

"Dad!" Caitlyn howled. "Alana won't give us a ride to the mall."

"Alana, give Becca a ride or *you* won't be taking the car."

Caitlyn and Chloe jumped into the backseat. Alana snarled at them, "I'm giving you a ride because Dad said I had to. When we get to the mall, stay out of our way. We don't want to be seen with you."

Read 2 Timothy 2:19–21

What does it mean to be mature?

You might call it your lucky day if your older siblings cared about you as much as they do the family dog. Sometimes parents seem to have forgotten what it's like to be your age. And teachers might assume you won't be issued a brain until you turn thirty.

What do *they* know that you don't, anyway?

A driver's license means someone can safely operate a car, nothing more. A diploma doesn't guarantee a person has graduated from the terrible twos. Making payments on a car and piling up birthdays doesn't always signify maturity.

So when the Bible urges you to become mature by being "made holy," like God—who's *reeeally* old—the thrill might not give you chills.

God may be really old, but he's also utterly cool. And acting like him is the secret to real life. Maturity is being what God wants you to be when he wants you to be it. It's becoming like him in every attitude and action.

When you grow in obedience to your Master, running away from what's wrong and chasing what's right, then you're "an instrument for noble purposes," ready for the best God has for you (2 Timothy 2:21).

> Those who cleanse themselves from the latter will be instruments for special purposes, made holy, useful to the Master and prepared to do any good work.
>
> *2 Timothy 2:21*

Day 302

Gnarly

You used to be such a nerd. Until you found your crowd on the beach.

At the beginning, you were drawn to the group with jungle-print surfboards and coordinated board shorts. They lay on the beach, not saying much. Just things like "Whoa." Seemed chill.

Your new friends didn't bathe. And they chain-smoked funny little cigarettes they rolled fresh. "I don't do it myself," you told people who worried about your new friends. "They're melding their minds toward universal peace. It's so cool. They see stuff." No doubt.

You start reevaluating your friendships when your skin blisters and sprouts suspicious precancerous growths, and then your hair gets gnarly and gnatted and you gnotice you can't get a comb through it. Bad scene.

Read Genesis 37:1–11

When is it stunning to have your own style?

Joseph couldn't have been more dumb, sharing a dream that his family would bow to him. Joseph's older brothers had decided to kill the dreamer, but it paid better to sell him as a slave.

But Joseph had a likeable side. He thought for himself. He spoke up, regardless of what others thought. He wanted to stand apart from his brothers, to lead, to be more than a seventeen-year-old herding sheep.

Years after he became a slave, God allowed Joseph to interpret a dream predicting seven years of bad crops. He rose to power when he helped the Egyptians store food and avoid starvation. When his brothers went to Egypt to scrounge food, they bowed before a great ruler who fed them. That ruler was Joseph. Joseph realized that God hadn't given him power to take revenge on his brothers. The Lord still had a part for him to play in his big plans.

God wants you to think hard about how he can use you—to do right at school, to tell teammates about him, to reach out and feed the homeless, teach kids to read, or help the elderly do what they can't do anymore.

Dream big about what God wants you to be. Be significant for God.

Joseph had a dream.
Genesis 37:5

Day 303
Whacky World

No one in the hall could miss the explosion.

"You're acting like a baby," Marin spat.

"Really? Well, you *are* a baby." Madeline laughed nastily.

Marin gulped. "What are you talking about?"

"You know what I'm talking about. You still wet the bed."

That was the secret Madeline had sworn never, *ever* to tell. Marin and Madeline met in third grade, and Marin stayed over at Madeline's house a couple times a month. She always brought blankets and sheets instead of a sleeping bag. Some weekends Marin had to toss her bedding in the wash or take stuff home in a plastic bag.

The girls were best friends. Marin's problem didn't matter.

Until now. And Marin was getting ready to take off Madeline's head.

Read Luke 22:47–54

How did Jesus react when Peter let his emotions overwhelm him?

With a kiss for a greeting, one of Jesus' twelve handpicked followers showed the guards which man was Jesus.

Peter watched, horrified. He'd given three years of his life to following Jesus. He was one of Jesus' three closest friends. Now his friend and master was being seized by soldiers, torn away to be tried and to die. Peter was terrified and angry.

He lashed out (John 18:10). It felt like the thing to do. But it wasn't.

A teacher gives you extra homework, and you cuss under your breath. Your parents make you mad, so you slam doors. You feel hurt, and you end a friendship. You see something you like, so you take it. Your emotions say it's right, so you do it.

But the emotions that swirl inside of you—anger, excitement, hatred, jealousy, boredom, laziness—can't distinguish right from wrong. Your sure guide is the calm, unchanging commands of the Bible (Psalm 19:7–11).

"No more of this!" Jesus says.

Think—don't just feel—before you act.

But Jesus answered, "No more of this!" And he
touched the man's ear and healed him.

Luke 22:51

Day 304
Life Is a Logroll

A year ago when his mom remarried, Matthew expected his life to stabilize. His biological father had started drinking again, so Matthew decided to move in with Mom and her new husband, Joe. Matthew hated switching schools, but it got him out of range of his father's yelling. Besides, his mom's new husband had a nice place.

Then his mom sat him down. "Joe and I are getting a divorce," his mom told him. "Things aren't working out. We'll need to pack up and find an apartment. We need to be out within a week."

"We're staying around here, aren't we?" Matthew protested. He was sick of shuffling schools.

"I don't know. I think I need some space. You understand, don't you?"

Sure. I always understand.

Read Hebrews 13:8

What stays the same when everything else changes?

Your LIFE swirls: You switch schools. You move. Your mom goes to work and your dad loses his job. Your classes, schedule, and teachers never stay the same. Your WORLD changes: Neighborhoods spring up. Malls multiply. TV shows premier and fizzle. You find a new favorite song. On top of it all, YOU change: Your brain and body expand. You redo your hair and buy new clothes. You swap friends. Your interests and hobbies and afterschool activities come and go. You get a job.

Even if your family isn't lurching, you can still feel like you're logrolling. Life shifts, spins, and bobs, threatening your balance and leaving you powerless. Sometimes you lose your footing and land in the drink.

Jesus never changes. Yesterday he showed himself to be God on earth (John 1:14). Today he's the one who won't leave you (Hebrews 13:5). And he prepares a forever home for you (John 14:3).

Jesus won't always stop the log from spinning. But if you ask for his help, he climbs on the log, holds your hand, puts cleats on your feet, and helps you dance.

Jesus Christ is the same yesterday and today and forever.

Hebrews 13:8

Day 305

Game Master

"Breakfast was great, Mrs. Dahmke." Aliyah groaned. "I'm stuffed. Thanks for letting me stay over."

"Thanks for coming, Aliyah," Jordahn's mom answered. "It sounds like you two had a good time. But I'll need to take you home now because I have errands to run."

Aliyah whispered to Jordahn, "But it's Saturday! Don't you want to watch videos or something? Then we could go to the mall."

"Sure, but Mom says she needs to take you now."

"I don't want to go. I always make sure I'm not home on Saturday mornings so I don't have to do chores. My brother will do them. He's so juvenile."

"You *what*?" Jordahn was amazed. "If I tried that my parents would never let me out of the house!"

Read Matthew 25:14–30

*What does God expect you to do with the skills
and strength that he gives you?*

You don't get to play ball without practicing, have friends over without picking up, or be part of a family without doing your part. There's no way to split responsibility and privilege.

Jesus said his Father's kingdom is like a master who trusts his servants with astronomical amounts of money—not a student's measly allowance, but more cash than you'll touch in your life.

Two servants work to increase the money entrusted to them. The master gives them even grander opportunities.

Nice. Or not. You do well, you get more work. Sounds like school.

Not quite. The servants hear their master's approval. They "share their master's happiness." It's like reaching the final level of a video game.

A third servant refuses to take risks. He hides what he has. He's tossed.

So how much do you have? What do you have? How can you wisely invest your life to serve God? The Lord has given you vast riches and a lifetime to give back to him what he's given you.

His master replied, "Well done, good and faithful servant!"

Matthew 25:21

Day 306

Wheeling the Wrong Way

Emma wanted everything perfect for her date. She puckered up to the mirror to get her lipstick right, then stepped back to check her outfit. *Just right.* She looked a lot older than she was. *My mother would hate this—if she bothered to notice.*

Emma heard Darren pull up. Emma hated the stunts he did with her on the back of his motorcycle, but she figured a few seconds of terror was worth the attention he gave her.

Emma ran outside. She hopped on, hung on, and hoped.

Read Romans 8:38–39

Where can you find total love and acceptance?

Trying to grow up fast is like jumping on the backseat of a motorcycle speeding the wrong way. Once you're on, it's tough to get off.

Some kids fly down dead-end roads—smoking, drinking, inhaling, or popping to feel cool; thinking they can get along without their parents; purging food or starving themselves; dating or hanging out with older kids. They push past the speed limit, thinking they can outrun the consequences.

But here's the surprise: We've *all* headed away from God (Romans 3:10–12). Every one of us tries to act grown-up—too grown-up—attempting to get along without keeping the Lord close or dodging his commands. We do life our own way to feel big, strong, and independent.

God has a better way for us to feel important. He offers us more love and acceptance and significance than we can ever manufacture for ourselves. *Nothing* is bigger than God's love for us in Jesus.

We need to stop trying to be something we're not and enjoy being the people God made us to be. We can say, "God, I'm not all grown-up. I never will be. I'll always need you. I want to follow and obey you because you love me. I'll never outgrow you."

It's like getting a ride back to where you belong.

> Neither death nor life . . . neither the present nor the future
> . . . neither height nor depth, nor anything else in all creation,
> will be able to separate us from the love of God.
>
> *Romans 8:38–39*

Day 307

Home?

"When are we going to leave?" Santiago whispered not too quietly to his parents. He didn't get an answer—other than "Shhh!"

Santiago loved Grandpa. Funeral homes, however, gave him the creeps.

Santiago got the message that he wasn't going anywhere, so he walked back over to the casket. Everyone remarked that Grandpa looked the best he had in years. Santiago thought he looked like an old mannequin with its cracks and chipped paint puttied over.

In fact, everything in the place felt unreal. Warbly music played in the background as ladies cried and men shook hands and talked baseball. Off to the side, the funeral director wore a well-rehearsed look of polite concern. He glanced at his watch a lot.

This isn't Grandpa, Santiago thought as he looked back in the casket. He worried how it would feel to be in Grandpa's place.

Read John 14:1–7

What will the end of your life be like?

It's scary. You don't just morph and grow up. You grow old. Your skin wrinkles, your brain starts to skip, and your body breaks. And that's not the end of your story. You don't just grow old. You die.

God stays with you even if you reside in a nursing home (Isaiah 46:3–4). A funeral home or cemetery isn't your final resting place. Christians have a better home. When Jesus told his followers that he was leaving soon (John 13:33), he said not to worry. He was going to prepare a mansion for them. He knew his followers would arrive safely, because he would come back for them (1 Thessalonians 4:13–17).

Jesus had a lasting home in mind—heaven. His disciples already had directions to get there. *Jesus* was the path. And because they knew his Son, the Father would welcome them in his mansion.

Death is just a door. Heaven is your forever home.

My Father's house has many rooms. . . . I am going
there to prepare a place for you.

John 14:2

Day 308

Loves Me Not

You signed up for German because you thought the girl you like would be there, but she took Spanish instead. So for the next two semesters you suffer through a teacher who spits on you when she says, "Ich liebe dich." If you plucked a daisy for insight into your love life, the petals would reach up and slap you and say, *She loves you . . . not.*

Or you're a girl and the hottie you adore from afar changes girlfriends quicker than you can change YouTube channels. He "goes with" a dozen girls a month. Never you. *He loves me . . . not.*

Rejection—the person you like doesn't like you back. You wonder: *What's wrong with me?* You worry: *Everyone thinks I'm a loser.* You wallow: *I'll spend my life as a nun.*

Read James 1:16–17

What does God have to do with finding someone for you?

Here's a big-picture truth to explain your every great moment, plus a lot of adverse situations. James says that "every good and perfect gift is from above." In other words, *God knows what you need when you need it.* You can trust him to give you the right gift at the right time, whether it's your driver's license, a date, or the guy or girl of your dreams.

That doesn't mean God doesn't care about you right now. He feels your rejection more than you can ever imagine, because he was rejected by the people he made (John 1:10–11). It's just that God's best gift might be *not* letting you go with that guy or girl—or *anyone*—right now. Dating the wrong person or just diving into dating too soon messes with all your other relationships and responsibilities. And it can make it harder to stay sexually pure before for marriage.

God sees your whole life from start to finish. He wants you to be ready for a marriage devoted to him. Your timetable might be that he should drop a cutie in your lap in the next ten minutes, but the gift he more likely wants to give is patience, character, and—at the right time, almost for sure—someone you're so crazed about that you want to spend the rest of your life together.

> Every good and perfect gift is from above, coming down from the Father of heavenly lights, who does not change like shifting shadows.
>
> James 1:17

Day 309
On the Couch

Evan kisses Ericka awkwardly on the cheek. Then the lips. And she kisses him back. Then he tries to touch her in ways that make her feel uncomfortable and wonderful at the same time. And now neither of them knows what to do. She's never been so close to a boy or felt so loved. She likes Evan's warm attention. And he wants more.

After a nervous minute, Evan blurts, "I love you." Ericka says the same. Both of them wonder what the words mean.

Freeze frame: Is love the reason Evan and Ericka are mashing lips?

Doubtful. Ericka enjoys Evan's affection. It makes her feel lovable and valuable. To keep him around, she's might do things she probably wouldn't do otherwise. So she's really using Evan. But Evan is using her too. Having a girlfriend proves to him and his friends he's a man. And groping Ericka is great fun.

Read Proverbs 5:15–23

What's God's awesome plan for sex?

Proverbs compares sex and love to water. In a desert, only a lunatic carelessly spills the water necessary to survive. Marriage is God's way of protecting sexual love as the priceless treasure God made it to be.

Love in marriage is for each other, not to prove something to others. It's the God-designed setting where Ericka won't worry about Evan dumping her, and Evan can treat Ericka right rather than just grabbing what he can. Real love is billion-dollar stuff, but Ericka and Evan are treating it like it's worth a few pennies.

But Ericka and Evan weren't having sex, so what's the big deal? Physical affection of the kissing kind isn't meant to be spilled all over either, because it's designed to lead to more. It's part of love, like a good warm-up band before the main concert.

Parents and other adults you trust can help you *set and keep* limits that will stop you from wasting one of God's best inventions. After all, if your parents didn't understand the feelings you're facing as you grow up, you wouldn't be here. Ugh. Really? Yeah. Talk to them.

Be faithful to your own wife, just as you drink water from your own well.

Proverbs 5:15 NCV

Day 310

A Sea of Eyeballs

Anthony found Lindsay fascinating—even in an ugly phys ed uniform.

Lindsay was, well, mature. The other guys talked smut about her, but Anthony just contemplated how amazing it would be if she were his girlfriend. He would be famous, or something like that, and more.

"We know you're dreaming about her," they yelled at Anthony as he stood staring. Dazed by her beauty, he didn't hear. "Forget it, Anthony. She thinks you're a moron." He still didn't break his stare.

The guys winged Anthony the basketball to wake him up. The ball, however, didn't hit in in the chest or knock the wind from his gut. It nailed his face, shattering his glasses and busting his nose.

Anthony was going to have a tough time explaining that to his mom.

Read Matthew 5:27–30

What does God say about thoughts of sex?

If people really gouged an eye every time their thoughts got red hot, the earth would be littered with eyeballs. Everywhere you look and listen—online, magazines, TV, movies, jokes, videos, T-shirts, billboards—your thoughts are shoved toward sex.

What Jesus calls "lust" isn't mere curiosity about the opposite sex. It isn't wanting a really close friend—or even, as you get older, having a body that feels sexually hungry. Lust is grasping for *what* you can't have *when* you can't have it.

The Bible is clear that adultery—sex outside of marriage—is wrong (Exodus 20:14; Hebrews 13:4). Jesus says purity runs even deeper. You don't have to roam under clothes or get pregnant to have gone "too far." Real purity is booting from your brain even thoughts of wrong things.

That's what Jesus means by his hyped-up language ("hyperbole") about getting rid of things that cause you to sin. Jesus doesn't want you to mutilate yourself but to cut off evil—to exit situations that tempt you, to look the other way when you need to (Job 31:1), and to crowd out bad thoughts by filling your head with good ones.

> But I tell you that anyone who looks at a woman lustfully
> has already committed adultery with her in his heart.
>
> *Matthew 5:28*

Day 311
See Ya Later

Stefan and friends crowded into the best comic book store in town—an over-grown newsstand that sold everything from bubble gum and baseball cards to magazines and papers from all over the world.

But his buddies were looking for more than a Spiderman issue.

"Don't think so hard, Stefan," they told him. "Just take it."

"It" was a magazine from the 18+ rack.

It wasn't that Stefan didn't have hormones or a raging curiosity. But he could think of several fatal reasons to say no: (1) getting arrested for shoplifting, (2) getting grilled by his parents for looking at porno, (3) the pledge he'd made to stay sexually pure, and (4) the awful churning stomach he felt whenever he deliberately did something wrong.

Four strikes—his friends were out. Stefan walked away. "If you want it," he told them, "*you* take it. I'm going home."

Read Matthew 5:6

Are you a fool to play by God's rules—like his rules about sex?

Cheaters grab good grades. Shoplifters score great stuff. Devious kids do wrong and then lie to get out of punishment. They all take what they want and almost always get to keep it. You feel deprived.

God will smoke people who don't abandon sin (Revelation 21:8). But that end-of-the-world truth probably feels irrelevant. Right now you just see the spectacular success of doing evil.

There's a great thing about doing good: If you do right, you don't fear (Romans 13:3). It beats being awash with worry about getting in trouble. But here's another great thing: When you hunger for God and his ways, he fills you up so you can be wildly happy doing what's best. When you actually want righteousness—right attitudes and actions, inside and out—he remakes you. You do good for your own sake and so the world around you works right.

And whenever you want God's right thing in God's right time, he'll give it to you.

Blessed are those who hunger and thirst for righteousness, for they will be filled.

Matthew 5:6

Day 312

The Skanks

Gracie had heard about "The Skanks" long before she graduated into her big new school. And she spotted Jasmine and Jayden her first day.

Jasmine and Jayden were twins who did everything they could to live up to their naughty nickname. They had a reputation for being, um, *skanky*. And from high atop their throne of popularity, they controlled the social scene of the entire school.

Any girl without a boyfriend—they had decreed—was a loser. Never mind that the boys at their middle school knew far more about honking their armpits than they did about dating the ladies. Or that no one needs a relationship that probably leads nowhere good.

Gracie was—by The Skanks' quite official rules of the school—a loser. And guess what? Knowing she was doing right didn't automatically make her feel better.

Read Matthew 5:8

What does purity look like in real life?

You ache when you're excluded for making excellent choices. If purity were just about following rules for the sake of rules, you'd have reason to feel awful. But it's better than that.

Yep, purity is about *performance—how you act*. It's about obeying and conforming to God's commands. But conforming isn't contorting—twisting yourself into a pretzel just because someone makes you.

Purity is also about *purpose—how you think and feel*. Jesus said that real purity starts with the heart (Matthew 5:21–22, 27–28). You'll never live up to his best expectations of you if your biggest goal in life is to hook up. Changing how you think and feel is how you permanently alter how you act.

Get this: Purity is most of all about a *person—how you live close to Jesus*. It's no mystery. Jesus said that anyone who serves him sticks tight with him (John 12:26). Real purity wants to stick close to Jesus' side. It's true: The pure in heart see God.

Having Jesus close by trumps holding hands with an armpit honker.

Blessed are the pure in heart, for they will see God.

Matthew 5:8

Day 313
On Your Side

Maya hadn't heard her older brother's friend come into the house. When Andrew shouted, "Anyone here?" she yelled, "In here!" She didn't think anything of it when he sat down next to her while she did her homework. They talked for a few minutes, and she explained that everyone else had gone to a movie. Andrew was always so nice.

Then he pinned her down and told her to be quiet.

Afterward he said not to tell anyone.

Maya crawled down in the corner, stuck between the bed and the wall. She felt filthy. Numb.

Read Psalm 146:5-10

Where can a victim of abuse—any abuse—go for help?

Nothing is as big a slap to God's plan for his world as sexual abuse—assault, date rape, incest, or being grabbed or molested.

Six Bible verses won't put life back together. God can.

Jesus was whipped and nailed naked to a cross. So he understands helplessness. No one rescued him. No one understood his pain.

God always takes the side of the beaten down. He always believes their side of the story. He wants them to feel clean, safe, and fearless; not dirty, threatened, or ashamed. Blessed ("peaceful," "happy," and "at rest") is the one who hopes in the Lord.

God doesn't leave the abused to suffer alone. When abuse steals love, God wants to give it back through his family and other caring people. If you or a friend has been abused, tell a trusted adult, or even a mental health telephone hotline what happened. They'll keep your story private but get you the help you need. *Don't wait.*

Abuse blends sex and violence and churns out helpless, hopeless victims, both guys and girls. It's a mess. But God knows how to put victims of abuse back together.

Blessed are those whose help is the God of Jacob, whose hope is in the Lord their God. He is the Maker of heaven and earth, the sea, and everything in them—he remains faithful forever. He upholds the cause of the oppressed . . . the Lord lifts up those who are bowed down.

Psalm 146:5-8

Day 314

Rescued or Barbequed

Knock, knock. Bamm. BAMM. You open your front door. A firefighter stands outside.

"Excuse me," he says with polite urgency. "This house is on fire. You must have noticed the flames and heat and smoke. I'm here to rescue you."

"Actually, I hadn't noticed," you reply. "We're having a party."

"In there? In that smoke?" Your living room is a cloud.

"Smoke? What smoke?" You cough as you finish pouring yourself a soda. "I can hardly see your guests. And look—the heat's melted your ice."

"Well, I don't want to leave. Everything I need is here."

"You don't understand. This house is burning down. I'm here to show you the only safe exit. Just follow . . ." *Slam.*

Read Exodus 6:6–12

What did the Israelites think about God's rescue plan?

For centuries, the people of God had rotted in slavery, a life "bitter with hard labor" (Exodus 1:14). Egyptian masters beat them to make bricks for the Pharaohs' building projects and even attempted to kill the Israelites' baby boys to prevent them from revolting as grown men.

Along came Moses, God's appointed leader. He brought a promise from God to save the Israelites from slavery, judge their masters, and guide them into a prosperous new land where they could live in peace as his people.

They didn't jump up and down with delight.

You might have the same reaction when God says he wants to usher you into a life of total devotion: *God, you couldn't possibly love me.* You're convinced you're too awful for God to love. *My life is too big of a mess.* You think your situation is too tough. *You don't care.* You suppose God doesn't understand the pressures you face. Or you think, *My friends don't want to come with. I don't want to follow anyone. I don't know where God will take me.*

None of those feelings change the fact that God wants to set you free.

> Moses reported this to the Israelites, but they did not listen to him because of their discouragement and harsh labor.
>
> Exodus 6:9

Day 315
Move

A secret message passed through camp. Prisoners should be ready to flee camp soon. A few nights later, the POWs jolted awake as helicopters roared over the camp before dawn, destroying guard towers and the camp command. What seemed like an eternity later, paratroopers stormed the prison itself. Cell doors swung open. The POWs were free. But they needed to walk out.

Crazed with fear, some prisoners wouldn't leave their cells. "We can't go out with no weapons! We're going to die!"

"Get out!" yelled the paratroopers, who knew they controlled the camp and a corridor to safety. "Trust us. Shut up and move!"

Read Exodus 14:10–18

What did God say to the Israelites when they thought they would die trying to escape slavery?

God sent frogs, gnats, hail, and death—all to force the Egyptians to free their Israelite slaves. He had more miracles up his enormous sleeve—like parting the Red Sea and drowning the Egyptian army. When Israel nevertheless doubted God knew what he was doing, he told them, "I mean it. I'll save you. Quit moaning. Start walking."

If they wanted to escape, they had to *believe*. And they had to *act* on their belief.

God sent Jesus to rescue you. Jesus died to bring you forgiveness and a life close to God. But you won't ever enjoy that freedom if you don't believe him and act on that belief. You've got to get out of your cell.

How? You decide to trust him. Then you grab hold of what he's done for you. If you believe that God has forgiven and accepted you, for example, then you talk to him confidently (Hebrews 10:19–22). If you're sure he protects you, then you fear nothing (Psalm 118:6). If you know that God uses hardship to teach you, then you resolve to learn from tough experiences you can't change (Hebrews 12:11). If you accept God's love for you, then you choose to love others (1 John 4:19). If you trust that God wants what's best for you, then you obey (Psalm 19:7–11).

If you don't act on good news, it can't change your life.

Then the Lord said to Moses, "Why are you crying out to me? Tell the Israelites to move on."

Exodus 14:15

Day 316
Show Me the Way

David's parents wondered why he had helped himself to cash from a teacher's purse. "She's really stupid," David told them. "She always leaves her purse out."

"It sounds like you're trying to blame *her*," his dad said as calmly as he could manage. "What we need to know is why you took the money."

"I didn't do it for myself. There's this girl I know whose coat was stolen. It wasn't fair. Our teacher knew it and didn't figure out who took it. I was sort of getting her back. I gave most of the money to this girl so she could get a new coat."

"David, don't you realize that was wrong?"

"But I only kept five bucks. That makes it not so bad, doesn't it?"

Read Exodus 13:21–22

Why did God show up in pillars of cloud and fire for Israel?

God didn't abandon the Israelites to wander alone through the desert in search of the land he had promised. He showed up by day in a pillar of cloud and by night in a pillar of fire, visible signs of his presence and protection. The people followed the pillar as it moved. It cleared their confusion and built their confidence.

God didn't stop at pointing out a route and rest stops. He spoke to Moses and revealed ten commands that told Israel how to act toward him and toward people (Exodus 20:1–17). After Israel entered the land, God continued to speak through his spokespeople, the prophets.

We need the same assurance about where to go—how to live, what to do, and what not to do. It's not that we're dumb. But we need help to think right about wrong. Lying is bad, but we still find reasons to fib, exaggerate, jumble, and distort. Stealing is crooked, but we excuse ourselves when we shoplift, copy homework, or fill our computers with illegal downloads. Spin us around once, and we're lost.

God doesn't dress in a cloud anymore, but he still guides you. He's given you the Bible to lead you where he wants to take you, to give you sure direction. It's your map. Don't leave home without it.

By day the Lord went ahead of them in a pillar of cloud to guide them
on their way and by night in a pillar of fire to give them light.

Exodus 13:21

Day 317

Just What You Need

Maurita screamed as Molly walked away, "I don't know why I tell you anything. You always talk behind my back."

Molly had been Maurita's best friend since kindergarten. At their small school where everybody knew everybody else's business, they didn't have many other friends. When Molly walked off, Maurita felt abandoned. Molly was all she had. Where would she find another friend like her?

When a girl moved in next door, Maurita's hopes rose. But that went nowhere. Then Maurita's math teacher paired her as a study partner with the girl who sat behind her. Jen was quiet, so Maurita didn't know her well. She was nice, though. And after a few months, Jen became a better friend for Maurita than Molly ever was.

Read Exodus 16:9–20

How did God feed the Israelites when they thought they would starve?

Not long after the Israelites fled slavery, they faced certain starvation in the desert. Where could they find food for two million people?

They didn't expect it to fall from the sky. Yet it did. God sent "manna," which literally means "What is it?" It was God's unexpected solution to an impossible problem, a sign that God was looking out for them. If they didn't trust that God would provide again the next day, the food they hoarded overnight would stink and crawl with maggots. God made them gather manna repeatedly to remind them that they needed him every day.

You face times when you think you're going to die—that you're going to wither with loneliness, shatter from stress, or melt with nervousness. One more ounce of pressure and you'll crumple. You know you need God. Yet you can't see a solution coming.

God will take care of you. Among other things, he promises to provide godly friends (1 Kings 19:14–21), encouragement (2 Thessalonians 2:16–17), and peace (Philippians 4:6–7), and to meet your physical needs (Philippians 4:19).

Where will help come from? God. What will it be? You never know. When will it come? On time.

Thin flakes like frost on the ground appeared on the desert floor.

Exodus 16:14

Day 318

Out Your Nose

Brody sat on the floor outside his room after Jason ejected him from Sunday school for mouthing off. After a while, Jason came out and asked Brody what was going on with him in class.

"I'm bored," Brody eventually answered. "I've been coming here ever since I was in first grade, and I can't make friends."

"Do you have friends at school?"

"Yes."

"What are your friends like at school?"

"They're fun. We get in trouble sometimes. But they aren't boring like kids here. My friends there are the best."

Read Numbers 11:4–6, 18–20, 31–34

How did the Israelites like the food God miraculously provided for them in the desert?

Sure, God gave us manna, the Israelites thought. *"It's good for you,"* he says. *I'll bet God doesn't eat bamanna muffins three times a day.* The Israelites' imaginations cooked up pots of fish, and their memories picked fresh fruits and veggies. They wanted to go back to Egypt.

What they remembered, however, was unbelievably better than what they ever actually had. Heading back to slavery for a bag of onions was like a dog going back to the pound because the biscuits were good.

God wasn't upset that his people were bored by his menu. He was angry that they would rather be bound as slaves than walk with him. Their complaints rejected not only his gift but himself. So for a month, God granted their wish—enough meat that it came "out of their nostrils."

God gives gifts meant only for your best (James 1:17). Your attitude toward all that God gives—however plain, simple, or even boring his gifts might seem—reveals your attitude toward God himself (Exodus 16:4). So don't whine for things you think are better. The Lord just might give you what you want.

You know how it feels to spit milk through your nose. Imagine blowing bird chunks.

But now we have lost our appetite; we never see anything but this manna!

Numbers 11:6

Day 319

Scared Off

God seemed so real on your trip with friends from church. So close. Utterly obvious. You decided that nothing would ever again come between you and God. You wanted to trust and obey him the best you knew how.

But the last night of the trip, you dreamed about your friends back home. You were going through a normal school day, except that every few minutes a friend told you what they thought about your faith in God: *You think you're better than us. That stuff isn't real. You were brainwashed—you would have signed up for the circus if that's what they told you to do. Being a Christian is the kiss of death. I wouldn't say this if I didn't care about you, but . . .*

By the time you woke up, you weren't so sure about following Jesus. And your own brain kept hounding you: *My friends are going to dump me. I won't survive. I'll be mocked. Or ignored.*

Read Numbers 13:26–33

What did the Israelite spies tell people about the land they saw?

When God brought the Israelites to the border of the land he promised to give them, twelve men snuck ahead to spy out the land. It was as good as God said, overflowing with milk and honey, bursting great globs of grapes so huge they took two men to carry.

Even so, ten of the spies focused on the downside—thugs who ran the land. They forgot God's promise—the land was theirs for the taking. True, there were giants. But God said the Israelites could whip them, not with their own skill but with his strength.

There's no doubt that what God promises us is good. We look at it, we want it. Friendship with the living God. Membership in his kingdom. Guidance and peace even amidst chaos. God's security, satisfaction, and splendor are a huge upside.

It's the giants that scare us—our friends' reactions, the things we need to give up, our fears and weaknesses.

Our eyes are fine. It's our hearts that fail.

Yes, there are giants in the land. But God is bigger.

> And they spread among the Israelites a bad report
> about the land they had explored.
>
> *Numbers 13:32*

Day 320

Stick or Get Stuck

On the first day back from summer vacation, the football team lined the school's main entrance. As Serge limped past, the team captain crooked his arm, cocked his head, opened his mouth, and flopped out his tongue. "Look, guys," John said as he drooled. "The retard is back! Everybody wave to the retard." The whole team copied John's cruel imitation.

Serge wasn't mentally retarded. Cerebral palsy slurred his speech and limited his muscle control.

Not everyone thought John was funny. When he chased Serge down the hall, John's girlfriend stuck out her foot to trip John. He sprawled. And she yelled at him as he lay on the ground. "I'm sick of you making fun of Serge," she steamed. "You're so mean!"

Read Numbers 14:1–9

Why did Caleb and Joshua stick up for what was right?

You're on the football team. Question: Do you applaud as John's girlfriend stomps on his chest?

It's great to want to stand apart from the crowd. It's more realistic to choose the crowd you want to stand with.

No matter where you go, there are two types of people. The first tries to do right. At school, they learn, listen, and do well. They treat others the way they want to be treated. At home, they respect their families. At church, they study to know God better and live what they know.

The other kind of people live for themselves and no one else. They push the limits. They do whatever they can get away with without getting busted.

The second group is often bigger. And louder.

That doesn't mean they're right or that they'll win. Joshua and Caleb stood against popular opinion. They ripped their robes to mourn sin. They chose to be on God's side. And they stood *together*. Because they did what God wanted, he elected them leaders of a new generation that stormed the promised land.

You may not have the guts to start the right crowd. But find a way to join them.

The land we passed through and explored is exceedingly good.

Numbers 14:7

Day 321

Missing the Best

Taylor wailed when the doctor confirmed her fears. "NO! You're wrong!" But as she watched her stomach grow, she couldn't deny reality. And when her abdomen wrenched with labor pains, she knew there was no easy escape.

For Taylor, the pain of giving birth was nothing compared to her baby boy being whisked away. He was perfect, the doctor said, but she didn't get to see him before he met his adoptive parents. Putting her baby up for adoption would let her finish school and get on with life. But a thousand times a day she wondered what her baby was doing and how he was.

Even years later, when she had a husband and family, she still imagined what the boy looked like, and she imagined him taking his spot at the table when she called for dinner.

Read Numbers 14:26–35

*What happened to the Israelites when they
decided to disobey God over and over?*

When we sin, we do damage to our relationship with God. Yet when we accept his offer of forgiveness, he mends the cracks. But sometimes the consequences of what we've done live on.

The Israelites sinned against him over and over (Numbers 14:22). They refused to storm the land. They accused the Lord of plotting to murder them and their children in the wilderness. They even vowed to choose a new leader and return to bondage in Egypt. God was beyond furious. "How long will they refuse to believe in me, in spite of all the signs I have performed among them?" (Numbers 14:11).

Moses pleaded with God, and God forgave the Israelites (Numbers 14:20). But they didn't live happily ever after. Forgiveness didn't eliminate the results of their sinful actions. Their guilt was gone, but the consequences weren't. God gave the people what they asked for. He locked them out of the land. They missed the best of what he planned.

In this wilderness your bodies will fall—every one of you twenty
years old or more . . . who has grumbled against me.

Numbers 14:29

Day 322
Comfy Cozy

Your legs and arms flow in perfect harmony, a symphony of grace and coordination. As you admire your powerful stride, you hum an old country tune, "O Lord, it's hard to be humble, when you're perfect in every way."

Glancing over your shoulder, you discover you're so far ahead of the pack that you decide to stop running. *I deserve a break. Training hard, looking good. Yep, I'm fine.* You plop down on the on the track and spread out a picnic. You bite into your hero sandwich. *Hero—how appropriate,* you think.

You lie back and fall into a deep slumber, dreaming of gold medals and world records.

Sleeping contentedly, you rouse only when a truck driver rolls down his window and yells, "Moron! Get outta the road!"

Read Deuteronomy 8:6–20

Why did God warn Israel against getting comfortable?

God saved Israel from repeated severe difficulties—slavery, snakes, scorpions, and starvation, for starters. And the new homeland he planned for them was sweet—filled with streams and springs, wheat and barley, grapes, figs, honey, sheep, silver, and gold. God had a worry, however—that his people would forget all about him when they settled into such a nice place.

It's usually not a problem to remember God when life turns rough. But when you feel safe and satisfied, you're easily distracted, wrapped up in what you're doing and in the good stuff God gives you. You're not alert or on track. You forget that everything you have and are comes from God.

You get back on pace when you rouse yourself with the fact that God is still God. He's worth thanking and chasing even when life goes great.

The risk in slowing your pace in the race of following Jesus isn't that other runners—other believers—will pass you by. The real danger is that your pride will run you over.

> When you have eaten and are satisfied, praise the Lord your God for
> the good land he has given you. Be careful that you do not forget
> the Lord your God, failing to observe his commands. . . .
>
> *Deuteronomy 8:10–11*

Day 323

Onward

You spent the past several days scribbling in yearbooks—spilling your most brilliant thoughts like, *"You're a great person." "Don't ever change." "Call me."* Even *"Friends Forever."*

Ugh. You didn't mean nine-tenths of what you wrote. You wanted your own yearbook to be covered in signatures from front to back, so you had to do your part for others.

You were eager to blow out middle school and never look back. But your graduation ceremony shook you. The ol' place meant more than your yearbook scribbles might indicate.

You're surprised that you might actually miss the place. But you're also looking forward to a place that's even bigger and better.

Read Deuteronomy 4:32–40

The Israelites were camped at the edge of the land God had promised, ready to enter. What did Moses want them to remember?

When Israel looked back at forty years of wandering in the wilderness, they had no problem recalling the hardships they faced in the desert. Moses worried they would forget how good God had been—and the difference God's goodness should make in how they lived.

The world had never witnessed anything like God's friendship with Israel. God conversed with them. Through pests, floods, fire, and miracles, he rescued them from slavery to make them his people.

They had only begun to see what God would do. And what God had done for them, Moses said, should change their lives. They had seen that God was God. Now they should follow him.

God's acts were real, not made-up mush scribbled in someone's yearbook. God's love for you is just as real. Through Jesus, he acted to rescue you. He's promised never to leave you.

What you've learned about God so far is just the beginning. And it should change you. God is God. Follow him.

You were shown these things so that you might know that the Lord is God; besides him there is no other.

Deuteronomy 4:35

Day 324

I Smell a Skunk

"Thawr's skuhnk in thuh pawrk, yuh know."

Skunks? *I don't think so.* You walk away laughing. No uptight park ranger is going to ruin your fun. *Anyone who talks that stupid* is *that stupid.* So you ignore his advice about keeping food in sealed containers inside a car so raccoons or skunks—or bears—don't ravage your camp. You spill chips and soda inside and out of your tent, and you put a stash of candy under your pillow as you tuck yourself in.

As soon as you lie quiet, you notice animal noises in the woods. *Maybe that stupid ranger knew what he was talking about. . . .*

When you hear claws scratch the tent wall, you burrow into your sleeping bag. And when you see claws shred nylon, you make a run for your car.

Read Judges 2:6–15

Why didn't Israel rest easy in the land God had promised them?

Just as God had warned, Israelites who refused to enter the land died in the desert. Their children became the heroes, conquering most of the peoples in the land. In time, however, a generation grew up that hadn't seen God's miracles firsthand. That's when the trouble began.

Instead of serving God, this new generation of Israelites followed the gods, or *Baals*, of their neighbors, who were worshiped through prostitution and child sacrifice. When God saw his people's disobedience, he allowed their sinful neighbors to survive. Their presence tested whether they would be devoted to him or turn away.

Because Israel let sin stick around, life became a sticky mess.

Doing wrong hurts you now. It's like volunteering to get beat up. But it also hurts you later. God wants to chase sin from your life by changing how you think and act. When you don't let him, your enemy lives on. It threatens you. It teases. And sometimes it wallops you all over again. God doesn't warn you for nothing.

Don't be surprised if you wake up wearing a skunk on your head.

Then the Israelites did evil in the eyes of the Lord and served the Baals.

Judges 2:11

Day 325

It's Okay to Be Alone

Claudia flopped on her bed, grabbed her pillow, squished her face into it, and cried.

After a while she rolled over and pulled out her diary and began to write.

LOSER! she scrawled in huge letters across two pages. *Dear Diary*, she started on a third page. *Today I made a total fool of myself. Jessie copied Michel's test. Ms. Williams found out and Jessie and Michel got kicked off the volleyball team. Everyone thinks I told Ms. Williams. It wasn't me.*

Claudia had tried to defend herself at volleyball practice, but no one believed her. At the end of practice, the team walked away from Claudia and flipped off the gym lights, leaving her alone in total darkness. *Why are they treating me like this? I didn't do anything. I don't have any friends left.*

Claudia knew that wasn't true.

I still have you, God, she wrote. *Please get me out of this mess.*

Read Psalm 31:9–16

What do you do when friends dump you?

It's no surprise when enemies lie about you, talk behind your back, leave you in the dark, or punch you in the stomach.

It's harder to understand when friends do those things. You do your best to be a good friend, you work out conflicts, you love like Jesus—and a friendship still blows up in your face. Sooner or later it happens to everyone. You moan and groan with hurt.

If you trust God to get you through the hurt, you'll survive. He can make it bearable to be alone because *he's* still your friend. He knows what you need in the dark or behind slammed doors—even inside your head or on a page of your diary: "The eyes of the Lord range throughout the earth to strengthen those whose hearts are fully committed to him" (2 Chronicles 16:9).

When you have God as your friend, pain is only part of what you write in a diary or journal. It's only part of what you think and feel. The last line you write—or the thought to focus on through an awful, lonely day—can always be, "God, I trust you. I belong to you. Help me."

> But I trust in you, O Lord; I say, "You are my God." My times are in your hands; deliver me from my enemies and from those who pursue me.
>
> Psalm 31:14–15

Day 326

He Ain't Ugly

Your cousin is switching to your school, and your life is over.

Minus the tail, James looks like an oversized prehistoric beaver—beady eyes and teeth that would make a mama beaver proud, topped by glasses like soda-bottle bottoms. You fake sick and stay home for the first three days he's at school. Then it hits you. *We have different last names. No one will ever know.*

Your solution works until someone swipes James' glasses. He's pitiful, with his teeth chattering as he begs to get them back.

"Give my cousin his glasses," you hear yourself say. "NOW!"

Read Ruth 1:1–16

Why be loyal?

While Ruth's husband was alive, she had a duty to her mother-in-law, Naomi. But then she *chose* to stick with Naomi—simply because Naomi had been kind to her. Ruth decided to join a new nation and follow God.

You're "loyal" when you meet the obligations you should—to God (1 Chronicles 29:17–18), family (Exodus 20:12), country (Romans 13:1), people who have helped you (Luke 17:12–16), other believers (Galatians 6:10), and people in need (Luke 10:29–37).

It's a mistake to misplace loyalty—to give it to material things (Matthew 6:24) or to people who hurt you (2 Corinthians 11:19–20). Being loyal doesn't mean you keep a friend's suicide note a secret or shield a friend who did wrong (Ephesians 5:11).

So what deserves your loyalty—and how much—and why? Think it through: (a) your bratty sister, (b) your homely next-door neighbor who's been your best friend since kindergarten, (c) a popular peer who brushes you off like dirt, (d) your dad when he dresses dumb, (e) your favorite football team, or (f) your best pair of shoes.

Don't die for something dumb. But don't hide when something important deserves your help.

Where you go I will go.

Ruth 1:16

Day 327
The Price Is Right

"This one. Definitely." Dmitri's friends each grab a hoodie with their school's logo and head to the cashier.

"Aren't you going to buy one?" Christopher asks. "We all are."

"Nope. Maybe later."

"How come you never have money?" Christopher noses.

Maxim snorts. "He doesn't make money. He volunteers as a handy wipe at the nursing home. He changes old people's diapers."

"I don't change diapers," Dmitri hits back. "Besides, so what if I did? My job's more important than mowing lawns for a stupid hoodie."

"You don't get paid?" Chris is shocked. "*That's* stupid."

Read Luke 21:1–4

What makes a gift really great?

Your dog won't know the difference if you stuff yourself *before* you flip a few measly scraps under the table. But that's no way to treat people.

Jesus says that when you love people, you don't just give leftovers. Even though the gift the widow gave was tiny, it was better than the bags of money the rich gave. She offered all she had.

Giving unselfishly might cost you *time*. Like helping little kids at church, volunteering at a latchkey program, or tutoring during free time at school. Being a giver often costs *money*. You could donate monthly to give a distant child school, food, shelter, and clean water. Or you can contribute to projects near to home.

Be aware that giving a real gift can cost you *popularity*. Jesus says to target people who can never pay you back (Luke 14:12–14), reaching beyond your friends to the poor, strange, sick, or trapped (Matthew 25:34–36). Going to "the least" can cause cool people to lose interest in you.

Loving unselfishly sometimes costs you *even more*. It can cost you everything. Like the widow. Or the gift Jesus gave you (1 John 3:16).

This poor widow has put in more than all the others. All these people gave their gifts out of their wealth; but she out of her poverty put in all she had to live on.

Luke 21:3–4

Day 328

Just Kidding

He'll never talk to her, thinks Hugh. He decides to help John out.

"Hey, Emily—John thinks you're so lovely," Hugh shouts. She looks at John like he's a nerd on a stick. John clamps his hand over Hugh's mouth and drags him around the corner to shut him up. "Ha ha," John says as he thumps Hugh in the stomach.

The next morning, Hugh tapes a homemade two-foot-high heart-shaped card on Emily's locker, complete with a sappy poem and John's name signed in big letters. A Snap goes viral before Emily gets to school and tears it down. "Why did you do that?" John yells.

"It was funny," Hugh jokes. "You're a coward."

John doesn't look amused. Five minutes later, both of them are wiping bloody noses. Hugh remains puzzled. *Why can't he take a joke?*

Read Matthew 5:21–24

What can you do when you've made someone mad?

The passage pictures someone busily worshiping God ("at the altar") when he realizes he's made someone mad. Jesus said the worshiper should go to the person he angered and set things right.

So picture this. You're sitting in church. You grow uneasy. A bit queasy. You break a sweat and rummage in the pew rack for a motion-sickness bag. You suddenly bolt out the back to beg forgiveness from a person you hurt.

Not likely.

When you make someone mad, you might not feel guilty, much less stabbed to the heart with an awareness that you've done wrong. But Jesus reminded his listeners that God hates not just "big sins" like murder but "small sins" like anger. In his eyes, they're a lot alike.

The situation you inflamed, by the way, isn't solved by a secret "Sorry!" tossed at God. He wants you to go to the person you angered and repair what you can.

Even tough guys and girls need to go.

Apologize. Set the situation straight. Change.

Go and be reconciled to them; then come and offer your gift.

Matthew 5:24

Day 329
Somewhere Better to Go

Miki sat on the curb, spurting tears and talking to herself and God and anyone who happened to walk by.

"Olivia started it. She says I'm her best friend, but then she said I was ugly and laughed at me and stabbed me in my back. She claimed I stole her boyfriend. He and I had three classes together. What was I supposed to do? I just talked to him. I'm not a flirt. She is.

"And then three weeks ago she said *really* bad stuff about me—stuff I wouldn't say about *anyone.*" Miki started crying again. "When I tried to defend myself it was even worse. It's been *three weeks* since any of my friends have talked to me. They all hate me now. And I hate *her.*"

Read 1 Peter 2:19–23

Why forgive people who hurt you?

You trash your sister's iPad and have to forfeit your allowance for the next year to buy a new one. You skip practice and get benched. You show up tardy to school and get detention.

You got punished. You deserved it. Buck up.

But you don't deserve every bad thing that comes your way—like when people lie about you, mock your beliefs, question your motives, quit your friendship, rip you off, broadcast your smallest mistake, or blame you for something you didn't do.

Jesus said believers should turn the other cheek (Matthew 5:39). That doesn't mean, however, that you should let people slap you up. He also said to confront people who cause you pain and to avoid them if they don't change (Matthew 18:15–17).

That still might not fix how you feel, because your hurt doesn't go away as long as you keep hating. When your enemies hit you hard, then hating them ropes and gags you. You won't feel free until you forgive.

Jesus forgave by praying for the people who hurt him (Luke 23:34). Then he refused to plot revenge or toss back insults. He let God defend him.

By forgiving his enemies, Jesus wrestled free from them.

> When they hurled their insults at him, he did not retaliate. . . .
> Instead, he entrusted himself to him who judges justly.
>
> *1 Peter 2:23*

Day 330

True Peace

Mayerly Sanchez remembers a close friend, Milton. "The day before he died," whispers Mayerly, "we had been playing soccer in the street." Stabbed in a gang fight in a suburb of Bogota, Colombia, Milton was one of thirty thousand people in his country to die violently that year.

At his funeral, Mayerly vowed to work for peace. She was soon leading a national peace movement of almost three million kids. Their work influenced more than ten million Colombians to vote "yes" to a Citizen's Mandate for Peace that highlights love, acceptance, forgiveness, and work. She discussed legislation with Colombian congressmen and spoke at leading universities. She's been nominated for a Nobel Peace Prize.

Mayerly still works hard for peace, teaching children about the dangers of land mines. And it all started when she was fourteen.

Read Matthew 5:9

How can you make peace in a world at war?

Statistically, you can count on 98.6 percent of beauty pageant contestants to stroll on stage and declare that world peace is their life's deepest wish. (Right after perfect hair and a beachside condo like Barbie's.)

They're blowing smoke to try to win a crown. Mayerly, in contrast, has done *real* stuff to try to stop the killing in a country where murders have exceeded fifteen times the rate of the United States.

To Mayerly, peacemaking is part of daily life. "We heard a lot about peace in the media," one fifteen-year-old Colombian said. "But Mayerly taught us that peace needs to be practiced. If we see two of our friends fighting, we need to intervene and try to motivate them to get along."

Mayerly's peacemaking didn't start with taking on drug lords. It began with how she acts at home and with friends. Your work begins with how you treat your siblings and the brat who sits behind you in science.

When you spread peace among friends and family and enemies, you prove you belong to the Prince of Peace (Isaiah 9:6–7).

Blessed are the peacemakers, for they will be called children of God.

Matthew 5:9

Day 331
Fungus Among Us

Your mom's question was innocent enough. "How was the party?"

"Oh, fine," you totally lie. How can you tell your mom that you spent the whole evening feeling like you had bad breath, body odor, and an incurable foot fungus? Morgan kept looking around to see if there was anyone better to chat with. When you tried to talk to Joshua, he left to fiddle with the music choices—six times during one song. Cameron ran off to refill his water so many times he was going to wet the bed. And Katherine was in the corner all evening, nose stuck in some guy's ear, telling stupid jokes and nibbling.

What's wrong with you?

Probably nothing. But as long as you try hard to break into the innermost circles of a class, party, team, even your friend group, you'll likely be unhappy with the results. There's a better way to find friendship.

Read Proverbs 18:24

What happens when you try too hard to be popular?

Seeking big-league popularity ruins you. It forces you to fit the expectations of people you want to impress—to be someone you're not, do things you don't want to do, and say things you normally wouldn't say. Besides that, your popularity lasts for only as long as your beauty or brains rank at the top. Then you're out, and someone else is in. Better to find a few select friends who "stick closer than a brother" than a crowd of fans who control you, use you, then despise you.

Parties might not be the place to meet those close friends. Jonathan and David were young men when David walloped the giant Goliath and was brought before Jonathan's father, King Saul. They met because David did what was right (1 Samuel 18:1–4). Ruth and Naomi were brought together by tough times (Ruth 1). The apostle Paul became Timothy's friend and mentor when Timothy started doing ministry as a teen (2 Timothy 1:6).

The crowd may never accept and appreciate you the way you are. But you can ask God to help you find real friends amid the crowd.

One who has unreliable friends soon comes to ruin, but
there is a friend who sticks closer than a brother.

Proverbs 18:24

Day 332
Awash in a Pool of Drool

"The inverse of the common denominator is multiplied by the square root of the algebraic cosine," your teacher drones, "which of course demonstrates that if x is greater than or equal to y, then z is the negative product of an imaginary number."

The rest is a haze. Mr. Ultradull keeps lecturing, too daft to see you losing consciousness in the back of his room. As you drift off, you wonder if there are laws against a teacher being so boring.

Half an hour later, the bell rings.

You awake. Your face rests on your desk in a pool of drool.

Through sleepy eyes, you see the last of your classmates exiting the room. You stumble after them and wipe your face on your sleeves, only to find that your shirt has sopped up spit like a sponge.

You nodded off and no one knocked you awake. So where are your friends when you need them?

Read Psalm 55:12–14

What's your best bet for avoiding friendship pain?

You sass. You talk behind each other's backs and spill each other's secrets. You tease with stinging bits of truth. You get in ugly moods and clam up. You borrow without asking and forget to give back. Even the best friendships often flip-flop between kindness and cutdowns, fondness and fights, cool times and cruelty.

They bite. You chomp. That's life with friends. Or is it?

A real friend, says Proverbs 18:24, "sticks closer than a brother." And Ecclesiastes 4:10 says that if one falls down, his friend can help him up. So what's up when friends stab you rather than stick close?

No one wants to go through life alone. But don't settle. You need friends who keep you from making a fool of yourself. Friends who keep you from destroying yourself. Friends who wake you up before you drool on the desk. Friends who stick with you even when your shirt is soaked. You only get that kind of care when you get the right kind of friends.

If an enemy were insulting me, I could endure it; if a
foe were rising against me, I could hide.

Psalm 55:12

Day 333

Team Sport

"She needs an answer now!" Clayton barked, muffling the phone against his shirt.

"We've talked about this before," Clayton's mom answered calmly. "We don't think it's appropriate for you to go out with Mara alone."

"We're not going out. We're just going to the mall. Don't you trust me?"

"It's not a question of trust, Clayton. It's not wise to put yourself in a situation where—"

"The kids at church are going to a hockey game tonight," Clayton's dad interjected. "You said you might go to that. Why don't you invite Mara to go with you? We'll pay. You can treat her."

Problem solved, supposed Mom and Dad. Clayton thought not. "I don't want to bring Mara around church people. She'll think I'm one of them."

Read Proverbs 16:18

What happens when you try to survive alone as a Christian?

You might not be tempted to become a porno star or sneak into a casino to blackjack away your college savings. But at times you may dream of ditching your Christian faith and friends for other things.

You might laugh if people—like your parents—think you're tottering on the fence between devotion and ditching God, between following Jesus and wandering away. Maybe they know that most people who stop being Christians don't dash toward the fence and pole-vault to the other side. They tiptoe along the top of the fence until they teeter over.

They need other believers to call them back from the edge—when, for example, they want to hook up with non-Christians, or they decide they'll do *anything* to be popular, or they choose to make relatively minor stuff like clothes or money majorly important.

When you dare to dance on the fence, sooner or later you slip. Don't be surprised if it hurts to slam the ground on the other side. There's no one over there waiting to catch you.

Pride goes before destruction, a haughty spirit before a fall.

Proverbs 16:18

Day 334

Blow Your Locker Open

Your parents tell you following Jesus is "the most important thing in life." No one else your age seems to think so.

Your youth pastor says you're supposed to "live for God" at school and "take a stand." God will be with you.

So where is he? *If God loves me,* you've been wondering, *why doesn't he blow my locker open?* You know—a mind-melting display of power. Like you twiddle the lock and suddenly KABOOM!—your locker door hangs by half a hinge. When the dust clears, you see God's blinding face whispering to you, entrusting you with a message for your school. Light fills the school and your classmates fall to their knees in awe of God and respect for you, God's spokesperson in their midst.

Impressive.

Read 1 Kings 19:10–18

How did God help when Elijah felt picked on?

Only a month had passed since Elijah stood on Mount Carmel, one man against 450 prophets of the fake god Baal. At Elijah's request, God flung fire from heaven to torch a sacrifice—stone altar and all. Baal failed. God won. Elijah was a hit. For a while.

What did Elijah get for doing everything right? He stood alone, or so he thought. From his vantage point, everyone else in Israel had abandoned their faith in the one true God to follow idols. And Queen Jezebel wanted to kill him. Lonely and scared, Elijah fled into the desert. He wanted to curl up and die.

Elijah's biggest complaint? He was alone! So God showed himself to Elijah—not in an earthquake, wind, or fire, but in a whisper. God gave him a partner—*Elisha.* And God told him he wasn't really alone. *Elijah had friends—* seven thousand other worshipers of God, at the ready.

God wants to display his power in your life. But he also wants to give you the truly potent gift of partners in following him. But you have to be able to spot them before you can join them.

Yet I reserve seven thousand in Israel—all whose
knees have not bowed down to Baal.

1 Kings 19:18

Day 335
Waffle Vomit

The lead singer of the band Waffle Vomit stared down from posters all over Jake's bedroom. "He has songs about prayer and stuff," Jake told his older brother Jeff. "He's got to be a Christian."

Jeff rolled his eyes. "Sure, Jake. He's foaming at the mouth because he's a rabid follower of Jesus. That's why he chews bat eyeballs for breakfast."

"That's just a ploy," Jake explained. "No one would listen to him if he didn't act like that. Besides—we're not supposed to judge."

"We're not supposed to condemn people," Jeff corrected. "But don't you think we're supposed to be able to tell who's a Christian?"

Read Ephesians 2:1–5

How do you know who is a Christian and who isn't?

If a dead guy were propped up in an easy chair with a newspaper and slippers, it might be hard to judge from across the room whether he was dead or just relaxing. But the closer you get, the more you know—a whiff or a poke tells you a lot. Other times it requires a pulse check or a search for brain waves.

It doesn't usually take the county coroner to tell a dead body from a live one, and you don't have to be a pastor to know a Christian when you see one. Being a Christian doesn't mean going to church or being nice or talking religious. It's having God's new life.

Without God, the part of you that wants to be friends with God is dead. Even if you look good, propped up on the outside, your insides are dead in disobedience—you've done what *you* want, not what God wants. But when you become a Christian, God freely forgives you. He makes you his friend and jump-starts your heart. You start to follow the One who saved you.

Sometimes when a person is reborn (John 3:1–16) you don't see much life right away—you can't directly observe the new friendship with God that's formed on the inside. But God's life doesn't take long to ooze to the outside to affect attitudes and actions.

You spot a Christian by the new life that's begun. Life grows. Life shows.

God, who is rich in mercy, made us alive with Christ.

Ephesians 2:4

Day 336

Head Above Water

"I guess I never thought of that, Mrs. Dalbey," Halley mumbled.

"There's a reason God sometimes doesn't seem real to us, Halley," she said quietly. "The wrong things we all do are a lot worse than we think. They put a wall between us and God. They make us his enemies."

Halley listened intently to her dear elderly neighbor. "God says we deserve eternal separation from him. God's Son—Jesus—took that punishment when he died on the cross. If we admit our sin and accept the fact that Jesus died for us, God forgives us. That's how each of us can become a Christian."

"Sweetie," Mrs. Dalbey continued. "I know you're hurting. You've been through so much. When you get to know Jesus and act on what you believe, your faith starts to feel real."

Mrs. Dalbey let Halley think. Then she asked if Halley wanted to pray to start a new relationship with God. She did. "God, I know I need you," they prayed together. "I've sinned. Thank you that Jesus died in my place for my sins. I want your forgiveness. I want to follow and obey you."

Read Colossians 1:9–14

What does it mean for God to "rescue" you?

Christians aren't corpses. They're back from the dead. But what does that look like? The first sign of God's life in you is knowing that you're *rescued* by God.

If you're in water over your head and don't know how to swim, you can pretend for only so long that you don't need help. The beginning point in becoming a Christian is realizing that you're in way past your eyeballs. The bad stuff you've done and the good stuff you've left undone has plunged you deep in sin. If you say you never sin, you're fooling yourself (1 John 1:8). And the penalty for sin is separation from God forever (Romans 6:23).

God doesn't leave you to rescue yourself, to yank yourself by your swimsuit to safety. If you admit your sin to God, he forgives you (1 John 1:9). He rescues you from going under.

> For he has rescued us from the dominion of darkness and brought us into the kingdom of the Son he loves, in whom we have redemption, the forgiveness of sins.
>
> *Colossians 1:13–14*

Day 337
It's Not a Small World

"That was truly wonderful," you squeal. "Let's do it again!"

With that, your hosts lead your tiny boat on another spine-tingling tour where multicultural munchkins brighten your day, singing "It's a Small World After All" over and over and over in 687 languages.

After your fourteenth trip aboard the happiest cruise that ever sailed, your hosts are exasperated. "May we suggest you look at your map?" they urge. "Really. There are so many other attractions in the park."

"This *is* the park," you protest. You slap the map away, pulling out some fancy-looking documents and waving them at the attendants. "This is it. The deed to Disneyland. My father gave it to me, and here I am. Enjoying it fully, I might add. Another round, please."

Read Titus 2:11–14

What does it mean for you to be "remade" by God?

If you owned the happiest place in la-la land, you wouldn't be content to float in a boat listening to motorized mannequins. Within minutes, you would be off on another ride. Within days, you would know every feature of the parks. And years later, you would appreciate every inch of your magic realm. Yet if you never broke out to explore, you might never know how much existed.

Settling for immaturity as a Christian is like getting stuck on the first ride you find. Christians—people who have let God rescue them—sometimes don't realize that God has more for them. A Christian is also someone who is being *remade* by God.

Being a Christian—possessing "salvation"—is way bigger than getting your sins forgiven. The word behind "to save" means "to be made whole." God wants not just to rescue you from drowning but to fix your broken parts and teach you how to swim. He wants to train you to say "NO!" to evil and "YES!" to good. He wants you totally devoted to him.

For the grace of God has appeared that offers salvation to all people.
It teaches us to say "No" to ungodliness and worldly passions, and to
live self-controlled, upright and godly lives in this present age.

Titus 2:11–12

Day 338

Turn on a Dime

Bryan swept the garage floor, feeling sick to his stomach.

He and his brother were having a bedtime snack when Bryan got so mad at Trent's teasing that he hurled a plate across the kitchen at his brother. He missed, but the plate gouged the cupboard and shattered on the floor.

What was I thinking? Bryan had been a Christian for a couple years, and he couldn't understand why he still got angry at his brother.

By the time Bryan finished his next chore—mowing the lawn—he felt even worse. He couldn't shake the look on his mom's face. She wasn't a Christian. And she looked at him as if she'd just found out her son was a serial killer or something. She might as well have said it: "You hypocrite! I thought Christians were supposed to be different."

What do I do now?

Read 1 John 1:9–2:6

How can a Christian stay close to God?

You don't have to watch Christians for more than a few minutes to discover they aren't perfect—and if you doubt that fact, look no further than your own flaws. The Bible also makes that reality clear. As a Christian, you're *rescued* from sin and hell. But you're not fully *remade*. In the meantime, you need to be *responsive*.

Suppose a car needs barely a twitch on the steering wheel to turn it. That's responsive—unlike a car that hardly budges no matter how far you crank the wheel. To John, a responsive Christian admits his or her sin and asks forgiveness. Paul said it almost the same: A responsive Christian gets up and goes on after stumbling (Philippians 3:12–14).

That's *your* goal. And if you're looking for friends, that's the best kind. Start by looking for the *rescued*—the ones who know God. Then look for those who are being *remade*—the ones who are growing. And if you find a friend who's *responsive* to God—one who turns when God says, "Turn!"—grab hold and hang on tight.

But if anybody does sin, we have an advocate with the
Father—Jesus Christ, the Righteous One.

1 John 2:1

More Than Skin Deep

Julie quizzed Edward. "You're wearing your shirt tomorrow, right?" Everyone in their youth group had bought T-shirts with the group's logo. Edward got one, but he felt stupid wearing it to church, much less anywhere else. As far as shirts went it was okay, although people always asked him questions he couldn't answer.

It would look bad if Edward didn't wear his shirt the next day. He was supposed to help advertise a concert that week.

"It's dirty," Edward lied.

"Can't you wash it?"

"I do my own laundry," he fibbed again—a real whopper. "I won't have time tonight."

"How else will people know about the concert?"

Edward could sense he wasn't winning. "Okay, okay. I'll wear it."

Indeed he did. Under a big flannel shirt.

Julie saw him. She told him that didn't count.

Read Acts 2:42–47

What good are Christian friends?

Random forces pull friends together. *Good things:* sports, hobbies, after-school clubs. *Hard things:* alcoholic parents, busted-up families, killer homework. *Stupid things:* foul mouths, partying, ganging up on others. Whatever it is, *something* pulls you together. You have things in common.

God doesn't plan for his followers to sit around and stare at each other because they have nothing to talk about. He wants our bond with other followers of Jesus to go beyond our matching T-shirts. Our job isn't to stick out but to stick together.

The book of Acts describes how the early church stayed tight, clinging to each other without becoming a clique. They cared. They shared. They did good. They got closer to Jesus. They told the world about him, so they became an always-expanding family.

Their shirts weren't the only reason they stood out (John 13:35).

Every day they continued to meet together in the temple
courts. They broke bread in their homes. . . .

Acts 2:46

Day 340

Pray for One Another

"Why are you over here all alone?" Danay prodded.

Natalie crumpled. "My dad told us last night that he and Mom are getting a divorce."

"No way!" Mark laughed. "Your parents are the best. You're kidding."

Danay hit Mark. "She's serious, Mark. Stop it."

Natalie told Danay and Mark that her parents acted nice when people were around but fought nonstop when they weren't. Mark apologized for laughing, and after a while he suggested they pray for Natalie. Right there. Right then. Mark and Danay prayed very simply for God to take care of Natalie and do whatever he could to help her parents.

Read Ephesians 6:18

How can you pray for friends?

You probably don't dissect conversations with friends like you slice and up a frog in biology. You just talk. Prayer, however, might not be so easy. Here's some help. In a single verse, the apostle Paul dissects the heart of prayer.

"Pray in the Spirit" says *how* to pray: Ask God to spark your prayers and to help you want what he wants.

"On all occasions" says *where* to pray: Prayer works when you're alone, but it becomes even more powerful when you team with other Christians (Matthew 18:19–20). And hey—talking to God together isn't any more complicated than talking to one friend in front of another. Keep it simple. No frothy words.

"All kinds of prayers and requests" tells you *what* to pray about: everything! "Always keep on praying" describes *when*: as often as you breathe. "All the Lord's people" says *who* to pray for: start with your Christian friends.

One question left. *Why* pray? Paul doesn't say, because it's an assumption underneath everything else he wrote. You pray because we all need God. Because we all need his help. And because God wants to answer (1 John 5:14–15).

And pray in the Spirit on all occasions with all kinds of prayers and requests.

Ephesians 6:18

Day 341
Talk It Up

For the duration of the weekend retreat, Anna played "secret angel," showing acts of kindness for a person whose name she had drawn. First she wrapped a small present and snuck it under her pillow. Then she wrote a long note detailing everything she liked about her "mortal." And when her mortal was assigned a turn doing dishes, she slyly volunteered and took her place.

Anna had no idea who had her own name. She hoped it wasn't the van seatmate who barfed all over her on the way to the retreat. It wasn't likely the guy who carelessly knocked her over on the skating rink.

On the night before the group heading home, everyone flopped on their stomachs around a single candle lighting the room, going around the circle to reveal the name of their mortal and say something nice. Anna described how she observed her mortal being kind. Everyone clapped. But no one said anything about Anna. They had lost her name.

Read Hebrews 3:12-13

How can you encourage your Christian friends?

Encouragement isn't about group hugs. It isn't forced gushy feelings, like squeezing the last toothpaste bubble from a tube. Encouragement inspires. It helps friends go higher.

The writer of Hebrews warned that it's easy for any of us to be fooled into thinking sin looks good and God looks bad. The remedy? Daily doses of reality dropped on you by other Christians.

Encouragement means reminding friends *who God is*: He never makes stupid rules (Psalm 19:7–9). He's always good and loving (Psalm 145:17). Encouragement means reminding friends *what's right*: obeying parents (Colossians 3:20), gulping back gossip (James 1:26), speaking with purity about others (Ephesians 5:3–4), plus many other things you know are right. And encouragement means reminding friends that *you'll make it together* (2 Timothy 2:22).

You don't have to say much. But you do need to talk it up. If you and your friends don't encourage one another, who will?

> But encourage one another daily . . . so that none of
> you may be hardened by sin's deceitfulness.
>
> *Hebrews 3:13*

Day 342

Unreal

"Really?" your best friend says. "You told Ms. Rasmussen you cheated on a spelling quiz? A stupid quiz?"

"Um, well," you stammer. "I agree that it's stupid we still have spelling in eighth grade."

"Don't change the subject," says your friend. "What did you do?"

"Um, the word was belligerent. *B-e-l-l-i-g-e-r-e-n-t*. I couldn't remember how to spell it, and there it it was, on the cover of a magazine Anthony had stashed under his seat. I copied the word and got it right. I had to fess up."

Your friend waves you away. "You're too good to be real. You're invisible to me. I can't talk to you anymore."

Read Revelation 5:6–14

Does God guarantee people will like you?

You can get lost in the seals, bowls, and thunder of Revelation. But what you just read is unmistakably clear: God is building a people who belong to him, a gaggle of friends who rely on his care now and forever. And there's a crowd of people following God.

Nevertheless, everybody faces days when they feel friendless. Honestly, doing the right thing might make your lonely days feel even lonelier.

Jesus has a promise for you. He said that anyone who leaves "home or brothers or sisters or mother or father or children or fields for me and the gospel" will receive "a hundred times" as much in "this present age" and "in the age to come eternal life" (Mark 10:29–30).

If God rewards leaving fields for his sake, he absolutely cares when following him means you lose friends. Revelation shows God keeping his promise on a big scale: Heaven will be full of people from every tribe and nation.

Those friends are here. Right now. Jesus said you'll see some of them soon, in "this present age." And Revelation shows you'll be hanging with them for all eternity. When you follow God, you have friends forever.

With your blood you purchased men for God from every
tribe and language and people and nation.

Revelation 5:9

Day 343
Snow Forts

"You can't come in here, runt," Ava scowled. "Build your own fort." Her brother trudged through the snow to the far side of their yard. He built his own snow fort and sulked in it by himself. He packed snowballs that froze into ice balls to lob at his sister and her friends.

Ava's fort is just like a clique.

Snow forts keep you warm even if outside it's cold enough to kill. Similarly, a clique can be good. Blowing through your world are cold winds of insecurity, peer pressure, and potential for failure. Inside a clique, you and your friends can stick together for warmth.

If you're on the outside, a clique is cold agony. If the group won't let you in, you could freeze to death. Just like a snow fort, a clique is toasty on the inside and freezing on the outside.

Read 1 John 4:7–12

If God built a snow fort, what would it be like?

God's snow fort is the group of people who believe in Jesus, and friendship with him is the only entrance requirement. God doesn't ice-out people from the wrong school or neighborhood, or people who dress wrong or who aren't quite *enough* of something.

God's snow fort never gets too crowded. He keeps ripping down walls and adding on rooms. He's always inviting more people in.

A crisis arises when people inside the fort decide not to let anyone else in. First John 4:19 says we have the power to welcome people into our group because God has welcomed us—we love because he has loved us. Including others isn't always cozy. There's a good chance we have to squish to fit in, but that's what makes God's snow fort different from Ava's.

Stay warm with your friends. But remember to welcome others in from the cold.

Dear friends, let us love one another, for love comes from God. Everyone who loves has been born of God and knows God. Whoever does not love does not know God, because God is love. This is how God showed his love among us: He sent his one and only Son into the world that we might live through him.

1 John 4:7–9

Day 344
Speak Up

Christopher didn't say a word, but his face screamed pain. Hearing he had leukemia was a shock. Learning what he would go through to survive was dismal. Nothing would be easy.

Jordan knew God could help. His insides were all jittery, knowing he should tell Christopher what he had experienced firsthand. Jordan had never been deathly sick, but his little brother once was. His family got through his illness with prayer and God's power.

Still, Jordan hesitated.

Read Hebrews 13:15

Why are you willing to speak up about Jesus—or not?

Jesus once said that what you think will sooner or later come gushing out of your mouth. He put it like this: "The mouth speaks what the heart is full of" (Matthew 12:34). You might be shy about saying what you really think, however, because your world pressures everyone to fit the norm. If you're short, you get pulled up by the hair to the "right" height. If you're tall, you get your head lopped off.

You don't need to invite rejection and ridicule for little things. But big things are worth standing up for. The Bible says, "If you openly declare that Jesus is Lord and believe in your heart that God raised him from the dead, you will be saved" (Romans 10:9 NLT).

Speaking openly about your faith doesn't get you a ticket into heaven, but it does reveal what's in your heart. And what you know about Jesus is worth spreading far and wide.

If you never spill that good news, others won't know how they can meet Jesus. Romans points out that truth: "But how can they call on him to save them unless they believe in him? And how can they believe in him if they have never heard about him? And how can they hear about him unless someone tells them?" (Romans 10:14 NLT).

When you speak up about your faith, you're saying thanks for what God has done for you. And you're letting others hear the great news too.

Through Jesus, therefore, let us continually offer to God a sacrifice
of praise—the fruit of lips that openly profess his name.

Hebrews 13:15

Day 345
Not Snots

Heather moved across the country in December, and her new school had an amazing rule that she could try out late for whatever group or team she wanted. The pom squad didn't exactly cheer when she picked their group. After Heather did some routines from her last school, the squad said they needed to talk alone.

"I think we should let Heather in," Alyssa suggested. "Have you seen her older brother? He's cute."

"I like our group the way it is," Emma announced. "There's no way she can learn our routines midyear. I think we should tell her to—"

"Shut up, Emma," Mackenzie interrupted. "Our routines aren't that hard. We don't have any reason to leave anyone out. Admit it. You just don't like Heather."

When the squad gives Heather a double thumbs down, we probably think *Meh. Everyone gets left out sometimes. So what?*

That might be true. But there's a kinder urge inside us that knows it's bad to exclude Heather without a bona fide reason. Doing life right is all about belonging—and inviting others in.

Read Matthew 28:16–20

In some of his last few words on earth, what
does Jesus say to his followers?

All the good things Jesus has done for us aren't ours to hog for ourselves. He welcomes us into a friendship with himself, and he expects us to welcome others into the same relationship. We don't get to pick who to let in and who to shut out.

It's mean to leave someone off a team. It's incredibly more than mean when we allow the smallest bit of *"Tough luck. I don't like you. I don't care about you"* to shut others out of a connection with God and his people, now and forever.

When Jesus called his followers together for his final words, most worshiped him, falling on the ground in awe. Some doubted. Yet Jesus said the same thing to all of them: "I am Master of all. Go invite others to join our crowd. I'll go with you."

Therefore go and make disciples of all nations.
Matthew 28:19

Day 346

You Know Him

After working a whole summer in hundred-degree-plus heat on an African mission trip, Travis shivered in a sweat shirt, jeans, and blanket.

His friends lounged comfortably in the cool evening air. They thought he was crazy.

Travis quietly talked about building a house at an orphanage, getting to know the kids, and letting God lead his life.

Talking came easy. The summer hadn't just toasted his outsides but lit his insides on fire. He burned to know Jesus. And obey him. Jesus was his one-of-a-kind friend.

His friends sat happily in their spiritual iciness. They thought he was loopy.

The next day, a bunch of friends had liked a post that said, "I think Travis should stop talking about Jesus. No one wants to hear about that."

Read Matthew 10:32–33

Why admit that you know Jesus?

Some people see Christians as the worst kinds of salespeople. They push stuff you don't want. They talk until your ears rot. If you're smart, you stop them before they start.

God isn't obnoxious. You don't have to wear your faith on a T-shirt or glue a fish to your family car. You do need to be okay being known for belonging to the Lord.

Peter notes that once you know God, you should have simple words ready: "Give an answer to everyone who asks you to give the reason for the hope that you have." Your words should also be kind: "Do this with gentleness and respect" (1 Peter 3:15).

Sometimes, however, even God's closest followers quake when people oppose their faith. Peter crumbled, for example, when a little servant asked if he knew Jesus (Luke 22:55–62). But Peter grew into a mighty preacher. He got bold.

You know God. You belong to Someone great. Don't be afraid to say it.

Whoever acknowledges me before others, I will also
acknowledge before my Father in heaven.

Matthew 10:32

Day 347

Grave Dust

"It's all a myth," Lucas argued. "You know—all that stuff about Jesus rising from the dead. People invented God when they didn't understand evolution—or astrophysics."

"Astrophysics?" Stephen pondered. "Isn't that the dog on *The Jetsons*?"

"No, stupid," Rick spat. "Astrophysics is the study of bodies in space. Before you could have evolution, you had to have stars and planets. It's okay to believe Jesus 'lives in our hearts.' You just can't say he's alive. He's dead."

"Where do you get this stuff?" Marin objected. "I could say Santa Claus and my grandma Jody 'live in my heart.' Jesus did more than that. He rose from the dead. Truly. Body and all."

Read Luke 24:36–49

Why does it matter that Jesus isn't dust in a grave?

If Jesus wasn't raised, our faith is useless (1 Corinthians 15:14, 17). And his early followers knew it. After their Lord was crucified, they hid in fear. They had hoped Jesus would set up the new kingdom he had promised. Suddenly he was dead, and nothing had turned out how they had expected. A few disciples claimed he was alive, gone from the grave where he had been laid, risen from the dead (Luke 24:6, 34).

It seemed too good to be true, until Jesus suddenly stood among them.

Jesus dared his followers to study the scars on his hands and feet where he had been nailed to the cross. He dined on a piece of fish. Jesus was no ghost, no figment from their wishes. He helped them understand that God had promised his resurrection all along.

So why does this matter?

By raising Jesus from the dead, God declared Jesus to be his Son (Romans 1:4). He confirmed that Jesus had paid in full for our sins (Romans 4:25). And because death couldn't keep Jesus in the grave, it won't hold his followers either. He lives with us now, and we'll live with him forever.

> This is what is written: The Messiah will suffer and
> rise from the dead on the third day.
>
> *Luke 24:46*

Day 348

High Voltage

"I got nothing," Maria sighed. "My grandparents are Christians. My parents are Christians. I grew up a boring Christian."

Maria's youth pastor, Monique, stuck her head in the door. "How's it coming?" she asked. Michelle had put Maria and five other kids in a room to brainstorm how to tell other students at school about Jesus.

"We could have a visitor's night at church," Camila bubbled. "We could have games, skits, and free pizza. We might even—"

Thom interrupted. "Nick thought we should have a Bible study before school."

Monique nodded. "Those are both good starts. But both of those tactics mean that your non-Christian friends have to come to *you*. What could you do to go to *them*?"

Read 1 Peter 2:9–10

What qualifies you to tell others about Christ?

You're hanging with your Christian friends. Praying for one another. Encouraging one another. You're charged up.

You'll blow a fuse if all that energy stays in one place.

When God formed the church, the early believers grew up and grew out. Jesus told his followers to "go and make disciples" (Matthew 28:19). They did. God "added to their number daily those who were being saved" (Acts 2:47). They told the world about Christ and his love—always with actions, often with words. Rather than becoming a clique, they formed a family. Instead of turning inward, they spread out.

You might assume you have nothing to tell. You probably didn't rack up a bunch of gory, sensational sins for God to save you from, and your decision to follow Jesus may have been quiet, made over time. But if you understand God's "mercy"—how God forgave, accepted, and befriended you—then you have a story. Tell people about the God who called you to live close to himself.

> But you are a chosen people, a royal priesthood, a holy nation,
> God's special possession, that you may declare the praises of him
> who called you out of darkness into his wonderful light.
>
> *1 Peter 2:9*

Day 349

Sure

"You used to be nice," Sasha complained. "You're changing."

"Me? Changing?" David faked innocence. "I'm just not a nerd anymore."

"You ignore me and everyone else from church."

"Oh—" David fought back. "So you're jealous of my new friends."

Sasha didn't answer right away. "That's not the problem," she said after a long silence. "It's bigger than that. You ignore everything about Jesus."

"So?"

"See? You act like it doesn't matter. I'm not sure who you are anymore. I thought you were a Christian."

"So did I," David finally admitted. "Now I'm not so sure."

Read Hebrews 10:19–23

How do you know that you're a Christian?

Who you are is the sum of what you like, how you act, how you feel, and what you believe. Most of all, it's about who you belong to.

God made us, so we belong to him (Psalm 24:1–2). Except we decided we didn't. We all chose to distance ourselves from him (Romans 3:23).

The Old Testament illustrated that separation concretely. God's presence dwelled in the temple, in the "Most Holy Place." Only one priest could pass through a curtain to get close to God's presence—and then only once a year. That high priest dared come close only if he carried the blood of an animal killed as a sacrifice for the people's sin (Leviticus 16).

The New Testament clarifies that an animal can't die for our sins. But Jesus could. He was the perfect sacrifice for all sins for all time. His blood opens a new way for us to "enter the Most Holy Place" with confidence. His death means God cleanses us, accepts us, and removes our guilt—and gives us eternal life with him that starts right now (John 3:16).

Becoming a Christian begins by saying, "Yes, God, I accept Christ's death for my sins. I admit I belong to you." You don't run from God anymore. You run toward him. You don't choose to be far away. You choose to follow.

Let us draw near to God with a sincere heart and
with the full assurance that faith brings.

Hebrews 10:22

Day 350
Doing the 'Tudes

Callie and William glared at their youth pastor. They hated their assignment—asking a non-Christian what she or he thinks of Christians.

"I asked Mr. Riley what he saw in me that made him want to be a Christian," William reported. "He said he didn't buy it, and that he hardly ever sees me being kind to people—nothing like Jesus. He called me a fake."

"And I talked to Miss Fernandez," Callie said. "I asked, 'How are Christians different from other people?' She said, 'Can I be blunt? They aren't different—they're *weird*.'"

Read Matthew 5:13–16

Why would anyone be crazy enough to follow Jesus' teaching?

You want to do right, but not if it's hopelessly hard. Or just "because God said so." Some of the Bible's commands might sound wacky to the point of unworkable. Like the "Beatitudes," the words Jesus uttered in Matthew 5:1–11, capped off with the passage you just read. Why "do the Beatitudes"?

(1) *Doing the Beatitudes makes you happy.* Different from the whizzy and woozy feelings you catch at an amusement park. But people who live by the words of Jesus experience God and his blessings.

(2) *Doing the Beatitudes makes a splash for good.* You're spice—tasty flavor. You're light—a beam on God's right way.

(3) *Doing the Beatitudes shows off God's power.* He makes you spiritually hungry, honest about pain, gentle, merciful, pure, peaceful, and patient in persecution. Those are powerful qualities—and powerfully attractive, even if others don't see it right away.

Non-Christians don't need public posts to hear about Jesus—they want to see God in our actions. Our health or wealth won't draw people—in fact, we hope for better riches. Rubbing our goodness in people's faces isn't what Jesus meant by being "a city set on a hill."

If you want to be happy, do good, make friends, and show off God, Jesus gave you a to-do list.

Let your light shine before others, that they may see your
good deeds and glorify your Father in heaven.

Matthew 5:16

Day 351
The Shock in Their Eyes

Martina glanced up from her Bible study notes and paused, startled to see Lila at the back of the room. Other shocked faces communicated the same thing: Why is *she* here?

Martina had met "Lila the Sleaze Queen" at a track meet. Even with a smoker's cough, Lila still ran fast. Lila, in fact, ran around a lot, Martina had heard.

"Hi, Lila!" Martina blurted. Lila grabbed a seat and listened quietly. A girl next to her helped her follow along in her Bible. At the end of the evening, she talked to a few people and then slipped out the back.

Martina found her the next day at track practice. "Did you see how they looked at me?" Lila asked. "I knew they wouldn't want me there."

"But it got better," Martina reminded her. Lila nodded. "They were just surprised to see you at a Bible study. You were a little shocked too, weren't you?" Lila had to admit she was—and that she felt welcome. And that she wanted to go back.

Read Mark 2:13–17

What kind of people did Jesus choose to hang out with?

You don't have to be a sleaze queen or an ax murderer to have offended God. When you grasp that God is good and sin is evil and how repulsive *all* evil is to God—well, none of us measures up.

Here's the good news: We walked away from God, but while we were still stuck in sin, he took the first step toward us (Romans 5:8). He didn't make people get morally perfect before he would be their friend.

The religious leaders watching Jesus hated his friendliness toward sinners. They mocked his choice of a crooked tax collector to be his follower and despised his dinners with sinners. But those who sneered at Jesus for chumming with the bad guys were blind to their *own* badness. They didn't think they needed a spiritual doctor, so they pushed Jesus away—and stayed sick. It was the ones who admitted they needed a spiritual doctor who let Jesus near—and got well.

Jesus said to them, "It is not the healthy who need a doctor, but the sick. I have not come to call the righteous, but sinners."

Mark 2:17

Day 352
When Truth Clashes

No one was surprised when Nina's older sister got pregnant. But Trinity was shocked when she heard about the abortion.

"She did *what?*" Trinity looked at Nina with sick eyes.

Nina stuck up for her sister. "I don't know what I'd do. I wouldn't want to have a kid."

"How can you say that?" Trinity blurted.

"I think you have to be there to know what you'd do." Nina looked at Trinity like she was unbelievably stupid. "You just can't make that choice ahead of time."

"There's not much choice," Trinity fought back. "Abortion is wrong."

Read 1 Peter 3:15

What can you do when your beliefs clash with your world?

Most people trust something other than the Bible as their prime source of truth. They follow their feelings and do what feels good. They think technology has all the answers and conclude God is unnecessary. Almost everyone appoints their own brains as absolute judge and decides what is right and true for themselves.

Some ask polite questions. Others criticize how Christians think and live. Many point out our hypocrisy, selfish narrowness, and un-Jesus-like attitudes and actions.

Sometimes they're right. Because we're imperfect, our view of the world and of ourselves is imperfect. Their critique challenges us to grow in what we know, to study ourselves in the mirror of the Bible and make sure we aren't a mess. We need to double-check that Jesus is really in charge of our lives and that we understand him and his Word correctly.

Then what? Go ahead and answer questions and objections as best you can. Tell what you think and why. It's okay to say "I don't know" and give an answer later, when you've had a chance to research the best answer.

Sharing Jesus is an enormous chance to express your devotion to Jesus. When you live for Jesus, questions inevitably come your way. So get ready!

Always be prepared to give an answer to everyone who asks
you to give the reason for the hope that you have.

1 Peter 3:15

Day 353
Step by Step

"Sure, I go to church," Madison fired back. "Got a problem with that?" Classmates had asked Madison about God a couple times before, and when her replies sounded stupid and less-than-satisfactory, they laughed. So this time she came out fighting.

Barking and biting like a cornered dog is one response to people confronting your faith—to peers grilling you, teachers asserting opinions you disagree with, maybe a non-Christian parent telling you to spend less time at church. Another reaction is hiding your faith—changing the subject or morphing your behavior to fit your surroundings.

Either way, fears can come crashing in: *Will I lose this friend? What should I say? Shouldn't I stand up for God?*

Read 1 Peter 3:15–16

How should you respond to people who question your faith?

When Peter says to be prepared to explain your faith, that sounds like a small step for Peter but a giant leap for you.

Yet Peter gives a reason to be unafraid—because Christ is Lord. *Jesus* deserves your deepest awe and obedience. Your first concern is what *he* thinks, not what others think (Luke 12:5). If you can halt fear from ringing in your ears, you'll better hear the Holy Spirit helping you know when to speak and what to say (Mark 13:11).

Having the right words is only half of sharing Jesus. Nothing beats real love and the example of a changed life for demonstrating that God is real. Gentleness and respect go a lot farther than loud debates—besides, God changes minds, not you (2 Timothy 2:24–26). Your job isn't to make a scene but to have a pure heart, "a clear conscience" that calms opponents.

God will help you share about him step-by-step.

Start by asking him for courage. Refuse to hide that you go to church, and don't duck when a Christian friend waves "hi" at school. Then start praying for your closest friends, and work on inviting one to church. Little steps give you practice for bigger steps, like speaking up about Jesus.

Do this with gentleness and respect.
1 Peter 3:15

Day 354
Heimlich Maneuver

"What was her question today?"

"She asked how we know that God made the world and that we didn't evolve."

"She thinks too hard. We're just supposed to accept stuff. Aren't we?"

"This all started when her grandma died. She asked Mr. Swanson if heaven was real and he gave her a huge lecture. She feels really bad."

"Did you see his face when she asked if Jesus really did a miracle to feed all those people? He almost choked. That's one thing I don't like. I don't like it when they don't even let us ask questions."

Read John 1:43–51

Does God dislike people who question Christian beliefs?

You can't swallow food whole. Either your esophagus will forcibly expel the intruder or your stomach will grind to a halt. At best, your gut asks who let the solids in. At worst, you choke and die.

God doesn't expect you to swallow truth whole. He invites you to chew.

Nathanael questioned whether Jesus was who Philip claimed: God's Son come to save the world.

Yet Nathanael also accepted Philip's invitation to come and see. That's significantly different from refusing to believe anything no matter what the evidence. That's not acting too cool for Sunday school—writing off Bible study or youth group or confirmation class without even trying to grapple with reasons your faith.

Jesus saw Nathanael under the fig tree—a customary spot for studying Scripture—so Nathanael knew where to look for answers. He was like the Bereans (Acts 17:11), who heard the message Paul preached about Jesus "with great eagerness and examined the Scriptures every day to see if what Paul said was true."

Nathanael wasn't making excuses. He loved truth enough to ask questions and consider the answers (2 Thessalonians 2:10). Being mature doesn't mean you know everything. It means you know the One who does.

When Jesus saw Nathanael approaching, he said of him,
"Here is a true Israelite, in whom there is no deceit."

John 1:47

Day 355
Stand Downwind

When Brock and his friends hit seventh grade, they started having weekly week-end parties. Back then, the boys stole phones and hid them in the microwave so the girls couldn't play their dance music. By eighth grade, couples were tongue-wrestling on the couch. By ninth grade, his friends were trying weed.

Brock knew other parties were a lot worse. Yet he had a queasy certainty he should have ditched the parties a *looooong* time ago. But these were his best friends. His only friends. All of his friends, actually.

They told Brock the stuff they did was no big deal. When he said it was, they turned on him. Before he could stop going to the parties, they stopped inviting him.

Read Matthew 5:10–12

What does it mean to be "persecuted for righteousness"?

You're in a situation and you're feeling weird. You wonder if it's you—or if it's Jesus.

You can't blame your own random weirdness on God. When people look at you funny, check if it's something you can fix. Do a deodorant check. Flip a breath mint. Stand downwind when you chat. Do your best to act normal—within God's limits, of course. And if you still wind up thinking, *I don't fit here . . .* and if you ponder *Is this about right and wrong? . . .* and if you conclude *If I decided to disobey Jesus, this problem would go away . . .* then the problem is about him.

People all over the world are persecuted—sometimes solely for their beliefs, sometimes because of a tangled knot of ethnic and economic and religious is-sues. You might never face persecution like that. Yet you'll surely catch some "all kinds of evil against you." Many times persecution means you get ignored with a fury. People don't mistreat you. They don't beat you. They just ignore you.

Massive is your reward.

Blessed are those who are persecuted because of righteousness,
for theirs is the kingdom of heaven . . . great is your reward.

Matthew 5:10, 12

Day 356
Monkey Pile

"One-monkey! Two-monkey!" Hannah counted. Then she rushed. *Bam!* Ben lay flattened, walloped in a quarterback sack.

Ben jumped up and shouted at Hannah. "Stop it! One more time and I'm quitting! It's *three* monkeys."

Hannah laughed at Ben. "Benny's such a baby," she taunted.

Next play. "One-monkey! Two-monkey!" Hannah counted—and rushed early, knocking Ben even harder. When Ben kept moaning and couldn't get up from the ground, his dad scooped him up and sped to the emergency room.

A scan showed Ben's exploded spleen, and emergency surgery saved him. When Hannah came to visit Ben, she started to cry. "Your dad told me what the doctors said," Hannah finally said. "I'm sorry I did this to you."

"It's okay, Hannah," Ben said. "I won't stay mad at you. I forgive you."

Read Psalm 103:8–12

You blew it. You know it. Now what are you supposed to do?

You can't unrupture a spleen you bounced to shreds. Or reel nasty words back into your mouth. Or uncheat on a test. Nothing can completely undo what you did—whether it's a sin or a mistake or a bit of both. But you *can do what you can* to make things right: Say you're sorry. Talk nicer. Turn yourself in to the teacher and take a zero or retake the test.

When we do wrong, the pain we cause people is only half our problem. Setting that straight is only half our job. Our sin also snubs God. "You are not a God who is pleased with wickedness; with you, evil people are not welcome," David wrote. "The arrogant cannot stand in your presence; you hate all who do wrong" (Psalm 5:4–5).

God's anger is bone-crushing, but his forgiveness is even bigger. When you blow it and you know it, admit your sin to God. He's not giving you permission to be bad; he's offering you a fresh start at following him.

As far as the east is from the west, so far has he
removed our transgressions from us.

Psalm 103:12

Day 357

Are We There Yet?

"Get off my side!" your little sister whines, swinging her Barbie at you. *Whack!* The hard plastic head cracks you across the nose.

"OW!" you howl. "Stop it! MOM—that HURT! Make her stop!"

The backseat has gotten way too tight on a trip that won't end. You've been riding for weeks. Each evening you write in your journal about *The Great American Road Trip*—under "Things I'd rather forget."

"This is so stupid!" you fuss. "Where are we going?"

Your parents don't disclose your destination. They won't trace on a map the route you're taking. "It's a surprise," they say.

One day you stop at a gas station. The clerk is nosy in a friendly sort of way. "You folks aren't from around here, are ya," she figures. "Where ya headed?"

"Wish I knew," you reply. "Ask them. This was their idea."

Read Philippians 1:9–11

Where is Jesus taking you as you follow him?

You won't enjoy a long road trip if you're clueless where you're headed. If all you're sure of is that your backside is glued to a car seat, you'll feel dragged to who-knows-where. And you'll yawn, snooze, and snore if you finally get to your destination and no one explains what you're looking at.

The White House is more than a house. The Grand Canyon is more than a hole. Following Jesus is an adventure. Not understanding where you're headed—and why—and what you'll see along the way—turns the ride into a chore.

The apostle Paul flips through some travel pictures to show off your destination—actually, to show you what *you* will look like when your journey is done: Your relationship with Jesus will change you completely. You will be "pure," "blameless," "filled with the fruit of righteousness."

The trip has already started. God is in the driver's seat. He guarantees he'll get you to the goal (Philippians 1:6). And you don't have to guess where you're going.

And this is my prayer: that your love may abound more
and more in knowledge and depth of insight.

Philippians 1:9

Day 358
Starting Over

"I'm not a murderer or anything," Mia told her Bible study friends. "But I have a mouth. I can talk nice when I'm around all of you, but the rest of the time I swear a lot. If my little brother hits me, I swear. If a teacher does something I don't like, I swear. It's a bad habit.

"I feel bad all the time about it. I know it's wrong, so I imagine God hating me. I wonder if I'm going to hell. Trying to follow Jesus just makes me feel like a failure. I don't want that."

Read John 7:53–8:11

What helped the woman who was caught sinning to start over?

Sometimes we assume we're perfect. We might actually be awful people who just never feel guilt. Or we could be like the Pharisees in the Bible—nice religious people who don't smoke, drink, or swear but ooze pride, anger, and selfishness.

Other times we admit our sin. But our honest guilt turns into fear that we do nothing right and that God won't forgive us when we mess up.

Jesus deals with the woman's sin matter-of-factly, like a doctor who says, "Yep, you're sick, but we can deal with that." Jesus doesn't cover up her sin. The woman was caught sleeping with someone's husband. He didn't say she didn't deserve death, the punishment Jewish law prescribed. But he set her free. He says simply, "I do not condemn you. . . . Leave your life of sin."

God treats us the same way: He expects us to admit our wrongdoing. But if we admit our sins, he promises to forgive us, washing away our guilt and putting our friendship with him back on track (1 John 1:8–9).

That's what gives us the freedom to start over. And over. And over again if we need to.

Christians aren't perfect. Unlike cows and horses, we can't run as soon as we get out of the womb. Like little babies, at first we lie helpless. Then we flip, roll, scoot, crawl, and stand. Muscles and balance develop. *Then* we walk. But we never walk—or run—without getting up from the pavement a lot.

Go now and leave your life of sin.

John 8:11

Day 359
Fakery

You worked so hard.

You got nothing for it.

With a hundred hours invested in your photography project, you had stalked sunsets for months to capture the perfect prize-winning photo.

Meanwhile, your arch-competitor downloaded a stock photo, printed it, and presented it as his own. He claimed he got the shot on a beach vacation. When the judges stuck a blue ribbon on his photo, a crowd gathered round and clapped loudly.

No one noticed. No one cried, "Fake! Unfair!"

You feel ripped off.

Read Hebrews 6:7–12

Why work hard when hard work doesn't always win the prize?

Every action has two audiences.

Fans on earth are fickle. In fact, they seldom know when to clap. You study for an exam until your brain overloads, but a classmate who steals the answers gets the best grade. You play tough all season long, yet the coach plays favorites when he hands out the MVP award. Or you leave a party to get home by curfew, and you hear your peers jeering as the door slams shut behind you.

Fans on earth sometimes clap for people who deserve to be loudly booed.

Your Fan in heaven is faithful. God always notices a job well done. Sure, he sees when you do something "spiritual," like praying, worshiping, or reading your Bible. But he notices *all* the ways you obey him—doing homework and chores, listening to your parents, playing hard, respecting teachers, treating people great.

When you dedicate yourself to doing good, you're like a patch of soil that soaks up rain and grows a bumper crop for its master. God is Master of your existence, and he won't forget what you've done.

Trust him. Be patient and you'll enjoy the harvest.

God is not unjust; he will not forget your work and the love you have shown him as you have helped his people and continue to help them.

Hebrews 6:10

"Just Do It" Doesn't Do It

Dirks and his dad returned from their hunting trip with a ten-point buck roped to the roof of their truck. "It should have been Dirks's," his dad told everyone when he bragged how they got the deer.

Dirks faked a smile. He knew he should feel disappointed, but he wasn't sure he was.

He didn't know what he felt. Up in a tree stand with his dad waiting for deer, Dirks pretended to be happy. When a buck finally wandered by, he wasn't sure he could kill it. He had never seen a deer that close, except for a stuffed head mounted above his grandparents' fireplace. But Dad had promised him the first shot, and Dirks didn't want to disappoint.

"Shoot! Just shoot!" his dad hissed. The buck's ears perked, and Dirks paused a second more before pulling the trigger. He hit ground. When the buck bolted, his dad quickly shot. Dad didn't miss.

Read Jeremiah 1:4–10

How did Jeremiah react to God's expectations of him?

When you fail—or you're scared you will—you might try to shrug it off or make excuses or say it doesn't matter. But in the back of your head, the truth rattles around: You want to do well. So you're bothered. You're embarrassed. And you probably would never admit your lack of perfection without checking who's listening.

When God made Jeremiah a prophet—someone who would speak to God's people, the nation of Israel—Jeremiah was terrified. The Lord sent Jeremiah to go nose-to-nose with kings and leaders and the entire nation.

Jeremiah didn't think God's expectations fit him. "God, you're way off. I'm too young. I can't speak."

But God's expectations always fit. He knows how he made us. He sees more in us than we see in ourselves. He knows he can make us able to do what he asks.

God let Jeremiah doubt for a second. Then he said, "Don't worry. *I* will send you. *I* will be with you. *I* will make you strong." He doesn't bark "Just do it" or "Just shoot it." God works patiently with us until we get to his goal.

But the Lord said to me, "Do not say, 'I am too young.'"

Jeremiah 1:7

Day 361

Faster, Higher, Stronger

Jun anxiously awaited her turn at her first all-district gymnastics meet. *There are so many people watching.* She did fine in her first two events, but in the floor exercise she missed a landing and bounced out-of-bounds. Her score dropped to the bottom of all the girls competing. She ran back to her team-mates furious with herself.

Her coach tried to encourage her. "Jun, you did great. We'll work on land-ings and some endurance training and next time you'll—"

"I made a fool of myself," she snapped. "I'm not any good at gymnastics. I'm not going to do this anymore."

Read Hebrews 12:4–11

If God loves you, why does he let you struggle?

You didn't stop toddling when you banged your face on the furniture a few times, and you kept trying at math even when 2+2=4 bewildered you. And no doubt you'll do whatever it takes to keep growing up—to get your driver's license, rent your first apartment, and build a career and family.

Life is hard. Just because something takes effort doesn't mean you're stupid or lazy or uncoordinated. It simply means God is working on you.

God uses your struggles with school, home, sports, lessons, and relationships to discipline you—to *train* you—to make you strong, tough, and more like him. That's not necessarily because you've done badly, but because he knows you can do better. God probably won't shoot lightning at your legs so you effortlessly win gymnastics meets. Nor does he zap your heart so you flawlessly obey him.

You practice to get good at anything. You need to practice to master life and to become a strong Christian. God doesn't put you into training because he's a mean coach who laughs while you run laps. He knows what it takes to make you mature—when to go easy and when to push hard—and his discipline is always perfectly planned for your good.

Practice hurts. But it works.

No discipline seems pleasant at the time, but painful.
Later on, however, it produces a harvest of righteousness
and peace for those who have been trained by it.

Hebrews 12:11

Day 362

Mow Me Down

When William's older brother went off to college, he arranged for William to take over his lawn-mowing business. All William had to do was finish the last month and a half of fall mowing, then start the business up again next spring. He could make three times more per hour than any of his friends.

William would be rolling in green stuff.

But he had to mow it before he could roll in it. After spending a whole Saturday mowing—and not finishing what he needed to do—he recalled that his brother was a foot taller and sixty pounds bigger. And it took him five years to build his business.

This was more work than William had figured.

His mom felt sorry for him. His dad said he couldn't quit.

William whined that this experience would forever ruin his attitude toward work, and he threatened to live at home until he was forty.

Read James 1:2–5

If you're supposed to persevere, when is it okay to quit?

Quitting a team or an activity or a job doesn't always mean you're a quitter. You need to quit when you're hurting yourself—when you can't get enough sleep, you cry your eyes out nightly, or you don't get your homework done. You don't have much choice but to quit when you're forced to do wrong—by a crooked boss, for example. And it's okay to quit when you can do better at something else, *after* you've stuck it out and kept your promises. Commitments you made first—not necessarily the ones you like best—come first. Get help while you sweat it out, even if that means someone else takes some of your jobs.

Bad times force you to rely on God. From the frontside, trials are terrifying. But from the backside you can see how God cared for you—and how he brought you through.

Consider it pure joy, my brothers and sisters, whenever you face trials of many kinds, because you know that the testing of your faith produces perseverance.

James 1:2–3

Day 363
Don't Play Dead

Part of Mort's job working the funeral home late shift was whisking the ashes of cremated customers into brass urns. The job didn't pay much, but it presented certain, shall we say, golden opportunities.

Night after night, Mort picked through the ashes of the dearly departed for hidden treasure. *Gold.* A filling here, a dental bridge there. Occasionally he hit the mother lode—a shiny mouthful from an elderly lady or gentleman who successfully resisted being fitted with dentures.

Mort accumulated enough spare cash to retire on beachfront property in the Bahamas. And the best part? His victims never fought back.

Read Philippians 2:3–8

Does being a Christian mean you always play dead—and get torched—and let someone steal your fillings?

As Christians, there's no better way to act with love than to "lay down our lives" (1 John 3:16). You can sacrificially give time or stuff, or show kindness to an enemy, or put others before yourself.

You have only so much to give. Give wisely.

If you hang your school locker open with a sign saying *Look here! Steal my stuff!* you'd have nothing left for yourself or to share with people who need your help. If you perpetually let people take advantage of you, then you won't be able to give when it really matters.

Jesus gave because he was strong, not because he was weak.

No one walked all over Jesus. No one stole anything from him. He *chose* to give, in both life and death, even when he "made himself nothing" and "humbled himself." When he was about to be taken by force to be beaten and crucified, he made clear that he was dying by choice (Matthew 26:53–54).

Being robbed and giving a gift have the same result. You pay a price. But when you give by choice, people don't see a fool. They see Jesus.

In your relationships with one another, have the same mindset as
Christ Jesus: Who, being in very nature God, did not consider equality
with God something to be used to his own advantage; rather, he
made himself nothing by taking the very nature of a servant. . . .

Philippians 2:5–7

Day 364

Fighting Forward

"Tragedy struck today in northwest Wisconsin," the newscaster announced. "A Polk County deputy sheriff was critically wounded after he responded to a call for help in capturing a man sought for a shooting in Minnesota last night. Deputy Mike Seversen was shot under the chin at close range as he attempted to . . ."

Three days later, Mike woke up in a hospital bed.

He couldn't move.

But he was alive.

Read Philippians 4:12–13

What's the toughest situation you could face without shattering?

You probably don't think your life is finished when your phone breaks. You probably don't doubt God's care when you blow a test or can't afford two-hundred-dollar shoes.

But what if you were paralyzed from the neck down—like Mike, a real-life guy? What if you couldn't walk, talk, or breathe on your own? Or if your brain failed? Life is over when you hurt that bad, isn't it? Then it's time to give up on God and life, right?

Wrong.

Mike still can't use his arms or legs. He understands what he's lost. He's no fool. But he also knows what he still possesses. He has God. He fought to learn to breathe and talk again. His brain works well. He hunts, works on his house, jokes with his family and friends. He teaches people about God's care.

The apostle Paul, like Mike, realized he could thrive with a less-than-perfect life. He was tougher than he knew. God was bigger than he thought. Paul wrote from prison that he could be happy in any circumstance, with little or plenty, because God made him strong.

You probably won't be shot trying to capture a criminal. But you won't escape bad times (John 16:32). Your life isn't finished when it falls apart—when the race turns into an uphill battle against the wind, with flies in your eyes and gnats up your nose. That isn't time to quit. It's time to see how tough God can make you. You can do all things.

I can do all this through him who gives me strength.

Philippians 4:13

Day 365

Where's the Finish Line?

A herd of cows glances up from grazing to stare at the students cycling down their bumpy back road. The cows are utterly content. The bikers, not so much.

"Stopping!" Thomas screeches from the back of the line. "Something's wrong. I've clocked eight miles since that last left turn. Shouldn't we be to another road by now? Hey, Eric—did you get us lost again?"

"Me? Don't blame me! You've got a map too."

Miles later, Sophie yells, "Stopping!"

"Why are we stopping this time?"

"Jon's barfing in the bushes. He can't take the heat."

"Eric, you lied," Savannah whines. "You said this would be fun. We should have gone someplace to lie on the beach. I can't ride any farther."

Read Jude 24–25

When you follow God, what's your ultimate destination?

Christians who don't focus on the finish line are like bikers wandering the countryside asking cows for directions. They wander. They hit bumps. They *fwang* over their handlebars. They forget to enjoy the rush as they blow downhill.

Knowing where and when you'll finish keeps you from quitting a tough ride. Being convinced that each push on the pedals propels you closer to the goal keeps you moving. If you sweat for nothing, you'll find something better to do. Yet when ice-cold drinks, crystal lakes, and a cushy sleeping bag await, you can endure.

As a follower of Jesus, your destination is sweeter than anything you've ever imagined. You're heading upward. Toward maturity. Toward heaven. Toward your Lord.

And because of his strength, God promises to get you there "without any wrong in you." Not because you're perfect, but because you cling to his forgiveness. Jesus is invading your life with his glory, greatness, power, and authority—for now and forever.

> God is strong and can help you not to fall. He can bring you
> before his glory without any wrong in you and can give you
> great joy. He is the only God, the One who saves us.
>
> *Jude 24–25 NCV*

About the Author

Kevin Johnson (www.kevinjohnsonbooks.com) is the bestselling author or coauthor of more than sixty books and Bible products for adults, students, and children. As a youth worker and pastor, Kevin served children and youth in a wide variety of settings. He and his wife, Lyn, live in Minneapolis, Minnesota, and have three grown children.